THE CAMBRIDGE COMPANION TO
JOHN HENRY NEWMAN

John Henry Newman (1801–90) was a major figure in nineteenth-century religious history. He was one of the major protagonists of the Oxford or Tractarian Movement within the Church of England whose influence continues to be felt within Anglicanism. A high-profile convert to Catholicism, he was an important commentator on Vatican I and is often called 'the Father' of the Second Vatican Council. Newman's thinking highlights and anticipates the central themes of modern theology including hermeneutics, the importance of historical-critical research, the relationship between theology and literature, and the reinterpretation of the nature of faith. His work is characterized by two elements that have come especially to the fore in postmodern theology, namely, the importance of the religious imagination and the fiduciary character of all knowledge. This *Companion* fills a need for an accessible, comprehensive and systematic presentation of the major themes in Newman's work.

Ian Ker is Senior Research Fellow in Theology at St Benet's Hall, Oxford. He has published over twenty books, mostly on Newman, including *John Henry Newman: A Biography* (1988, 1999).

Terrence Merrigan is Professor of Systematic Theology at the Katholieke Universiteit Leuven. His many publications include *Newman and Truth* (2008).

T0370557

THE CAMBRIDGE COMPANION TO REFORMATION THEOLOGY
edited by David Bagchi and David Steinmetz (2004)
ISBN 0 521 77224 9 hardback   ISBN 0 521 77662 7 paperback

THE CAMBRIDGE COMPANION TO AMERICAN JUDAISM
edited by Dana Evan Kaplan (2005)
ISBN 0 521 82204 1 hardback   ISBN 0 521 52951 4 paperback

THE CAMBRIDGE COMPANION TO KARL RAHNER
edited by Declan Marmion and Mary E. Hines (2005)
ISBN 0 521 83288 8 hardback   ISBN 0 521 54045 3 paperback

THE CAMBRIDGE COMPANION TO FRIEDRICH
SCHLEIERMACHER
edited by Jacqueline Mariña (2005)
ISBN 0 521 81448 0 hardback   ISBN 0 521 89137 x paperback

THE CAMBRIDGE COMPANION TO THE GOSPELS
edited by Stephen C. Barton (2006)
ISBN 0 521 80766 2 hardback   ISBN 0 521 00261 3 paperback

THE CAMBRIDGE COMPANION TO THE QUR'AN
edited by Jane Dammen McAuliffe (2006)
ISBN 0 521 83160 1 hardback   ISBN 0 521 53934 x paperback

THE CAMBRIDGE COMPANION TO JONATHAN EDWARDS
edited by Stephen J. Stein (2007)
ISBN 0 521 85290 0 hardback   ISBN 0 521 61805 3 paperback

THE CAMBRIDGE COMPANION TO EVANGELICAL THEOLOGY
edited by Timothy Larsen and Daniel J. Trier (2007)
ISBN 0 521 84698 6 hardback   ISBN 0 521 60974 7 paperback

THE CAMBRIDGE COMPANION TO MODERN JEWISH PHILOSOPHY
edited by Michael L. Morgan and Peter Eli Gordon (2007)
ISBN 0 521 81312 3 hardback   ISBN 0 521 01255 4 paperback

THE CAMBRIDGE COMPANION TO THE TALMUD AND
RABBINIC LITERATURE
edited by Charlotte E. Fonrobert and Martin S. Jaffee (2007)
ISBN 0 521 84390 1 hardback   ISBN 0 521 60508 3 paperback

THE CAMBRIDGE COMPANION TO LIBERATION THEOLOGY,
SECOND EDITION
edited by Christopher Rowland (2007)
ISBN 9780521868839 hardback   ISBN 9780521688932 paperback

THE CAMBRIDGE COMPANION TO THE JESUITS
edited by Thomas Worcester (2008)
ISBN 9780521857314 hardback   ISBN 9780521673969 paperback

THE CAMBRIDGE COMPANION TO CLASSICAL ISLAMIC
THEOLOGY
edited by Tim Winter (2008)
ISBN 9780521780582 hardback   ISBN 9780521785495 paperback

THE CAMBRIDGE COMPANION TO PURITANISM
edited by John Coffey and Paul Lim (2008)
ISBN 9780521860888 hardback   ISBN 9780521678001 paperback

THE CAMBRIDGE COMPANION TO ORTHODOX CHRISTIAN
THEOLOGY
edited by Mary Cunningham and Elizabeth Theokritoff (2008)
ISBN 9780521864848 hardback   ISBN 9780521683388 paperback

THE CAMBRIDGE COMPANION TO PAUL TILLICH
edited by Russell Re Manning (2009)
ISBN 9780521859899 hardback   ISBN 9780521677356 paperback

Forthcoming

THE CAMBRIDGE COMPANION TO THE TRINITY
edited by Peter C. Phan

THE CAMBRIDGE COMPANION TO THE VIRGIN MARY
edited by Sarah Boss

THE CAMBRIDGE COMPANION TO BLACK THEOLOGY
edited by Dwight Hopkins and Edward Antonio

THE CAMBRIDGE COMPANION TO

JOHN HENRY NEWMAN

edited by
Ian Ker and Terrence Merrigan

CAMBRIDGE
UNIVERSITY PRESS

University Printing House, Cambridge CB2 8BS, United Kingdom

Cambridge University Press is part of the University of Cambridge.

It furthers the University's mission by disseminating knowledge in the pursuit of
education, learning and research at the highest international levels of excellence.

www.cambridge.org
Information on this title: www.cambridge.org/9780521692724

© Cambridge University Press 2009

First published 2009

A catalogue record for this publication is available from the British Library

ISBN 978-0-521-69272-4 Paperback

Contents

Preface

John Henry Newman continues to attract the attention of students and scholars from a range of disciplines, including theology, philosophy, and literature. The extent and range of the interest in Newman and his work is in itself an argument for a book that brings together essays that provide a comprehensive introduction to his theology. The fact that much of the work devoted to Newman is of a specialized nature reinforces the need for a systematic presentation of the major themes of his work and the context in which his thought developed.

The ongoing interest in Newman is easily explained.

In the first place, Newman was a major historical figure in his own right. His life (1801–90) spans a fascinating century and Newman was a witness to and a commentator on much nineteenth-century history. Moreover, Newman was directly involved in a number of significant developments throughout the century. He was the major protagonist in the so-called Oxford Movement, the author of the seminal text, *The Idea of a University*, an important commentator on Vatican Council I, and an innovative thinker in the field of theological epistemology.

His significance to his own age perhaps pales in comparison to the stature he has enjoyed in the twentieth and twenty-first centuries. Newman's work is regarded as marking a watershed in the development of modern (especially Catholic) theology. He is regarded as a leading representative (and in Catholic theology, one of the forerunners) of the turn to the subject in modern thought. His own theology highlights and anticipates themes that are characteristic of modern theology, including the importance of historical-critical research, the hermeneutics of doctrinal development, the place of experience in the life of faith and in theology, the relationship between theology and literature, and the re-interpretation of the nature of faith. In regard to the latter theme, Newman's work is characterized by two elements that have come especially to the fore in contemporary (postmodern) theology, namely, the importance of the religious imagination and the fiduciary character of all knowledge.

Newman's novelty and his relevance to modern theology are evidenced in the fact that he was appealed to by leading figures in the movement known as Catholic Modernism, and that he is regarded as the precursor of the movement for the retrieval of the scriptural and patristic sources of theology (ressourcement or 'nouvelle théologie') and of the Second Vatican Council (of which he is often called the 'Father' or the 'invisible peritus').

Newman is a thinker whose influence and concerns extend well beyond the nineteenth century into the (modern) twentieth and (postmodern) twentieth-first centuries. Recent studies have highlighted the postmodern themes in Newman's writings and contemporary authors continue to find inspiration in his work.

In conclusion, then, first, Newman is an excellent point of entry to the history and development of theology since the nineteenth century. Second, Newman's work is significant in its own right. He was a seminal thinker who anticipated modern and postmodern concerns and themes and who explored these in an original fashion. The ongoing interest in Newman is ample testimony to his contemporary relevance. And third, in the face of more and more specialized studies of Newman, there is a great need for an accessible, comprehensive and systematic presentation of the major themes in his own work.

Ian Ker
and
Terrence Merrigan

Abbreviations and references

References to works published during Newman's lifetime are to the uniform edition, which was published by Longmans, Green & Co. of London between 1868 and 1881.

Posthumously published works of Newman, which are identified here according to the edition used, include the following: *Letters and Correspondence of John Henry Newman during his Life in the English Church*, ed. Anne Mozley, 2 vols. (London, 1891); *My Campaign in Ireland, Part 1*, ed. W. Neville (privately printed, 1896); *Correspondence of John Henry Newman with John Keble and Others: 1839–1845*, ed. at the Birmingham Oratory (London, 1917); *John Henry Newman: Autobiographical Writings*, ed. Henry Tristram (London and New York, 1956); *Meditations and Devotions of the late Cardinal Newman* (London, 1893); *The Philosophical Notebook of John Henry Newman*, ed. Edward Sillem, 2 vols. (Louvain, 1969–70); *The Theological Papers of John Henry Newman on Faith and Certainty*, ed. Hugo M. de Achaval, SJ, and J. Derek Holmes (Oxford, 1976); *The Theological Papers of John Henry Newman on Biblical Inspiration and on Infallibility*, ed. J. Derek Holmes (Oxford, 1979); *On Consulting the Faithful in Matters of Doctrine*, ed. John Coulson (London, 1961); Henry Tristram, 'Cardinal Newman's *Theses de Fide* and his Proposed Introduction to the French Translation of the University Sermons', *Gregorianum* 18 (1937), 219–60; *The Letters and Diaries of John Henry Newman*, ed. C.S. Dessain *et al.*, vols. i–xxxii (Oxford and London, 1961–2008).

All dates indicated below refer to the original date of publication.

Apo.	*Apologia Pro Vita Sua*
Ari.	*The Arians of the Fourth Century*
Ath.	*Select Treatises of St Athanasius*, 2 vols.
A.W.	*John Henry Newman: Autobiographical Writings*, ed. Henry Tristram (London and New York, 1956)
Call.	*Callista: A Tale of the Third Century*

xiv *Abbreviations and references*

Campaign	*My Campaign in Ireland, Part 1*, ed. W. Neville (privately printed, 1896)
Cons.	*On Consulting the Faithful in Matters of Doctrine*, ed. John Coulson (London, 1961)
D.A.	*Discussions and Arguments on Various Subjects*
Dev.	*An Essay on the Development of Christian Doctrine*
Diff.	*Certain Difficulties Felt by Anglicans in Catholic Teaching*
Ess.	*Essays Critical and Historical*
G.A.	*An Essay in Aid of a Grammar of Assent*
H.S.	*Historical Sketches*
Idea	*The Idea of a University*, ed. I.T. Ker (Oxford, 1976)
Jfc.	*Lectures on the Doctrine of Justification*
K.C.	*Correspondence of John Henry Newman with John Keble and Others, 1839–1845*, ed. at the Birmingham Oratory (London, 1917)
L.D.	*The Letters and Diaries of John Henry Newman*, ed. Charles Stephen Dessain *et al.* (Oxford and London, 1961–2008), vols. i–xxxii
L.G.	*Loss and Gain: The Story of a Convert*
M.D.	*Meditations and Devotions of the late Cardinal Newman* (London, 1893)
Mir.	*Two Essays on Biblical and on Ecclesiastical Miracles*
Mix.	*Discourses Addressed to Mixed Congregations*
Moz.	*Letters and Correspondence of John Henry Newman during his Life in the English Church*, ed. Anne Mozley (London, 1891)
O.S.	*Sermons Preached on Various Occasions*
P.N.	*The Philosophical Notebook of John Henry Newman* (1969–70)
P.S.	*Parochial and Plain Sermons*
Prepos.	*Present Position of Catholics in England*
S.D.	*Sermons Bearing on Subjects of the Day*
S.N.	*Sermon Notes of John Henry Cardinal Newman, 1849–1878*, ed. at the Birmingham Oratory (London, 1913)
T.P. i	*The Theological Papers of John Henry Newman on Faith and Certainty*, ed. Hugo M. de Achaval, SJ, and J. Derek Holmes (Oxford, 1976)
T.P. ii	*The Theological Papers of John Henry Newman on Biblical Inspiration and on Infallibility*, ed. J. Derek Holmes (Oxford, 1979)

T.T.	*Tracts Theological and Ecclesiastical*
Theses	*Cardinal Newman's Theses de Fide and his Proposed Introduction to the French Translation of the University Sermons*
U.S.	*Fifteen Sermons Preached Before the University of Oxford*
V.M.	*The Via Media*
Ward	Wilfrid Ward, *The Life of John Henry Cardinal Newman*, 2 vols. (London: Longmans, Green & Co., 1912)

Notes on contributors

David B. Burrell, CSC, is Theodore Hesburgh Professor Emeritus in Philosophy and Theology at the University of Notre Dame. His books include *Analogy and Philosophical Language* (1973), *Exercises in Religious Understanding* (1975), *Aquinas: God and Action* (1979), *Knowing the Unknowable God: Ibn-Sina, Maimonides, Aquinas* (1986), *Freedom and Creation in Three Traditions* (1993), and *Friendship and Ways to Truth* (2000).

Brian E. Daley, SJ, is Catherine F. Huisking Professor of Theology at the University of Notre Dame. He is the author of *The Hope of the Early Church* (1991), *On the Dormition of Mary: Early Patristic Homilies*, and *Gregory of Nazianzus* (2006).

Cardinal Avery Dulles, SJ, is Laurence J. McGinley Professor of Religion and Society at Fordham University. His books include *Models of the Church* (1974), *Models of Revelation* (1983), *The Assurance of Things Hoped For: A Theology of Christian Faith* (1994), *Newman* (2002), *The Splendor of Faith: The Theological Vision of Pope John Paul II* (rev. edn, 2003), *A History of Apologetics* (rev. edn, 2005), and *Magisterium: Teacher and Guardian* (2007).

Sheridan Gilley is Reader Emeritus in Theology at Durham University. He is the author of *Newman and his Age* (1990) and co-editor of *The Irish in the Victorian City* (1984), *The Irish in Britain 1815–1839* (1989), *Religion, State and Ethnic Groups* (1992), *A History of Religion in Britain* (1994), *The Irish in Victorian Britain: The Local Dimension* (1999), and *World Christianities c. 1815–c. 1914: The Cambridge History of Christianity*, vol. viii (Cambridge University Press, 2006).

Gerard J. Hughes, SJ, is Tutor in Philosophy at Campion Hall, Oxford. His books include *The Nature of God* (1995) and *Aristotle on Ethics* (2001).

Ian Ker is Senior Research Fellow in Theology at St Benet's Hall, Oxford. His books include *John Henry Newman: A Biography* (1988), *Newman the Theologian: A Reader* (1990), *The Achievement of John Henry Newman* (1990), *Newman on Being a Christian* (1990), *Newman and the Fullness of Christianity* (1993), *Healing the Wound of Humanity: The Spirituality of John Henry Newman* (1993), and *The Catholic Revival in English Literature, 1845–1961* (2003).

Gerard Loughlin is Professor of Theology and Culture at Durham University. He is the author of *Telling God's Story: Bible, Church and Narrative Theology* (1996) and *Alien Sex: The Body and Desire in Cinema and Theology* (2004).

Gerard McCarren is Assistant Professor of Systematic Theology at Immaculate Conception Seminary, New Jersey.

Terrence Merrigan is Professor of Systematic Theology at the Catholic University of Leuven. He is the author of *Clear Heads and Holy Hearts: The Religious and Theological Ideal of John Henry Newman* (1991) and co-editor of *Newman and the Word* (2000), *Newman and Faith* (2004), and *Newman and Truth* (2008).

Thomas Norris is Lecturer in Systematic Theology at St Patrick's College, Maynooth. He is the author of *Newman and his Theological Method* (1977) and *Only Life Gives Life: Revelation, Theology and Christian Living According to Cardinal Newman* (1986) and co-author of *Christianity: Origins and Contemporary Expressions* (2004).

Denis Robinson, OSB, is President-Rector of St Meinrad School of Theology and Seminary, Indiana. He is co-editor of *Theology and Religious Pluralism* (2003).

Thomas L. Sheridan, SJ, is Professor Emeritus of Theology at St Peter's College, New Jersey. He is the author of *Newman on Justification* (1967).

Francis A. Sullivan, SJ, is Professor Emeritus of Ecclesiology at the Gregorian University, Rome. He is the author of *Magisterium* (1983), *The Church We Believe In* (1988), *Salvation Outside the Church, Creative Fidelity* (1992), and *From Apostles to Bishops* (2001).

1 Life and writings

SHERIDAN GILLEY

NEWMAN THE ANGLICAN

Childhood and youth

John Henry Newman was born in London on 21 February 1801, the eldest of the six children, three sons and three daughters, of a banker, John Newman, an easygoing member of the Church of England without strong dogmatic convictions, and of his wife Jemima *née* Fourdrinier, whose ancestry was French Huguenot. Newman was baptized an Anglican in the London church of St Benet Fink on 9 April, though he was only to make his first communion as an undergraduate in Oxford in November 1817. His religious upbringing was a conventional, non-sacramental middle-class one. His childhood religious education was the then commonplace Anglican undoctrinal Bible-reading of his aunt Elizabeth Good Newman, and his paternal grandmother Elizabeth *née* Good, but he brought to it a profound sense of the superior reality of the supernatural, as in his wish that the Arabian Nights were true and in his imagining that he was an angel and the world was a deception played upon him by his fellow-angels.

This state of mind was interrupted by an adolescent reading of the Deist Tom Paine and the sceptic David Hume. His conversion to a more dogmatic form of Christianity, Calvinist Evangelicalism, occurred, according to his own account, at the age of fifteen in the autumn of 1816. It took place during the summer holidays while he was staying on at his boarding school as a result of the failure of his father's bank and under the influence of his Anglican Calvinist schoolmaster mentor, the Rev Walter Mayers. Newman was thereby caught up into the Evangelical Revival, the most vital religious movement of his youth. The basis of his conversion was his sense of the ultimate reality of 'two and two only absolute and luminously self-evident beings', himself and his Creator. These are the subjective and objective twin poles of his subsequent thought: the self, with its feelings and intellect and conscience, and the God in whom the self finds the means of escape from its own selfishness and subjectivity. He later summed up this private and personal religion in Cicero's aphorism, 'never less alone than when alone', and it was the permanent foundation of his growth into a stronger public institutional and intellectual understanding of the doctrine of the Church.

Newman later came to consider his experience to be quite unlike the standard form of Evangelical conversion, of conviction of sinfulness and the sensation of transforming release by the divine deliverance from it. Rather, he 'fell under the influence of a definite Creed'.[1] It was, moreover, accompanied by a stern moralism. Newman read the autobiography, *The Force of Truth*, by the Evangelical Anglican clergyman Thomas Scott of Aston Sandford, to whom 'humanly speaking' he said he almost owed his soul. Newman summarized Scott's teaching, deriving from Scott's conversion from Unitarianism to Trinitarian orthodoxy, in the phrases 'Holiness rather than peace' and 'Growth the only evidence of life'. Holiness is the principle of growth within the soul; and it is only by growth in holiness that the soul can know it is alive. This emphasis upon personal holiness preserved Newman from any hyper-Calvinist tendency to antinomianism, or an assurance of salvation which had freed him from the need to obey the moral law. It accompanied his private dedication to the celibate life.

Newman's conversion was also, however, the beginning of his serious intellectual life, giving him the 'impressions of dogma' which remained at the heart of his religion, and which at first included the doctrines of the Trinity, the Incarnation and Atonement, and of the Lutheran apprehension of Christ, or the doctrine of justification by faith alone. He also embraced the idea of his own 'final perseverance' through predestination to eternal life, in his strong sense of his own divine calling, but like other moderate Calvinists, he did not embrace the concurrent doctrine of reprobation, of God's preordained rejection of sinners, which he later pronounced 'detestable', thinking only of the mercy to himself. His belief that the pope was Antichrist, deriving from the Evangelical Joseph Milner's *Church History*, put him in the radical Evangelical camp, and gave him an odd tendency to millennial speculation. Long after he had outgrown it intellectually, the image of the papal Antichrist stained his imagination. He remained ever after more certain of his conversion than that he had hands and feet, but his belief in predestination was fading by the age of twenty-one. From that time, his faith would always seek to balance the light of reason with the life of experience: true religion must satisfy the demands of both head and heart.[2]

Oxford

The Oxford in which Newman became resident as an undergraduate in 1817 was a bulwark of the Church of England, the principal training ground, with Cambridge, for its ministry, governed by the Heads of Houses and Fellows of the Colleges who were usually Anglican clergy (and as Fellows, had to be celibate). Newman's Evangelicalism made him an outsider to the heavy-drinking undergraduate culture of Trinity College, but his poor performance at his Finals in schools in 1820 was the result, he thought, of overwork and a crisis of seeking intellectual excellence over moral. In 1822, however, he triumphed in his election by examination to a Fellowship at the intellectually progressive Oriel College, where he came under the influence of Richard Whately, later Anglican Archbishop of Dublin, whom he helped to write a textbook on logic. Whately was accounted a radical thinker, teaching Newman not only to think, but to rely upon himself, yet, despite this liberal influence, Newman also learned about the doctrine of the Church in an Anglican tradition rooted in the writings of the sixteenth-century Richard Hooker and the Caroline divines of the reign of Charles I. Whately showed Newman the importance of the independence of the Church from the State in its own separate sphere, while another Fellow, Edward Hawkins, taught him the value of tradition beside the Bible, and the Rev William James imparted a version of the idea of the apostolic succession of the clergy, of their descent through long lines of bishops from the first apostles.

These three principles – tradition, the apostolic succession, and the Church's own independent authority – were to be fundamental to the Oxford Movement in the 1830s; but the major change in Newman's mind took place in the year between his ordination to the diaconate and the priesthood, between 1824 and 1825, over the issue of baptismal regeneration, the spiritual rebirth of the child at the font. This doctrine, taught by the Anglican *Book of Common Prayer*, was a stumbling block to some Evangelicals, as it appeared to contradict their understanding of God's justification of the sinner at conversion, a free and undeserved pardon for sin which led to regeneration or the second birth into a new state of life. Such a true converted Christian was thereby distinguished from the merely 'nominal' unconverted one. Whether a vital Christian, a real Christian, was created by baptism or conversion, was an issue fraught with significance for the Anglican doctrine of the Church as well as for her pastoral theology.

The matter was still a grey area in the 1820s, and Evangelicals like Mayers could adopt the compromise of a conditional or partial or ecclesiastical change of state to the child at baptism, to be completed, in some cases at least, at conversion. Newman, however, like another young Evangelical, William Ewart Gladstone, chose to embrace the full Prayer Book doctrine. This was partly because of his sense that the sharp distinction between the regenerated convert and the unregenerate, the saved and the lost, was an unreal one, as Hawkins had told him. It did not describe the people at St Clement's in Oxford where Newman was a curate, raising the money to rebuild the church, and would therefore not work in a parish. But with this belief came a new sense of the importance of the sacrament, and of sacraments in general, and of the Church which by sprinkling with water and pronouncing a formula could make all the difference to the spiritual character of her children.

There were two possible developments arising from Newman's drift from Evangelicalism. The first was into some form of liberalism, by which he meant not so much unbelief as the principle of indifference towards doctrine, that one religion is as good as another. By his own account, he flirted briefly with liberal views in 1827, but this ended with his own breakdown as an examiner in schools in autumn 1827 and the death of his favourite and youngest sister, Mary, early in 1828. Or he could move forward into the High Church tradition. In 1828, he acquired and began to read systematically the writings of the Fathers of the early Christian centuries, finding his hero in St Athanasius, who had defended the Nicene faith, in St Jerome's phrase, *contra mundum*, against the world. Complementing the influence of the eighteenth-century Anglican Bishop Joseph Butler, he also imbibed the philosophy of the ancient theological school of Alexandria, its mystical interpretation of Scripture, its love of learning, its belief in a divine revelation to the gentiles in the pagan philosophers, as well as to the Jews, and its understanding of nature as a mysterious sacrament and symbol of the Godhead. Newman's patient labour of careful scholarship in this area inspired his first book, *The Arians of the Fourth Century* (1833), and continued through his remaining years as an Anglican, bearing its final fruit in his *Essay on the Development of Christian Doctrine*.

It was a High Anglican tradition to appeal to the Fathers as well as to the Bible, but no one wrote about them with quite the intensity of Newman. His new High Churchmanship inspired this quest for the proper fourth-century pattern of the Church, as he sought out the origins of the modern heresies in the early ones, in the darkening world of ecclesiastical politics around him. In 1828, he succeeded Hawkins as Vicar of the University Church of St Mary the Virgin, and from its pulpit preached the succession of wonderful, uncontroversial parochial sermons which beyond his ordinary congregation of tradesmen attracted the fascinated interest of generations of undergraduates for the height of their spiritual teaching and the simplicity and beauty of their prose. He also preached the university sermons in which he expounded the role of reason as subordinate to conscience and experience in forming the conception of God. Partly inspired by Bishop Butler, he attacked those who treated belief as a matter of deductive logic and evidence and proof, regardless of the moral and spiritual dispositions of the believer, and tried to distinguish the forms of argument helpful to religion from those hurtful to religion. The university sermons embodied Newman's response to much of the conventional divinity of his own day as well as to the scoffers of the eighteenth century. Newman's teaching that faith is personal in character, as heart speaks to heart, passed into the very personality of the Oxford Movement itself, as a band of brothers devoted to one another, and to an ideal intellectual and spiritual community in Oxford. It was this sense of a common cause that Newman depicted in all its intensity in his later spiritual autobiography the *Apologia Pro Vita Sua* (1864), and it entered into the classic account *The Oxford Movement* (1891) by Newman's great Anglican disciple, Dean Richard Church, which both have a readership today.

Controversy was inevitable, with such intensity of feeling, and in 1829, Newman abandoned his own former support for Catholic Emancipation to oppose the re-election of the Home Secretary Robert Peel as a member of parliament for the University of Oxford. Newman called Peel a 'rat' for changing his mind on the issue when it was his duty to represent the Anglican interest of Oxford, but Newman also found himself in conflict with his former mentors Whately and Hawkins, now Provost of Oriel. Newman assumed the leadership of a younger set of dons, including his bosom friend, Richard Hurrell Froude, and the older but quietly inspirational John Keble. Keble's volume of poems, *The Christian Year*, published in 1827, with a poem for every service of the *Book of Common Prayer*, made the dangerous new imaginative world of early nineteenth-century Romanticism pioneered by Sir Walter Scott and William Wordsworth safe for the Anglican tradition, in what Newman, with reference to the Caroline poets, described as the revival of the music of a school long dead in England.

The Oxford Movement

The election of a new Whig government in 1830, after four decades of almost unbroken Tory rule, raised fears of reform of the Church as of the other parts of the constitution which radicals called the 'Old

Corruption'. There were popular attacks upon the bishops, most of whom opposed the Reform Bill of 1832, and the government decided as a first ecclesiastical measure to reform the over-privileged minority Protestant Church of Ireland, united to the Church of England in 1800. The Oxford Movement began in a paradox, in effect the defence of the aggressively Protestant Irish Church against a Roman Catholic crusade to reduce her power. Newman was stirred by the news of the government bill when on a holiday in Italy, but nearly died on revisiting Sicily. His recovery convinced him that God had preserved him for a purpose, reflected in his hymn, 'Lead, kindly light', and that he had a work to do in England. The poems written on his continental journey were published as the 'Lyra Apostolica' in the *British Magazine* and with those of other High Churchmen in the *Lyra Apostolica* in 1836.

After Newman's return to Oxford, John Keble preached his sermon on National Apostasy from the pulpit of St Mary's, and ever after Newman kept the date, the 14 July, as the beginning of 'the religious movement of 1833', or as it was to come to be known after 1839, the Oxford Movement. The Movement opened its campaign in September by publishing the *Tracts for the Times*, originally brief productions only a few pages long. Newman was to publish or edit or contribute to thirty of the ninety *Tracts*. In the first, he began in militant manner by calling for a reassertion of the authority of the office of the bishop as the local and present embodiment of apostolic authority in the Church, signifying her independent foundation by Christ. The *Tracts* taught that the Church was a supernatural society with her foundations in the heavens, Christ's body and bride, 'His very self below', bearing the divine message even to the end of the world.

Though this was partly a response to the claim by the State to reform the Church, there was another paradox here, that the Movement began among arch-conservative Tories traditionally attached to notions of sacral monarchy, and to the British constitution in which Church and State were one. Thus High Anglicans might protest at the Church's Babylonian captivity, and set out to make the Church a popular power, yet they would never agree on the desirability of disestablishment, which might have weakened the Church though giving it her freedom. There was, however, now a tension between the principle of the Church as established by the State, once all but a High Church article of faith, and the Church's Catholicity. To the new High Churchmen, or Apostolicals, like Newman, the Church was Catholic, or she was nothing.

The *Tracts* also rejected the ecclesiastical status of the Nonconformist Churches which, under Evangelical influence, had grown massively in membership in England and Wales during the preceding thirty years. On High Anglican theory, they lacked bishops and were therefore not Churches. With the accession of Edward Bouverie Pusey, the young and erudite Professor of Hebrew, to the Movement, the *Tracts* increasingly became learned treatises, with a strong stress upon re-establishing High Churchmanship from the writings of the theologians of the Anglican tradition as well as from the Fathers.

The publication of a separate library of the Fathers began in 1838, and of the Anglo-Catholic divines in 1841. Newman's own patristic essays, another effort to change the whole spiritual and intellectual atmosphere or 'ethos' of Anglicanism, originally appeared in the *British Magazine*. They were republished as *The Church of the Fathers* in 1840.

There was good Anglican precedent for claiming a special ecclesial excellence for the Church of England, as superior to the other Protestant Churches, but the High Church tradition had usually acknowledged the benefit of the sixteenth-century Reformation, considering the Church of England to be Reformed as well as Catholic. Yet the Church of England had the special virtue of preserving the traditional Catholic threefold apostolic order of bishop, priest and deacon, as had the Roman and Orthodox Churches, while being free from their corruptions. On this basis, on the 'branch theory', Rome and Orthodoxy were 'branches', with the Church of England, of the original undivided primitive Church. Or on a different perspective, Rome, while corrupt, had a proper ministry which continental and dissenting Protestants lacked, and Canterbury held to a middle way between Rome and Geneva, or between Popery and a more radical Protestantism or Puritanism.

In *Tracts 38* and *41, The Via Media*, Newman suggested that the Church of England had become more Protestant than she once had been. In his *Lectures on the Prophetical Office of the Church* of 1837, a work which grew out of his controversy with the Abbé Nicolas Jager, and which was delivered in the Adam de Brome chapel of St Mary's Church, Newman redefined the *via media* or 'Anglicanism' as lying midway between popular Protestantism and Roman Catholicism. Yet even here he declared that unlike Rome and Protestantism, which had reality, forming the character of nations, 'Anglicanism' was only a 'paper theory', in the writings of a distinguished body of High Anglican theologians, not yet realized in concrete terms in the real experience of a living Church. Moreover, Newman distinguished, within the Church's teaching, the 'episcopal tradition' which he identified with the Catholic creeds, and which resembled the Anglican idea of the fundamentals of the faith, passed from bishop to bishop, from the 'prophetical tradition' within the broad current of the Church's theological reflection in its widest sense, including its worship in the *lex orandi*. This idea, of the subtle and complex relationship of the *lex credendi*, of what is believed, to the *lex orandi*, or how the Church prays, has had a profound effect on theology since, and it reaffirmed the importance for Newman of the Prayer Book. In stressing, however, the vitality and vigour of the 'prophetical tradition', Newman widened the possibility for change and growth in the Church's teaching way beyond the primitive creeds, while identifying the faith with the whole range and scope of it in a manner nearer to Roman Catholicism. Significantly, Newman renamed 'Anglicanism' 'Anglo-Catholicism' in his second edition of the *Lectures* in 1838.

Newman had some basis in the Anglican tradition for his *Lectures on the Doctrine of Justification* of 1838, his principal attempt to apply his understanding of the *via media* to a particular dogma, in which he took to pieces the Reformation principle on which the Church was said to stand or fall. Newman united the Protestant position, that justification is being declared just, that is given a full and free pardon regardless of one's sins, in a new relationship with God, with the Roman Catholic understanding that justification is being made just, that is restored, regenerated, renewed, in holiness and righteousness, God effecting what He declares. To the Protestant who argued that the formal cause of justification is the imputation of Christ's death to the sinner, and to the Roman Catholic who made the formal cause the infusion of Christ's merits through his death upon the cross, Newman preferred the language of the 'impartation' of Christ's merits through God's indwelling Trinitarian presence in the soul.

Newman made the instrumental cause of justification both baptism, as Catholics do, and faith, as do Protestants. The work of salvation is begun in baptism, sustained by faith, hope and love, good works and sacraments, and transforms the believer in holiness and righteousness in the image of Christ, from glory into glory. Newman thought that the Protestant formula, justification by faith alone, had some merit, in pointing to Christ as our sole justifier. Its defect in English popular Protestantism is that it produces the neglect of hope, love, good works, sacraments, holiness and righteousness, with a reliance not on Christ but on one's subjective feelings about Him, so that Christians are justified not by their faith but by their feelings. On the other hand, Newman argued polemically that the Roman Catholic position made righteousness a human possession to be trafficked with, as between equals, but his conclusion that justification includes regeneration was obviously closer to the Catholic position than to the Protestant one, as a process rather than an act, even while his emphasis upon the divine indwelling widened the subject with the teaching on deification by Athanasius and the Greek theological tradition.

The Oxford Movement's repudiation of the Reformation became still clearer with the posthumous appearance of the first two volumes of Hurrell Froude's *Remains*, also in 1838. *Tract 85*, Newman's 'Lectures on the Scripture Proof of the Doctrine of the Church', showed a radical awareness of the difficulties in the Protestant appeal to Scripture worthy of a German Higher Critic. There was, however, also controversy with the new Anglican liberals, and with the cloudy theology of the Oxford professor Renn Dickson Hampden. Newman had questioned whether another sometime Oriel liberal, Thomas Arnold, the celebrated reforming headmaster of Rugby School, was formally a Christian; in 1836, Arnold attacked him as one of the 'Oxford Malignants'. By 1837, Newman's attempt to define a new Anglican ecclesiology was inflaming the hostility of Protestants of every stripe and was worrying old-fashioned High Churchmen, whose conservatism was as remote as it could be in its moderate tone and temper from Newman's own innovative and quicksilver mind.

Newman's activities, however, were as much spiritual as intellectual: with editions and translations of the Breviary hymns; with *Tract 75*, on the Roman Breviary, and the revival of daily services and of auricular confession. His construction of a church in the hamlet of Littlemore gave him another field of responsibility, assisted by his mother and sisters. His belief in the Anglican *via media* was first shaken in the summer of 1839 by an apparent parallel between Anglicanism and moderate Monophysitism as a mediating position. It was even more shaken in 1839 on reading an essay on the Donatists of North Africa in the *Dublin Review* by Nicholas Wiseman, the principal intellectual figure in the Roman Catholic revival in England. Wiseman quoted St Augustine's phrase, 'Securus judicat orbis terrarum' ('the whole (Catholic) world judges surely'), to distinguish the local Donatist schismatics from the African Catholics in full communion with the world-wide Church. Newman recovered from the shock, which came to him with an incantatory power, distressing him with the thought that the Church of England, for all her claim to be apostolic, was in difficulty in claiming to be Catholic. He had applied the doctrine of apostolicity as one of union with his bishop, the sympathetic Richard Bagot – he regarded his bishop as his pope – but Augustine's universalism had emerged to resolve the problem of heretical bishops, through the need for a living authority superior to the bishop himself.

Newman assumed a heavy journalistic responsibility from 1838 to 1840 as an editor, as well as a frequent contributor, to the *British Critic*, and in 1841 he wrote a series of letters to *The Times* attacking his old adversary Sir Robert Peel's speech opening a reading room at Tamworth, which recommended religious neutrality. Newman's letters, subsequently published as 'The Tamworth Reading Room', contain a brilliant dissection of the powerlessness both of Peel's non-denominational Christianity and of a faith claiming to be based on reason and culture. The letters include some of Newman's most powerful writing on the role of reason in religion, so that he quoted certain passages from them nearly thirty years later in the formal and systematic conclusion to the argument of the *University Sermons, An Essay in Aid of a Grammar of Assent*.

In 1841, however, Newman unwittingly unravelled his enterprise of catholicizing Anglicanism. The Church of England, according to a famous aphorism, had a Catholic Prayer Book, but its sixteenth-century formulation of faith, the Thirty-nine Articles, was Protestant. The Articles were important as the guarantee of the Anglican monopoly in Oxford, where undergraduates had to subscribe to them at matriculation and the clergy on ordination and on becoming Fellows. They therefore had to be shown to be compatible with Newman's developing Catholicism. The authors had been Protestants, but Newman chose 'to take our reformed confessions in the most Catholic sense they will admit; we have no duties towards their framers'. By Catholic, he did not mean primarily Roman Catholic, but according to the faith of the primitive Church, and he specifically rejected such popish doctrines as prayer before images and the papal supremacy. But damagingly, he spoke of the Church as 'teaching with the stammering lips of ambiguous formularies' in the Articles, which had been deliberately phrased obscurely to include the Catholic-minded in the Tudor era, and could therefore be understood in a Catholic sense as well as a Protestant one.

Newman then set out, like a lawyer, to take them in their literal or legal sense. Thus the Articles recommend the official Tudor sermon collections, the *Books of Homilies*, which shed a Catholic light upon the Articles if these last are interpreted by them. He sailed closest to the wind of seeming sophistry in arguing, over Article XXII, which condemns 'the Romish doctrine' of purgatory as 'a fond thing vainly invented', that this did not condemn the official Roman Catholic doctrine, which was published by the Council of Trent after the Article had been drawn up, but only the abuses among ill-educated papists. So too, Article XXXI, on the 'sacrifice of Masses' (in Latin, 'sacrifices') as 'blasphemous fables and dangerous deceits', was directed against the widespread abuse of the doctrine, in private Masses, and not against the idea that the Mass was in some sense a sacrifice. Here Newman was thinking, as in much of his writing, of the distinction between popular religious practice and the Church's formal theology, a key not likely to occur to the ordinary reader. Yet far from being a dishonest document, enabling a man to hold the best living in the Church of England with the worst teachings of the Church of Rome, the most noticeable aspect of *Tract 90* was its artless candour about the difficulties of its author's own Anglo-Catholicism. In the storm of controversy which followed, Newman brought the *Tracts for the Times* to an end.

The din of condemnation of Newman by the Anglican bishops and the joint establishment of a Protestant bishop in Jerusalem by the State Church of Prussia and the Church of England brought Newman in 1841 to his deathbed on the Church of England. From 1842, he lived at Littlemore with a few disciples, engaged on his translations of the *Select Treatises* (1842–44) and *Historical Tracts* (1843) of St Athanasius, while editing the translation of the Abbé Claude Fleury's *Ecclesiastical History* (1842–44), for which he wrote an essay on ecclesiastical miracles (1843), and commissioning the *Lives of the English Saints*. On his resignation from St Mary's in 1843, he preached his most affecting sermon, 'The Parting of Friends', at Littlemore, evoking the mutual love and loyalty of his companions which had made the Oxford Movement what it was.

The theory of doctrinal development

Yet Newman still hesitated to become a Roman Catholic. The fifteenth and last of his *University Sermons*, published in 1843, 'The Theory of Developments in Religious Doctrine', derived the development of doctrine from the character of divine revelation, which was given as the impression of facts and actions on the mind, from which it reasons into doctrine. The Blessed Virgin, pondering the mystery of the Christ Child in her heart, had received an implicit knowledge of His person which would only later be made explicit in the doctrine of the Church. The same was true of the Apostles. The formulation of the doctrine deriving from this implicit knowledge would be part of inspired Scripture, but would go beyond it in the formulae which became the creeds, and which would admit of further doctrinal development down the centuries.

But perhaps the principle of development dealt with Newman's difficulty, that modern Roman Catholicism seemed to him to look so unlike primitive Christianity, especially in a matter like the papal primacy. Although revelation had ceased, doctrinal development continued to elucidate the original divine deposit, given in revelation, through the Spirit's presence in the Church. Just as an acorn looks unlike an oak, or a baby can only foreshadow the appearance of the man he becomes, so the Church could not exactly resemble her early self, but, if she is indeed still that original, must bear the evidence of nineteen centuries of development and growth upon her.

The principle of the development of doctrine has become so important in modern Roman Catholic theology that it is difficult to imagine a world in which Catholic theologians defended dogma by insisting that it was simply unchanging. No sentence in Newman has, however, been more misunderstood than his remark that 'In a higher world it is otherwise; but here below to live is to change, and to be perfect is to have changed often'. This ignores the preceding sentence, which urges that the idea of Christianity changes as it enters the world 'in order to remain the same'. Thus Newman has been wrongly taken to justify any and every kind of change, when his whole point is that development, properly understood, has its own laws, by which the idea of Christianity unfolds itself in every form of intellectual and institutional expression, making the Church ever more herself. It is true that by change an organism shows that it is alive, but it can only alter according to its own nature: a gazelle cannot grow up a gorilla. This is the very opposite of the Protestant notion of change, of a corruption of the original message which requires constant correction according to the principle of *semper reformanda*, a continuing revolution of returning to Scripture for the reinvention of the New Testament Church.

The Catholic, on the other hand, has to take into account the complete Christian story. Newman admits the possibility of corruption, and discusses seven criteria for distinguishing true developments from false ones: preservation of type, continuity of principles, power of assimilation, early anticipation, logical sequence, preservative additions, and chronic continuance. On the vexed issue of the papal primacy, he argues that there is more early evidence for it than for the doctrine of the real presence, which he received as an Anglican, and that if development accounts for the Athanasian Creed, it also explains the sixteenth-century creed of Pope Pius IV. In short, the work of spirit had never failed in the Church, any more than it had failed in him, as he projected his own personal capacity for life and growth to the whole of Christian history.

Newman's argument was complete, but the *Essay on the Development of Christian Doctrine* was still unpublished when he was received into the Roman Catholic Church by the Italian Fr (now Blessed) Dominic Barberi of the Passionist Order on 9 October 1845. Nicholas Wiseman, as assistant Vicar-Apostolic of the Central District, advised Newman to publish the work as it was, as the evidence of his intellectual movement into the Catholic Church. In that sense, the book was written for a particular purpose, not to prove Roman Catholic Christianity to be true but to remove a widely held objection to it, that Rome had changed, by making this change an argument in her favour. Like Darwin in *On the Origin of Species*, Newman offers his thesis modestly, as an hypothesis to account for a difficulty. Newman illustrates Bishop Butler's principle that conviction rests, not on binding syllogistic proof, like a chain, which is only as strong as its weakest link, but insofar as it is reasonable, on converging probabilities, like a rope, in which the weaker strands reinforce the stronger. The *Essay* carries the whole power of his personal pilgrimage, especially in its concluding passage – 'Time is short, eternity is long'. In the end, as Butler had taught, action cannot wait on perfect argument, but must make a definite choice.

Newman also brought to Roman Catholicism certain of his Anglican teachings, on the sovereign role of conscience, the importance of the laity and the development of doctrine. Above all, he saw himself as the same man before and after his submission to Rome, in a continuity unbroken by his new allegiance, in his quest for holiness and truth. Benjamin Disraeli may have exaggerated in claiming that Newman's conversion was the blow from which the Church of England still reels, but it is notable that the greatest of modern Anglican theologians ceased to be an Anglican. He had, moreover, given some of his best thought to the question of the identity of Anglicanism, and concluded that it was essentially Protestant.

On the centenary of Newman's death in 1990, the celebrations tended to stress his role as a bridge between the Roman Catholic Church and the Church of England, a judgement summed up by Adrian Hastings's view of him as 'the supreme reconciler', ignoring his many anti-Anglican remarks after his submission to Rome while remembering his reunion with his old Anglican friends who never ceased to love him, including Keble and Richard Church. The republication of his Anglican sermons in eight volumes by another Anglican friend, the Rev William Copeland (1868), testifies to his surviving influence in the Church of England, which he continued to regard as a bulwark against the rising tide of unbelief.

But the recommendation was a negative one, and Newman's legacy to the Church of England was ambiguous. His own insistence as a Roman Catholic that the Oxford Movement had its end in Rome from the first was denied by his Anglo-Catholic followers who tried to maintain his earlier teaching. His repudiation of the Reformation and of Protestantism gave rise to a very one-sided reading of Anglican history among Anglo-Catholics, and it turned Anglican Protestantism in a more radically anti-Catholic direction and fostered innumerable local Anglo-Catholic disputes with Evangelicals within the Church and with Nonconformists outside it. With the development of a more radically liberal Anglican school of thought by the 1850s, the heirs of Whately and Hampden, the successors to the Oxford Movement helped to precipitate the Church's division into warring parties of High, Low and Broad Churchmen with their own theological colleges and newspapers, so that Newman's own quest for a clearer theology resulted in a kind of undeclared but permanent state of Anglican theological civil war. Does the Church of England belong to the Reformation, or the Counter-Reformation, or the Enlightenment, or to some judicious amalgam of all three, and in what degree? Newman himself had weakened the Articles as a security for the Church's Protestantism, in a manner which benefited theological liberalism, as liberals like A.P. Stanley saw. The Anglo-Catholics were forced by episcopal persecution to practise a liberal congregationalism, with an infallible priest-pope in every parish, and the failure of the State and the bishops to control the ritualist clergy who introduced medieval or modern Roman ceremonial into their churches left unrealized Newman's own original programme for the restoration of Anglican episcopal authority. He had tried to exalt the office of the bishops, as angels of the Church, and the angels had knocked him down. He looked back over his shoulder at the lack of an ultimate authority in the Church of England, and having found a true authority, however marred by the flaws inseparable from mere humanity, he was not going to surrender it now.

NEWMAN THE ROMAN CATHOLIC

Newman's conversion to Roman Catholicism meant that he no longer had to create a Catholic ecclesiology, though he was to refine the one that he found. His position, however, was a paradoxical one. In the *Essay on the Development of Doctrine*, he justified his submission to Rome not on the usual ground of an appeal to Rome's claim to be *semper eadem*, always the same, but on the argument that Rome had remained the same by its capacity for change. A form of the idea of doctrinal development, deriving from the German Catholic theologian J.A. Möhler, had influenced Newman's disciple William George Ward, but Newman's own reference to Möhler shows that he had not read him. Newman's thesis puzzled the Roman Jesuit theologian Giovanni Perrone, who had written of Newman's Anglican writings that he mixed up and confounded everything ('Newman miscet et confundit omnia'). Newman was denounced as heretical by the American convert journalist Orestes Brownson because he seemed to strengthen the arguments for Unitarianism from the Bible, by insisting that belief in the Trinity historically rested on tradition as well as Scripture. Newman knew little of Roman scholasticism, which had still been familiar to seventeenth-century Anglicans. There had been no modern Anglo-Catholic library of medieval theology to complement the library of the ancient Fathers. On the other hand, his own very literary mode of self-expression was unlike the logical precision and argument by definition of ordinary Latin theology, even while the Roman theologians lacked his expert knowledge of the Fathers.

In any case, Newman was to be immersed for years in the sheer practical business of establishing himself at old Oscott College near Birmingham in 1846 and then in Rome, where he was ordained to the priesthood on 30 May 1847, and published a four-part Latin dissertation, the first part on Athanasius against the Arians. He was then busy establishing his institute of secular priests, the Oratory, in Birmingham. He thought of this as a Catholic version of an Oxford college, but the sixteenth-century founder of the Roman Oratory, the Florentine St Philip Neri, the 'apostle of Rome', had been one of the saints of the Counter-Reformation, and Newman, like his disciple Frederick William Faber, began his Catholic life with strongly pro-Roman loyalties. While not being opposed to Gothic architecture as such, if brought into line with modern rubrics, Newman favoured classical forms as a style more appropriate to the modern church, and like Faber, was in conflict with the Gothic Revival architect, Augustus Pugin, especially over Pugin's insistence on rood screens in front of the sanctuary. Newman also defended Faber's collection of lives of the continental Counter-Reformation saints, which aroused controversy among the more restrained native English Catholics for their emphases, particularly in the life of St Rose of Lima, on an extreme of self-mortification and mystical experience.

Loss and Gain and *Callista*

Newman's first major new publication as a Roman Catholic was the novel *Loss and Gain* (1848), which he wrote while in Rome. It is a witty satire on the extremes of Oxford religion as he had encountered it, as in holding up to ridicule the tea parties of the Evangelical Freeborn and the Gothic aestheticism of the High Church Bateman, but the sharp cut and thrust of the theological debate requires some specialist knowledge of what he was parodying. The novel's account of the interior development of its hero, Charles Reding, from Oxford to Rome, is a moving one, and the portrait of Oxford has its interest, especially in Newman's pioneering quotation of university slang, some of which seems to appear in print in the book for the first time. But Reding is a solitary figure. Although Newman himself briefly appears under two aliases, there is no real narrative of the collective activities of the Oxford Movement itself, and it does not touch the spiritual and intellectual heart of the Movement, about which Newman was to write so movingly in the *Apologia*.

Newman also began another novel, *Callista: A Sketch of the Third Century*, with its story set in North Africa, which is depicted in luxuriant and sometimes gory detail, enriched from its author's patristic reading. The narrative of the plague of locusts and of the subsequent persecution of the Christians of the decaying North African Church, and various horrors to do with the native paganism, are part of Newman's oppressive picture of the tropical over-richness of its setting. The heroine, Callista, with her natural purity deriving from her Hellenic inheritance, is by imaginative contrast with her sensual surroundings a convert and a virgin-martyr, like the heroine of Cardinal Wiseman's novel of the same period, *Fabiola* (1854), which is set in Rome, and was to be the first in a new Catholic library of fiction. Newman's work was not published until after Wiseman's, in 1856.

Early Catholic writings

Newman's *Discourses Addressed to Mixed Congregations* (1849) is a sermon collection notable for the terror of the address on hell, 'Neglect of Divine Calls and Warnings', depicting the damnation of an ordinary man no worse than most are. The *Lectures on Certain Difficulties Felt by Anglicans in Submitting to the Catholic Church* (1850) is Newman's most anti-Anglican publication, and still arouses Anglican hostility. The first half is addressed to his old High Church brethren, with its thesis that 'communion with the Holy See [was] the legitimate issue of the religious movement of 1833': the Oxford Movement always had its proper end in Rome. The second part of the work addresses some of the standard objections to Roman Catholicism beginning with the social and religious state of Catholic countries, which Newman painted in no unsparing hand, acknowledging the characteristic excesses of popular Romanism in a fashion which tries to weaken the objections to them by the very entertaining frankness of the description. Here Newman's brilliance is at scene painting, in a sort of impressionism before the impressionists. Yet Newman also recalled the happier dimension of his Anglican faith: 'Can I wipe out from my memory, or wish to wipe out, those happy Sunday mornings, light or dark, year after year, when I celebrated your communion-rite, in my own church of St Mary's; and in the pleasant- ness and joy of it heard nothing of the strife of tongues which surrounded its walls?' On the other hand, he found the Church of England as a national establishment to be ultimately unreal, however outwardly impressive, when 'as in fairy tales, the magic castle vanishes when the spell is broken, and nothing is seen but the wild heath, the barren rock, and the forlorn sheep-walk.'[3] A papal doctorate followed soon after, and it was as Dr Newman that he was known to the public until he was made a Cardinal.

Newman's 'best-written work', in his own view, the *Lectures on the Present Position of Catholics in England* (1851), addressed to the Brothers of the Birmingham Oratory and delivered in the Birmingham Corn Exchange, followed on the national anti-Catholic furore over the so-called 'Papal Aggression' of the pope's restoration of the Roman Catholic hierarchy of bishops in 1850, under Wiseman as Cardinal Archbishop of Westminster. This shows Newman at the very height of his powers as a satirist, in his attack on the great British monster of No Popery, as in his comparison of the Anglican bishops' thunderous charges against Rome to a very English phenomenon, a peal of bells. He also parodied No Popery as a tradition in the speech of a fabulous Russian Count Potemkin (supposed to be a junior member of the family of Catherine the Great's alleged builder of phantom villages) about the infernal British Constitution and 'the atheistical tenets and fiendish maxims of John-Bullism'.[4] Quoting Blackstone's *Commentaries*, Potemkin speaks in horror to his shocked audience of the maxim '*The King can do no wrong*', ascribing 'ABSOLUTE PERFECTION' to the monarch, who is 'the fount of justice', and works by 'grace', whose parliament claims 'OMNIPOTENCE', whose ancestor James I had called himself 'a god', who has 'UBIQUITY' in her courts, and whose 'ABSOLUTE IMMORTALITY' is asserted in the maxim, 'THE KING NEVER DIES'. To these must be added the past horrors of the British penal system and the evil actions of Britain down the centuries. The speaker multiplies the 37 in the year of the Queen's accession in 1837 with her then age of 18 years to give 666, 'the number of the beast' in the Book of Revelation. Clearly Queen Victoria is the Antichrist itself.[5]

The outcome of the work for Newman was a tragic one, for he attacked the character of Giovanni Giacinto Achilli, an ex-Dominican friar, and a mass seducer of young Italian women, who had become a Protestant and a popular speaker on the anti-Catholic lecture circuit. Newman relied for his charges on an essay by the inefficient Cardinal Wiseman, who had lost the documents on which his charges had been based. Newman faced the possibility of prison, and had to send emissaries to Italy to find the women to testify on the truth of his remarks, but though he was found guilty by a prejudiced judge and jury, he was let off with a lecture from the bench on the moral deterioration of converts and with a fine of £100. This was quickly paid from the large sums raised to assist him throughout the Catholic world, part of which went to the building of the University Church in Dublin. The further editions of the *Lectures* presented a gap where the pages on Achilli had been, with asterisks and in Latin the words, 'About these things which followed let posterity judge'.

This did nothing to diminish his stature among his fellow Catholics, and Newman remained at the heart of the Catholic Revival. His brilliant sermon, 'The Second Spring', preached to the assembled Fathers at the First Synod of Westminster at Oscott in 1852, drew an over-pessimistic picture of the meagre survivals of Catholicism in England after the Reformation, while predicting a glorious future. The preacher like some of his hearers, including Wiseman, broke down in tears, as Newman evoked the feelings of its time and place, in the mood of optimism created by the Church's rapid expansion, and the aspiration of some to reconvert the nation to the Catholic faith.

The Catholic University of Ireland

Newman's chief services to the Church in the 1850s came in connection with his Rectorship (1854–58) of the Catholic University of Ireland in Dublin, which he modelled partly on Oxford and partly on the Catholic University of Louvain. His most celebrated works of the decade were his lectures on university education in Dublin, published as *Discourses on University Education* (1852) and *Lectures and Essays on University Subjects* (1859). Most of these were reshaped and re-assembled as *The Idea of a University* in 1873. *The Office and Work of Universities*, a collection of articles in the Dublin *Catholic University Gazette*, appeared in 1856. Newman's inspiration for the idea of a university came partly from the conflict between Oxford and Edinburgh in 1808–10, and the defence of Oxford by Edward Copleston of Oriel against the Scots of the primary end of a university as a training of the mind, in a love of knowledge for its own sake, through a 'liberal education' in the true sense of 'liberal', as the free work of a free man rather than the servile work of a slave. For Newman, this training, in 'a habit of mind', a 'philosophical habit', in an enlargement of mind, like the intellectual contemplation which Aristotle considered the highest good, is an ultimate value, and requires no religious or moral defence, as it is an end in itself regardless of any use it might possess for the learned professions and religion.

Newman thought the university should teach universal knowledge, and impart a synoptic vision of all the sciences in their relations with one another, though he also commended as a basis for any education, the inculcation of intellectual habits like a disciplined mastery of detail, 'the idea of science, method, order, principle, and system; of rule and exception; of richness and harmony'. Again, while creating a curriculum based on the humanities, he did not undervalue the university's useful contribution to the professions like medicine, for which he founded a school in Dublin. With his insistence on a balance among the disciplines, he also accorded a large place to both the classics and theology, the latter as a science indispensable in a Catholic institution, which might yet produce an educated Catholic laity. His famous semi-satiric passage on the virtues and vices of the gentleman as the product of knowledge and culture, 'the creation, not of Christianity but of civilization', shows both the scope and limitations of the university ideal, as a good in itself, requiring supplementation by another. The Church exists to create saints, not gentlemen, and all saints are not gentlemen as all gentlemen are not saints. The rhetorical splendour of Newman's evocation of the long history of the papacy belongs to the argument for the Church's role as an agent of civilization. A university need not be Catholic, and Newman's name lives on among non-Catholics as the most distinguished of Victorian theoreticians of higher education. Indeed Newman shows an Oxonian devotion to the idea of the university in itself, as to the life of the mind. But Newman thought that if Catholic theology is true, the only complete university is one in which it is taught, and a Catholic university also makes its own kind of necessary contribution to the life of the Church.

Yet Newman's woes in Ireland wore him down. He later thought that he had been sent to Ireland trusting that any work blessed by the pope would prosper, when the pope knew no more about Ireland than he did. He felt that he was inadequately supported by his own patron Archbishop Paul Cullen, who declined to answer his letters, against some of the other Irish bishops, like the ultra-nationalist John MacHale,

Archbishop of Tuam, and that he was suspected of Anglo-Oxonian elitism by those in the Irish hierarchy who had been prepared to accept the government's own secular Queen's colleges, or who saw the main function of the institution as a utilitarian one, the creation of an educated professional class of teachers, doctors and lawyers. Newman caused political disquiet in different quarters by appointing both English converts and Irish nationalists. He resigned from his Irish post in 1858.

The Rambler

Newman's Rectorship coincided with his conflict with Faber, as superior of the London Oratory, over a case which began with a dispute over whether it was the proper work of the Oratory to hear nuns' confessions but was related to different visions of what the institute was, the subject of a number of Newman's addresses to his brethren. The Birmingham Oratory was a large responsibility in itself, and its numerous good works were complemented from 1859 by one in which Newman took the keenest interest, the foundation of a public school, whose early pupils included Newman's future patron, the young Duke of Norfolk.

Yet Newman's rate of publication in the 1850s was an extraordinary one: it included writings on a range of historical subjects, including the *Lectures on the History of the Turks*, published in 1854, the year of Crimean War, and essays on the Northmen and Normans, the mission of St Benedict and the Benedictine schools, later gathered together with other matter in three volumes of *Historical Sketches* (1872–73). This productivity came to a sudden end. In 1859, Newman briefly undertook the editorship of the journal *The Rambler* which was in trouble with the Roman authorities over its lack of enthusiasm for the pope's Temporal Power in the papal states, then under threat from Italian nationalists and the House of Savoy. Newman himself did not think the Temporal Power essential to the papacy's survival, a position in which time has proved him right. His own essay, 'On Consulting the Faithful in Matters of Doctrine', which appeared in *The Rambler* in July 1859, was delated to Rome by Bishop Brown of Newport, later his champion. The essay has been regarded as the charter of freedom of the laity in the Church, though as Newman protested, it only allowed laymen a passive role, to be consulted as one does one's watch or a sundial, whenever authority wished to know what the faithful believed as a spirit-given witness to the truth.

But Newman's failure to explain himself in Rome, for which the dilatory Wiseman was partly responsible, left him under a cloud until 1867. He suffered from depression and wrote little during the five years from 1859, and there were rumours that he intended returning to the Church of England, which he indignantly repelled with the response that the 'thought of the Anglican service makes me shiver'.[6] His experience did not alter his fundamental loyalty to the pope, of whom he was personally fond, but it confirmed him in his conviction that Rome's place in the Church, while essential, had become over-weighted into a kind of tyranny through contemporary circumstances, especially the Church's loss of her theological schools at the French Revolution.

Apologia Pro Vita Sua and 'The Dream of Gerontius'

Newman was aroused from this state by Charles Kingsley's attack upon him for having no love of truth for its own sake like other Catholic clergy, in the December 1863 issue of *Macmillan's Magazine*. Newman's response, standing at his desk for hours to write while weeping, appeared in weekly instalments, beginning with the thirty-nine blots in Kingsley's charges, in a backwards reference to the Thirty-nine Articles. The resulting work, the *Apologia Pro Vita Sua* (1864), despite its knockabout reply to Kingsley, is a spiritual autobiography, lacking much normal autobiographical detail like the names of his parents. But the sheer beauty of its prose and its strength of feeling, as an account of a personal pilgrimage, in a transparently sincere quest after religious truth, make it worthy to stand beside St Augustine's *Confessions*, and carried all before it to convince most of its Protestant readers that however great were his difficulties in showing the complexities of a state of mind which changed over time, here was an honest man. Subsequent attempts to convict Newman of error in his detail have not shaken the general acceptance of his integrity which was the general reaction to the work.

The *Apologia* also gave Protestant England an understanding of the romance of the Oxford Movement, as a spiritual and intellectual force for transforming the Church of England. It thereby did a high service to Anglo-Catholicism, as well as to the Roman Catholic Church, and occasioned Newman's resumption of his old friendships with Richard Church and Keble, who died only two years later, while making Newman himself a respected figure in the Victorian pantheon of great men, as one of whom the ordinary Briton could be proud.

There was a further triumph, as yet unforeseen in 1865, in Newman's publication in the Jesuit periodical *The Month* of 'The Dream of Gerontius', a poem describing the soul's departure through death to Purgatory. As well as softening the harshness of much Catholic teaching on the last things – the soul is cleansed in water as well as fire – 'The Dream' supplied popular Victorian popular hymnody with two of its favourite hymns, 'Praise to the holiest in the height' and 'Firmly I believe and truly', and later gained a further popularity among Protestants, astonishing in so 'popish' a production, through the setting of most of the text by Edward Elgar.

Newman and Vatican I

Newman's new moral stature confirmed his standing with the less aggressively neo-Ultramontane body of English Catholics, including much of the aristocracy and gentry, apprehensive of the policies of Newman's sometime friend and fellow convert, Henry Edward Manning, who in 1865 succeeded Wiseman as Archbishop of Westminster. Manning was responsible for the failure of Newman's various attempts to establish an Oratory at Oxford, on the grounds of Rome's policy of opposition to religiously mixed education: after all, it was that opposition, embodied in the person of Paul Cullen, which had inspired the creation of the Catholic University in Dublin. Newman's reply in 1865 to the attack in Edward Bouverie Pusey's *Eirenicon* on Faber's extravagant Mariology defended the moderation of the Church's Marian teaching in both the English and Roman traditions, by invoking an argument, persuasive to Anglo-Catholics, which cited the second-century St Justin's description of the Virgin as the Second Eve.

Newman did not respond to Pusey's twin assault on Manning's doctrine of the papacy. Newman himself believed in papal infallibility, as a private opinion: he was not a Gallican, or a Liberal Catholic, but a moderate Ultramontane. He thought, however, that it was 'inopportune' at the time to define the doctrine, and held this position consistently throughout the period before and during the First Vatican Council (1869–70), which made the dogma binding on Roman Catholics. Yet the Council's definition, however outrageous it might seem to Protestants and liberals, disappointed the more extreme neo-Ultramontanes by keeping to the narrow confines of the Roman tradition of teaching on the matter. Newman suffered embarrassment when his private letter to his bishop, William Bernard Ullathorne, then in Rome, became public, describing the keener partisans of defining the doctrine as 'an insolent and aggressive faction'.

But Newman was impressed by the gradual submission of the whole episcopal hierarchy to the new decree, and after it had been intemperately attacked by William Ewart Gladstone, he defended it in the traditional restricted sense in his *Letter to the Duke of Norfolk* in 1875. The *Letter* pointed out that the pope's infallibility did not mean impeccability or sinlessness, and disarmed critics by listing numerous instances of past papal bad behaviour. Infallibility does not endorse the pope's private theological opinions, and only extends to an official definition concerning faith and morals, and not to matters of secular fact or history, or to particular commands. In an infallible utterance, the pope must intend to address the whole Catholic world, *ex cathedra Petri*, from St Peter's chair, and not just order or instruct a part of it. Such definitions are not a primary means of moral teaching, which arises from conscience. Infallibility belongs only to the words of the definition itself, and does not extend to its supporting documents or arguments.

Newman's understanding of infallibility has been generally accepted by the modern Church, and has been clearly exercised only twice in the modern era, to define the Immaculate Conception of the Virgin, in 1854, and the Assumption in 1950. Newman also had to answer Gladstone's charge that the doctrine had made a difference to the civil allegiance of Roman Catholics to the Crown. Newman replied that infallibility did not apply to such a political loyalty, and that in after-dinner etiquette, he would toast the pope, but conscience first, thereby restating his primary loyalty to this inner 'aboriginal Vicar of Christ' as the pope within: belief in Rome depends upon the very obedience to conscience which the pope could not disturb without undermining himself.

Newman's reference to the 'malaria' at the foot of St Peter's caused disquiet in Rome, as referring to the papal curia, which took exception to parts of the document, and proposed in 1876 to censure it.[7] The move was stopped by Manning, now a cardinal, on the grounds that Newman had provided the most sympathetic and winning interpretation of the Vatican decrees to the British Protestant public. Indeed Manning supported the Duke of Norfolk's action in 1879 to secure for Newman a cardinal's hat, but Manning chose to interpret literally Newman's formal refusal of the honour: a non-episcopal cardinal had normally to reside in Rome, and Newman did not wish to negotiate the point with Pope Leo XIII. In the end, Newman received the hat, declaring that the cloud had lifted from him forever. His motto as cardinal, 'Cor ad cor loquitur' ('heart speaks to heart'), summed up his experience of both the communion of believers and of God Himself. His long ordeal of trial by the very authorities which he had tried to uphold, both as an Anglican and as a Roman Catholic, was at an end.

Newman was brought up against the issue of authority in republishing his Anglican works. Here he saw that it was impossible to alter the record of his past opinions, but for the two-volume collection

The Via Media, containing both the third edition of his *Lectures on the Prophetical Office* and a miscellaneous body of Anglican publications, including his retractions of his anti-Roman opinions, he wrote a long corrective Preface answering the charge of corruption, in which he set out his mature thoughts on the distribution of functions within the Church. The key, he thought, lay in Christ's three offices as Prophet, Priest and King, which are exercised by the Church in His name. The Priestly Office includes worship, piety and the spiritual life. Its credal note is Holiness, its instrument the affections, its aim or end is devotion, and its bad tendency is to superstition. It is chiefly the activity of priesthood and people. The Prophetical Office is intellectual, theological and philosophical. Its credal note is Apostolicity, its instrument is reason, its aim or end is truth. Its bad tendency is towards rationalism or heresy, and it is chiefly the activity of the theologian. The Regal Office has the care of rule, government and administration. Its credal marks are Oneness and Catholicity, its instrument is command, its end or aim is order, its bad expression is tyranny, and it is chiefly exercised by the papacy and curia. In short, given that the Church consists of peccable mortals, there is a natural tendency of the offices to exceed their proper sphere and to collide, giving rise to the conflict and scandal that the enemies of the Church always hold against her.

The implications, which Newman delicately suggested rather than spelled out in detail, are clear, in a lesson in common tolerance. The theologian should respect the old Neapolitan crone who chattered to her crucifix, for within her seeming idolatry lies a kernel of true devotion. The theologian cannot be the final arbiter of truth, and Rome should provide space for theological disagreement and debate, and only condemn when the faith is in danger. Newman's categories were enlarged by the Baron Friedrich von Hügel as the 'ethico-mystical', the 'intellectual' and the 'institutional' in his work *The Mystical Element of Religion* (1908) into a general theory of religion, but Newman's work also suggests that, as in contemporary economic or evolutionary theory, a true balance can emerge should conflict occur.

The 'Preface' could be taken as the ecclesial summit of Newman's long religious pilgrimage. He had found his early Evangelicalism lacking in a defence in reason. His brief flirtation in liberalism showed its deficiency in faith, his Anglo-Catholicism proved to be deficient in order. He thought that Liberal Catholicism leaned too far towards reason, neo-Ultramontanism too far towards order. There was a balance, a classic position, which held each with its due weight in its proper relation to the others.

The *Grammar of Assent*

This attempt to analyse the constitutional complexity of the Church had its complement in Newman's effort to show the structural complexity of personal belief. Whereas his works usually were written for particular occasions, to answer a case or meet a challenge, *An Essay in Aid of a Grammar of Assent* (1870), which had a large number of false beginnings over the years, was an uncharacteristically systematic study from its rebarbative opening sentence, 'Propositions (consisting of a subject and predicate united by the copula) may take a categorical, conditional, or interrogative form'.[8] With a theory of knowledge resting on empiricists like John Locke, Newman argued that the mind operates by receiving the real images or impressions of individual objects, which are private and personal to the receiver. General public notions are based upon them, but there are many such notions of which a person may have no personal experience but of which he has only heard or read. But that gives rise to two modes of argument, about matters of which individuals have a real personal experience, from the inside, and notions which they only know from externals or at second hand. Newman calls the first real inference, leading to conclusions which as assents or assertions are held with certitude. He thereby explained the fundamental conflicts in conviction between one person and another as arising ultimately from the differences in what they find in experience to be real.

Of course, the same real forms of experience give rise to wider loyalties, as to a flag, a nation or a Church. But because such loyalties are ultimately rooted in what the individual finds real, they lead to divergences in any argument about them. In this, religion is like other subject areas in which differences are not to be resolved by reason alone. Yet such convictions are not simply irrational, though the arguments supporting them are only implicit and unstated. The mind may find a certitude in conclusions from probable arguments which accumulate to reinforce one another, and indeed, as Wittgenstein was to recognize, holds a host of propositions as certain which it has never thought to confirm, such as the claim that Great Britain is an island. Here, in spite of Locke's argument that beliefs should be held with a degree of conviction which is in proportion to the evidence for them, such propositions do not become more certain if further proofs are found for them. Certitude is absolute, not proportional to evidence, and is a normal and natural state of mind, even where it does not arise from a conclusion based on the binding formal logic of the syllogism or mathematical proof.

Yet such a certitude is not unreasonable, even though the mind may take a synoptic view of concrete particulars without propositional or linguistic intermediaries, as it brings to its materials a surplus which is not obviously in those materials themselves. A weather-wise peasant surveying the clouds, or a Napoleon concluding his strategy from a swift survey of his opposing armies, or even in mathematics, a Newton pointing to the rule for finding the imaginary root of equations, seems to have a power of argument, which is common sense in the multitude, in matters of practical everyday judgement, but is a special skill in the gifted and genius in the few. Newman called this power to judge (with reference to Aristotle's *Nicomachean Ethics*) the Illative Sense, and was thereby seeking to show the complex rationality of disciplines outside mathematics and logic, in a manner which has had its influence on philosophers to the present day. The *Grammar* was Newman's last independent major book, his attempt to show the new scientific spirits, who insisted on mathematical or empirical proofs for everything, that religious belief is, with other kinds of mental activity, a normal and natural activity of the mind, as indeed are such other areas in which the mind makes reasoned judgements on the basis of real experience, from aesthetics to human relations.

Newman's legacy

Newman devoted much of his remaining old age to the revision and republication of his complete works. This, however, left much in manuscript which has seen the light of day since, and he has been shown to be one of the greatest letter-writers of the nineteenth century by the publication, from 1961, of his letters in thirty-one volumes. They show him exercising his full literary powers in all his moods, from tenderness and affection to sarcasm and rebuke.

Newman would have disapproved the opinions of those secular admirers who think that his genius conjured masterpieces from passing dead-and-gone theological controversies. His output was mainly ecclesiological, a gigantic exercise in showing the compatibility of the critical spirit with Roman Catholicism. His wider reputation has grown with time, but this has been especially true in his own communion, in which Rome has declared him Venerable. He did, however, confront a major historic difficulty as a Roman Catholic. His career in the Church coincided with the neo-Ultramontane movement among Catholics to reaffirm their loyalty to Rome, as the papacy became the symbol of Catholic resistance to liberal and anticlerical attacks upon the Church in Catholic countries, and the heart of her demands for spiritual independence from the State. This was especially so in Italy where nationalists assailed the States of the Church. The personal benevolence of Pius IX (1846–78), the longest ruling pope in history, helped to redefine him as the centre of a cult aided by new technologies, as cheap colour printing made his picture available to every Catholic home, and the popular press and the telegraph carried his words to the remotest corners of the earth.

Neo-Ultramontanism had much to be said for it: it helped to inspire the largest efflorescence of the religious life in the Church's history, not least in the new orders of women, and through a figure like Cardinal Manning, sustained a renaissance of interest in social justice. Above all, it had defended, often heroically, a principle which was more to Newman than life itself, both as an Anglican and as a Catholic, the sovereignty and independence of the Church. But though many of the leading neo-Ultramontanes were also laymen like Ward, the movement reinforced clericalism and central authority, in a Church which Newman thought had enough of both already. So it was that Newman's lack of enthusiasm for the Temporal Power, and his defence of the role of the laity and of the critical role of the theologian, made him suspect as less than wholeheartedly Ultramontane to Rome's more embattled defenders, such as his sometime Anglican disciples Frederick William Faber and William George Ward.

But the chief English Liberal Catholic critic of Rome, Lord Acton, and his great German theologian ally Ignaz von Döllinger, found Newman equally unsatisfactory as an ally, especially in his refusal to attack Rome openly. Newman's first major biographer Wilfrid Ward made Newman the spokesman for a lonely 'Via Media' in the Catholic Church, between liberal Catholics and neo-Ultramontanes, reflecting Ward's own 'Via Media' between the Modernists and the integralists around St Pius X. Even this, however, had the disadvantage of turning Newman, who was always surrounded by friends and sympathizers, into a solitary martyr for the truth. The Modernists like George Tyrrell themselves confessed that however stimulating they found Newman, especially in framing a non-propositional understanding of divine Revelation, he would never have been a recruit to their cause. More recent liberal Catholics who invoke his name tend to ignore his massive and fundamental orthodoxy. Newman's mature insistence that the theologian is not the sovereign power in the Church but must defer to the pope and curia placed severe limits on his own radicalism.

On the other hand, to call him a conservative or a traditionalist is to ascribe to him a defensiveness which he did not possess, and to misunderstand his sheer originality and quality of mind. He did not repeat the past, but offered a new interpretation of it. He aspired to show that orthodoxy and criticism were compatible with each other, and that above all, the Church could only welcome truth.

Notes

1.   *Apo.*, 4.
2.   *Apo.*, 4.
3.   *L.D.*, xxvi:115.
4.   *Prepos.*, 5.
5.   *Prepos.*, 28, 30, 32–3, 35, 38–9.
6.   *L.D.*, xx:216.
7.   *Diff.*, ii:297.
8.   *G.A.*, 3.

Further reading

Chadwick, Owen. *The Victorian Church*, Part 1. London: A. & C. Black, 1966, 168–202.
Chadwick, Owen (ed.). *The Mind of the Oxford Movement*. London: A. & C. Black, 1960, 11–64.
Dessain, Charles Stephen. *John Henry Newman*. London: Thomas Nelson, 1966.
Gilley, Sheridan. *Newman and his Age*. London: Darton, Longman & Todd, 1990.
Ker, Ian. *John Henry Newman: A Biography*. Oxford: Clarendon Press, 1988.
Merrigan, Terrence. *Clear Heads and Holy Hearts: The Religious and Theological Ideal of John Henry Newman*. Louvain: Peeters, 1990.

2 The Church Fathers

BRIAN E. DALEY

When John Henry Newman looked for words and images to express his understanding of authentic Christian faith and practice, it seemed almost beyond question to him to reach for the writings of the theologians we generally call the 'Church Fathers': pastors, exegetes, polemicists, preachers who had witnessed – in Greek, Latin, Syriac, and a variety of other ancient languages – to a growing understanding of the full meaning of the Gospel during the first seven or eight centuries of Christian history. Newman, after all, was born an Anglican, living at a time of crucial importance for the development of the Anglican Church's self-understanding; in the wake of his friend John Keble's celebrated 'Assize Sermon' of 14 July 1833, he found himself caught up in a new movement in the Church, which consciously sought to present the Church of England as rooted in classical Christian doctrine, in the traditional structures of Church office and sacramental worship, yet in critical opposition to the central leadership and teaching authority of the Roman papacy – a *via media* or middle way, as Newman and his friends described it, between the Evangelical or liberal Protestantism of the time and Catholicism.[1] Newman tells us, from the distant vantage point of his *Apologia*, written in 1865, that it was his own confidence in the unique position of the Church of England, as classically Catholic in its central beliefs and practices, but irreversibly opposed to the post-Reformation papal system, which drove him in the years after Keble's sermon to study the Church Fathers with new intensity and thoroughness: it was in the doctrines and worship of the 'primitive Church', Newman was convinced, expressed and regulated by the first four of the councils recognized by Christians as 'ecumenical' or universally authoritative,[2] that Anglicans could find a common Christian identity with both Orthodox and Catholic Christians and with the doctrinally faithful communities of the Reformation. Studying the Fathers, Newman was convinced in the early 1830s, could only make him a better Anglican, by revealing the shape of a purer and more universal brand of Christianity.[3]

In fact, Newman had begun studying the early Church even before Keble's sermon had launched the 'Oxford Movement' on its fateful course. In March 1831, he had been approached by Hugh James Rose, an Anglican clergyman of High Church commitments, to write a history of the councils of the Church as part of a new series to be published by Rivington's, dedicated to raising the Church's awareness of its own doctrinal and liturgical tradition.[4] Newman agreed, but as he worked on the project, he became more aware of the complex relationship between theological debate and its resolution in conciliar formulas, on the one hand, and the broader currents of piety, preaching, and customary biblical exegesis, on the other. He would at least need to produce two volumes, he thought – one for the Eastern councils, one for the Western – to do justice to the project; and the content would have to be not simply an explanation of conciliar teaching as a set of authoritative decisions and principles, but an attempt to evoke the developing consciousness in the Church of its fundamental interpretation of the Gospel of Christ.[5] Aided by a new thirty-six-volume set of Patristic texts presented to him by his pupils, Newman threw himself into studying the theological and spiritual background of the first council, the Council of Nicaea, and ended by producing a broad survey of the forms and central content of Christian doctrines on God and Christ during the second and third centuries, as the context of Arius's particular approach and of the ultimate Nicene response, as well as a detailed narrative of the reception of the Nicene Creed in the later fourth century. The result, finished at the end of July 1833, was Newman's first book and first major theological achievement: *The Arians of the Fourth Century*.[6]

This book – eventually published by Rivington's apart from Rose's projected series because of its length and detail, as well as the theological misgivings of its editors about Newman's reading of doctrinal development – begins with Newman's analysis of the religious forces at work in second-century Christianity: the Jewish and pagan philosophical traditions, as well as two very distinct approaches within the Christian family to interpreting the person of Jesus Christ and his relationship to the God of Israel, whom he called 'Father'. Newman devotes roughly the first third of the book to developing his own hypothesis of two distinct doctrinal and exegetical 'schools' in the early Church of the East: the approach of the Church of Antioch and its surrounding region, heavily influenced by the Jewish element in the Syrian population as well as by Platonic speculation, which took a somewhat rationalistic, historicist approach to interpreting Scripture and saw in Jesus at best an inspired prophet or a superhuman created mediator between a transcendent God and the world; and the contrasting approach of the Church of Alexandria, which cherished a loftier view of Jesus as truly Son of God, sharing the mysterious divine substance as his own, and which found support for this view in a figural or spiritual, rather than a historically literalist reading of the biblical canon. Arius, Newman suggests (with minimal historical evidence), was trained in Antioch, and shared the Antiochene approach to theology, even though he was an Alexandrian by birth and clerical appointment; his teaching that the Son of God was himself created before all things, and because he is a creature can act as appointed mediator between a transcendent Creator and finite reality, stands in radical contrast to the conviction later formulated in the creed of Nicaea against Arius, and defended almost single-handedly by St Athanasius for some fifty years: that Jesus is literally God as Son, in full possession of the unique, immeasurable divine reality that also belongs to his Father and to the Spirit he sends on the Church. Christian orthodoxy, in Newman's reconstruction of the early Church's debates, had its first home in Alexandria, not in Antioch, and in Alexandria's way of reading the Bible.[7]

The argument, as even Newman came to realize, was somewhat hastily contrived, and more than a little tendentious. It is easy enough, from our perspective, to see the contemporary connections behind Newman's reconstruction: the Antiochene tradition, given its full expression by Arius, combined the 'Jewish' biblical literalism of modern Evangelicals with the broad, philosophical relativizing of religious doctrine practised by the liberal wing of the English Church; both groups mistakenly took the Church's Protestant character as an invitation to reject classical doctrine and sacramental practice; and the key to resisting both, for those who took classical doctrine seriously, was to seek out a more spiritual, God-centred understanding of Jesus and the Church, as represented by the tradition of Alexandria. As Rowan Williams puts it, in his introduction to the 2001 edition of *The Arians of the Fourth Century*,

> Newman's 'Antioch' is an ideal type not an historical reality. It is the type of a theology dictated by human wisdom, human desire, the reluctance to be humble before revelation. Alexandria, the home of true theology, is characterized by reverence, by the expectation that the Bible will always be deeply mysterious, working through elusive symbolism over a lifetime of contemplation; this is a theology giving priority to God. Newman's purpose in terms of the 1820s was

evidently to challenge any English assimilation of German critical scholarship and doctrinal revisionism.[8]

Perhaps the most interesting element in Newman's argument, however, is his attempt to explain the apparent silence of ancient written sources, even in Alexandria, about Trinitarian doctrine and Christological orthodoxy before the late fourth century. The Alexandrian scriptural interpreter and theologian Origen, for instance, writing in the first half of the third century, presents us with a highly developed understanding of Father, Word and Spirit as sharing in a single, dynamic divine reality at the heart of created history; yet the three are also clearly ranked, in ways that at least echo the traditional Platonic understanding of God and his mediating agents.[9] Elements in Arius's discussion of the relation of Son to Father clearly echo the language and thought-patterns of Origen's Trinitarian theology, even though – as Rowan Williams has shown in detail – there are still more substantial differences between the two Alexandrians.[10] Tertullian, too, writing in Roman North Africa, and Hippolytus, his Greek-speaking contemporary in the first two decades of the third century, elaborated understandings of God as a single transcendent being, irreducibly composed of Father, Son, and Spirit; ultimately, they based their argument on the confession of those three names together in the baptismal creed.[11] Yet none of these authors uses the ontological language of one substance and three persons, as classical Trinitarian doctrine would begin to do from the 370s on. The question, then, inevitably rises out of the fourth-century Arian controversy and its context: is this central doctrine of Christianity, itself inextricably linked with the early councils' view of Christ as truly the Son of God, simply an invention of fourth-century Christian theologians? Is it the product of some form of development in theological thinking, which took time to reach its full articulation? Can it really be regarded as part of the original, apostolic faith of the Church – the faith expressed in the New Testament canon?

The classical Anglican view, represented in the early seventeenth century by Hooker and his contemporaries, and later in that century by Bishop Bull, was that the substance of the Church's faith in a Trinitarian God – the faith of the early councils – had been present in a recognizable form in Christian teaching since New Testament times, even if the technical language in which the dogma is expressed took time to develop. A prominent Roman Catholic approach, on the other hand, formulated by the seventeenth-century French Jesuit historian and theologian Dionysius Petavius (Denys Pétau), was to admit that many early

Christian conceptions of God, Christ and human salvation were impre-
cise and even erroneous by later standards, and that a gradual development of orthodox doctrine, as it would eventually be normative for the
whole Church, was only possible through the guidance of the Holy Spirit
and the leadership of the Church's hierarchical *magisterium*. Although
Newman would gradually adopt Petavius's view himself, his position
in *Arians* stood somewhere between these two positions. Pointing to the
ancient practice of the *disciplina arcani*, by which the central Mysteries
of the Christian faith were not publicly available through creedal formulas or written treatises, but were only communicated to full members
of the Church at the time of baptism, Newman suggests that the central
dogmas of the Trinity and the Incarnation remained within this orally
communicated tradition until public controversy, in the fourth century,
made it impossible to keep them private any longer.[12] Although
Newman realized, when writing *Arians*, that formulation and dogmatic
clarity is eventually a necessity for theology, as the Church takes on a
more public role in society, they are always at best a mixed blessing, an
invitation to rationalism and philosophical wrangling as well as to a
purer faith. The formulation of faith, in other words, can also become a
cause of its being cheapened, commodified, distanced from the gaze of
the contemplative heart.[13]

In his introduction to the most recent edition of the work, Rowan
Williams points out that this view must have seemed unacceptable to
the High Churchmen of the 1830s, who saw the Church as founded
on serious continuity with the doctrines and structures of primitive
Christianity, guaranteed by state patronage, just as it would have seemed
to the liberals of the time, for whom doctrine was dispensable, or to the
Evangelicals who clung to the text of Scripture alone:

> The effect [of Newman's argument] is a strikingly intense rhetoric of
> initiation, revealed-but-concealed mystery, the holy community
> guarding its integrity against a hostile world ... Orthodoxy has become
> more of a quality of spiritual life than a public system by which a
> community may govern itself. If you hold Newman's view of the
> Church, the legal privileges of the Church of England, with the ideology
> that went with them, could hardly be at the top of a polemical agenda.[14]

Even in this first book, Newman finds in the early Church a model of an
intensely spiritual brand of Christianity that invites the modern
Christian, too, to move beyond sectarian debates and religious politics.

Through the 1830s and early 1840s, Newman continued to develop
his vision of the Christian life in a dazzling variety of works: sermons and

lectures delivered at St Mary's, contributions to the series *Tracts for the Times*, essays in *The British Critic* (the Tractarian journal which he edited from 1838 until 1842) and other journals, and a variety of occasional letters to newspapers and other publications. Much of this vast output was centred on the effort he and his colleagues in the movement were now making to present a fresh and lively picture of early Christianity, one that would totally engage both the heart and the mind of sympathetic readers. From the ecclesiastical and political demands of the day, Newman found himself now a Patristic scholar.

In March 1834, for instance, he began working on an edition of the Greek fragments of the works of Bishop Dionysius of Alexandria, a third-century pupil of Origen's who engaged in an important correspondence with his contemporary, Bishop Dionysius of Rome, on the proper way to conceive of Father, Son, and Holy Spirit as God. This was, for Newman, a new venture into the technical, philological side of Patristic scholarship, and may have grown out of his own sense that *Arians*, for all its passion and energy, lacked a hard scholarly edge; unfortunately, he never finished the work.[15] During the 1830s, too, Newman wrote a number of more popular biographical pieces for the *British Magazine* on various key figures in the early Church – Basil of Caesaraea, Gregory of Nazianzus, Antony of Egypt, Augustine, Martin of Tours, and others – most of which would later be gathered, along with similar works he wrote as a Catholic, in three volumes of *Historical Sketches*. In 1836, Newman and Pusey began the *Library of the Fathers*: a new series of translations of key Patristic texts, which was the first systematic attempt to make the most influential theological and spiritual works of early Christianity available to the English reader. He also shepherded a team of translators (including his disciples Mark Pattison, John Dalgairns, and T.D. Ryder) in producing a translation of St Thomas Aquinas's collection of Patristic excerpts, arranged as a running commentary on the Gospels: the *Catena Aurea* ('Golden Chain'), published in 1841. In the summer of 1841, Newman began to work on his own translation of Athanasius's main doctrinal works for the *Library of the Fathers* – a translation that he radically revised, towards the end of his life, in the interest both of greater readability and of more recognizable Catholic orthodoxy.[16]

Throughout these years, however, Newman seems still to have been wrestling, in his own mind, with the central issue he had sensed in his study of the Arians and their opponents on the question of Jesus's divinity and its implications for our understanding of God: how can one account for the apparent distortions and omissions we find in early Christian theology, alongside its obvious strengths? How can one see in the early Church a model for contemporary Christianity, if the classical dogmas acknowledged by modern Christians are often still obscure or even missing in the more 'primitive' Patristic works of the second and third centuries? By the early 1840s, Newman seems no longer to have been content with pointing to the 'discretion' of early Church teachers in expressing doctrine, as he had done in *Arians*, and to have moved more and more directly towards the conviction that the conceptual content of Christian doctrine – what the Church knows and says of God – itself develops, in an organic but unpredictable way, within the bounds of a living community that is itself the sole herald and interpreter of the Gospel: a theory that clearly relied, for intelligibility, on some kind of institutional teaching office within the Church's leadership.

A first articulation of this position, now closer to that of Petavius than to that of Bull, is visible in the fifteenth (and last) of his Oxford University Sermons, delivered on 2 February 1843: 'The Theory of Developments in Religious Doctrine'. Here Newman attempts to work out an epistemology of faith, based on the assumption that religion involves an encounter with realities that lie beyond the ordinary grasp of the senses, and yet that offer us genuine, life-transforming knowledge – 'the possession of those living ideas of sacred things, from which alone change of heart or conduct can proceed'.[17] Newman argues:

> Further, I observe, that though the Christian mind reasons out a series of dogmatic statements, one from another, this it has ever done, and always must do, not from those statements taken in themselves, as logical propositions, but as being itself enlightened and (as if) inhabited by that sacred impression which is prior to them, which acts as a regulating principle, ever present, upon the reasoning, and without which no one has any warrant to reason at all. Such sentences as 'the Word was God,' or 'the Only-begotten Son who is in the bosom of the Father,' or 'the Word was made flesh,' or 'the Holy Ghost which proceedeth from the Father,' are not a mere letter which we may handle by the rules of art at our own will, but august tokens of most simple, ineffable, adorable facts, embraced, enshrined according to its measure in the believing mind. For though the development of an idea is a deduction of proposition from proposition, these propositions are ever formed in and round the idea itself (so to speak), and are in fact one and all only aspects of it.[18]

This priority of 'simple, ineffable, adorable facts' over our linguistic expressions of them, this *experience* of ultimate divine reality which serves as the foundation of all attempts to define it or argue about its limits, explains, according to Newman, the way in which the Church Fathers tended to interpret Scripture, and to use scriptural texts in argument with those they considered heretics: Scripture offers 'the main outlines and also large details of the dogmatic system', but does not contain its full development:

> Scripture, I say, begins a series of developments which it does not finish; that is to say, in other words, it is a mistake to look for every separate proposition of the Catholic doctrine in Scripture ... There is one view concerning the Holy Trinity, or concerning the Incarnation, which is true, and distinct from all others; one definite, consistent, entire view, which cannot be mistaken, not contained in any certain number of propositions, but held as a view by the believing mind, and not held, but denied by Arians, Sabellians, Tritheists, Nestorians, Monophysites, Socinians, and other heretics ... The question, then, is not whether this or that proposition of the Catholic doctrine is *in terminis* in Scripture, unless we would be slaves to the letter, but whether that one view of the Mystery, of which all such are the exponents, be not there. One thing alone has to be impressed on us by Scripture, the Catholic idea, and in it they all are included.[19]

What Newman here suggests as the reason that the life and faith of the early Church is normative for later centuries is not the conviction that the whole Catholic system of doctrine and practice is literally to be retrieved from the New Testament and the earliest Christian documents, or supposed to be part of early secret oral teaching, but rather a perceptible continuity between earlier and later forms of belief, already visible in early Christian debates and documents, that is rooted in a common experience of the saving Mystery of God.

What is still missing, of course, is an explicit acknowledgement that this perception of the Mystery, which lies behind all genuine development of doctrine, is authoritatively articulated within a universal teaching Church, one that is not identical with any national or political institution. Newman would finally come to express this conviction in the *Essay on the Development of Christian Doctrine*, completed in October of 1845, just before his reception into the Roman Catholic Church. Here Newman returns to the issue he had begun to deal with in *Arians*: the obvious reality of change – in practice, language, and even the conceptual content of teaching – within the Christian community. For some more liberal modern Christians, Newman observes, change of doctrine and practice is simply a normal fact of historical life, as the

Church 'accommodates itself to the circumstances of times and seasons'; but for them the idea of a divinely revealed truth and 'the supernatural claims of Christianity' are usually unimportant.[20] The classical
Anglican position, on the other hand, often justified by the dictum of the
fifth-century Gallic writer Vincent of Lérins that Apostolic doctrine can
only be recognized in 'what has been held always, everywhere, and by
all', restricts normative Church dogma and practice to what can be
demonstrated as common to all orthodox communities in Christian
antiquity. While conceding the attractiveness of Vincent's principle as
an ideal, Newman shows that such consensus cannot always be found
among major Christian writers and Churches of the first four centuries,
especially in what has come to be recognized by Anglicans as central
dogma: the doctrine of the Trinity, or the composition of the person of
Christ, or the reality of original sin. In contrast, other doctrines which
Anglicans and other Reformation Churches rejected, as not forming part
of Apostolic teaching, like the purgation of souls after death, the real
presence of Christ in the Eucharist, and even the teaching authority of
the Roman see, are, he suggests, commonly affirmed by the Church of the
first four centuries in both East and West.[21] Even Newman's own thesis,
developed in *Arians*, that the early consensus of Christian teachers on key
doctrines has been masked by the ancient practice of the *disciplina arcani*,
no longer seemed to him to be tenable, simply on historical grounds:
'because the variations continue beyond the time when it is conceivable
that the discipline was in force, and because they manifest themselves on
a law, not abruptly, but by a visible growth which has persevered up to this
time without any sign of its coming to an end'.[22] So Newman here
proposes, instead, the very thesis he had tried to avoid ten years before,
what he calls the 'theory of development of doctrine':

> That the increase and expansion of the Christian Creed and ritual,
> and the variations which have attended the process in the case of
> individual writers and Churches, are the necessary attendants on any
> philosophy or polity which takes possession of the intellect and
> heart, and has had any wide or extended dominion; that from the
> nature of the human mind, time is necessary for the full comprehen-
> sion and perfection of great ideas; and that the highest and most
> wonderful truths, though communicated to the world once for all
> by inspired teachers, could not be comprehended all at once by the
> recipients, but, as being received and transmitted by minds not
> inspired and through media which were human, have required only
> the longer time and deeper thought for their full elucidation.[23]

Newman goes on to illustrate his thesis in elaborate detail, and draws his examples almost exclusively from the doctrinal controversies of the early Church, as the period when the commonly accepted Christian dogmas cherished by the Anglican High Church were still in formation. Development, he concludes, is simply a natural aspect of the teachings and practices of any community that lives in history; development is given consistency, checked for authenticity, by the discerning promulgation and reception of the community itself in which it occurs; and this process requires leaders, teachers, recognized structures of authority and communication, in order to function effectively. His conclusion, based on the phenomenon of doctrinal continuity and change in the Fathers, was for him now inevitable: 'Of all existing systems, the present communion of Rome is the nearest approximation in fact to the Church of the Fathers ... Did St Athanasius or St Ambrose come suddenly to life, it cannot be doubted what communion he would take to be his own.'[24] As he would later remark to his former colleague Pusey, 'the Fathers made me a Catholic'.[25]

Newman discovered the reality of historical development in the Church by reading the Fathers. He was not drawn to their works, however, simply as a museum of evidence for the Church's struggle to discern heresy from orthodoxy, or as a collection of clues to the ecclesial conditions for authentic change in doctrine and practice. In a celebrated passage in his *Apologia Pro Vita Sua* (1865), he describes how, while working on *Arians* in the early 1830s, he found in Patristic texts, especially texts from the Alexandrian tradition of exegesis, a still deeper implication of the ever-changing character of worship and dogma, an invitation to see the world around him not simply as brute fact, but as a door to eternal, invisible reality:

> What principally attracted me in the ante-Nicene period was the great Church of Alexandria, the historical centre of teaching in those times ... The broad philosophy of Clement and Origen carried me away; the philosophy, not the theological doctrine; and I have drawn out some features of it in my volume [*The Arians of the Fourth Century* (1833)] with the zeal and freshness, but with the partiality, of a neophyte. Some portions of their teaching, magnificent in themselves, came like music to my inward ear, as if the response to ideas, which, with little external to encourage them, I had cherished so long. These were based on the mystical or sacramental principle, and spoke of the various Economies or Dispensations of the Eternal. I understood these passages to mean that the exterior world, physical

and historical, was but the manifestation to our senses of realities greater than itself. Nature was a parable: Scripture was an allegory: pagan literature, philosophy, and mythology, properly understood, were but a preparation for the Gospel. The Greek poets and sages were in a certain sense prophets ... In the fullness of time both Judaism and Paganism had come to nought; the outward framework, which concealed yet suggested the Living Truth, had never been intended to last, and it was dissolving under the beams of the Sun of Justice which shone behind it and through it. The process of change had been slow; it had been done not rashly, but by rule and measure, 'at sundry times and in divers manners,' first one disclosure and then another, till the whole evangelical doctrine was brought into full manifestation. And thus room was made for the anticipation of further and deeper disclosures, of truths still under the veil of the letter, and in their season to be revealed. The visible world still remains without its divine interpretation; Holy Church in her sacraments and her hierarchical appointments, will remain, even to the end of the world, after all but a symbol of those heavenly facts which fill eternity. Her Mysteries are but the expressions in human language of truths to which the human mind is unequal.[26]

In one strong tradition of Patristic literature, at least, which Newman identifies (with some over-simplification) as that of Alexandria, he found the ability to find eternal significance in temporal things, typological revelations of Christ in earlier biblical events, the presence of Christ as saviour in the present sacraments of Christian worship. The Fathers offered him not just a theory of Church authority, but a spirituality.

Central to the attraction that the Alexandrian Fathers held for Newman, it seems, was their strong emphasis on the organic unity, and the divine subjective centre, of the person of Christ.[27] This is particularly clear in his long-lived predilection for the theological position of Athanasius, the fourth-century opponent of Arius and promoter of the Nicene formulation of Christ's person, and for that of Cyril, his fifth-century successor as Bishop of Alexandria, who opposed the tendency of the later Antiochene theologians to see in Christ two closely entwined but ultimately distinct realities, one eternal and divine, one historical and human. In one of the revised notes Newman originally added to his translation of Athanasius, for instance, he explains the Alexandrian's understanding of Jesus's status as Son of God in extremely strong terms:

The Son of God must be God, granting that the human word 'Son' is to guide us to the knowledge of what is heavenly; for on earth we understand by a son one who is the successor and heir to a given nature ... The Son then participates in the Divine Nature, and since the Divine Nature is none other than the One individual Living Personal True God, he too is that God, and since that One True God is eternal and never had a beginning of existence, therefore the Son is eternal and without beginning ... Thus there are two infinite Persons, in each other because they are infinite. Each of Them being wholly One and the Same Divine Being, yet not being merely separate aspects of the Same. Each is God as absolutely as if the Other were not.[28]

This emphasis on the personal and substantial reality of Christ's divine identity characterizes Newman's own thought and preaching, as early as his Anglican days. So, for instance, in a Passiontide sermon given at St Mary's probably in 1841 or 1842, while he was at work on translating Athanasius, Newman makes it clear that the Jesus who suffered is literally God, in the full sense:

Here we are brought to the second point of doctrine which it is necessary to insist upon, that while our Lord is God He is also the Son of God, or rather, that He is God because He is the Son of God. We are apt, at first hearing, to say that He is God though He is the Son of God, marveling at the mystery. But what to man is a mystery, to God is a cause. He is God, not *though*, but *because* he is Son of God ... The great safeguard to the doctrine of our Lord's Divinity is the doctrine of his Sonship: we realize that He is God only when we acknowledge Him to be by nature and from eternity Son.[29]

And this emphasis on Jesus's divine identity, even in the midst of his human words and activities, leads Newman also to make his own the distinctive Greek Patristic idea of Christian salvation not simply as a change in the believer's relationship with God, thanks to the work of Jesus – as most Protestants had taught since Luther – but as actual transformation, as participation through the Spirit in the divine life and Trinitarian relationships of the Son. Thus he urges in a Christmas homily, probably from 1842,

Let us steadily contemplate the mystery, and say whether any consequence is too great to follow from so marvelous a dispensation; any mystery so great, any grace so overpowering, as that which is already manifested in the incarnation and death of the Eternal Son ... Men we remain, but not mere men, but gifted with a measure of all those perfections which Christ has in fullness, partaking each in his own degree of the Divine Nature so fully, that the only reason (so to speak) why His saints are not really like Him, is that it is impossible – that He is the Creator, and they His creatures; yet still so, that they are all but Divine, all that they can be made without violating the incommunicable majesty of the Most High.[30]

The theme of Christian salvation as divinization, first developed explicitly by St Irenaeus at the end of the second century, embraced by St Athanasius and St Gregory Nazianzus in the fourth and St Cyril of Alexandria in the fifth, and presented with even more radical clarity by St Maximus the Confessor in the seventh, is by the 1840s, at least, an integral aspect of Newman's increasingly Patristic interpretation of the Gospel of Christ.[31]

Newman's Christ-centred piety and theology, in fact – his sense of who and what Christ really is – remain anchored in the Alexandrian tradition throughout his life; it was not simply the Alexandrians' Platonic sense of meaning, or their tendency to search for types and mysteries in the narrative of Scripture that attracted him, but their deeply affective interpretation of the person of Christ, as well. So in the summer of 1858, Newman published a long, rather technical essay in the Irish journal *Atlantis*, defending the correctness of Cyril of Alexandria's favourite way of expressing the mystery of Christ, in his mature works: that in him we recognize 'one nature of the Word, made flesh'.[32] While the essay is couched as 'a purely historical investigation into the use and fortunes of certain scientific terms',[33] Newman is clearly intent on defending Cyril's language as being well within the mainstream of orthodox theology. The point was not obvious; the Council of Chalcedon (451), whose formulation of the concepts in which the Church traditionally understands the distinctive constitution of Jesus – as 'one *hypostasis* or person' subsisting 'in two natures, without confusion or change, without division or separation'[34] – expressly set out to find a theological middle ground, a *via media*, between Cyril's insistence on the 'natural' unity in Christ of the divine, saving Word of God with the humanity he made his own, and the more symmetrical picture of distinct but co-inherent human and divine natures promoted by Antiochene theologians and echoed, in the late 440s, by Pope Leo of Rome. Faithful adherence to Cyril's formula, especially by major Eastern theologians of the late fifth and early sixth centuries like Patriarch Severus of Antioch, led large bodies of the faithful in Syria, Egypt and Palestine to break communion with the Church of Constantinople and to ordain their own hierarchies – the beginning of a new set of Christian divisions, which continue to this day. As an Anglican and a Catholic, Newman was clearly committed to the two-nature language of Leo and Chalcedon as expressive of later Catholic dogma; yet his own theological sympathies, evident in his sermons since the 1830s and in his work on Athanasius, just as clearly lay with the more 'mystical', unified, God-centred approach of Cyril. In a Lenten sermon of the early 1840s, for instance, Newman reminds his hearers that Christ, the agent of salvation, always remains God in person and being:

> He took upon Him our nature, as an instrument of His purposes, not as an agent in the work. What is one thing cannot become another; His manhood remained human, and his Godhead remained divine. God became man, yet was still God, having His manhood as an adjunct, perfect in its kind, but dependent upon His godhead. So much so, that unless Scripture had expressly called Him man, we might well have scrupled to do so. Left to ourselves, we might have felt it more reverential to have spoken of Him, as *incarnate* indeed, come in human flesh, human and the like, but not simply as man.[35]

Newman suggests in his article on Cyril's formula, in fact, that this Alexandrian, strongly unitive interpretation of the person of Christ is the one that finds the most support in the whole Patristic tradition, and that the more symmetrical language of the Council of Chalcedon represented something relatively new, guaranteed as doctrinally adequate only by the intervention of Leo, 'who saw with a Pope's instinctive sagacity the need of the times, to explain the old truth ... under the comparatively new formula'.[36] Newman's reading of the central meaning of the Chalcedonian formula – like the interpretation of Chalcedon by mainstream Greek and Latin theology until at least the seventeenth century – was to take it in an Alexandrian rather than an Antiochene sense: as expressing the intuition of Athanasius and Cyril, in language that included, for the sake of Church unity, terminology favoured by their Antiochene critics.

The reasons for Newman's interest in Patristic theology, it seems, were not simply formal or historical, not simply that most of the classical doctrines on which the unity of Christians is founded were originally expressed in an authentic way in the first five or six centuries of the Church's history. Newman also seems to have felt a deep religious kinship with many of the early theologians who formulated, in conflict and meditation, what was to become the core of Christian orthodoxy. In an early Christmas sermon, for instance, he remarks that the early controversies and creeds not only set the boundaries for our own thinking about the Mystery of salvation in Christ, but 'rouse in us those mingled feelings of fear and confidence, affection and devotion towards [Christ], which are implied in the belief of a personal advent of God in our nature'. Patristic formulations of faith are suitable for use in the modern liturgy, he suggests, precisely because 'they kindle and elevate the religious affections'.[37] And in a later sketch, on the bitter political struggles of St John Chrysostom as Patriarch of Constantinople at the turn of the fifth century, Newman offers a gentle and attractive portrait of the Patristic style of theological argument that seems also to be a portrait of the kind of theologian (and perhaps correspondent) he wants to be:

> Now the Ancient Saints have left behind them just that kind of literature which more than any other represents the abundance of the heart, which more than any other approaches to conversation. I mean correspondence ... Instead of writing formal doctrinal treatises, they write controversy; and their controversy, again, is correspondence. They mix up their own persons, natural and supernatural, with the didactic or polemical works which engaged them. Their authoritative declarations are written, not on stone tablets, but on what Scripture calls 'the fleshly tables of the heart.' The line of their discussion traverses a region rich and interesting, and opens on those who follow them in it a succession of instructive views as to the aims, the difficulties, the disappointments, under which they journeyed on heavenward, their care of the brethren, their anxieties about contemporary teachers of error. Dogma and proof are in them at the same time hagiography. They do not write a *summa theologiae*, or draw out a *catena* [i.e., an anthology of excerpts from earlier sources], or pursue a single thesis through the stages of a scholastic disputation. They wrote for the occasion, and seldom on a carefully-digested plan.[38]

For Newman, who always strove to listen and to speak with the heart, the Fathers always remained in touch, always were ideal partners in conversation.

Notes

1. For a full description of his position in the 1830s, see *Apologia Pro Vita Sua*, ed. Martin J. Svaglic (Oxford: Clarendon Press, 1967), 54–60.
2. These are the Council of Nicaea, called by the Emperor Constantine in 325 as the first intentionally world-wide gathering of Christian bishops, to deal with the crisis of faith raised by the teaching of Arius that the Son of God, who became flesh, was created in time; the First Council of

Constantinople (381), which reaffirmed the faith of Nicaea and expanded its teaching on the Holy Spirit; the Council of Ephesus (431) and the subsequent document produced by its main participants in 433, expressing a common Christian understanding of the person of Christ as 'perfect in divinity, perfect in humanity'; and the Council of Chalcedon (451), which further refined this complex understanding of Christ, as a normative guide to the correct interpretation of the earlier creeds of Nicaea and Constantinople. This focus on the first four ecumenical councils as normative for Christian faith – rather than on the first seven, recognized together by Catholic and Orthodox Christians, or on the twenty-one general councils affirmed by the Catholic Church – has been characteristic of Anglican dogmatic theology since the sixteenth century.

3. See *Apologia*, ed. Svaglic, 60.
4. See Ian Ker, *John Henry Newman: A Biography* (Oxford: Clarendon Press, 1988), 42.
5. Ker, *John Henry Newman*, 43–4.
6. The most accessible modern edition of this work, based on Newman's third edition of 1871, is published by the Birmingham Oratory (Leominster: Gracewing, and Notre Dame: Notre Dame University Press, 2001). For recent, magisterial surveys of the fourth-century 'Arian' controversies over the divinity of Christ and the triune nature of God, see R.P.C. Hanson, *The Search for the Christian Doctrine of God* (Edinburgh: T & T Clark, 1988); Lewis Ayres, *Nicaea and its Legacy* (Oxford: Oxford University Press, 2004); John Behr, *The Nicene Faith*, 2 vols. (New York: St Vladimir's, 2004).
7. It is important to remember, as a backdrop for High Church concerns in Newman's time, that Arius's understanding of Christ as a created mediator between God and humanity continued to play a role in Christian theological discussions, and was revived with considerable enthusiasm by a number of Anglican divines in the seventeenth and eighteenth centuries. See Maurice Wiles, *Archetypal Heresy: Arianism Through the Centuries* (Oxford: Oxford University Press, 1996).
8. Rowan Williams, in John Henry Newman, *The Arians of the Fourth Century*, xxxix.
9. For Origen's view of the divine Trinity, see especially *On First Principles* Preface 4; i:1–3; ii:4; ii:6–7; iv:4.
10. Rowan Williams, *Arius: Heresy and Tradition* (London: Darton, Longman and Todd, 1987), 131–48.
11. See Tertullian, *Against Praxeas*, and Hippolytus, *Against Noetus* – both treatises opposing the 'modalist' or 'Sabellian' tendency of a number of early third-century Church leaders to suggest that the names of Father, Son and Holy Spirit really refer to three distinct ways believers have encountered the single God of the Bible, rather than to any distinctions within God's own being.
12. *Ari.*, 44–56.
13. For Newman's reflections on the negative aspect of doctrinal formulation, see *Ari.*, 36–7.

14. *Ari.*, xxxiv.
15. See Stephen Thomas, *Newman and Heresy: The Anglican Years* (Cambridge: Cambridge University Press, 1991), 68–70.
16. Newman's translation of Athanasius's works for the *Library of the Fathers*, published in 1844, included the *Contra Gentes*, the three authentic *Orations against the Arians*, the *De Decretis* and *De Synodis*, *De Oratione Dionysii*, and the *Defence before Constantius*. In addition, his notes on Athanasius's *Defence of his Flight* and his letter *To the Bishops of Egypt* appeared with translations by others. All of these works, except the early *Contra Gentes*, reveal Athanasius in full polemical engagement with those who rejected the language of Nicaea. Newman's revised version of his translation of Athanasius, which appeared in 1881, admits to being 'free,' and in many places is really more of a summary or paraphrase; he is interested now in making what he sees as the crucial sense of Athanasius's theology as clear as possible.
17. *U.S.*, 332.
18. *U.S.*, 334.
19. *U.S.*, 335–6.
20. *Dev.*, 10.
21. *Dev.*, 122–34.
22. *Dev.*, 29.
23. *Dev.*, 29–30.
24. *Dev.*, 27–8.
25. *A Letter to Dr Pusey* [1865], later published in *Difficulties Felt by Anglicans in Catholic Teaching* (London: Pickering, 1876), ii:24. Newman makes the same point, at somewhat more length, in the last of his 1850 lectures, *Certain Difficulties Felt by Anglicans in Catholic Teaching*, which deals with the significance of ecclesiastical history: 'I say, then, that the writings of the Fathers, so far from prejudicing at least one man against the modern Catholic Church, have been simply and solely the one intellectual cause of his having renounced the religion in which he was born and submitted himself to her' (*Diff.*, i:367).
26. *Apologia*, ed. Svaglic, 36–7.
27. For further details, see Daley, 'Newman and the Alexandrian Tradition: "The Veil of the Letter" and the Person of Christ', in Terrence Merrigan and Ian Ker (eds.), *Newman and Truth* (Louvain: Peeters, 2008).
28. *Ath.*, ii:287–8, 292. The Rev Benjamin King, in a yet-unpublished dissertation, has shown in some detail that when Newman republished his translation of Athanasius in 1881, along with an alphabetically arranged version of the original annotations to his translation, he made significant changes to align the text and notes more closely with scholastic Catholic orthodoxy. I am grateful to Benjamin King for allowing me to read this chapter of his work.
29. 'Christ, the Son of God Made Man', in *P.S.*, vi:53–82, at 56–7. This sermon, for the Fifth Sunday of Lent, was delivered before 1842. For a similar position, see his earlier sermon, 'The Humiliation of the Eternal Son' [before 1834]: *P.S.*, iii:156–72.
30. Religious Joy [probably 1842]: *P.S.*, viii:244–55, at 252–3.

31. The fullest and most recent treatment of this central Patristic theme is Norman Russell, *The Doctrine of Deification in the Greek Patristic Tradition* (Oxford: Oxford University Press, 2004).
32. 'On St Cyril's Formula, μία φύσις τοῦ Θεοῦ Λόγου σεσαρκωμένη *Atlantis* (July 1858), 331–82; later published in *T.T.*, 287–336.
33. *T.T.*, 332.
34. J. Neuner and J. Dupuis (eds.), *The Christian Faith in the Doctrinal Documents of the Catholic Church* (New York: Alba House, 1981), 154.
35. 'Christ the Son of God Made Man' [before 1842]: *P.S.*, vi:61–2.
36. *T.T.*, 376.
37. 'The Incarnation' [before 1835]: *P.S.*, ii:29.
38. 'The Last Years of St Chrysostom', first published in *The Rambler* (1859–60); republished in *H.S.*, ii:221, 223.

Further reading

Daley, Brian E. 'Newman and the Alexandrian Tradition: The Veil of the Letter and the Person of Christ', in Ian Ker and Terrence Merrigan (eds.), *Newman and Truth*. Louvain: Peeters, 2008.

Harrold, Charles Frederick. 'Newman and the Alexandrian Platonists', *Modern Philology* 37 (1940), 279–91.

Ker, Ian. *Newman and the Fullness of Christianity*. Edinburgh: T & T Clark, 1993, 83–122.

Strange, Roderick. *Newman and the Gospel of Christ*. Oxford: Oxford University Press, 1981.

Thomas, Stephen. *Newman and Heresy: The Anglican Years*. Cambridge: Cambridge University Press, 1991.

Williams, Rowan. 'Newman's *Arians* and the Question of Method in Doctrinal History', in Ian Ker and Alan G. Hill (eds.), *Newman after a Hundred Years*. Oxford: Oxford University Press, 1990, 263–85.

3 Revelation

TERRENCE MERRIGAN

THE IDEA OF REVELATION

The English word 'revelation' is derived from the Latin 'revelare' which means 'to remove the veil'. The Latin is in turn a rendition of the Greek 'apokalypsis' that literally means an uncovering, a laying bare. The term revelation is not, strictly speaking, a religious term. It can be employed to denote any act of disclosure, of making known what was hitherto unknown or unseen. As such the idea of revelation belongs to the entire realm of human experience and is applicable to the whole field of human knowledge. The theological discussion of revelation as a distinctive and even unique source of knowledge is a fairly recent phenomenon, a response to the Enlightenment insistence that the only valid knowledge is that which conforms to the standards of modern empirical science.

It is important to keep the broader understanding of the term in mind when one considers John Henry Newman's reflections on revelation. Newman was absolutely committed to the idea that the Christian religion contained truths that would not have been known had they not been disclosed by God in and through the life, death and resurrection of Jesus Christ. But he was also prepared to countenance the idea of God's universal self-disclosure, at least as a sort of (ongoing) preparation for the reception of the Gospel. It is here, in his reflections on what he called 'natural religion', that Newman's broad understanding of the notion of revelation comes into its own. And it is here, too, that we must begin if we are to fully appreciate Newman's presentation of the distinctiveness of specifically Christian revelation.

'NATURAL RELIGION' AND REVELATION

The experience of conscience

In his *Philosophical Notebook* (a collection of reflections and jottings which was only published in 1970), Newman ponders Descartes's celebrated 'Cogito, ergo sum'. He writes as follows: 'Though it is not easy to give a list of those primary conditions of the mind which are involved in the fact of existence, yet it is obvious to name some of them. I include among them, not only memory, sensation, reasoning, but also conscience.'[1] So Newman can write that it is as legitimate to say 'Sentio ergo sum' ('I feel, therefore I am'), or 'Conscientiam habeo, ergo sum' ('I have a conscience, therefore I am'), as it is to say 'Cogito, ergo sum'. In all these formulations, however, the linking 'ergo' is the product of a 'post-factum' analysis of what is originally 'one complex act of intuition', in which the 'apprehension' and the 'judgment' are simultaneous.[2]

According to Newman, conscience is characterized by two indivisible, but not indistinguishable, dimensions which he described as a 'moral sense' and a 'sense of duty'. As a 'moral sense', conscience is manifest in the awareness that 'there is a right and a wrong', which is not, of course, the same as knowing, in a particular instance, what is right or wrong. As a 'sense of duty', conscience is manifest as a 'keen sense of obligation and responsibility', namely, to do good and avoid evil.[3] Newman speaks of these two dimensions, respectively, as 'a rule of right conduct', and 'a sanction of right conduct'.[4] It is peculiar to conscience that it 'has an intimate bearing on our affections and emotions'. Indeed, in Newman's view, conscience 'is always emotional'. Hence, he sometimes speaks quite simply of 'the feeling of conscience' to describe its operation. Newman describes this feeling as 'a certain keen sensibility, pleasant or painful – self-approval and hope, or compunction and fear' which follows upon the performance of certain actions. For Newman, the feelings generated by conscience – or, more accurately, by our behaviour – are possessed of profound theological significance. As he expresses it:

Inanimate things cannot stir our affections; these are correlative with persons. If, as is the case, we feel responsibility, are ashamed, are frightened, at transgressing the voice of conscience, this implies that there is One to whom we are responsible, before whom we are ashamed, whose claims upon us we fear. If, on doing wrong, we feel the same tearful, broken-hearted sorrow which overwhelms us on hurting a mother; if, on doing right, we enjoy the same sunny serenity of mind, the same soothing, satisfactory delight which follows on our receiving praise from a father, we certainly have within us the image of some person, to whom our love and veneration look, in whose smile we find our happiness, for whom we yearn, towards whom we direct our pleadings, in whose anger we are troubled and waste away. These feelings in us are such as require for their exciting cause an intelligent being; we are not affectionate towards a stone, nor do we feel shame before a horse or a dog; we have no remorse or compunction on breaking mere human law: yet, so it is, conscience excites all these painful emotions, confusion, foreboding, self-condemnation; and on the other hand it sheds upon us a deep peace, a sense of security, a resignation, and a hope, which there is no sensible, no earthly object to elicit. 'The wicked flees when no one pursueth' [Proverbs, 28:1]; then why does he flee? Who is it that he sees in solitude, in darkness, in the hidden chambers of his heart? If the cause of these emotions does not belong to this visible world, the Object to which his perception is directed must be Supernatural and Divine.[5]

For Newman, then, religion or at least religious consciousness is a profoundly ethical affair. It is born out of the inevitable requirement – the necessity – to act. One might say, then, that the soul's encounter with God in conscience is as much a question of volition as of sentiment – i.e., the emotions attendant on the performance of particular deeds – though it is, of course, the presence of these emotions which implies 'a living object, towards which [conscience] is directed'.[6] J.H. Walgrave says as much when he writes that while the apprehension of God by conscience is 'spontaneous', it remains a free act which 'supposes' a serious moral commitment, a willingness to obey the moral imperative, and a fundamental choice for generosity.[7] The relationship between the soul and God which attention to conscience makes possible is not therefore merely a matter of present religious experience – it is, above all (to use another of Walgrave's formulations) an 'absolute religious goal'.[8] And for Newman, this goal is only realizable in and through a sustained moral commitment made incarnate in the mundane routine of every day. As he explains:

> Whether [the image of the Divine within us] grows brighter and stronger, or, on the other hand, is dimmed, distorted, or obliterated, depends on each of us individually ... Men transgress their sense of duty, and gradually lose their sentiments of shame and fear, the natural supplements of transgression, which ... are the witnesses of the Unseen Judge.[9]

For Newman, then, in the experience of conscience the subject apprehends not only itself, but itself as subject in relation to God. In other words, 'Conscientiam habeo, ergo sum' is also – and more or less simultaneously – 'Conscientiam habeo, ergo Deus est' ('I have a

conscience, therefore God exists').[10] This conviction explains Newman's
oft-cited remark that, for him, there were 'two and two only absolute and
luminously self-evident beings, myself and my Creator'.[11] It accounts,
too, for his declaration that 'If I am asked why I believe in God, I answer
that it is because I believe in myself, for I feel it impossible to believe in
my own existence (and of that fact I am quite sure) without believing also
in the existence of Him, who lives as a Personal, All-seeing, All-judging
Being in my conscience'.[12]

Newman acknowledged that his claim on behalf of conscience,
namely, that 'it has a legitimate place among our mental acts', or 'that
we have by nature a conscience', constituted an unproved 'assumption',
a 'first principle', the rejection of which made further discussion mean-
ingless.[13] He makes no apology for this. In his *Lectures on the Present
Position of Catholics in England* (1851) he declared that to think at all
one must be possessed of at least some 'opinions which are held without
proof', and these are rightly called 'first principles'.

> If you trace back your reasons for holding an opinion, you must stop
> somewhere; the process cannot go on forever; you must come at last
> to something you cannot prove, else life would be spent in inquiring
> and reasoning, our minds would be ever tossing to and fro, and there
> would be nothing to guide us. No man alive, but has some First
> Principles or other.[14]

Of course, for Newman the 'inevitability' of 'first principles' does
not divest the individual of responsibility in regard to them. It is basic
to Newman's philosophical outlook that humanity is 'emphatically self-
made', and charged with the task of 'completing his inchoate and rudi-
mental nature, and of developing his own perfection out of the living
elements with which his mind began to be'.[15] Where conscience is
concerned, the implications of this principle are staggering. Not only
is it one's 'sacred duty' to acknowledge conscience's legitimate place
among those 'living elements' with which the mind begins (in accordance with 'the law of our being'), the failure to do this prejudices, if it does
not entirely pervert, the elaboration of a whole body of derivative principles. For Newman then, the task of thinking soundly is, from the
outset, a moral, as well as a practical imperative, one to be fulfilled
most 'conscientiously' in fidelity to our being.[16]

Conscience and the emergence of 'natural religion'

For Newman, the apprehension of God in the phenomena of conscience is not the product of a rational analysis of our experience (though

such an analysis might well, in his view, issue in a proof of God's existence). It is instead an immediate, 'existential'[17] awareness – an instinct or intuition[18] – that we stand before One who is to us as a father, One in whose presence we feel a 'tenderness almost tearful on going wrong, and a grateful cheerfulness when we go right'.[19]

There is no suggestion here of private revelation or of some sort of mystical encounter with God. God is present as the source of the phenomenon, and the person – most obviously the child – who has been secured from influences hostile to religion or moral behaviour, spontaneously apprehends Him in the sanction (and its attendant emotions) which accompanies his decisions.[20] Hence, conscience is described as the 'voice' of God, or more accurately as the 'echo' of God's voice in us.[21]

As we have seen, Newman holds that the experience of conscience impresses on the mind a 'picture' or 'image' of God.

> These feelings in us are such as require for their exciting cause an intelligent being ... If the cause of these emotions does not belong to this visible world, the Object to which his perception is directed must be Supernatural and Divine; and thus the phenomena of Conscience, as a dictate, avail *to impress the imagination* with the picture of a Supreme Governor, a Judge, holy, just, powerful, all-seeing, retributive.[22]

It is precisely in view of its role in generating an 'image' of God in the minds of men and women that Newman describes conscience as the 'creative principle of religion'. Religion here – or 'natural religion' as Newman preferred to call it – is that living relationship between the believer and a personal God which comes to expression in stories and myths (narrative), rituals and devotions (spirituality), and codes of conduct (ethics).[23]

Newman displayed a remarkable appreciation for the religious traditions of paganism. In the *Apologia*, he records his discovery of the Alexandrian Church's view that 'pagan literature, philosophy, and mythology, properly understood, were ... a preparation for the Gospel'.[24] In the *Arians of the Fourth Century* (1833), he speaks of the 'vague and uncertain family of religious truths, originally from God', which permeate the 'Dispensation of Paganism'.[25] Indeed, Newman goes so far as to affirm 'the divinity of traditionary [i.e., pagan] religion'.[26] 'All knowledge of religion', he wrote, 'is from [God], and not only that which the Bible has transmitted to us. There never was a time when God had not spoken to man, and told him to a certain extent his duty.' Hence, Newman could write that, 'Revelation, properly speaking, is an universal, not a local gift'.[27]

Newman did not simply adopt the Alexandrian doctrine of the 'economy of salvation' with its attention to selected elements of pagan life. Instead he adapted it in the light of his own sensitivity to the demands of concrete history. Hence, Newman does not pay much attention to the doctrine of the Logos, which had served the Fathers in accounting for the wisdom of Greek philosophy, but turns instead to the actual practice of the 'natural religion' of paganism, since this was a more widespread phenomenon, more accessible to the great mass of non-Christians.[28] This is perfectly in keeping with his lifelong conviction that 'the one great rule on which the Divine Dispensations with mankind have been and are conducted [is] that the visible world is the instrument, yet the veil, of the world invisible'.[29]

This attention to concrete forms is reflected in Newman's conviction that God uses the rites and customs of pagan religions to realize His salvific will. In the *Idea of a University*, he writes as follows:

> He [God] introduces Himself, He all but concurs, according to His good pleasure, and in His selected season, in the issues of unbelief, superstition, and false worship, and He changes the character of acts by His over-ruling operation. He condescends though He gives no sanction, to the altars and shrines of imposture, and He makes His own fiat the substitute for its sorceries. He speaks amid the incantation of Balaam, raises Samuel's spirit in the witch's cavern, prophesies of the Messiah by the tongue of the Sibyl ... and baptizes by the hand of the misbeliever.[30]

In a similar vein, Newman in 1832 observed that God 'can sustain our immortality without the Christian sacraments as He sustained Abraham and the other saints of old time'.[31] And, on another occasion, he reflected that, 'As just men existed before Christ came, why not at a distance from the Church? For what the former is of time, so just men among the heathen is of space'.[32] In a most remarkable declaration, he even goes so far as to reflect that, 'it does not follow, because there is no Church but one, which has the Evangelical gifts and privileges to bestow, that therefore no one can be saved without the intervention of that one Church'.[33] The suggestion that God might indeed employ non-Christian forms of religious practice and association to work His salvific will is an idea that has only recently come to the fore in theological reflection.[34] While we cannot take this passage as proof that Newman thought in these terms, we must at least acknowledge that his reflections were not simply incompatible with this view. In this regard, it is interesting to note that the co-editor of the series within which Newman's *Arians of*

the Fourth Century appeared, objected to Newman's defence of the
principle that all religion comes from God.[35]

Newman's willingness to regard humanity's concrete religious history as the expression of a genuine (if deficient) relationship to God is
reflected in his acknowledgement that much of what is characteristic of
Christianity has parallels in non-Christian thought and practice. 'When
Providence would make a Revelation', Newman observes, 'He does not
begin anew, but uses the existing system ... Thus the great characteristic
of Revelation is addition, substitution.'[36] In line with this conviction,
Newman notes that, a 'great portion of what is generally received as
Christian truth, is in its rudiments or in its separate parts to be found
in heathen philosophies and religions. For instance, the doctrine of a
Trinity is found both in the East and in the West; so is the ceremony of
washing; so is the rite of sacrifice. The doctrine of the Divine Word is
Platonic; the doctrine of the Incarnation is Indian; of a divine Kingdom
is Judaic', and so on. Upon discovering this fact, some theologians
argue that since 'these things are in heathenism, therefore they are not
Christian'. Newman replies,

> We, on the contrary, prefer to say, 'these things are in Christianity,
> therefore they are not heathen'. That is, we prefer to say, and we
> think that Scripture bears us out in saying, that from the beginning
> the Moral Governor of the world has scattered the seeds of truth far
> and wide over its extent; that these have variously taken root, and
> grown up as in the wilderness, wild plants indeed but living; and
> hence that, as the inferior animals have tokens of an immaterial
> principle in them, yet have not souls, so the philosophies and reli-
> gions of men have their life in certain true ideas, though they are not
> directly divine ... So far then from [the Church's] creed being of
> doubtful credit because it resembles foreign theologies, we even
> hold that one special way in which Providence has imparted divine
> knowledge to us has been by enabling her to draw and collect it
> together out of the world.[37]

Whereas those who resist this view maintain that 'Revelation was a
single, entire, solitary act, or nearly so', Newman maintains that 'Divine
teaching has been in fact ... "at sundry times and in divers manners",
various, complex, progressive, and supplemental of itself'.[38]

Newman's discussion of 'natural religion' mixes historical and what
we would now call phenomenological analysis. As history, Newman's
presentation is certainly not up to contemporary standards. The heart
of his reflections, however, is not the history of religions, but the growth

of religious consciousness. And on this point, Newman displays a remarkable sensitivity to the insights of modern psychology. He is, for example, well aware that the development of an 'image' of God is heavily dependent on all sorts of 'external' factors and circumstances:

> How far this initial religious knowledge comes from without, and how far from within, how much is natural, how much implies a special divine aid which is above nature, we have no means of determining ... Whether its elements, latent in the mind, would ever be elicited without extrinsic help is very doubtful.[39]

Newman insists that the 'image' of God must be expanded, deepened and completed 'by means of education, social intercourse, experience, and literature'.[40] At least initially, and this remains the case if one's education and religious practice do not contribute to a 'filling out' of one's emergent image of God, the individual experiences Him primarily as 'Lawgiver' and 'Judge'.

However, while conscience reveals God primarily as a lawgiver, it also reveals Him as One who wills our happiness and has ordered creation accordingly. From the outset then, the individual looks to the divine lawgiver as to a benevolent ruler, who has one's best interests at heart.[41] Walgrave gives expression to this when he observes that, unlike Max Scheler or Albert Schweitzer and others, Newman does not reduce the experience of conscience to that of 'bad conscience'. Instead, he views it as a dialectical relationship between 'good' and 'bad'.[42] This tensile experience issues in two major characteristics of 'natural religion', namely, prayer and hope, with the former serving as the vehicle par excellence for the expression of the latter.[43] The hope of which Newman speaks is perhaps best described as an irrepressible existential longing or perhaps even anticipation that the One who calls us to perfection will come to our aid:

> One of the most important effects of Natural Religion on the mind, in preparation for Revealed, is the anticipation which it creates, that a Revelation will be given. That earnest desire of it, which religious minds cherish, leads the way to the expectation of it. Those who know nothing of the wounds of the soul, are not led to deal with the question, or to consider its circumstances; but when our attention is roused, then the more steadily we dwell upon it, the more probable does it seem that a revelation has been or will be given to us. This presentiment is founded on our sense, on the one hand, of the infinite goodness of God, and, on the other, of our own extreme

misery and need – two doctrines which are the primary constituents of Natural Religion.[44]

So it is that the expectation of a revelation, that is to say, of some initiative on the part of the divine, emerges, for Newman, as an 'integral part of Natural Religion'.[45] The naturally religious person is, as it were, 'on the lookout' for God, and ascribes even the rites and ceremonies by means of which he seeks to appease the Deity to the latter's revelatory activity.[46]

All this being said, however, Newman was insistent that the dispensation of paganism could never satisfy the religious hunger (or disquiet) engendered by the experience of conscience. On a number of occasions throughout his life, he offered differing accounts of the reason for this failure. So, for example, he speaks of conscience's lack of a sanction, beyond itself, for its elevated claims about the Moral Governor and Judge.[47] These are therefore prey to societal pressures and to the individual's own inclination to abandon the moral ideal as impracticable.[48] In an early University sermon (and, it would seem, again in the *Grammar*), Newman maintains that it is, above all, the obscurity of the object of one's religious instincts and aspirations, that is, the dearth of information about God's 'personality', which saps one's moral resolve and raises the spectre of the futility of the moral and religious enterprise.[49] In the *Grammar* and, to some extent, in the *Parochial and Plain Sermons*, and in *The Arians of the Fourth Century* it is the sense of one's culpability and one's inadequacy to the moral task which exposes natural religion's inherent insufficiency.[50] In all three cases, Newman proposes that the only adequate complement to the essentially incomplete natural religion of man is 'revealed' religion, which is to say, 'the doctrine taught in the Mosaic and Christian dispensation, and contained in the Holy Scriptures', which does not supplant, but builds on, nature's authentic teaching.[51] That 'religion' is the subject of the following section.

REVELATION AND THE CHRISTIAN RELIGION

The 'idea' of Christianity

Christianity, for Newman, is not the mere perfection of humanity's natural religious instincts, though it does involve the perfection of all the authentic elements of natural religion. It is the introduction into history of something hitherto unknown. It is a revelation of God that would be unthinkable were it not already realized in the person of Jesus, and 're-presented in the Church by means of certain sacramental "extensions of the Incarnation"'.[52] According to Newman, Christianity has provided us with a fuller vision of the divine person than conscience ever could. Great though our (potential) knowledge of God may be under natural religion, Newman reflects, it is but 'twilight' in comparison to 'the fullness and exactness' of 'our mental image of the Divine Personality and Attributes' furnished by 'the light of Christianity'. Newman actually speaks of an 'addition' to our image of God, and maintains that it is 'one main purpose' of revealed religion to 'give us a clear and sufficient object for our faith'. Indeed, 'the Gospels ... contain a manifestation of the Divine Nature, so special, as to make it appear from the contrast as if nothing were known of God, when they are unknown'.[53]

Christianity is a 'revelatio revelata',

> a definite message from God to man conveyed distinctly by His chosen instruments, and to be received as such a message; and therefore to be positively acknowledged, embraced, and maintained as true, on the ground of its being divine, *not as true on intrinsic grounds*, not as probably true, or partially true, but as absolutely certain knowledge ... because it comes from Him who can neither deceive nor be deceived.[54]

Christian faith is not simply the recognition of the suitability of certain doctrines to the human condition; nor does it emerge naturally out of the experience of conscience. It is instead a response to God's unprecedented action in history in Jesus Christ.[55] Newman's theology is radically incarnational. 'All the providences of God centre' in Christ, he wrote in the *Grammar*.[56] His salvific work 'is the sole Meritorious Cause, the sole Source of spiritual blessing to our guilty race',[57] and the Church, especially via its sacramental life, exists to render that blessing accessible to humanity.[58] As Ian Ker has pointed out, Newman did not hesitate to ally himself, as a Catholic, with the view of Duns Scotus, against Thomas Aquinas, that the Incarnation would have taken place even if humanity had never sinned.[59] The 'various economies of salvation' find their focus in the Christ-event. The Incarnation constitutes the unifying principle of salvation history in all its diversity.[60] Hence, Newman is quite insistent that faith in Christ and a share in the Church's life are the 'ordinary' and most reliable way to salvation.[61]

It is, above all, the radically 'historical' character of Christian teaching, its rootedness in concrete facts and historical events which, according to Newman, accounts for its appeal to the beleaguered practitioner of natural religion.

> Revelation meets us with simple and distinct *facts* and *actions*,
> not with painful inductions from existing phenomena, not with
> generalized laws or metaphysical conjectures, but with *Jesus and
> the Resurrection* ... The life of Christ brings together and concen-
> trates truths concerning the chief good and the laws of our being,
> which wander idle and forlorn over the surface of the moral world,
> and often appear to diverge from each other.[62]

'The revealed facts are special and singular',[63] though the 'principles'
these facts display are manifest in natural religion as well. So, for example, 'the doctrine of the Incarnation is a fact, and cannot be paralleled
by anything in nature; the doctrine of Mediation is a principle, and
is abundantly exemplified in its provisions'.[64] Revelation 'conveys the
"things" of heaven, unseen verities, divine manifestations, and them
alone – not the ideas, the feelings, [or] the aspirations of its human
instruments'.[65] Since it consists of 'facts revealed to us [which] are not
of this world, not of time, but of eternity ... and essential in themselves',[66] revelation is 'objective truth'.[67] It exists 'in itself, external to
this or that particular mind'.[68]

The 'res revelata' ('things revealed') are communicated through
human signs, words, and events. These media are inadequate to the
great truth of which they are the vehicles, but without them there
would be no communication of the truth at all. 'Such sentences as "the
Word was God" ... or the Word was made flesh ... are not a mere letter
which we may handle by the rules of art at our own will, but august tokens
of most simple, ineffable, adorable facts, embraced, enshrined, according
to its measure in the believing mind.'[69] In short, 'our ideas of Divine things
are just co-extensive with the figures by which we express them'.[70]

In the Incarnation of Christ, above all, 'the revealed doctrine ... takes
its true shape, and receives an historical reality; and the Almighty is
introduced into His own world at a certain time and in a definite way',
namely, 'in the form and history of man'.[71] For Newman, Christ is the
perfect realization of the sacramental principle – in Him, God is visibly
and tangibly active in history. 'Surely His very presence was a Sacrament',
writes Newman. In Him, 'God has made history to be doctrine'.[72] The
Incarnation is an unparalleled 'theological-historical' fact, that is to say,
an historical event charged with theological significance.

Speaking of the Christian appropriation of God's self-disclosure
through the Incarnation, Newman observes that 'the original instrument' of conversion and the 'principle of fellowship' among the first
Christians was the 'Thought or Image of Christ'. Moreover, he argues,

this 'central Image' continues to serve as the 'vivifying idea both of the Christian body and of individuals in it'.[73] The 'image' or 'idea' of Christ (Newman uses these words interchangeably) is the principle of Christian fraternity. As Newman expresses it:

> [Christ] is found, through His preachers, to have imprinted the Image or idea of Himself in the minds of His subjects individually; and that Image, apprehended and worshipped in individual minds, becomes a principle of association, and a real bond of those subjects one with another, who are thus united to the body by being united to that Image; and moreover that Image, which is their moral life, when they have been already converted, is also the original instrument of their conversion. It is the Image of Him who fulfils the one great need of human nature, the Healer of its wounds, the Physician of the soul, this Image it is which both creates faith, and then rewards it.[74]

The Church and the idea of Christianity

The Christian 'idea', in its completeness, is the possession of the Church viewed in its entirety. It exists in the 'mind of the Church', as the correlate to the 'fact of revelation', in the fashion of the image or impression which the individual mind forms of material objects. Newman acknowledges that 'religious impressions' may be made on the mind by 'supernatural' operations on the part of the Divine, such as those presumably manifest in the process of 'inspiration', or by 'illuminating grace' at baptism. However, in keeping with his general principle that God usually acts 'through, with, and beneath those physical, social, and moral laws, of which our experience informs us',[75] Newman insists that the 'secondary and intelligible' means by which one receives the 'impression of Divine Verities', are, for instance, 'the habitual and devout perusal of Scripture ... the gradual influence of intercourse with those who are in themselves in possession of sacred ideas ... the study of Dogmatic Theology ... a continual round of devotion, or again, sometimes, in minds both fitly disposed and apprehensive, the almost instantaneous operation of a keen faith'.[76]

The idea is not, properly speaking, the object of faith. It is, however, the means by which the object of faith is apprehended. In the words of Coulson, 'an "idea" is not reality at its most real but an image of what acts upon us in the manner of objects of sense-perception'.[77] Christianity is at once possessed of, and possessed by, the 'idea' of the Incarnate Christ (Newman's preferred focus for the appropriation of the mystery of Christ).[78] This 'idea' was communicated to the apostles 'per modum unius' in and through Jesus's life, death and resurrection (though their knowledge of it was to a great extent implicit), and there-after preserved, by the operation of the Holy Spirit, in the mind of the Church as a permanent and integral 'idea', 'impression', or 'image' (1843),[79] or as a 'deep internal sense' (1847),[80] or as a 'real apprehension' (1870).[81]

The 'idea' realizes itself in the Church's life and history as the shared property of the whole body of the faithful and as the principle of their union. It is manifest in their communal life, the shared life of the pastors and the faithful ('pastorum ac fidelium conspiratio') – such that communal witness is the only truly adequate criterion for determining what belongs to the idea and what is foreign to it. Though this latter insight – in fact, the theory of reception – only found explicit expression in Newman's Catholic works such as 'On Consulting the Faithful', and in his correspondence relative to Vatican I, it is implicit in the *Essay on Development* which, as Lord Acton observed, employs the ancient maxim that 'the voice of the people is the voice of God'.[82] Lash observes that 'it is fundamental to [Newman's] argument [in the *Essay on Development*] that the gospel is communicated to, and lives in, the church as a *whole*',[83] and Coulson rightly observes that, for Newman, 'Christ is not encountered directly or introspectively as an "alter ego", but always through the Church as a public body".[84]

Nicholas Lash has argued that, in the final analysis, the dynamism and organizing power of the Christian idea is born of its foundation in the risen Christ, God's living Word in history. It is this same rooted-ness in Christ which accounts for Newman's tendency 'to express the transcendence of the "idea" by hypostatizing, or personalizing it'.[85] The true 'object' of the Christian 'idea', then, is Christ Himself, the living Word of God who 'exists underneath and before all of the expressions which Christians have invented to expound it'.[86] He is the ground, the source of coherence, and the continuing dynamic, of Christian life and reflection, in and through which He is now known and apprehended.

The idea of Christianity and the Church's doctrinal tradition

The need to communicate the original apostolic experience, and the natural penchant of the mind for conceptualization and systematization (which is particularly evident in the case of heresies) entailed that attempts were quickly made to cast the grounding 'idea' in the form of meaningful propositions. In his fifteenth University sermon, Newman observed that, the mind which is habituated to the thought of God, of Christ, of the Holy Spirit, naturally turns ... with a devout curiosity to the contemplation of the Object of its adoration, and begins to form statements concerning Him before it knows whither, or how far, it will be carried. One proposition necessarily leads to another, and a second to a third; then some limitation is required; and the combinations of these opposites occasion some fresh evolutions from the original idea, which indeed can never be said to be entirely exhausted. This process is its development, and results in a series, or rather body of dogmatic statements, till what was at first an impression on the Imagination become a system or creed in the Reason.[87]

A dogmatic statement is, then, the fruit of the interaction between the imagination and the reason. In the words of John Coulson, these 'are to each other as implicit to explicit, inarticulate to articulate, and pre-conceptual to conceptual. They modulate into each other, therefore, and may be said to share a common grammar.' In view of this fact, as Coulson points out, Newman 'does not press the distinction between assents to the primary forms of religious faith (expressed in metaphor, symbol, and story), and to the beliefs and doctrines derived from them'.[88]

This explains why, in the *Grammar of Assent*, Newman argues that a religious truth-claim (such as, 'The Son is God') can be held 'either as a theological truth, or as a religious fact or reality'. In the first instance, 'the proposition is apprehended for the purposes of proof, analysis, comparison and the like intellectual exercises'. That is to say, it is regarded 'as the expression of a notion'. In the second instance, the proposition is apprehended 'for the purposes of devotion'. In this case, it is 'the image of a reality'.[89] According to Newman, religion 'lives and thrives in the contemplation' of images. It is this which provides the believer with 'motives for devotion and faithful obedience'. Precisely because it is 'an image living within us', precisely because it occupies 'a place in the imagination and the heart',[90] a dogmatic proposition, such as the claim that 'the Son is God', is able to 'work a revolution in the mind', to inflame the heart, and to shape our conduct.[91]

This is not – and need not – be the case where the same proposition is looked upon as the expression of a notion and subjected to critical scrutiny. Indeed, Newman observes that the application of the intellect to religious issues may well issue in a diminishment of lively faith. 'In the religious world', he observes, 'no one seems to look for any great devotion or fervour in controversialists ... theologians, and the like, it being taken for granted, rightly or wrongly, that such men are too intellectual to be spiritual, and are more occupied with the truth of doctrine than with its reality'.[92]

That being said, however, Newman's religious and theological ideal was a tensile or polar unity between both activities – 'religion using theology, and theology using religion'.[93] It is against this background that we must understand Newman's celebrated remark to the effect that, 'From the age of fifteen, dogma has been the fundamental principle of my religion: I know no other religion; I cannot enter into the idea of any other sort of religion; religion, as a mere sentiment, is to me a dream and a mockery'.[94] Dogmas, Newman explains, are related to specific 'facts', to events in history and to realities which precede us and which call for an appropriate response. These 'facts' are the foundation and the object of any and every sentiment, thought, and action which might be characterized as authentically religious.

Despite his insistence on the necessity of dogma as a pointer towards the appropriate response to God's revelatory deeds in history, Newman was profoundly aware of the limitations of every doctrinal formulation. As he explained:

No revelation can be complete and systematic, from the weakness of the human intellect. When nothing is revealed, nothing is known, and there is nothing to contemplate or marvel at; but when something is revealed, and only something for all cannot be, there are forthwith difficulties and perplexities. A Revelation is religious doctrine viewed on its illuminated side; a Mystery is the selfsame doctrine viewed on the side unilluminated. Thus Religious Truth is neither light nor darkness, but both together; it is like the dim view of a country seen in the twilight, with forms half extricated from the darkness, with broken lines, and isolated masses. Revelation, in this way of considering it, is not a revealed 'system', but consists of a number of detached and incomplete truths belonging to a vast system unrevealed, of doctrines and injunctions mysteriously connected together; that is, connected by unknown media, and bearing upon unknown portions of the system.[95]

Christian faith in revelation is therefore not reducible to the acknowledgement of a body of dogmatic propositions. Already in 1840, Newman had observed that, 'No analysis is subtle and delicate enough to represent adequately the state of mind under which we believe or the subjects of belief, as they are presented to our thoughts'.[96] Writing in 1858, Newman had pondered Christianity's 'poetic' and therefore 'immeasurable, impenetrable, inscrutable, [and] mysterious' character.

Poetry, Newman wrote, 'does not address the reason, but the imagination and affections; it leads to admiration, enthusiasm, devotion, and love'.[97] Elsewhere, Newman observed that 'Revealed Religion should be especially poetical – and it is so in fact'.[98]

The Church requires both the poetical spirit (represented by St Benedict) and the scientific spirit (represented by St Dominic), as well as the spirit of pragmatism (exemplified in Ignatius of Loyola). 'Imagination, Science, Prudence, are all good', Newman declares, and the Church 'has them all'. 'Things incompatible in nature, coexist in her.' 'Her prose is poetical on the one hand, and philosophical on the other.'[99]

The ideal which Newman espoused for the Church, as it seeks to appropriate the great gift of revelation, was the union of 'clear heads and holy hearts',[100] that is to say, the union of critical intellection and deeply held faith. This is what Newman had in mind when he spoke, in the *Grammar*, of 'the theology of a religious imagination'.[101] One of the fruits of the achievement of this ideal would be a profound sensitivity to the limitations of each and every articulation of the faith, whether by an individual theologian or by the Church in the exercise of its teaching authority.

In a letter to an agnostic correspondent, dated 29 April 1879, Newman wrote: 'What then you say of mechanical science, I say emphatically of theology, *viz.* that it "makes progress by being always alive to its own fundamental uncertainties"'.[102] The most stirring statement of this principle can be found in papers preparatory to the *Grammar* which date from 1863. There, reflecting on the poverty of our language when it is called upon to express the 'real thing'[103] which is the object of Christian faith, Newman lays down what might be described as a 'charter' for the exercise of both the individual and the communal intellect. The essence of that charter is the willingness to live with the limitations that inevitably accompany the science of God, and, even more, to see in them some clue to God's very being. Newman writes as follows:

> From the nature of the case, all our language about Almighty God, so far as it is affirmative, is analogical and figurative. We can only speak of Him, whom we reason about but have not seen, in terms of our experience. When we reflect on Him and put into words our thoughts about Him, we are forced to transfer to a new meaning ready made words, which primarily belong to objects of time and place. We are aware, while we do so, that they are inadequate, but we have the alternative of doing so, or doing nothing at all. We can only remedy

their insufficiency by confessing it. We can do no more than put ourselves on the guard as to our own proceeding, and protest against it, while we do ... it. We can only set right one error of expression by another. By this *method of antagonism* we steady our minds, not so as to reach their object, but to point them in the right direction; as in an algebraical process we might add and subtract in series, approximating little by little, *by saying and unsaying, to a positive result.*[104]

REVELATION IN HUMAN HISTORY

A great idea, such as the 'idea' of Christianity, does not unfold itself in the mind alone. 'In proportion to its native vigour and subtlety', it will 'introduce itself into the framework and details of social life', thereby realizing itself in a whole range of social forms, such as ethical codes, systems of government or thought, ritual practices, and so on.[105] These, in turn, shape the way in which the idea is manifest, influencing its development for better or worse as the case may be.[106] Christianity, Newman wrote, had first appeared 'as a worship, springing up and spreading in the lower ranks of society ... Then it seized upon the intellectual and cultivated class, and created a theology and schools of learning. Lastly it seated itself, as an ecclesiastical polity, among princes, and chose Rome for its centre.'[107]

Christianity is, accordingly, a complex, comprehensive fact of history, and its invigorating 'idea' is subject to history's permutations and convolutions.[108] This is indeed the case with any 'philosophy [idea] or polity which takes possession of the intellect and heart, and has any wide or extended dominion'.[109] In the case of Christianity, however, the question of the impact of history on the 'idea' embodied therein is particularly acute, since the Churches allege – and justify their existence by an appeal to – a real and unbroken continuity between 'the religion taught by Christ and His apostles' and their own.

Newman struggled with the inescapable ambiguity of Christian revelation – namely, that while it is very much a matter of human words and their history, it is ultimately the history of the Word. He himself was not prepared 'to abandon the tension between immutability and change, between the transcendent and the historical', which this entailed.[110] He was, therefore, obliged to provide an account of how revelation could be preserved in a changing world that was scarred by human sinfulness. Only by doing so could he justify the claim, made in the *Essay on Development*, that the whole 'superstructure' of Christian tradition ('this body of thought ... laboriously gained') – is 'the proper representative of one idea, *being in substance what that idea meant from the first*, its complete image as seen in a combination of diversified aspects, with the suggestions and corrections of many minds, and the illustration of many experiences'.[111] Newman poses the problem quite directly:

> If Christianity be a social religion, as it certainly is, and if it be based on certain ideas acknowledged as divine, or a creed (which shall here be assumed) and if these ideas have various aspects, and make distinct impressions on different minds, and issue in consequence in a multiplicity of developments, true, or false, or mixed ... what power will suffice to meet and to do justice to these conflicting conditions?[112]

Newman's answer to his own question was the Church, understood as a community invested with authority. As an Anglican, Newman identified the Church's authority primarily with its 'rule of faith' which he regarded as apostolic in origin. This 'rule of faith', succinctly expressed in the 'Creed', had been 'committed and received from Bishop to Bishop' (hence, Newman called it the 'episcopal tradition'), and 'expounded' by so-called 'prophets' (or teachers) who 'unfold and define its mysteries' (these expositions constituted what Newman called 'prophetical tradition').[113]

In the course of writing his *Essay on Development*, however, Newman came to the conclusion that 'tradition' alone did not suffice to guarantee the transmission of the apostolic faith. There was, he claimed, also need for 'a supreme authority ruling and reconciling individual judgments by a divine right and a recognised wisdom',[114] 'an infallible expounder' of Christian truth.[115] As he puts it, 'A revelation is not given, if there be no authority to decide what it is that is given'.[116] In his *Essay on Development*, he observed that the perception of the need for such an authority can be antecedent to its identification, and has, in fact, called forth a variety of solutions.[117] Newman, however, finds it self-evident that 'if development must be, then, whereas Revelation is a heavenly gift, He who gave it virtually has not given it, unless He has also secured it from perversion and corruption'.[118]

Accordingly, Newman identifies as the very 'essence' of revealed religion 'the supremacy of Apostle, or Pope, or Church, or Bishop', and this as a 'substitute' for 'the voice of conscience' that is paramount in 'natural religion'.[119] One might venture to say that, for Newman, as far as Christianity is understood in relation to natural religion, the terms 'revelation' and 'authority' are interchangeable. He himself writes that 'Revelation consists in ... the substitution of the voice of a Lawgiver for the voice of conscience'.[120] The 'subjective authority' of the natural order has been replaced by an 'objective' authority in the revealed order – be it 'the voice of Scripture, or of the Church, or of the Holy See'.[121]

In any case, natural religion itself is not subject-centred, if by this one means 'ego-centred'. It is, from the outset, directed to the (generally fearsome) deity revealed in the experience of conscience. Moreover, precisely insofar as conscience 'reaches forward to something beyond itself, and dimly discerns a sanction higher than self for its decisions',[122] it already involves what Erich Przywara describes as an 'anticipation' of the divine authority exercised by an authoritative Church.[123] It is in view of the sameness, as it were, in fundamental 'orientation' – i.e., towards an authority beyond self – that exists between natural and revealed religion, that Newman, fully cognizant of the absolutely unique and unmerited character of revelation, can write that both conscience and revelation 'recognize and bear witness to each other'.[124]

> The guide of life, implanted in our nature, discriminating right from wrong, and investing right with authority and sway, is our Conscience, which Revelation does but enlighten, strengthen, and refine ... Nature warrants without anticipating the Supernatural, and the Supernatural completes without superseding Nature.[125]

Newman's vision of the integral union between natural and revealed – i.e., dogmatic – religion leads Przywara to describe him, most aptly, as 'the great synthesizer of interiority and the Church'.[126] In the same vein, Otto Karrer observed that, in Newman's conception of things, the fruitful and life-giving tension between authority on the one hand, and personal thought and conscience on the other, is part of the whole system of religion.[127] Indeed, as Przywara observes, in Newman's scheme, these two constitute 'one living principle' of revelation, revelation promised and initiated in conscience, and brought to completion in the doctrine of Christ which the Church proclaims.[128]

Notes

1. *P.N.*, ii:43. See also ii:31–3.
2. *P.N.*, ii:71; see also ii:33, 43, 45, 63, 83.
3. *G.A.*, 107; see also 105; *P.N.*, ii:49.
4. *G.A.*, 106.
5. *G.A.*, 110.
6. *G.A.*, 109.

7. J.H. Walgrave, 'La preuve de l'existence de Dieu par la conscience morale et l'experience des valeurs', in *L'existence de Dieu*, Cahiers de l'actualité religieuse, no. 16 (Paris: Casterman, 1961), 117.

8. J.H. Walgrave, *Newman vandaag*, Periodieke uitgave van het Geert Groote Genootschap, no. 698 (Marienburg- and Hertogenbosch, 1957), 25.

9. *G.A.*, 116. See also *U.S.*, 80–1.

10. *P.N.*, ii:59: '[As] our consciousness [of thought] is a reflex act implying existence (I think, therefore, I am), so this sensation of conscience is the recognition of our obligation the notion of an external being obliging, I say this, not from any abstract argument from the force of the terms (e.g., "a law implies a lawgiver") but the peculiarity of that feeling to which I give the name of Conscience'.

11. *Apo.*, 4.

12. *Apo.*, 198.

13. *G.A.*, 105, 60.

14. *Prepos.*, 279.

15. *G.A.*, 349.

16. *Prepos.*, 279: 'From what I have said, it is plain that First Principles may be false or true; indeed, this is my very point, as you will presently see. Certainly they are not necessarily true; and again, certainly there *are* ways of unlearning them when they are false: moreover, as regards moral and religious First Principles which are false, of course a Catholic considers that no one holds them except by some fault of his own.' These words date from 1851. By the time Newman came to write the *Grammar of Assent* (1870), he expressed himself much more cautiously regarding the problem of defectiveness in first principles, and recognized the possibility of inculpable error. See *G.A.*, 241, 249, 259. The 'decisiveness' of Newman's position in the 1851 lectures must be viewed in the light of the apologetic character of the lectures, and his status as a convert, that is to say, his concern not to seem to call into doubt traditional thinking.

17. J.H. Walgrave, 'Conscience de soi et conscience de Dieu: Notes sur le "Cahier philosophique" de Newman', *Thomist* 71 (1971), 377.

18. *G.A.*, 46–7, 71–3. For a discussion of 'instinct' and 'intuition' in Newman, see Father Zeno, *Our Way to Certitude* (Leiden: E.J. Brill, 1957), 95–7.

19. John Henry Newman, *Parochial and Plain Sermons*, 8 vols. (London: Rivington, 1868), ii:61.

20. *G.A.*, 105–10. The sanction is 'conveyed in the feelings which attend on right or wrong conduct' (106).

21. *G.A.*, 106–14.

22. *G.A.*, 110 (emphasis added). For an extensive discussion of the nature and function of the imagination in Newman's work, see Terrence Merrigan, *Clear Heads and Holy Hearts: The Religious and Theological Ideal of John Henry Newman*, Louvain Theological and Pastoral Monographs, 7 (Leuven: Peeters; Grand Rapids, MI: W.B. Eerdmans, 1991), 48–81, 177–8, 186–92; Merrigan, 'The Image of the Word: John Henry Newman and John

Hick on the Place of Christ in Christianity', in T. Merrigan and Ian Ker (eds.), *Newman and the Word* (Louvain: Peeters; Grand Rapids, MI: W.B. Eerdmans, 2000), 1–47.

23. See, in this regard, *G.A.*, 389; see also 55, 98–102, 119.

24. *Apo.*, 27.

25. *Ari.*, 80–2. See also *Ess.*, ii:231–2, where Newman speaks of the 'seeds of truth' in 'the philosophies and religions of men ... though they are not directly divine'. See Ian Ker, 'Newman and the Postconciliar Church', in Stanley L. Jaki (ed.), *Newman Today* (San Francisco: Ignatius Press, 1989), 124, who points out that Newman's acknowledgement of elements of truth in paganism led him 'to what was then the radical conclusion that the Christian apologist or missionary should, "after St Paul's manner, seek some points in the existing superstitions as the basis of his own instructions, instead of indiscriminately condemning and discarding the whole assemblage of heathen opinions and practices", thus "recovering and purifying, rather than reversing the essential principles of their belief"'. See *Ari.*, 80–1, 84. Compare Newman's remarks in this regard and Vatican II's *Decree on the Missionary Activity of the Church* (*Ad Gentes*), no. 9: 'Whatever truth and grace are already to be found among peoples – a secret presence of God, so to speak – it [missionary activity] frees from evil infections and restores to Christ their source ... accordingly, whatever good is found to be sown in the minds and hearts of human beings or in the particular rites and cultures of peoples, not only does not perish but is healed, elevated and perfected, to the glory of God, the confusion of the devil and the happiness of humankind'.

26. *Ari.*, 79, 81. See Erwin Ender, 'Heilsökonomie und Rechtfertigung: Zur Heilsfrage im Leben und Denken Newmans', in H. Fries, W. Becker, *et al.* (eds.), *Newman Studien* (Heroldsberg bei Nürnberg: Glock und Lutz, 1948–), x:164 n. 32. As Ender points out, Newman in his later writings (*V.M.*, i:248) does not speak of the 'divinity of paganism', but of the 'doctrine ... of the indirectly divine character of Paganism', as opposed to 'the exclusive divinity of the Mosaic theology' (*U.S.*, 164).

27. *Ari.*, 79–80. See Francis McGrath, *John Henry Newman: Universal Revelation* (Tunbridge Wells: Burns & Oates, 1997), 42.

28. Ender, 'Heilsökonomie und Rechtfertigung', 155.

29. *Ess.*, ii:192.

30. *Idea*, 65–6; *Ari.*, 82; see Ender, 'Heilsökonomie und Rechtfertigung', 156.

31. *P.S.*, i:275.

32. *S.N.*, 328.

33. *Diff.*, ii:335.

34. See Terrence Merrigan, 'The Anthropology of Conversion: Newman and the Contemporary Theology of Religions', in Ian Ker (ed.), *Newman and Conversion* (Edinburgh: T & T Clark, 1997), 117–44.

35. Ian Ker, *John Henry Newman: A Biography* (Oxford: Clarendon Press, 1988), 52.

36. *Ess.*, ii:194–5.

37. *Ess.*, ii:231–2. See *G.A.*, 386, where Newman claims that 'Our Supreme Master might have imparted to us truths which nature cannot teach us, without telling us that He had imparted them, – as is actually the case now as regards heathen countries, into which portions of revealed truth overflow and penetrate, without their populations knowing whence those truths came'.
38. *Ess.*, ii:233.
39. *G.A.*, 115.
40. *G.A.*, 116.
41. *G.A.*, 113–14. See also Terrence Merrigan, '"One Momentous Doctrine which Enters into my Reasoning": The Unitive Function of Newman's Doctrine of Providence', *Downside Review* 108 (1990), 254–81. Note that on p. 59 of the *Grammar of Assent* Newman places the 'thought' of 'Divine Goodness' before the thought of 'future reward,' or 'eternal life' as objects of real assent. See our discussion of this point in Terrence Merrigan, '"Numquam minus solus quam cum solus": Newman's First Conversion – Its Significance for His Life and Thought', *Downside Review* 103 (1985), 99–116, at 106–7.
42. J. H. Walgrave, 'Newman's leer over het geweten', in G. De Schrijver and J. J. Kelly (eds.), *Selected Writings – Thematische Geschriften* (Leuven: Peeters, 1982), 195.
43. *G.A.*, 400–3.
44. *G.A.*, 422–3. See also *Dis.*, 277–9.
45. *G.A.*, 403–5.
46. *G.A.*, 404, 417–18.
47. *Mir.*, 19–20; *U.S.*, 26–7; *O.S.*, 66; *Idea*, 515–16; *L.D.*, xxvii:54–5; *Diff.*, ii:253–4; *D.A.*, 133; *Ari.*, 80–1.
48. *U.S.*, 23; *Mir.*, 19; *Diff.*, ii:253–4; *Idea*, 515–16; *P.S.*, ii:103; *H.S.*, iii:79–81.
49. *U.S.*, 26–7; *S.N.*, 302; *G.A.*, 118.
50. *G.A.*, 487; *P.S.*, ii:155; *Ari.*, 146; *L.D.*, xxvii:55.
51. *Ari.*, 79. See also *U.S.*, 24, 115–18, 242–50; *Ess.*, i:22; *P.S.*, i:320–4; ii:18–19; *Apo.*, 46. See also Merrigan, 'One Momentous Doctrine', 265–6.
52. E. R. Fairweather, 'Introduction' to *The Oxford Movement*, Library of Protestant Thought, ed. J. Dillenberger *et al.* (New York: Oxford University Press, 1964), 11.
53. *G.A.*, 118.
54. *G.A.*, 387 (emphasis added).
55. *Ess.*, i:39.
56. *G.A.*, 57.
57. *P.S.*, ii:304.
58. See on this theme, Ian Ker, *Healing the Wound of Humanity: The Spirituality of John Henry Newman* (London: Darton, Longman & Todd, 1993), 60–7; see also Ender, 'Heilsökonomie und Rechtfertigung', 160–1.
59. Ian Ker, *Newman on Being a Christian* (Notre Dame: University of Notre Dame Press, 1990), 41–2; see also Ker, *Healing the Wound of Humanity*, 27–8; *Mix.*, 321–2, 358.

60. See Ender, 'Heilsökonomie und Rechtfertigung', 158–9.
61. See Ender, 'Heilsökonomie und Rechtfertigung', 160–3. Newman insists that the Roman Catholic Church is the only 'religious body ... in which *is* salvation'. (See *L.D.*, xxvi:364; xxx:33–4; emphasis in original.) However, he also insists that the teaching, *extra ecclesiam nulla salus*, did not apply to people in invincible ignorance. See *L.D.*, xxv:71. For a full discussion of Newman's views and their relevance to contemporary theology of religions, see Merrigan, 'The Anthropology of Conversion', 117–44; Merrigan, 'Christianity and the Non-Christian Religions in the Light of the Theology of John Henry Newman', *Irish Theological Quarterly* 68 (2003), 343–56.
62. *Mix.*, 347; *U.S.*, 27 (emphasis in the original).
63. *Dev.*, 84.
64. *Dev.*, 85. See also *U.S.*, 31; *Ari.*, 134: ' The great doctrines of the faith ... were facts, not opinions'. See also *Diff.*, ii:86: 'Christianity is eminently an objective religion. For the most part, it tells us of persons and facts in simple words.' See also *D.A.*, 241.
65. *Idea*, 290.
66. *Ess.*, i:69–70.
67. *Ess.*, i:34.
68. *Ess.*, i:134, 47; see also *Dev.*, 55, 79.
69. *U.S.*, 334.
70. *U.S.*, 338; see *D.A.*, 241–2.
71. *Mix.*, 347; *P.S.*, ii:155, 32, 39; iii:156.
72. *P.S.*, ii:62, 227; iii:114–15.
73. *G.A.*, 464.
74. *G.A.*, 464.
75. *Ess.*, ii:190, 192.
76. *U.S.*, 333. See also *T.P.*, i:138, 132–3; *P.S.*, iii:160–1, 169; *G.A.*, 118–19; Perrone, 409–10, 436–7.
77. John Coulson, *Newman and the Common Tradition* (Oxford: Clarendon Press, 1970), 64.
78. See Nicholas Lash, *Newman on Development: The Search for an Explanation in History* (London: Sheed & Ward, 1975), 140–1: 'Although, in 1845, Newman insisted that the task of ascertaining the "leading idea," as it has been called, of Christianity ... is beyond us ...,' in 1878 he admitted the propriety, "for the convenience of arrangement," of considering "the Incarnation the central truth of the gospel, and the source whence we are to draw out its principles" (*Dev.*, 324).' Lash observes that 'in making explicit that centrality of the fact and doctrine of the incarnation which most deeply characterises his conception of Christianity, Newman was not, in 1878 reversing the judgement made, in 1845, concerning the impossibility of ascertaining the "leading idea" of Christianity'. Lash sees the later emphasis as, in part, the consequence of 'apologetic considerations' (i.e., the refusal of Liberalism) and as, in any case, consistent with Newman's constant 'theological conviction'. He notes that Newman speaks of the doctrine of the Incarnation as the 'central', not the 'leading' idea.

79. *Dev.*, 316, 320, 321, 323, 327, 329, 330.
80. John Henry Newman, *Roman Catholic Writings on Doctrinal Development*, trans. and comm. James Gaffney (London: Sheed & Ward, 1997), 19: 'Initially the word of God enters the mind of the Catholic world through the ears of faith. It penetrates that mind, recedes inside it, and remains hidden there, becoming a kind of deep internal sense. It is brought into play by the ministering and teaching Church.'
81. *G.A.*, 22–30. For a discussion of the role of 'real apprehension' in the assent of faith, see Terrence Merrigan, 'Newman on Faith in the Trinity,' in Ian Ker and Terrence Merrigan (eds.), *Newman and Faith*, Louvain Theological and Pastoral Monographs, 31 (Leuven: Peeters; Grand Rapids, MI: W. B. Eerdmans, 2004), 93–116, especially 96–9.
82. See, for example, *G.A.*, 464–6, especially 466; *Cons.*, 464–6. The quote from Acton is taken from his *Lectures on the French Revolution*, ed. J. N. Figgis and R. V. Lawrence (London, 1932), 17, and is contained in Lash, *Newman on Development*, 134.
83. Lash, *Newman on Development*, 134 (emphasis added).
84. Coulson, *Common Tradition*, 64.
85. Nicholas Lash, *Change in Focus* (London: Sheed & Ward, 1973), 92; *Newman on Development*, 74–5, 48.
86. H. Francis Davis, 'Newman and the Theology of the Living Word', in *Newman Studien*, vi:171, 173.
87. *U.S.*, 329.
88. John Coulson, *Religion and Imagination: 'In Aid of a Grammar of Assent'* (Oxford: Clarendon Press, 1981), 51.
89. *G.A.*, 119.
90. *G.A.*, 140.
91. *G.A.*, 126.
92. *G.A.*, 216. For a consideration of the polar character of Newman's thought, see Terrence Merrigan, *Clear Heads and Holy Hearts*.
93. *V.M.*, i:xlvii. See Terrence Merrigan, 'Newman's Experience of God: An Interpretive Model', *Bijdragen* 48 (1987), 444–64; Merrigan, 'Newman on the Practice of Theology', *Louvain Studies* 14 (1989), 260–84.
94. *Apo.*, 49.
95. *Ess.*, i:41–2.
96. *U.S.*, 267.
97. *H.S.*, ii:387.
98. *Ess.*, i:23.
99. *H.S.*, ii:369.
100. *V.M.*, l:lxxv. See also 1:xlviii.
101. *G.A.*, 117.
102. *L.D.*, xxix:118.
103. *T.P.*, i:98.
104. *T.P.*, i:102 (emphasis added). For a reflection on the implications of this view for the relationship between the theologian and the Church, see Terrence Merrigan, 'Newman and Theological Liberalism', *Theological Studies* 66 (2005), 605–21.

105. *Dev.*, 37.
106. *Dev.*, 38–9, 92.
107. *V. M.*, i:41; see also *Dev.*, 77–8.
108. *Dev.*, 39.
109. *Dev.*, 29.
110. Lash, *Newman on Development*, 53.
111. See *Dev.*, 36, 38 (emphasis added). In *Dev.*, 36 Newman equates a 'living idea' with an 'active principle'. Elsewhere in his writings (*D.A.*, 379; *G.A.*, 465–6; *Jfc.*, 53, 198; *P.S.*, ii:288; iv:170, 315; v:41, 93; vii:208–9; *U.S.*, 29), he refers to the presence of Christ and His Spirit as the 'principle' of Christianity. See Lash, *Newman on Development*, 106–9. There are at least some grounds for thinking that 'complete' here (*Dev.*, 38) means not so much 'definitive' as 'adequate'. Seen in this light, the life of the contemporary Church can be regarded as an adequate 'representative' of the 'idea', just as the patristic Church was (and Newman clearly thought it was). In other words, it would seem that there is, in Newman, a tendency to see the Church, as 'realization' of the idea, in terms of a sort of 'continuum', that is to say, as 'sufficient' at any given moment.
112. *Dev.*, 89.
113. *V. M.*, i:249–50.
114. *Dev.*, 89.
115. *Dev.*, 90.
116. *Dev.*, 89.
117. *Dev.*, 31, 86, 87–8.
118. *Dev.*, 92.
119. *Dev.*, 86.
120. *Dev.*, 86.
121. *Dev.*, 86.
122. *G.A.*, 107.
123. Erich Przywara, 'Newman: Möglicher Heiliger und Kirchenlehrer der neuen Zeit?' in *Newman Studien*, iii:31.
124. *H.S.*, iii:79.
125. *H.S.*, iii:79; see *Diff.*, ii:252–3.
126. Przywara, 'Newman: Möglicher Heiliger?', iii:31.
127. Otto Karrer, 'Die geistige Crise des Abendlandes nach Newman', *Newman Studien*, i:276.
128. Przywara, 'Newman: Möglicher Heiliger', iii:31.

Further reading

Coulson, John. *Religion and Imagination: 'In Aid of a Grammar of Assent'*. Oxford: Clarendon Press, 1981, 46–83.
Daly, Gabriel. 'Newman, Divine Revelation, and the Catholic Modernists', in Terrence Merrigan and Ian Ker (eds.), *Newman and the Word*. Louvain Theological and Pastoral Monographs, 27. Louvain: Peeters; Grand Rapids, MI: W. B. Eerdmans, 2000, 49–68.

Dulles, Avery. 'From Images to Truth: Newman on Revelation and Faith', *Theological Studies* 51 (1990), 252–67.

Merrigan, Terrence. *Clear Heads and Holy Hearts: The Religious and Theological Ideal of John Henry Newman*. Louvain Theological and Pastoral Monographs, 7. Louvain: Peeters; Grand Rapids, MI: W. B. Eerdmans, 1991.

'Newman on Faith in the Trinity', in Ian Ker and Terrence Merrigan (eds.), *Newman and Faith*, Louvain Theological and Pastoral Monographs, 31. Louvain: Peeters; Grand Rapids, MI: W. B. Eerdmans, 2004, 93–116.

4 Faith

THOMAS J. NORRIS

John Henry Newman not only had much to say about faith in its many dimensions.[1] He was above all a striking instance of the journey and the drama of a lived faith. The Psalmist praises the person who decides in his heart to go on the holy journey (Ps 84:5). This praise seems altogether appropriate in the case of the leader of the Oxford Movement who traced an itinerary that a recent pope described as 'the most toilsome, but also the greatest, the most meaningful, the most conclusive, that human thought ever travelled during the last [nineteenth] century, indeed one might say during the modern era'.[2] That itinerary put Newman into a living contact with what Ian Ker calls 'the varieties of Christianity'.[3] This *ecumenical* experience gives his theology of faith both a providential ecumenical flavour and a vividly Catholic tone since his was a sustained search for the fullness of 'the faith given once for all to the saints' (Jude 3) and so for catholicity.[4] There is in his theology of faith a palpable tension between the devout Catholic and the dedicated ecumenist who could write that 'the absence of visible unity between ... different communions is so great a triumph, and so great an advantage to the enemies of the cross'.[5]

However, the ecumenical dimension of Newman's own life of faith also identifies an important hermeneutical tool for the reading of his texts, namely, one has to pay attention to the precise *context* of his various works. 'Never was a mind so unceasingly in motion. But the motion was always growth, and never revolution.'[6] The context within which Newman worked was quite variegated. Sometimes he is writing as a controversialist or a theologian, other times as a pastor or a guide to those seeking guidance in very personal journeys of faith, and still other times as an educator or soul-friend. And always there is that ever-expanding horizon of truth opening up in parallel with his personal itinerary of faith. His principal works, in fact, bear this out, being what may be called 'vocational', works undertaken in response to major shifts of perspective along his journey of faith.

One may locate the central axis of Newman's whole life in his very deliberate decision to follow Christ in 'the obedience of faith' (Rom 16:26; II Cor 10:5–6) whatever the cost, and to assist others in the breathtaking adventure[7] that inevitably follows such a decision. That adventure was intensified by the context of his time, a time when he felt 'love was cold',[8] and the tremors of the Enlightenment were being felt by many in his beloved England.[9] Towards the end of his life he wrote lines that seem to catch the thrust of his whole life, 'From the time that I began to occupy my mind with theological subjects I have been troubled at the prospect, which I considered to lie before us, of an intellectual movement against religion, so special as to have a claim upon the attention of all educated Christians'.[10] It is that 'claim' that provides the true co-ordinates of his whole life as disciple and pastor, educator and thinker. The purpose of this chapter is to expound the key themes in Newman's theology of Faith, both as act or virtue and as content (*fides qua* and *fides quae*).

This chapter will first attempt a formulation of his teaching on faith as a Catholic. Then it will consider faith as a principle of action in the life of believers. Next, reverting to his life's itinerary, we will look at the *Oxford University Sermons* as the principal formal texts addressing the topic of Christian faith during the Anglican years. This will be followed by a brief study of his engagement with the Roman schools of theology between 1846 and 1848. In a fourth moment we will study his thinking as a Catholic on the topic of faith. Finally, we will state some key conclusions concerning his theology of faith.

FAITH: A CATHOLIC DEFINITION

Newman often preferred to initiate a reflection by leaping *in medias res*.[11] Perhaps it is best for us to throw ourselves into the analysis of a text dealing directly with the theme of faith in the great theologian. In the *Discourses to Mixed Congregations*, delivered in 1849, four years after he had become a Catholic, he provides a succinct statement of the nature of faith. He writes as follows: '[Faith] is assenting to a doctrine as true, which we do not see, which we cannot prove, because God says it is true, who cannot lie. And further than this, since God says it is true, not with his own voice, but by the voice of his messengers, it is assenting to what man says, not simply viewed as man, but to what he is commissioned to declare, as a messenger, prophet, or ambassador of God.' One notices at once in this definition that the object of faith is God and the doctrine he has made known by means of 'a messenger, prophet, or ambassador'. Faith is by its very constitution an effect of God speaking and communicating: it is not primarily the result of our own thinking: 'we do not see, we cannot prove'. Faith, in other words, is not immanently generated knowledge, truth gained 'by sight or by reason'. Faith rather is knowledge generated in believers by the action of grace and the gift of the Holy Spirit. Faith has two qualities or 'peculiarities: it is most certain, decided, positive, immovable in its assent; and it gives this assent not because it sees with eye, or sees with the reason, but because it receives the tidings from one who comes from God'. Newman goes on at once to illustrate his teaching by reference to the Apostles who, as ambassadors of Christ, handed on to others what they themselves had received (see I Cor 11:23; 15:1-2). 'They preached to the world that Christ was the Son of God, that he was born of a Virgin ... Could the world see all this? Could it prove it? How then were men to receive it? Why did so many embrace it? On the word of the Apostles, who were, as their powers showed, messengers from God.'[12] The key question in the ancient Church, as in all subsequent centuries, was, has God spoken? And if he has spoken, who are the appointed hearers of his Word, his spokespersons? That means that the Apostles 'were nothing in themselves, [but] they were all things, they were an infallible authority, as coming from God'.[13]

Here he locates the apostolic credentials of Catholic faith: 'No one can be a Catholic without a simple faith, that what the Church declares in God's name, is God's word, and therefore true'. The word of the Church, spoken with the authority of 'the oracle of God', constitutes what is specific to Catholic faith and gives a definite coloration to the faith of Catholics. The Catholic view is that 'the object of faith is *not* simply certain articles ... contained in dumb documents, but the whole word of God, explicit and implicit, as dispensed by his living Church'.[14] An aspect of this distinctiveness is the principle that the believer assents to all that is revealed and taught by the Church, 'No one could say, "I will choose my religion for myself, I will believe this, I will not believe that"'.[15]

The implications of the text which we have analysed are great indeed. Faith presupposes divine revelation which is 'the initial and essential idea of Christianity'.[16] Revelation and dogma thus 'precede' faith which is the correlative of dogma,[17] itself the illuminated face of divine revelation.[18] Newman explains this order in a work of 1874 written to explain the teaching of Vatican I on papal infallibility, *The Letter to the Duke of Norfolk*. 'Our Divine Master might have communicated to us heavenly truths without telling us that they came from him, as it is commonly thought he has done in the case of heathen nations; but he willed the Gospel to be a revelation acknowledged and authenticated, to be public, fixed, and permanent; and accordingly, as Catholics hold, he framed a society of men to be its home, its instrument, and its guarantee. The rulers of that association are the legal trustees, so to say, of the sacred truths which he spoke to the Apostles by word of mouth.'[19] Since the topic of revelation is treated at length in the previous chapter there is no need to elaborate it further here.

FAITH A PRINCIPLE OF PERSONAL ACTION

By means of his own conversion in the summer of 1816 through the influence of Walter Mayers – 'the human means of the beginning of divine faith in me'[20] – when he 'received into his mind impressions of dogma, which through God's mercy, have never been effaced or obscured',[21] the teenager began to live a serious Christian life. Through mentors such as Thomas Scott he adopted the motto, 'Holiness before peace'. Newman's faith was to be rooted in revealed truths, for 'as well can there be filial devotion without the fact of a father as devotion without dogma'. This aspiration after a 'creedal holiness' must come to expression in obedience to the Word of God and adherence to the Christian system of belief. When in 1828 he succeeded in resisting a preference for intellectual achievement over holiness of life, and began to read the Fathers as the youthful diary of the Church, his faith-life took a second quantum leap. By means of the Fathers, he entered what he described much later as 'a paradise of delight'.[22]

He stresses the fact that the New Testament sees in faith the chosen instrument connecting heaven and earth. Faith opens to the believer a whole world inviting to action and driving such action with a unique inspiration and energy. Faith is not only an access to an otherwise inaccessible world, 'a world of overpowering interest, of the sublimest views, and the tenderest and purest feeling',[23] but also to a new life that fulfils the present life in superabundant fashion. Taking as his text, 'Now faith is the substance of things hoped for, the evidence of things not seen' (Heb 11:1), he contrasts faith and reason as habits of mind. He stresses the fact of 'faith ... as an instrument of knowledge and action, unknown to the world before ... independent of what is understood by reason'. As 'a novel principle of action', faith is much more than a 'believing upon evidence, or a sort of conclusion upon a process of reasoning'.[24] Through faith a unique principle of action enters history and transvalues all human thinking and acting. Ordinary mortals take upon themselves divinely appointed roles.[25]

His discovery of the Fathers of the Church had shown him this principle in action. In Ambrose, Athanasius[26] and Augustine he noticed a style of living and thinking appropriate to Revelation and its mysterious profundity. This style was at the same time at variance with merely logical forms of thought whose presuppositions would eliminate on principle the very notion of mystery. 'If the Fathers were not cold, and the Schoolmen are, this is because the former write in their own persons, and the latter as logicians and disputants. St Athanasius or St Augustine has a life, which a system of theology has not.'[27] Faith has to do with life and living it is the only proof of its authenticity. 'It is the new life, and not natural reason, which leads the soul to Christ.'[28]

Still, faith is only a beginning. It has to advance to hope and charity or love. If it is not animated as it were by the greatest of the theological virtues (I Cor 13:13), faith can become defective. In fact, it can easily decline into superstition. Faith may even justify bigotry or fanaticism, as Church history tragically witnesses.[29] It needs a safeguard. Since 'faith is a test of a man's heart', that safeguard is logically 'a right state of heart'.[30] That is why 'it is love which forms it out of the rude chaos into an image of Christ; or, in scholastic language, justifying faith, whether in Pagan, Jew or Christian, is *fides formata charitate*'.[31] This prepares the way for this famous principle, 'We *believe* because we *love*'.[32] The perfecting of faith through charity 'does not change its nature ... It remains what it is in itself, an initial principle of action.'[33]

THE ANGLICAN NEWMAN

This personal context of his own faith-journey, however, was to be challenged and, in the event, still further enhanced as he grappled with the religious and cultural context he diagnosed around him. He described that context towards the end of his life, on the occasion of receiving the cardinalate in 1879, as 'religious liberalism'. 'I rejoice to say, to one great mischief I have from the first opposed myself. For thirty, forty, fifty years I have resisted to the best of my powers the spirit of Liberalism in religion. Never did Holy Church need champions against it more sorely than now, when, alas! it is an error overspreading, as a snare, the whole earth.'[34] What was 'this spirit of Liberalism'? His definition is both succinct and theoretically penetrating. 'Liberalism in religion is the doctrine that there is no positive truth in religion, but that one creed is as good as another ... It is inconsistent with the recognition of any religion, *as true*. It teaches that all are to be tolerated, for all are matters of opinion. Revealed religion is not a truth, but a sentiment and a taste;

not an objective fact, not miraculous; and it is the right of each individual to make it say just what strikes his fancy.'[35]

Newman acutely felt the rising tide of this liberalism. He decided to act. Among the first things that needed serious attention was the truth-claim of Christianity. Between 1826 and 1843 he composed a set of fifteen sermons on the topic of faith and reason. He did so with 'no aid from Anglican theologians and no knowledge of Catholic theologians'.[36] The only exception in relation to Anglican theologians was Joseph Butler, the author of the *Analogy of Religion* which Newman read in 1823. This work was destined to exert a profound impact on his evolving method of theological reasoning.[37]

The sermons before the University of Oxford

In the *University Sermons* he plots the phases in the journey towards faith in God. The *Sermons* are a modern *itinerarium mentis in Deum*. He advances slowly, drawing insight from his knowledge of individuals and, in particular, from the manner in which living people *actually think and reason* as opposed to the manner in which they are *supposed* to perform these activities. He concentrates on this difference between *practice* and *theory*. The path to spiritual and moral reality, and so to divine truth and life, is not the path of demonstration and logic. He saw this fact personified in the Fathers who stressed the need to change one's own mindset and behaviour in order to perceive and embrace the Word of God. In the *Apologia* many years later, he put it in these terms, 'And then I felt altogether the force of the maxim of St Ambrose, *Non in dialectica complacuit Deo salvum facere populum suum*; – I had a great dislike of paper logic ... It is the concrete being that reasons; pass a number of years, and I find my mind in a new place: how? The whole man moves: paper logic is but the record of it.'[38] This explains a patent fact, namely, that 'logic makes but a sorry rhetoric with the multitude; first shoot around corners and you may not despair of converting by a syllogism'.[39] It is the concrete being, the whole man[40] who is in any case a unity, who thinks and reasons. 'After all', he writes in 1838, 'man is not a reasoning animal; he is a seeing, feeling, contemplating, acting animal'.[41]

It is fatal to assume that 'truth may be approached *without homage*'.[42] Now the forum where the person is most immediately and vitally invited to seek and to *do the truth* is conscience. The experience of conscience constitutes therefore the first phase in the soul's itinerary to faith. In Newman's epistemology, conscience plays a central role as 'a connecting principle between the creature and his Creator'.[43] Since conscience is both a 'moral sense' or 'judgement of reason' *and* a 'sense of duty' or a 'magisterial dictate', it opens up the way to the most vivid grasp of moral and spiritual reality. Still, it is the second aspect of conscience which acts as a 'a certain commanding dictate, not a mere sentiment, not a mere opinion, or impression, or view of things, but a law, an authoritative voice bidding him to do certain things and avoid others'.[44] The result of that experience, as real as the experience of thinking or choosing or remembering, is that the individual knows him/herself to be under address by *Someone*! One understands how conscience provides the most vivid grasp – 'real apprehension' he will say much later in the *Grammar* – of spiritual reality, whether natural or supernatural. It is through conscience, then, that 'a primal remembrance of the good and true is bestowed on us by God. If man does not hide from his own self ... he comes to the insight: this is where I want to go'.[45] Obeying the good and the true, he begins to walk towards the light and the truth and the life (John 3:21; 14:6).

With his gift for introspection and phenomenological analysis, Newman describes the appearance of God in conscience, detecting three stages in the process. The first stage is the 'emotional' one where the specific 'phenomena of conscience'[46] make their appearance. These phenomena are the familiar classifications of a 'good' and a 'bad conscience'. The second stage involves an unavoidable quest. We 'are not affective towards a stone, and do not feel shame before a horse or a dog', so that the exciting cause of these emotions cannot belong to this world. Rather, 'these feelings in us are such as require for their exciting cause an intelligent being'. They argue the existence of a Person 'to whom we are responsible, before whom we are ashamed, whose claims upon us we fear'.[47] Conscience discerns this Person acting in nature even before it hears him in revelation. It is in this sense that Newman drinks to conscience first and to the pope afterwards.[48] Conscience in fact is the aboriginal Vicar of Christ.[49] Finally, this search for the adequate cause of these emotions not only brings home the existence of a Personal Being speaking in the abyss of this most human faculty of conscience, it also points up for us the attributes of the Supreme Being. This phase, given such importance by Newman in the ascent towards the 'ethical character' of the Creator, will have the impact of enabling us to apprehend imaginatively or really. This theme will return very centrally in the *Grammar* where he will show that a delicate and obedient conscience is capable of apprehending the attributes of God in the 'phenomena of conscience'.

A special effect of heeding this Voice is the emergence in the soul of sets of value-convictions and truth-perceptions. These he calls '*first principles'* and are the second phase in the itinerary to faith. What are they precisely? They 'are the means of proof, and are not themselves proved ... they are to the mind what the circulation of the blood and the various functions of our animal organs are to the body ... they are in short the man'.[50] Thus someone who loves status and notoriety, or someone who focuses life on eating, drinking and being merry 'does not wish the Gospel to be true, and therefore is not a fair judge of it'.[51] But someone who loves truth, who acts justly and who lives by respect for the dignity of every other person, even when he has to disagree in the particular, is well disposed towards the Gospel and the message it carries from on high. If we forget this stage of the itinerary to faith, we become 'theoretical and unreal'[52] in our thinking about faith and the act of believing. Besides, we will not understand the fact that 'the most powerful arguments for Christianity do not *convince*, only *silence*'.[53]

If the second phase of the itinerary to faith consists in 'first principles', the third consists in what Newman calls *'antecedent probabilities'*. They constitute a kind of prism through which we view and assess all moral and religious questions. Thus 'a good and a bad man will think very different things probable'[54] in accordance with the tenor of their first principles. From Joseph Butler he had gleaned the principle that 'probability is the guide to life', a principle that was to land him in serious difficulty when he went to the Church of Rome.[55] As if aware of this danger, Newman spelled out the true meaning of 'antecedent probability'. 'I do but say that it is antecedent probability that gives meaning to those arguments from facts which are commonly called the Evidences of Revelation: that, whereas mere probability proves nothing, mere facts persuade no one; that probability is to fact, as the soul to the body; that mere presumptions have no force, but that mere facts have no warmth.' When positive antecedent probabilities are in place, 'the heart is alive'[56] with the result that evidences are truly heard and seen and accepted. Otherwise people 'may indeed look, but not perceive, and may indeed listen, but not understand' (Mark 4:12; Is 6:9–10).

The *University Sermons* underline the central role of antecedent probabilities in coming to spiritual truth and so to faith. This must not be taken to mean that he dismisses the role of 'the Evidences of Revelation' as they stand out in prophecy, miracles and holiness. However, the mind has need of a heart that is truly converted or on the way to conversion before evidences can speak and convince. Bernard Lonergan seems to hit the nail on the head here. He sees in Newman's approach to the act of faith a transition from the classic approach to the concreteness of method. 'On the former view, what is basic is proof.

On the latter view what is basic is conversion. Proof appeals to an abstraction named right reason. Conversion transforms the concrete individual to make him capable of grasping not merely conclusions but principles as well.'[57] After all, man is not a rational animal only, but, as we have seen already, a feeling and suffering one also. When these antecedent probabilities accumulate and converge in an adequate number, a number which may vary from person to person, they convince the person of the particular truth under consideration. As soon as the person reaches the point where he is convinced that *he ought to believe*, reason has done all it can do. The conviction that one ought to assent unconditionally to the message of the Gospel as God's Word is as far as reason is able to go. The final step of assent requires an act of the will and this involves our freedom. Faith, in other words, is 'not a conclusion from premises, but the result of an act of the *will*, following upon a *conviction* that to believe is a *duty*'.[58] At this stage 'what is wanted for faith is, not proof, but *will*',[59] since faith 'is the consequence of willing to believe'.[60] To cross the gap from knowing that *I ought to believe the Catholic Faith as God's Word* to saying, *Yes, I believe in the Catholic Faith as God's Word*, is an act of the will enabled by grace. This grace has of course been operative all during the previous phases of the journey. This view is characteristic of the entire theological tradition.[61]

The *University Sermons* in summary

Thus far we have largely followed Newman the Anglican in his analysis of *the phases through which the inquirer passes on his journey towards faith*. The *University Sermons*, however, also deal with *the relationship of faith and reason*. In fact, some regard them 'as perhaps the most useful analysis of the relationship between faith and reason, for our time'.[62] It is only proper, then, to investigate that relationship. That task is wonderfully facilitated by the fact that in 1871 Newman wrote an extended Preface to the third edition of the *Sermons*. There he states 'their doctrine ... in a categorical form, and, as far as possible, in the words used in the course of them'. He admits that, given the circumstances of their composition, he is surprised that 'the errors are not of a more serious character', especially in the case of 'the Discourses upon the relation of faith to reason' which are the last five of the fifteen.[63]

Clearly addressing the widespread perceptions of the day, he first sets down the popular notion of faith and reason. 'Whatever be the real distinction and relation between faith and reason, the contrast which should be made between them on a popular view, is this – that reason requires strong evidence before it assents, and faith is content with weaker evidence.'[64] Faith, then, is in all cases an exercise in 'weak reason'.[65] His strategy in dealing with the popular belittling of faith is to explore the many senses of the word 'reason'. One perceives his prowess in what Jan Walgrave perceived as 'a method of phenomenological investigation'[66] or in what Edward Sillem has called 'personal liberalism'.[67]

He detects 'three senses of the word "Reason" over and above the large and true sense'. The first sense consists in 'expertness in logical argument'. It has to follow that 'unless the doctrines received by faith are approvable by reason, they have no claim to be regarded as true'.[68] The second sense of the word reason viewed relatively to religion is as 'a faculty of framing evidences'.[69] The model of such a reason is reason as operative in demonstration through the clear exhibition of the appropriate evidences. 'The mind is supposed to reason severely, when it rejects antecedent proof of a fact, rejects every thing but the actual evidence producible in its favour.'[70] If this is the one and only sense of reason allowed, it is obvious that religion can have no dogmas or revealed truths, and only opinions.[71]

The third popular meaning of reason involves 'a certain popular abuse of the faculty; *viz.*, when it occupies itself upon Religion without a due familiar acquaintance with its subject-matter, or without a use of the first principles proper to it. This so-called reason is in Scripture designated "the wisdom of the world".'[72] In this third operation of reason there is absolutely no recognition of Christianity's proper subject-matter as supplied by revelation and dispensed by a living Church. It involves a rejection of the duty to observe the *'sacrificium intellectus'* when dealing with revealed mystery. This *'sacrificium'* 'was understood from Athanasius to Kant ... [as] the obligation not to operate with the human intellect in regions inaccessible to it'.[73]

These, then, are the three popular senses of the word 'reason'. They cover reason as explicit, evidential and secular. The first refers to the process of reasoning, the second to the method, and the third to the field of its operation. Whatever, of course, does not enter under these rubrics or criteria will not be considered rational or scientific. Thus faith and theology will inevitably suffer relegation to the realms of opinion and the pre-scientific.

The question asserts itself: are these the only operations of reason? May there not be other and even more vital operations of our capacity to know, understand and decide? Besides explicit reasoning, may there not also be implicit reasoning? And as for secular reasoning, may there not also be authentic operations of mind in the field of moral, spiritual and faith realities? The answer of Newman in each case is in the affirmative. In fact, 'faith viewed in contrast with reason in these three senses, is implicit in its acts, adopts the method of verisimilitude, and starts from religious first principles'.[74] Newman *enlarges* the sense of reason and reasoning against its trivialization. 'By the exercise of reason ... is properly meant any process or act of the mind, by which, from knowing one thing it advances on to know another; *whether it be true or false reason, whether it proceed from antecedent probabilities, by demonstration, or on evidence.*'[75] The drawing out of these processes and methods, together with their appropriate deployment in the understanding of faith and in the work of theology, will very largely constitute the warp and the woof of the remainder of Newman's life and ministry. Thus, for example, the way of antecedent probability coupled with the way of evidences might turn out to be a quick, powerful and effective method in the field of faith and that faith-thinking we call theology. A personally dramatic instance of such coupling was about to break upon him.

The phenomenon of *An Essay on the Development of Christian Doctrine*

As John Henry Newman began to see that developments of doctrine, as the very unfolding of the mystery of Christ and its riches (see Eph 3:3–13), were possible, even probable in the circumstances of history and humanity, his antagonism towards Rome began to mellow somewhat. Such developments of dogma now began to appear as antecedently likely. This was to be the theme of the greatest and concluding contribution in the *Sermons*, 'The Theory of Developments in Religious Doctrine'. In other words, it was *probable, antecedent* to the investigation of the annals of history and the facts of Church history, that there *would* be developments of Christian doctrine. From 1841 onwards he turned his mind increasingly towards the history of dogma, in particular, the phenomenon of new dogmas of faith being taught with the passing of time. This very insight of Newman is the key to the method of the *Essay on the Development of Christian Doctrine*.

Antecedent probability will have to be verified by a critical interfacing with the facts of history, in particular, the annals of the Church's teaching record. This results in a fascinating encounter between antecedent probability and the facts of doctrinal history which then yields a principle of verification of the harmony between probability and fact, what he called 'tests' or 'notes'.[76] Probability, historical fact and verification provide both the logical *and* the theological structure of the *Essay*. As his research advanced he was increasingly amazed at the harmony between antecedent probability and historical fact. They began to dovetail perfectly. In fact, long before he had concluded the *Essay* he was convinced that he had the 'answer (to) an *objection against Catholicism*',[77] namely, that the Catholic Church was guilty of the corruption of the apostolic faith.

Some observers concluded that Newman had been converted by probabilities, and not by facts. They went even further and contended that for Newman Catholic faith was only probably true. Having accepted from John Locke the principle that a conclusion cannot rise above its premises, this conclusion was inescapable.[78] Added to this was the notion that Newman had learnt from John Keble and his version of Butler's famous maxim, 'Probability is the guide of life'.[79] His critics were of the view that for the learned Oxford scholar the Catholic Church is probably the true Church. The truth was simply the opposite: the anticipation engendered by probability had put soul into the corpus of historical and doctrinal fact. In that way the warmth of probability had bonded with the force of fact and evidence.

INTERFACING WITH THE ROMAN SCHOOLS (1846–1848)

The stage was well set for Newman's arrival in Rome to study for the priesthood in September 1846. His views of the moral certainty of faith, as outlined in the *Sermons* and employed in the *Essay on the Development*, had preceded him. He was soon to learn that the leading Roman theologian of the day, Giovanni Perrone, SJ, had not understood them. 'Here persons at first misunderstood me', he wrote, 'and because I talked of "probable arguments", they thought I meant that we could not get beyond a probable conclusion in opposition to a moral certainty; which is a condemned proposition'.[80] It was disconcerting to be 'accused of denying moral certainty, and holding with Hermes[81] (that) we cannot get beyond probabilities in religious questions'.

He had to explain. 'This is far from my meaning. I use "probable" in opposition to "demonstrative", and moral certainty is a *state of mind*, in all cases however produced by probable argument which admits of more and less, the measure or probability necessary for certainty varying with the individual mind ... I do but say that the great line of argument which produces moral certainty is not evidence, but antecedent probability.'[82] He defended the position that none of the ideas in the *University Sermons* is as important or as 'original' as the idea of antecedent probability. In fact, 'antecedent probability is the great instrument of conviction in religious (nay in all) matters'.[83] The *Essay on the Development* had served to show it in action: it had verified the principle that 'antecedent probability' is in fact 'the great instrument' in reasoning, especially in the field of religion. Allen Brent contends that the reason for Perrone's misunderstanding of Newman had to do with the reaction to Kant in Roman circles, and, more specifically, with Perrone's 'synthetic and syllogistic method of theology originally developed as a specifically anti-Hermesian polemic'.[84]

Newman set about working up the theology of faith in his new setting. He read Holden's *Divinae Fidei Analysis*. He found it to be 'worth reading, though it has acknowledged faults'. He also read Perrone's *Treatise on Faith and Reason* and he liked it better than that of Holden. He was much relieved to find that his views largely coincided with those of Perrone.[85] He now composed a set of theses on the nature of the act of faith. His room in the Oratory in Birmingham contains no fewer than four copies of the *Theses de Fide*, the last being done in 1877 with a note appended, 'The Theses were drawn up by me at Rome in 1847, and corrected by our theological tutor. J. H. N.' He submitted them for correction to a *repetitore*, in spite of which they seem to be exactly as he wrote them.

The Roman Schools held that unaided reason could achieve a definite judgement of 'credibility' based on the external signs of prophecy, miracles and holiness. This judgement with regard to revelation came *before* the act of faith. In his *Theses* Newman tries to harmonize the *Sermons* with this Roman Theology. In doing so he draws from scholastic theologians such as Suarez and de Lugo and others. In the judgement of Avery Dulles, however, 'these theses ... do not represent an advance in Newman's thinking, but rather a defensive maneuver in which he clothed his thought in the ill-fitting suit of scholastic armor'.[86] This is obvious in the very first Thesis where faith is defined as 'a certain, non-evident assent of the *intellect* given to divine truth',[87] or again in the fourth Thesis where he adopts the position of Suarez that faith is absolutely certain of itself and does not admit any contribution whatsoever from antecedent probabilities.

Still the shock he felt at the Roman reaction to his theology of faith was acutely felt. He decided to write an *Introduction* for a French translation of the *Sermons* which was in the offing from 1846 onwards. A French priest, the Abbé Deferrière, encouraged by Newman's friend, Dalgairns, took up the project in France. Newman's *Introduction* 'would give him [Newman] elbow-room to explain himself on the subject of probability'.[88] Since time was of the essence, and the French translation lagged, he initially wanted the last six of the *Sermons* published in Rome under the title, *Remarks on the Relation of Faith and Reason*, together with a Preface explaining their origin and the likelihood that not all points would be accurate. He hoped, besides, that this might respond to the concerns raised by the *Essay*. In particular, the Sermons selected brought out two principles prominent in the *Essay*, namely, 'I. that no real idea can be comprehended in all its bearings at once; and 2. that the main instrument of proof in matters of life is antecedent probability'.[89]

In the end he composed in Latin a Preface for the French translation of the *Sermons* to be done by Dalgairns. It is particularly significant that Newman should have felt compelled to explain his theology of the act of faith in both the Roman and French milieus. Although he was conscious that 'throughout he is pursuing a process of investigation',[90] 'an exploring expedition into an all but unknown country',[91] the doctrinal integrity of his efforts was a source of preoccupation for him during the first five or so years after his becoming a Roman Catholic. However, when he returns to the theme of faith and reason formally, and begins the 'inquiry which will occupy him for about twenty years'[92] until the *Grammar* appears in 1870, he will seek his inspiration from the *Sermons* and the *Essay*, and *not* from the *Theses*.

THE CATHOLIC NEWMAN

Between 1860 and 1865 Newman carried on a deeply engaging correspondence with his friend, the scientist William Froude.[93] Froude challenged Newman to deal with his first principle, 'More strongly than I believe anything else I believe this. That on no subject whatever ... is my mind (or as far as I can tell the mind of any human being) capable of arriving at an absolutely certain conclusion ... Our "doubts" in fact, appear to me as *sacred*, and I think deserve to be cherished as *sacredly* as our beliefs.'[94] Froude wanted 'perfect logical demonstration'.[95] This is the very antithesis of what Newman had outlined in the *University Sermons*. It would also prove devastating for theology and dismissive of the faith of Catholics and of all Christians. 'If children, if the poor, if the busy, can have true faith, yet cannot weigh evidence, evidence is not the simple foundation on which faith is built.'[96]

Newman saw that a fresh endeavour on his part was simply necessary. His great concern 'would be to show that a given individual, high or low, has as much right (has as real rational grounds) to be certain, as a learned theologian who has the scientific evidence'.[97] He could see already that there were numerous certainties that people lived by but which could not be justified at the bar of logical demonstration. From Aristotle he knew of *phronēsis* as the faculty of practical judgement and he wondered if it might be indicative of the way in which people know concrete facts. Of course, this could not be a privileged route to truth, but one coincident with the universal one. To look for a privileged route would mean simple capitulation to fideism; to deny there was a way to know concrete truths and spiritual reality was to capitulate to rationalism.

As for the philosophical underpinning of the syllogistic method, Newman saw it typified in the philosophy of John Locke. The test of loving the truth is the principle of 'not entertaining any proposition with greater assurance than the roots it is built on will warrant'. For Locke, 'there are degrees of assent ... and ... as the reasons for a proposition are strong or weak, so is the assent'. Newman adjudicates Locke's viewpoint, so widely accepted then and even more so now, as 'a view of the human mind, in relation to inference and assent, which ... seems theoretical and unreal'.[98] He sees in Locke the outcome of an '*a priori* method of regarding assent in its relation to inference'. He does not go 'by the testimony of psychological facts' in order to determine 'our constitutive faculties and our proper condition'. It seems as if he wants to keep us 'under the narrow wings of his own arbitrary theory'.[99]

Both the science and the philosophy of the day converged on positions hostile to the meaning and integrity of faith and faith-life. In a 'Note' appended to the second edition of the *Apologia* in 1865, he formulated the resulting principles. The second and the fourth of his eighteen theses provide an incomparable summary of the issues involved.

2. No one can believe what he cannot understand.

    Therefore, e.g., there are no mysteries in religion.

4. It is dishonest in a man to make an act of Faith in what he has not had brought home to him by actual proof.

    Therefore, e.g., the mass of men ought not to believe in the divine authority of the Bible.[100]

TOWARDS A 'THIRD WAY': A 'GRAMMAR OF ASSENT'

An *organum investigandi* was needed.[101] The *organum* would have to confront the two principles just enunciated. Having gone on year after year in search of an *entrée*, he found the breakthrough during a vacation in Switzerland. 'At last when I was up at Glion over the lake of Geneva, it struck me: "You are wrong in beginning with certitude – certitude is only a kind of assent – you should begin with contrasting assent and inference." On that hint I spoke, finding it a key to my own ideas.'[102] He had discovered the organizing centre of the opus he wanted to write on the structure of believing and of faith-life, in order to vindicate the faith of ordinary believers. He had felt this task on his conscience for years so that 'it would not do to quit the world without doing it'.[103]

The precise structure of the *Grammar* bears out his intuition. In the first part Newman deals with Assent (the acceptance of a proposition as true) viewed in relation to Apprehension (the grasping of the meaning of the terms of the proposition), in the second in relation to Inference (the argumentation supporting the assent). He does so because he has suddenly grasped the contrast between formal inference and assent. That contrast turns on two facts or rather differences. First, in formal inference the conclusion is necessary but its truth *is conditional upon the truthfulness of the premises*, whereas in assent the conclusion is simply unconditional. In fact, 'assent is the acceptance of truth, and truth is the proper object of the intellect'.[104] Second, in formal inference it is not necessary to understand the terms of the premises, whereas in assent such an understanding or 'apprehension' is necessary. As we have already stressed, the theological aim was ultimately the legitimation of certitude in the belief of the man on the top of the Clapham omnibus. 'But Newman puts the question on a wider philosophical basis and inquires into the actual forming or development of certitude in general, and its legitimacy.'[105]

He succeeds in outlining an epistemology of faith by 'interrogating human nature, as an existing thing, as it is found in the world'.[106] The route to assent is through 'apprehension', as well as through what he called the 'Inductive' or 'Illative Sense'. Apprehension may be real or notional, depending on whether the object indicated by the terms of a proposition is understood as a 'thing' (an object of experience) or a notion (a concept or idea).[107] The 'real' deals with particulars, and real apprehension and assent are dependent upon the imagination's capacity to render the 'object' somehow present. At times Newman even speaks of 'imaginative apprehension' instead of 'real apprehension'.[108] He illustrates the two modes of apprehension and assent in terms of religion and theology: the former employs notional apprehension, the latter real or imaginative.[109] Hence, as Newman explains, a religious doctrine can be held 'either as a theological truth, or as a religious fact or reality'.[110] *In this way he shows the indispensable role of doctrinal statements in religion.* Newman concludes his discussion with a chapter applying his thought to the quality of our apprehension of the central doctrines of Christian faith. Real apprehension issues in real assent and inspires devotion. Dogma grounds devotion.

Still it was the step from apprehension to assent that principally preoccupied him. He wanted to show how the faithful can believe what they cannot absolutely prove in the sense of 'the highest degree of formal correctness of proof'. He was convinced that 'spontaneous mental reasoning precedes verbal arguing. There may be plain people who reason well, but produce only bad arguments. Even in science spontaneous reasoning precedes correct formal proof.'[111] As we have seen earlier, he had laid the foundations of such understanding in the *University Sermons*.

But now Newman saw that such a rational faith, as the Catholic tradition demanded, could be 'the result of converging probabilities, and a cumulative proof' from 'cumulating probabilities'.[112] He did so without prejudice to the mainstream position of Catholic theology which underlines the 'motives of credibility' in miracles, prophecy and holiness. His preference, however, is for the former. As he puts it, religious conviction arises out of 'the cumulation of probabilities, independent of each other, arising out of the nature and the circumstances of the particular case ... probabilities too fine to avail separately, too subtle and circuitous to be convertible into syllogisms, too numerous and various for such conversion, even were they convertible'. *This living logic* of proof differs from 'the rude operation of syllogistic treatment' as much as a portrait differs from a mere sketch 'in having, not merely a continuous outline, but all its details filled in, and shades and colours laid on and harmonized together'.[113]

Can one be more precise regarding this living reasoning of the mind? Newman answers in terms of what he calls the 'Illative' or 'Inductive' Sense. The Illative Sense, with roots in Aristotle's notion of *phronēsis*,[114] is 'the sole and final judgement on the validity of an inference in concrete matter'.[115] In a letter to a friend he explains further the meaning of the term as follows, 'There is a faculty of the mind which I think I have called the inductive sense, which, when properly cultivated and used, answers to Aristotle's *phronēsis*, its province being, not virtue, but the "*inquisitio veri*", which decides for us, beyond any technical rules, when, how, etc., to pass from inference to assent, and when and under what circumstances etc. etc. not.'[116] This faculty is nothing less than the faculty of judgement. As 'the power of judging about truth and error in concrete matters' it constructs the passage from inference to assent, and so from the conditional to the unconditional, to that which *is*. In that way the

Illative Sense 'determines what science cannot determine, the limit of converging probabilities, and the reasons sufficient for a proof'.[117]

In the concluding chapter of the *Grammar* he applies his thinking in the realms of both natural and revealed religion. This will allow us to see his epistemology of faith in action. He compares and contrasts his 'methods of reasoning'[118] with those of two eminent theologians, namely, Eusebius Amort (1692–1775) and William Paley (1743–1805). The former 'has dedicated to the great Pope, Benedict XIV, what he calls a "new, modest, and easy way of demonstrating the Catholic Religion." In this work he adopts the argument merely of the *greater* probability.' Newman holds with Amort that 'from probabilities [we] may construct legitimate proof, sufficient for certitude'. However, he differs from Amort in as much as Amort adds up probabilities in his argument while he highlights the fact of their '*accumulation*' and convergence.[119]

As for Paley, his famous work, *A View of the Evidences of Christianity* (1794), is content to exhibit the evidence for miracles and to prove the truth of Christianity in that fashion. A 'clear-headed and almost mathematical reasoner', Paley's 'argument is clear, clever, and powerful'. Still, Newman does not warm to it at all. He is convinced that 'modes of argument such as Paley's encourage … men to forget that revelation is a boon, not a debt on the part of the Giver; they treat it as a mere historical phenomenon'.[120] Paley assumes that one can 'compel men to come in', by the strength of 'a smart syllogism', forgetting that 'some exertion on the part of the persons whom I am to convert is a condition of a true conversion'.[121] The kind of person one is determines what one seeks and accepts. 'Truth there is, and attainable it is, but … its rays stream in upon us through the medium of our moral as well as our intellectual being'.[122] Here again, one is face to face with a recurring theme in Newman: his personalism.[123]

CONCLUSION

Newman read 'the tendency of the day' as the increasing propensity 'to deny that the proofs of Revelation are sufficient for faith – not only do unbelievers deny, but believers seem to grant'. To bring out the genuine *rationality* of faith as act and content, however, was personally necessary, pastorally essential and culturally urgent. If he did not attempt this project, he believed his life would be unfinished. Faith would be seen as an exercise in 'weak reason', believers as weak-minded, and faith-life as nothing more than a certain cultural or aesthetic option. He highlighted the fact that 'all men reason ... but all men do not reflect upon their own reasonings, much less reflect truly and accurately, so as to do justice to their meaning'.[124] He undertook such reflection. He succeeded in showing the reasonableness of the act of faith against fideists and protected the supernatural character of that act against naturalists.

Newman fought all his life against the reduction of reason to the dimensions of formal inference. He struggled for 'a wider concept of reasoning than had been current since the seventeenth century'.[125] Just as the great Christological controversies of the early centuries were instrumental in forging the language of 'person' and 'nature' and 'relation', in a similar way Newman, responding to the debates engendered by the attacks on faith in his own day, was able to forge a fresh language in this field. This is the great value of his notions of 'weak and strong reason', the 'real' and the 'notional', 'accumulation and convergence of probabilities', 'formal, informal and natural inference', 'Illative Sense', the 'unconditional' and others. He has enhanced the theology of the act of faith in a manner reminiscent of St Augustine's handling of the theology of the Trinity in the fifth century.[126]

From his conversion at the age of fifteen, John Henry Newman stressed and defended the fact that Christianity is a revealed religion. 'The Gospel revelation is divine and ... it carries with it the evidence of its divinity.'[127] However, he highlighted the harmony of revealed and natural religion, for 'we find in Scripture our Lord and His Apostles always treating Christianity as the completion and supplement of Natural Religion, and of previous revelations'.[128] Conscience is the lynchpin of that harmony as a 'connecting principle between the creature and his Creator'.[129] In fact, 'what conscience is in the history of an individual mind, such was the dogmatic principle in the history of Christianity'.[130]

In the process of this life-long project, he recovered the range of human reasoning, spelled out the gift-quality of faith, and exhibited its reasonableness against both rationalists and fideists. In doing so, he forged a rich philosophical and theological vocabulary which still awaits appropriate deployment. His first account of the relation between faith and reason in the *University Sermons* caused more than a little anxiety within the Roman School of Theology after he became a Catholic. However, a little over a century and a half later, a major papal encyclical 'gladly mentions' him as first among those 'more recent thinkers' who, in 'the Western context' in modern times, have shown through 'courageous research' the fruitfulness of the relationship between 'the Word of God' and philosophy.[131]

Notes

1. *U.S.*, 177. I have written on the general subject of faith in the life and thinking of the Venerable John Henry Newman in various places: 'Newman and the Act of Believing', *Doctrine and Life* 51 (2001), 84–90; 'Newman's Approach to the Act of Faith in the Light of the Catholic Dogmatic Tradition', *Irish Theological Quarterly* 69 (2004), 239–61. The latter has been of some help in the writing of the current chapter.
2. Pope Paul VI, *Acta Apostolicae Sedis*, 1963, 1025: from the homily delivered on the occasion of the beatification of Blessed Dominic Barberi, the Italian Passionist and missionary who received John Henry Newman into the Catholic Church in 1845.
3. Ian Ker, *Newman and the Fullness of Christianity* (Edinburgh: T & T Clark, 1993), 1–9.
4. See *Ess.*, ii:231–3.
5. *L.D.*, xxiv:22. See Thomas J. Norris, *Only Life gives Life: Revelation, Theology and Christian Living According to Cardinal Newman* (Dublin: Columba, 1996), 155–73.
6. Owen Chadwick, *Newman* (Oxford: Oxford University Press, 1983), 5.
7. See 'The Ventures of Faith', *P.S.*, iv:295–306.
8. *U.S.*, 197; see *P.S.*, ii:27: 'when love waxed cold'.
9. *Apo.*, 30-1.
10. *S.E.*, 104.
11. See, for example, the opening of the *Grammar of Assent*.
12. *Mix.*, 194–7; in the *U.S.*, 202–3, he writes, 'The Word of Life is offered to a man; and, on its being offered, he has faith in it. Why? On these two grounds – the word of its human messenger, and the likelihood of the message'.
13. *Mix.*, 197.
14. *L.D.*, xxiii:105; *Mix.*, 98–100.
15. *Mix.*, 197.
16. *V.M.*, i:xlvii, Preface to the third edition, 1877.
17. See *Dev.*, 326–35, 'The Supremacy of Faith'; in *Jfc.*, 217, he defines faith as 'the correlative, the natural instrument of the things of the Spirit'.
18. *Ess.*, i:41–2.
19. *Diff.*, ii:322; see n. 137.
20. *A.W.*, 181.
21. *Apo.*, 4.
22. *Diff.*, i:370.
23. *Ess.*, i:23.
24. *U.S.*, 177, 179.
25. See the following sample sermons on faith which emphasize faith as a principle of unique activity: 'Faith and Obedience' (*P.S.*, iii, Sermon 6); 'Subjection of the Reason and Feelings to the Revealed Word' and 'Faith without Demonstration' (*P.S.*, vi, Sermons 18 and 23); 'Obedience to God, the Way to Faith in God' (*P.S.*, viii, Sermon 14).

26. Newman translated and published Athanasius's *Orations against the Arians* in two volumes in 1844. The second volume is a treasure-house of Athanasian theology.
27. *Jfc.*, 31.
28. *U.S.*, 235.
29. See *Memory and Reconciliation: The Church and the Faults of the Past*, International Theological Commission (London: Jonathan Cape, 2000), 30–8.
30. *U.S.*, 226, 234.
31. *U.S.*, 234; see 193.
32. *U.S.*, 236. In a note in the third edition he explains that this is 'not love precisely, but the virtue of religiousness, under which may be said to fall the *pia affectio,* or *voluntas credendi'*.
33. *U.S.*, 250. Newman backs up his contention here with numerous loci from the Scriptures of both the Old and the New Testaments.
34. *Ward*, ii:460–1.
35. *Ward*, ii:460–1.
36. *U.S.*, ix–x.
37. *Apo.*, 67–8 and 78–9; see K. Dick, *Das Analogieprinzip, Newman Studien*, V Folge (Nürnberg: Glock & Lutz, 1962), 9–228, especially 122–3.
38. *Apo.*, 225; the Ambrose quote is in his *De fide ad Gratianum Augustum*, PL, 16, 42.
39. *D.A.*, 294; he quotes this text many years later in the *Grammar* 90 with glowing approval; see *L.D.*, xxix:106.
40. J. Boekraad, *The Argument from Conscience to the Existence of God According to J.H. Newman* (Louvain: Nauwelaerts, 1961), 103.
41. *D.A.*, 294.
42. *U.S.*, 198.
43. *G.A.*, 117.
44. *O.S.*, 64.
45. Paul Kokoski, Letter to the Editor, *The Irish Independent*, 23 June 2007.
46. *G.A.*, 110. Newman is clearly aware of David Hume's reduction of conscience to the level of mere moral emotion.
47. *G.A.*, 110, 109.
48. See *Diff.*, ii:261; see Pope John Paul II, *Crossing the Threshold of Hope* (London: Jonathan Cape, 1994), 191.
49. *Diff.*, ii:248.
50. *Prepos.*, 283–4; see Hans-Georg Gadamer, *Wahrheit und Methode* (Tübingen: J.C.B. Mohr, 1965); English translation, *Truth and Method* (London: Sheed & Ward, 1975).
51. *P.S.*, viii:114.
52. *U.S.*, 225.
53. Text quoted in Ian Ker, *Newman on Being a Christian* (Notre Dame: Notre Dame University Press, 1990), 1.
54. Ker, *Newman on Being a Christian*, 191.
55. See Norris, 'Newman's Approach to the Act of Faith', 246–7.
56. *U.S.*, 200.

57. Bernard Lonergan, *Method in Theology* (London: Darton, Longman and Todd, 1972), 338. When several years later Newman returns to the theme of faith in the *Grammar*, he will stress the same point. He will speak to inquirers and not to controversialists. 'I say plainly I do not care to overcome their reason without touching their hearts' (*G.A.*, 425).

58. *Ward*, i:242; see Josef Pieper, *Faith, Hope, Love* (San Francisco: Ignatius Press, 1986), 35–6.

59. *Ward*, i:242; see also *Ward*, ii:276–7.

60. *Mix.*, 225.

61. For interesting texts see Pieper, *Faith, Hope, Love*, 35–6.

62. New York: Doubleday, 1973, 47.

63. *U.S.*, x.

64. *U.S.*, x, 17.

65. *U.S.*, 202, 204. Here Newman anticipates by a century and a half recent philosophic discourse: see Arnella F. Clamor, 'In Search of a "Via Media" between Atheism and Catholicity: A Dialogue with John Henry Newman' (diss., Katholieke Universiteit Leuven, 2006).

66. J. Walgrave, 'Newman's beschrijving en verantwoording van het werkelijke denken', *Tijdschrift voor Philosophie* 1 (1939), 541–55.

67. *P.N.*, i:5.

68. *U.S.*, x, 13.

69. *U.S.*, xv.

70. *U.S.*, x, 26.

71. Much later, in a discourse as Rector of the fledgling Catholic University in Dublin, he will spell out the devastating implications of this thinking for faith and belief. See 'A Form of Infidelity of the Day', in *Idea*, 381–404.

72. *U.S.*, xv.

73. Eric Voegelin, 'On Christianity', in P.J. Opitz and Gregor Sebba (eds.), *The Philosophy of Order: Essays on History, Consciousness, and Politics* (Stuttgart: Klett-Cotta, 1981), 451.

74. *U.S.*, xvi–xvii.

75. *U.S.*, 223 (italics added).

76. Newman substitutes the word 'note' for the word 'test' in the third edition of 1878.

77. *L.D.*, xii:332.

78. See Stanley L. Jaki, 'Newman's Assent to Reality, Natural and Supernatural', in Stanley L. Jaki (ed.), *Newman Today* (San Francisco: Ignatius Press, 1989), 189–220.

79. *Apo.*, 30–1.

80. *L.D.*, xi:293; for the Church's teaching, see Denzinger-Schoenmetzer 2738–2740. See A. Brent, 'The Hermesian Dimension of the Newman–Perrone Dialogue', *Ephemerides Theologicae Lovanienses* 61(1985), 73–99; see also his article, 'Newman and Perrone: Unreconcilable Theses on Development', *The Downside Review* 102 (1984), 276–89.

81. Georg Hermes (1775–1831), Professor of Dogmatic Theology at Bonn.

82. *Ward*, i:168 as quoted by Henry Tristram in 'Cardinal Newman's *Theses de Fide* and his Proposed Introduction to the French Translation of the University Sermons', *Gregorianum*, 18 (1937), 223.

83. *L.D.*, xi:293.
84. Brent, 'The Hermesian Dimension of the Newman–Perrone Dialogue', 99.
85. *Ward*, i:168.
86. Avery Dulles, 'From Images to Truth: Newman on Revelation and Faith', *Theological Studies* 51(1990), 264.
87. Tristram, *Theses*, 226: 'Actus divinae fidei est intellectus assensus, Divinae veritati praestitus, certus, inevidens'.
88. Tristram, *Theses*, 242.
89. Tristram, *Theses*, 242.
90. Tristram, *Theses*, 244.
91. *U.S.*, x.
92. See *L.D.*, xxv:34.
93. The correspondence was published by G. H. Harper as *Cardinal Newman and William Froude, F.R.S., A Correspondence* (Baltimore, 1933). Nicholas Lash is critical of Harper's evaluation of the exchange because Harper 'took for granted just that restricted, monochrome notion of human rationality which, in the *Grammar* as in the *University Sermons*, Newman sought to undercut'. See Nicholas Lash, 'Introduction', *An Essay in Aid of a Grammar of Assent* (Notre Dame and London: University of Notre Dame Press, 1979), 3.
94. *L.D.*, xix:270.
95. *L.D.*, xxiv:104–5.
96. *U.S.*, 231; see also 253–4.
97. *L.D.*, xix:294.
98. *G.A.*, 155, 152, 157.
99. *G.A.*, 157.
100. *Apo.* (1865), 499.
101. Note II appended to subsequent editions of the *Grammar of Assent* describes this *organum*.
102. *A.W.*, 270. In 1878 he discussed the purpose of the work with Fr Edward Caswall of the Birmingham Oratory who wrote on his copy of the work these words. 'Object of the book twofold. In the first part shows that you can believe what you cannot understand. In the second part that you can believe what you cannot absolutely prove.'
103. *A.W.*, 273.
104. *G.A.*, 165.
105. Johannes Artz, 'Newman as Philosopher', *International Philosophical Quarterly* 16 (1976), 273.
106. *G.A.*, 157; see 168–9.
107. See Terrence Merrigan, 'Newman on Faith in the Trinity', in Ian Ker and Terrence Merrigan (eds.), *Newman and Faith*, Louvain Theological and Pastoral Monographs, 31 (Leuven: Peeters; Grand Rapids, MI: W.B. Eerdmans, 2004), 93–116. See p. 96: '*Real apprehension* occurs when religious doctrines are "regarded" as referring to "some-thing" which can be experienced. *Real assent* is the recognition that what the doctrine says is true, *in the sense* that it resonates with some aspect of our actual experience of life.' See also p. 99: '*Notional apprehension* occurs when religious doctrines are thought of as referring to

generalizations, to "creations of the mind". *Notional assent* is the unconditional acceptance of the truth of such generalizations. That is to say, notional assent is the conviction that the results of the reasoning process are sound.' See *G.A.*, 10–12, 13, 102–5, 195.

108. See Terrence Merrigan, *Clear Heads and Holy Hearts: The Religious and Theological Ideal of John Henry Newman*, Louvain Theological and Pastoral Monographs, 7 (Leuven: Peeters; Grand Rapids, MI: W.B. Eerdmans, 1991), 50–1; see pp. 48–81 on the imagination.
109. *G.A.*, 115–16. According to H.H. Price, *Belief* (London: Allen & Unwin, 1969), 315–16, this distinction is 'Newman's most original contribution to the epistemology of belief'.
110. *G.A.*, 119.
111. Artz, 'Newman as Philosopher', 273, 274–5.
112. *L.D.*, xv:457–8. The letter is dated 7 October 1853 and is evidence of his early preoccupation with the topic.
113. *G.A.*, 281.
114. See G. Verbeke, 'Aristotelian Roots of Newman's Illative Sense', in James D. Bastable (ed.), *Newman and Gladstone: Centennial Essays* (Dublin: Veritas, 1978), 177–96; and Jaki, *Newman Today*, 197.
115. *G.A.*, 338.
116. *Ward*, ii:589.
117. *G.A.*, 346.
118. *G.A.*, 383.
119. *G.A.*, 406.
120. *G.A.*, 418–19.
121. *G.A.*, 419–20.
122. *G.A.*, 304.
123. See *P.N.*, i:67–148. In *The Theological Method of John Henry Newman: A Guide for the Theologian Today* (Leiden: Brill, 1977), I have attempted to show that for Newman conversion, religious, moral and intellectual, is the bedrock of theological method and, *a fortiori*, for understanding the structure of the act of faith (see chapter IV, 'Theology and its Methodical Foundations', 84–111).
124. *U.S.*, 258–9.
125. Ker, *Newman on Being a Christian*, 1. Nicholas Lash endorses the contention of Maurice Nedoncelle that the *University Sermons* already had as one of their 'incontestable merits' the broadening of 'the concept of intelligence, too narrowly defined by classical rationalism'. See Lash, 'Introduction', 9; see M. Nedoncelle, 'Le drame de la foi et de la raison dans les Sermons Universitaires de J.H. Newman', *Etudes* 247 (1945), 75.
126. See Jean Guitton, *The Modernity of St Augustine* (London: Geoffrey Chapman, 1959), 65–70.
127. *G.A.*, 381.
128. *G.A.*, 383.
129. *G.A.*, 117; see *U.S.*, 194–5.
130. *Dev.*, 361.
131. Pope John Paul II, *Fides et Ratio* (Dublin: Veritas, 1998), 108.

Further reading

Dulles, Cardinal Avery, SJ. *John Henry Newman: Outstanding Christian Thinkers*. London: Continuum, 2002, 34–47.

Ker, Ian. *The Achievement of John Henry Newman*. Notre Dame: Notre Dame University Press, 1990, 35–73.

Meynell, Hugo. 'Newman's Vindication of Faith in the *Grammar of Assent*', in Ian Ker and Alan G. Hill (eds.), *Newman after a Hundred Years*. Oxford: Oxford University Press, 1990, 247–62.

Mitchell, Basil. 'Newman as a Philosopher', in Ian Ker and Alan G. Hill (eds.), *Newman after a Hundred Years*. Oxford: Oxford University Press, 1990, 223–46.

Pieper, Josef. *Faith, Hope, Love*. San Francisco: Ignatius Press, 1997, 13–85.

Tristram, Henry (ed.). 'John H. Newman on the Acta of Faith', *Gregorianum*, 17 (1937), 219–60.

5 Justification

THOMAS L. SHERIDAN

THE YOUNG EVANGELICAL'S CREED (1817–1822)

From 1 August to 21 December 1816 a very young John Henry Newman underwent a conversion which Louis Bouyer has described as an experience which 'left its seal upon him forever'.[1] Newman never repudiated that conversion, nor did he ever question its authenticity. Many years later he said of it: 'When I was fifteen (in the autumn of 1816) a great change of thought took place in me. I fell under the influences of a definite creed and received into my intellect impressions of dogma which, through God's mercy, have never been effaced or obscured.'[2]

Later he specified that this creed was 'at the time Calvinistic in character', adding that the religious impressions he then received 'were to him the beginning of a new life'.[3] In calling it 'Calvinistic' Newman was not referring to Calvinism as understood on the European continent at the time but rather to the doctrines of the Evangelical party of the Church of England.

The Evangelical Revival of the eighteenth century was basically a reaction to the cold, lifeless form of religion which prevailed within much of the Church of England of the time. As such it was an appeal more to the heart than to the head. Nevertheless, despite allowing for a wide variety of doctrinal interpretations, there were certain essential points on which all Evangelicals were agreed. Fundamental to all of these was the firm conviction of the total depravity of human nature as a result of Adam's sin. But to remedy this there was the great good news of the Gospel: the Atonement, which for Evangelicals meant that Christ was punished not only on behalf of, but instead of, sinful human-kind. Equal stress was placed upon the doctrine of grace, or God's free mercy, with a consequent rejection of the 'Roman blasphemy' of merit, and upon the doctrine of justification by faith alone as the sole instrumental cause of salvation. For those who were justified by the free gift of the Holy Spirit there was the certainty of the state of grace and of final salvation. Finally, the sole authority for all their teaching was the Bible.

Newman first encountered Evangelicalism in the person of one of his teachers at Ealing School, the Rev Walter Mayers, himself a recent convert.[4] In addition to Mayers's personal influence, mention must be made of the books he gave the young boy to read, most notably the works of Thomas Scott of Aston Sandford, of whom Newman later said that he was 'the writer who made a deeper impression on my mind than any other, and to whom (humanly speaking) I almost owe my soul'.[5] It was principally from him that Newman received those doctrines that would comprise his Evangelical creed. 'What, I suppose, will strike any reader of Scott's history and writings', Newman wrote, 'is his bold unworldliness and vigorous independence of mind. He followed the truth wherever it led him, beginning with Unitarianism, and ending in a zealous faith in the Holy Trinity ... It was he who first planted deep in my mind that fundamental truth of religion.'[6] It was his deep sense of the majesty of the Triune God and the purity of His Law, of the utter incompatibility between God and the sinfulness of His creatures, that inspired Scott in his life-long crusade against antinomianism, the view that Christians are freed by the Gospel from the obligation of observing the moral law. It was from him that Newman adopted the adage that sustained him in so many of the controversies in which he would later be embroiled, 'Holiness rather than peace'.

It was while he was at Trinity College, Oxford, that in 1821, 'the date, be it observed, when he was more devoted to the evangelical creed and more strict in his religious duties than at any previous time',[7] Newman penned a document, entitled *A collection of Scripture passages setting forth in due order of succession the doctrines of Christianity*, in which he summed up his Evangelical creed.[8] It is written in a florid style in which he seems to be consciously imitating Bishop William Beveridge, whose *Private Thoughts* Mayers had given him in 1817 and which he said had also exercised a most powerful influence on his thinking.

In this document are found all of the main tenets of Evangelicalism: the cardinal principle of justification by faith and faith alone, with the consequent disparaging remarks about baptismal regeneration; the dim view of human nature as corrupted by original sin ('man does *only* evil continually', and even of the justified man it is said that 'his understanding is still darkened and his heart polluted'); insistence upon the complete gratuity of election; the predestination of individuals to salvation (whereas the rest are simply *left* to the condemnation which they have deserved); final perseverance; and a certain vindictive quality in God's justice, which demands that redemption be not merely a question of Christ's obedience, but of punishment as well.

Newman would later question, not the reality of his conversion, but whether it was a truly Evangelical conversion as understood by Evangelicals themselves. Many years later he would write of himself: 'In truth, much as he owed to the evangelical teaching, so it was he had never been a genuine evangelical ... He had indeed been converted to it by spiritual life, and so far his experience bore witness to its truth; but he had not been converted in that special way which it laid down as imperative, but so plainly against rule, as to make it very doubtful in the eyes of normal evangelicals whether he had really been converted at all.'[9]

THE GRADUAL REJECTION OF EVANGELICALISM (1822–1825)

Newman was elected a fellow of Oriel in April of 1822 although, as he himself confessed, he did not fully 'come out of his shell' until 1826. His initial feeling of isolation was due not only to his natural shyness but also, as he himself pointed out, 'the result of his Calvinistic beliefs'.[10] In order to see what could be done with this shy young fellow, the members of the Oriel Common Room enlisted the aid of Richard Whately, of whom Newman would later say: 'I owe him a great deal ... While I was still awkward and timid in 1822, he took me by the hand, and acted towards me the part of a gentle and encouraging instructor. He, emphatically, opened my mind, and taught me to think and to use my reason.'[11]

Nevertheless, Newman still clung to his Evangelical creed, although he had already noted 'a gradual fading away' of his belief in the final perseverance of the just.[12] E. B. Pusey was elected a fellow of Oriel in April 1823 and Newman immediately recognized a kindred spirit in him, but in his journal he regretted that he seemed to be 'prejudiced against Thy children'.[13] The two spent many hours discussing religion, Newman arguing for imputed righteousness and Pusey against, Newman 'inclining to separate regeneration from baptism, he doubting its separation, etc.'.[14]

Another Oriel fellow who contributed to Newman's development at this time was Edward Hawkins, Vicar of St Mary's. In June of 1824 Newman had been ordained a deacon in the Church of England and begun to serve as curate of nearby St Clement's. Hawkins read Newman's sermons, criticizing not just their style, but also their content. He came down hard on Newman's first sermon, which by its implicit denial of baptismal regeneration 'divided the Christian world into two classes, the one all darkness, the other all light'. Hawkins denied that there was any such line, insisting that people 'are not either saints or sinners; but they are not so good as they should be, and better than they might be',[15] a truth which Newman was to discover for himself very shortly when he instituted a programme of parish visitation at St Clement's.[16]

Hawkins continued to criticize his sermons, but Newman did not give in easily. His early sermons at St Clement's continued to be strongly Evangelical in tone and content. But Hawkins also influenced Newman in a way that was to have more far-reaching consequences; he taught him what Newman later referred to as 'the *quasi*-Catholic doctrine of Tradition, as a main element in ascertaining and teaching the truths of Christianity'.[17] This, of course, struck at another Evangelical principle, namely, that Scripture is the sole source of Christian teaching.

Two days after completing his parish visitation, on 15 August 1824, he wrote in his private journal: 'The question of regeneration perplexes me very much'. He had been reading John Bird Sumner's *Apostolic Preaching*, which he said 'threatens to drive me either into Calvinism, or baptismal regeneration, and I wish to steer clear of both, at least in preaching'.[18] By the beginning of the year 1825 he was all but decided to 'give up the doctrine of imputed righteousness and that of regeneration as apart from baptism'. But in that same journal entry he immediately added: 'Let me, however, explain myself on the latter subject. It seems to me the great stand is to be made, *not* against those who connect a spiritual change with baptism, but those who deny a spiritual change altogether.'[19]

Having recently discovered the importance of tradition, Newman's investigations had convinced him that there was no escaping the fact of the constant and universal practice of infant baptism. But this posed a tremendous problem, with which he wrestled in a course of six sermons on faith preached on Sunday mornings from 20 February 1825 to 27 March: if baptism is the rite of admission into the true Church of Christ – and not just the visible Church (a distinction which he would soon reject) – this meant that infants are capable of being regenerated, that is to say, changed in their minds and hearts. But Newman was still reluctant to accept this. Instead he fell back on a solution suggested to him many years earlier when he had posed this problem to Walter Mayers: while baptism does not convey the Holy Spirit as thereby regenerating in the proper sense of the word, it does 'place a person in a state of favour such, that God is henceforth bound by covenant to favour him with His Spirit, as he can bear it'.[20]

But in 1825 Newman was still a long way from accepting the full doctrine of baptismal regeneration.

THE FINAL REJECTION OF EVANGELICALISM (1825–1827)

Reviewing, in his 'Autobiographical Memoir' of 1874, the various influences that led to his gradual rejection of Evangelicalism, Newman wrote:

> Mr Newman, then, before many months of his clerical life were over [he had been ordained a priest on 29 May 1825], had taken the first step towards giving up the evangelical form of Christianity; however, for a long while certain shreds and tatters of that doctrine hung about his preaching, nor did he for a whole ten years altogether sever himself from those great religious societies and their meetings which then as now were the rallying ground and the strength of the Evangelical body. Besides Sumner, Butler's celebrated work, which he studied about the year 1825 had, as was natural, an important indirect effect upon him in the same direction, as placing his doctrinal views on a broad philosophical basis, with which an emotional religion could have little sympathy.[21]

Recounting in the *Apologia* how in 1827 the reading of Keble's *Christian Year* had reinforced in his own mind the two principles he had learned from Butler, Newman refers to the one which is germane to our inquiry as 'the sacramental system', the realization that the material world is not just a sign, pointing to the world of the supernatural; it is the *instrument*, the means whereby we enter into contact with this world.

Butler's influence is to be seen in three sermons preached towards the end of 1825. In the first of these, in order to encourage those who feel that they must wait for some extraordinary visitation of God's grace before they can repent of their sins and be converted, he says: Not so: 'God's time is already come, it was the time of baptism. He *has* given grace and will give more to all who ask Him ... All are invited to Christ through baptism as the *means* of his grace.' The second sermon, 'On the Communion of Saints', echoes this same theme of the Holy Spirit given to the Church as a whole. In the third sermon, 'The Use of the Visible Church', we see that Newman still held that distinction between the visible and the invisible Church, but he stresses the importance of the visible Church as the ordinary means of instruction in God's revelation.[22]

But Newman still does not speak of 'baptismal regeneration'. For Newman 'regeneration' is sanctification, and at least at this stage of his development, holiness for Newman is essentially *moral* holiness. Now moral holiness must show itself in action. So in the sense that the newly baptized child has been given the Holy Spirit in baptism as the principle of change of mind and heart, the child can be said to be regenerated, but only in a less proper sense. Regeneration is a life-long process, a never-ending struggle in which the inspirations of the indwelling Spirit are constantly needed to repulse the attacks of indwelling evil.

Nevertheless, in a paper of over sixty pages on 'Infant Baptism' in answer to his brother Frank's objections to the direction in which he had been going, we can see that Newman had finally abandoned the distinction between the visible and the invisible Church.[23] The members of the true Church are the baptized. In his rejection of the Evangelicals' subjective criterion of membership in favour of the objective criterion of baptism, we see Newman's definitive break with Evangelicalism.

'SHREDS AND TATTERS' OF EVANGELICALISM (1829)

Beginning on 25 January 1829 and continuing on Sunday afternoons to 28 June, with one long interruption during March and April for a Lenten series, Newman delivered a series of sermons on the Epistle to the Romans.[24] The series is interesting because it incorporates many, though not all, of the changes we have seen in Newman's thought while still exhibiting what he would later call the 'shreds and tatters of Evangelicalism'.

The entire series may be summed up under two headings: (1) justification by faith only, and (2) the necessity of obedience, even for the just. (1) Since man is incapable of pleasing God by his own efforts at justification, his only recourse is to faith: that is to say, to trust in God's mercy for his only justification, a trust which is founded on the realization of his own sinfulness and helplessness. Whereas this is the only means of justification in any dispensation, the Christian is more blessed in this respect than others in that he has the assurance that he *will* be so justified. (2) This inability to please God by his obedience does not, however, take away the obligation and the necessity of obedience to the Law of God for all men, the Christian included. For the Law of God still stands, as both conscience and Bible testify. Obedience is a necessity for the further reason that it is only by acts of obedience proceeding from faith that a man can grow in that holiness which is necessary to fit him for the enjoyment of heaven. The obedience of the Christian, however, is different from the obedience of other men in that it is characterized by a freedom which proceeds from love and by an absence of fear.

Some of these individual sermons will be preached again later on by Newman, and it is interesting to see certain changes he made in editing them. For example, in the 1829 redaction of sermon no. 4 he had written: 'If he is saved, it must not be by an obedience to which he cannot attain but as the next best way, by confession and trust towards God, by *faith*'. In the 1834 redaction this is changed to read (changes are indicated in capital letters): 'If he is saved, it must not be by THAT PERFECT obedience to which he cannot attain but as the next best way, by confession and trust towards God, AND OBEYING AS WELL AS HE CAN AND by faith IN ORDER THAT HE MAY OBEY AND BY FAITH SO FAR AS HE CANNOT OBEY'.

The definitive solution to the problem of faith and obedience will be found in the idea of the Indwelling of the Holy Spirit, which will be the heart of Newman's doctrine in the *Lectures on Justification*. In these sermons on Romans there is frequent mention of the Holy Spirit, but almost as it were in passing, except for one passage in the very last sermon which presages that further development:

> Now the agent producing in our hearts this spiritual state, be it more or less developed within us, is the *Holy Spirit* ... By him it is said Christians are born to a new life ... We are baptized before we begin to think, as an acknowledgment that He must come to us before we move a step towards Him – and not only must His grace *once* precede us, but *ever*, throughout our lives. He must *dwell in us* according to His own gracious promise ... Faith, the first principle of the spiritual mind, is from Him, and all graces springing from faith come too from His guardian care – so the whole new man – according to the words 'God worketh in us to will and to do of his good pleasure'. (Phil 2)

DEEPENING OF THE ANGLO-CATHOLIC PERSPECTIVE (1830–1835)

By the year 1830 his investigations into the question of baptismal regeneration had led Newman to the great discovery of the Church. But now he saw that same Church threatened by new developments, particularly what he referred to as 'Liberalism', namely 'the mistake of subjecting to human judgment those revealed doctrines which are in their nature beyond and independent of it, and of claiming to determine on intrinsic grounds the truth and value of propositions which rest for their reception simply on the external authority of the Divine Word'.[25] News of developments in England, which reached him while on a Mediterranean voyage, further added to his anxiety, all the more so because of the helplessness he felt at such a distance from home.

Arriving home on 9 July 1833 Newman found that others beside himself were dismayed by the Liberal threat and ready to do something to combat it. Their answer was what came to be called the Oxford Movement, and one of its principal instruments was the *Tracts for the Times*. Prior to deciding to write his own treatise on baptism, Pusey had asked Newman to write on the subject. When Pusey's volume appeared in 1835, Newman's much shorter tract, though almost ready for the publisher, was never sent. Instead, as he notes at the head of the manuscript, it was 'turned into sermons'.[26]

Writing in an irenic spirit which contrasts sharply with the polemical tone of the subsequent *Lectures on Justification*, Newman explains from the outset that he is not so much interested in proving the doctrine of baptismal regeneration as in explaining what is meant by it. For 'a great number at least of members of the Church who are suspicious of it, would receive it, if they understood it'. Newman hopes thereby to enlist the Evangelicals as allies in the struggle against Liberalism. Many of these were at first sympathetic to the Tractarians, only to turn against them later on when they detected what they took to be signs of 'papist sympathies'.

Newman approaches the subject gradually. He does not speak of *regeneration* until page 18 of his thirty-five-page manuscript, and the word 'baptism' does not appear until page 23. Instead he begins with a common starting-point: election, original sin, and the kingdom of heaven. Throughout the treatise the stress is on the mysterious nature of the divine dispensation, in contrast to the rationalistic mentality of the common adversary. The gift which is bestowed on man by the Holy Spirit in regeneration is the imparting of a new nature; it is something holy and mysterious, different in kind from anything possessed by nature, raising the soul to what it was not before. Newman wants to reassure the Evangelicals that he is not reducing the gift of regeneration to a mere outward formality, as they might have feared. But at the same time he is careful to guard against their mistaking his concept of regeneration for their own. Thus the imparting of a new nature is 'only the beginning of the future gift of perfection and immortality'.

Newman meets the principal objection of the Evangelicals, and one which he himself had once shared, namely the lack of holiness in so many of the baptized, by showing that the regeneration of which he is speaking does not consist in holiness, but in something higher. Certain characteristics are given, for example, that it is completely uncondi-tioned and the imparting of it is sudden and complete. Mostly it is described in its effects: 'It brings the soul into a mysterious state ... man regenerate is initiated into the unseen world'. But what *is* this gift? The answer is given in the sermons which Newman preached during the period immediately following the writing of this tract. It is the gift of the Indwelling Spirit whereby, as St Peter tells us, we are made partakers of the Divine Nature.[27]

It is here that we see the influence of the Fathers of the Church whom Newman had been reading avidly all during these years. The doctrine of humanity's divinization, of their restoration into the image and likeness of God which they had lost by sin, and this through baptism and the Eucharist, is so much a part of the teaching of the Fathers that it could not have failed to make an impression on Newman. This impres-sion was undoubtedly confirmed by the reading which he was also doing at this time of the works of the great Anglican divines of the seventeenth century such as Launcelot Andrewes and George Bull.

This special indwelling of the Holy Spirit is directly linked to regeneration:

> The Holy Ghost ... dwells in body and soul, as in a temple. He pervades us (if it may be so said) as light pervades a building, or as a sweet perfume the folds of some honourable robe, so that, in Scripture language, we are said to be in Him and He in us. It is plain that such an inhabitation brings the Christian into a state altogether new and marvellous, far above the possession of mere gifts, exalts him inconceivably in the scale of beings, and gives him a place and an office which he had not before ... This wonderful change from darkness to light, through the entrance of the Spirit into the soul, is called Regeneration, or the New Birth; a blessing which, before Christ's coming, not even Prophets and righteous men possessed, but which is now conveyed to all men freely through the Sacrament of Baptism.[28]

THE FINAL SYNTHESIS (1837–1838)

By the year 1837 Newman had reached the final stage in the develop-ment of his thought on the subject of justification, and it was time for a synthesis. The needed synthesis came, to a certain extent, in the *Lectures on Justification* published in 1838 – 'to a certain extent', because the theology of the *Lectures* is not systematic, but polemic. Newman had failed in his attempt to win the Evangelicals over to his side in the struggle against Liberalism. In fact, in the unpublished tract on baptism he implied that they themselves had given in to the Liberal temptation. For in maintaining that 'the lives of baptized Christians show that they are not regenerate' and that 'it is inconceivable that children should have a moral change wrought in them', were they not being led rather by reason than by faith?

And so it is the Evangelicals who are now clearly the adversary, though the greater danger of Liberalism is never far from Newman's mind.[29] Oddly enough, it is Martin Luther on whom Newman principally trains his guns. Whether the *system* that Newman was refuting should be traced back to Luther himself is open to question. But I think that anyone who compares what Newman says about Luther himself and his doctrine would have to agree that Newman is not, in fact, entirely fair to Luther. For, in actual fact, Luther's own doctrine had much in common with the position that John Henry Newman was defending, as will be shown in the course of this chapter.

Newman had become convinced that the Catholic position on justification and regeneration was being rejected outright by many members of the Church of England because of a one-sided view of the doctrine of 'justification by faith only' which, he believed, was not the traditional teaching of that Church, namely, an interpretation of that axiom which was widespread in the Evangelical party, particularly among its more enthusiastic members. The fact of the matter, as Newman viewed it, was that many members of his Church simply did not know what their Church stood for. Hence the need to construct what he called a *via media*, not as a compromise between two contrasting opinions, but as a return to primitive Christianity as it existed prior to what he called Protestant 'exaggerations' and Roman Catholic 'corruptions'. Such a return was possible, he felt, by gathering into a systematic body of theology the wisdom of the golden era of Anglican theology, the sixteenth and seventeenth centuries. The *Lectures on Justification* were to be one contribution to this all-important task. As we have seen, to the extent that Newman's thought developed away from Evangelicalism, he gradually came to see that the blessings of justification and regeneration were conferred not in the Evangelical experience of conversion but by admission into the Church through the sacrament of baptism. He did not arrive at this conclusion, however, independently of a doctrine which he had received from his Evangelical masters, namely that justification and regeneration are the work of the Holy Spirit. Even in his Evangelical

days he was willing to admit that baptism might under certain circumstances bring a person within the sphere of influence of the Holy Spirit.
The reason, then, why he finally accepted baptismal regeneration was
that he came to see that baptism admitted to the Church which *was* that
sphere of influence in its concrete realization.

On the other hand, while Newman's thought was developing along
these lines, his understanding of the proper role of the Holy Spirit was
also deepening. He came to see that the Spirit's work of regeneration did
not consist merely in moral betterment, but in a communication of the
divine nature to a person through His indwelling presence, that regeneration was in fact this divine Indwelling.

These two ideas achieve a final synthesis in the *Lectures on
Justification*.[30] 'The great benefit of justification ... is this one thing –
the transference of the soul *from* the kingdom of darkness *into* the kingdom of Christ'.[31] On the other hand, '*this* is to be justified, to receive the
Divine Presence within us, and be made a Temple of the Holy Ghost'.[32]
It stands to reason, therefore, that incorporation into this Kingdom and
the entrance of the divine Presence into the soul are one and the same
thing. The Spirit does not enter into us to leave us what we were before.
'For what in truth is the gift [of justification] but a grafting invisibly into
the Body of Christ; a mysterious union with Him, a fellowship in all the
grace and blessedness which is hidden in Him?'[33] Hence 'our justification, or being accounted righteous by Almighty God, consists in our
being grafted into the Body, or made members of Christ, in God dwelling
in us and our dwelling in God, and the Holy Ghost is the gracious Agent
in this wonderful work'.[34] The indwelling of the Holy Spirit is directly
linked by Newman with the Resurrection of Christ. Newman distinguishes two moments in the act of salvation: the Atonement, of which
Christ in his body 'of flesh' was the 'sole Agent', and justification, of
which the Holy Spirit is the 'sole agent'. But justification is still termed a
'part' of 'Christ's work of mercy'. For not only is it the 'application of the
Atonement', but that application is made by the 'Spirit of Christ', the
One sent by Christ upon His Resurrection. There is some mysterious
connection between Christ's rising and the Spirit's coming, so close that
we can say that 'His going to the Father was, in fact, the same thing as
His coming to us spiritually'.[35] The Spirit sent by Christ, because He is
the Spirit of Christ, unites us to the risen Body of Christ and transforms
us into Him. The Resurrection then is not just a condition, but a true
cause of our justification.

Although the divine Indwelling lies at the heart of Newman's theology of justification, his main object in writing the *Lectures on*

Justification was to show how the Church of England understands the axiom 'justification by faith only'. His adversaries interpreted it to mean two things: (1) that justification is a question of mere imputation, 'a change in God's sight', and (2) that faith, by which is meant a special kind of trust, is the only instrument of justification, excluding not only works but also sacraments. In addition, says Newman, they held that faith is also the only means of regeneration, the 'change within', which is not to be identified with justification, since we are not justified by anything 'in us'.

As regards the first point, Newman agrees that the word justification itself does mean a declaring righteous, in other words an imputation. But, he says, this is a *divine* imputation. It is 'a declaring righteous while it proceeds to make us righteous'.[36]

> 'The Voice of the Lord is mighty in *operation*, the Voice of the Lord is a glorious Voice'. It is not like some idle sound, or a vague rumour coming at random, and tending no whither, but it is 'the Word which goeth out of His mouth'; it has a sacramental power, being the instrument as well as the sign of His will. It never can return 'unto Him void', 'but it accomplishes that which He pleases, and prospers in the thing whereto He sends it'. Imputed righteousness is the coming in of actual righteousness. They whom God's sovereign voice pronounces just, forthwith become in their measure just. He declares a fact, and makes it a fact by declaring it. He imputes not a name, but a substantial Word, which, being 'ingrafted' in our own hearts, 'is able to save our souls'.[37]

Or, as he says so beautifully later on: 'Justification is an announcement or fiat of Almighty God breaking upon the gloom of our natural state as the Creative Word upon chaos'.[38]

With statements such as these we can see Newman's care to show that the Catholic position on justification safeguards all the positive values that a mere-imputation theory wishes to vindicate, and more. Far from detracting from God's mercy and liberality, it magnifies His power and His love. Nor is the creature given undue credit: our justification, while in us, is not of us. It is the indwelling presence of God: 'He imputes, not a name, but a substantial Word'. This is not to deny that it is intrinsic to us: we *are* made righteous. But ours is a participated righteousness, depending entirely on the righteousness of Christ as its source: 'None but the Eternal Son, who is incommunicably like the Father, can be infinitely acceptable to Him or simply righteous. Yet in proportion as rational beings are like the Son, or partake of Him, so are they really righteous; in proportion as God sees His Son in them, He is well-pleased with them.'[39]

Newman never questioned the validity of the axiom 'justification by faith only'. It was accepted by the Church of England in its eleventh Article as 'a most wholesome Doctrine'. His problem was to show how it was to be understood without admitting what he called the 'ultra-Protestant' interpretation of the formula. The key to the solution of this problem was furnished by the Article itself, which refers to the 'Homily of Justification' for a fuller explanation of it. The Homily states that: 'The very true meaning of this *proposition* or *saying*, we be justified by faith only (according to the meaning of the old ancient authors) is this, We put our faith in Christ, *that we be justified by Him only*'.[40] The emphases are those supplied by Newman in citing this passage. In other words: 'Salvation by faith only' is but another way of saying salvation by *grace* only. Again, it is intended to humble man, and to remind him that nothing he can do of himself can please God; so that 'by faith' means 'not by works of ours'.[41] In short, faith is 'a *symbol* of the nature and mode of our justification, or of its *history*'. This is the special 'office' of faith: 'It magnifies the grace of God, and is a sort of witness of its freeness and its largeness'.[42]

But is faith only a *symbol* of the gratuity of our justification? Does it not also have an instrumental role therein? Newman realizes that he is obliged by the Homilies to grant that it does. How is he also to maintain the equally unique role of baptism? This is where matters become a bit more complicated.

First of all, it is clear that whether speaking of faith as symbol or faith as instrument, what Newman means by faith remains the same. Faith is:

an original means of knowledge, not resolvable into sense, or what is commonly called reason, confirmed indeed by experience, as they are, but founded on a supernaturally implanted instinct; an instinct developed by religious obedience, and leading the mind to the word of Christ and of His Apostles as its refuge.[43]

When Newman is speaking of faith as an instrument, he is clearly talking of either the act or the habit of faith. On the other hand, when he is referring to faith as a symbol, he is not speaking of either of these, but of faith considered in the abstract. It is almost as if all he meant by 'faith' here was the word itself. Take for example the comparison he draws between faith in this context and the name 'rock' or 'foundation' which our Lord gave to Peter, not intending thereby to exclude the other Apostles from being foundations also:

His *name* expresses what all of them, including himself, really *are*, – foundations. In like manner, on the explanation before us, faith is *said* to justify, not that it really justifies more than other graces, but it has this peculiarity, that it signifies, in its very nature, that nothing of ours justifies us ... Faith heralds forth divine grace, and its name is a sort of representation of it, as opposed to works.[44]

By adding the words 'on the explanation before us' Newman carefully qualifies the statement 'not that it really justifies more than other graces'. Elsewhere he will maintain that, in another sense, it does. For he is also committed to holding an instrumental role of faith which is exclusive of other graces. What then is that truly instrumental role such as to exclude any other internal instrument from the role of justifying?

For Newman faith is an instrument of justification only after baptism. It does not 'convey' justification; it 'preserves' it. Hence the expression 'by faith only' does not rule out baptism, which is the 'sole external instrument'. But it does rule out 'all other graces', that is to say, love, trust, repentance, etc., 'from the office of justifying'. Why this is, Newman does not pretend to know: 'Faith surely, and not any other grace, is that which operates in keeping us in it. *Why* it does so is altogether a distinct question, and one perhaps which we cannot adequately determine. But whatever be God's inscrutable designs for thus connecting faith with His evangelical gifts, so has He done.'[45] That last statement provides an important clue to his thinking here. For it shows that his claim of the sole instrumentality of faith rests not upon the exigencies of his system, but upon his conviction that it is a datum of revelation found both in Scripture and in the teaching of his Church. To deny it *a priori* would be to yield to that same Liberal way of thinking that he so decries. And so he has recourse to mystery. In the third edition (1874), as a Roman Catholic, he will deny it, albeit in a footnote: 'Catholics hold that, not faith only, but faith, hope and charity are the "sustaining causes" of justification'.[46] But, as long as he was an Anglican, he felt obliged by the tradition of his Church, whose teachings he was ready to defend, as events were to prove, with his career and his reputation.

But faith alone, in the sense of faith existing by itself, in no wise justifies. So true is this that Newman can go so far as to say that 'when we say that God justifies by faith on our part, we mean by acts of whatever kind done in faith'.[47] Hence there is a true sense in which he can say that 'though we are justified as St Paul says, by faith, and as our

Articles and Homilies say, by faith only, nevertheless we are justified, as St James says, by works'.[48] For Newman faith is the 'quality' or 'mode' of obedience which makes it acceptable.[49] Faith 'lives in outward works'.[50] Faith, because of its power to focus our attention upon the divine Indwelling as the source of all our justification, gives to our works an orientation to Christ and away from ourselves which makes them acceptable.

Here then are the main lines of Newman's theology of justification: by the sacrament of baptism the Christian is made a member of the Body of Christ and a temple of the Holy Spirit. It is in this that justification properly consists. God declares the sinner just, not leaving him to his sin, but by a real imputation of the Incarnate Word, the risen Christ, through the agency of the Holy Spirit and the instrumentality of the sacrament of baptism, which is God's very act. This union with the risen Christ is further consolidated and intensified through the reception of that Sacred Body in Holy Communion. But man is not passive in his own justification. He 'receives' it by faith, which is transformed by the actual communication of the presence of Christ from a mere condition into an instrument of justification. Faith, in turn, lives in works of love, or obedience, which are themselves the fruit of this indwelling Spirit, who imparts a gracious quality to them and makes them acceptable. A person can therefore 'obey unto justification', not that his righteousness in any sense proceeds from himself, but only from that divine Presence which is their source. Faith stands guard here, preventing these works from degenerating into mere acts of self-righteousness by keeping the mind fixed on Christ who is their source. In short: 'Justification comes *through* the sacraments; is received *by* faith; *consists* in God's inward presence, and *lives* in obedience'.[51]

POSTSCRIPT

While it is clear throughout the *Lectures on Justification* that it is an extreme branch of the Evangelical wing of his Church that Newman has in view, the Evangelicals are never mentioned by name. Instead it is principally Martin Luther at whom Newman directs his polemic. This is strange since, as Alister McGrath has pointed out, 'From 1600 onwards, the main Protestant influence upon English theology was *Reformed*, rather than *Lutheran* – due to Calvin and Beza ... rather than Luther'.[52] It is also unfortunate since, in actual fact, Martin Luther's own teaching on justification, while differing on many points, was very close to that of Newman on the most essential points.[53]

Luther too taught that our justification consists first and foremost in Christ dwelling in us: 'The righteous man himself does not live; but Christ lives in him, because through faith Christ dwells in him and pours his grace into him, through which it comes about that a man is governed not by his own spirit, but by Christ's'.[54] Thus Luther did not hold that we are justified by mere imputation, as Newman would maintain. Using a line of argumentation similar to Newman's, Luther taught that 'divine imputation may not be regarded as amounting to nothing outside God, as some think that the apostle's word "grace" means a favorable disposition rather than a gift'. He continued: 'For when God is favorable, and when he imputes, the Spirit is really received, both the gift and the grace. Otherwise grace was there from eternity and remains with God, if it signifies only a favorable disposition in the way that favor is understood among men. For just as God loves in very fact, not in word only, so, too, He is favorably disposed with the thing that is present, not only with the word.'[55]

Newman's harshest criticism of Luther comes when he says: 'He [Luther] found Christians in bondage to their works and observances; he released them by his doctrine of faith; and he left them in bondage to their feelings'.[56] While he might have said this of his Evangelical adversaries' understanding of faith, it does not apply to Luther himself. To be sure, Newman understood faith as primarily an intellectual assent, while for Luther it was primarily a question not of feelings, but of the will.[57] But in their understanding of the symbolic meaning of the axiom 'justification by faith only' they were in essential agreement. Luther, in fact, never spoke of faith as the instrument of our justification. For Luther, as for Newman, that axiom showed forth the total gratuity of our justification. Newman was correct in his assessment of Luther's motivation for insisting upon the truth of the axiom: 'The reasons which led to his insisting upon it were chiefly the two following, both arising from his opposition to the Roman doctrine concerning good works; – first his wish to extirpate all notions of human merit; next, to give peace and satisfaction to the troubled conscience'. But unfortunately he drew from this the conclusion that 'He taught that the Moral Law is not binding on the conscience of the Christian'.[58] Many others had drawn this same conclusion, leading Luther in 1520 to write his *Treatise on Good Works*, in which he explained how each of the Ten Commandments applied to the Christian, while insisting that faith must be the driving force behind all good works, and that it is because of that faith that they are pleasing to God.[59] This is the very point that Newman himself would make in Lecture XII.

Part of the reason why Newman failed to see the extent to which, however much they differed on certain points, Luther's own teaching was in many respects in substantial agreement with his own was that Newman had most probably never read Luther firsthand.[60] Then, too, the *Lectures* were essentially a polemical work, and in polemics the tendency is to stress differences rather than similarities.[61] Be that as it may, the question remains: in view of the fact that Newman's polemic is directed against an extreme branch of the Evangelical wing of his own Church, why does he single out Martin Luther for especial condemnation?

Part of the problem may lie with the Evangelicals themselves, who regarded Luther as 'a hero larger than life', but whose understanding of him made him out to be like one of themselves rather than the sixteenth-century figure that he was.[62] As Henry Chadwick has pointed out, 'Perhaps Newman chose Luther for his target because relatively few English people knew much of his writings, whereas they knew Calvin much better' and were better disposed to Calvin and the Calvinists than to Luther, with whom they felt far less comfortable.[63]

And then it must be remembered that Luther was a German. Is it not possible that Newman wanted to imply that the roots of the doctrine he was opposing were not English but a foreign import? In the very first Lecture he speaks of 'the Lutheran, or what might be called the Continental view, that faith is the proper instrument of justification'.[64] And he reminds us that Luther is 'the German Reformer'.[65] More importantly, conservative Anglicans (such as Newman's friend H. J. Rose) tended to accuse Luther of being responsible for German Rationalism, because of Luther's rejection of Church authority in the interpretation of the Scriptures.[66] And for Newman it was that rationalistic spirit which he called 'Liberalism' which would always remain the deadliest of all enemies to the Faith.

Notes

1. L. Bouyer, *Newman: His Life and Spirituality* (London: Burns Oates and Washbourne, 1958), 8.
2. *Apo.*, 4.
3. *A.W.*, 29.
4. Ian Ker, *John Henry Newman: A Biography* (Oxford: Clarendon Press, 1988), 4.
5. *Apo.*, 5.
6. *Apo.*, 5.
7. *A.W.*, 80.
8. Birmingham Oratory Archives A-9-1. There are two redactions of this document, the second of which is incomplete.

9. *A.W.*, 79. See also p. 82. For Newman's critique of the Evangelicalism of his day, as well as its positive contributions to his own spiritual development, see Ian Ker, 'Evangelical Christianity', in *Newman and the Fullness of Christianity* (Edinburgh: T & T Clark, 1993), 19–30.

10. *A.W.*, 65–6.

11. *Apo.*, 11.

12. *Apo.*, 4.

13. *A.W.*, 191.

14. *A.W.*, 203.

15. *A.W.*, 77.

16. On 17 July 1824. See *L.D.*, i:179; *A.W.*, 79, 206.

17. *A.W.*, 78. Newman's italics.

18. *A.W.*, 202.

19. *A.W.*, 203.

20. Birmingham Oratory Archives, A-17-1, Sermon nos. 57, 61 and 67; A-7-1, outlines of these and of nos. 59, 63 and 65.

21. *A.W.*, 78. The reference is to Joseph Butler's *The Analogy of Religion Natural and Revealed to the Constitution and Course of Nature*. It was first published in 1736.

22. Birmingham Oratory Archives, B-3-IV, Sermon no. 118; A-50-2, Sermon nos. 120 and 121.

23. Birmingham Oratory Archives, A-9-1.

24. Six of the sermons in their entirety, and fragments of five others, have been printed in V. F. Blehl, SJ (ed.), *John Henry Newman: Sermons 1824–1843* (Oxford: Clarendon Press, 1993), ii:133–206. The eighth in the series was published as 'Holiness Necessary for Future Blessedness' in *P.S.*, i:1–14. Two of the sermons are missing entirely.

25. *Apo.*, 288.

26. Birmingham Oratory Archives A-9-1. The sermons referred to are nos. 16, 17 and 18 of *P.S.*, iii:220–35, 236–53, 254–70.

27. *P.S.*, ii:26–40, 217–31; iii:254–70; iv:282–94.

28. *P.S.*, ii:222–3.

29. Newman himself said that the Lectures were written against 'the so-called Evangelical school' and 'against their system'; see *L.D.*, vi:129.

30. The *Lectures on Justification* were originally delivered in the Adam de Brome Chapel of St Mary the Virgin, beginning on 13 April and ending on 1 June 1837. In the ensuing months they were extensively revised for publication, the first edition finally appearing in March 1838. Unless otherwise indicated, references will be to the substantially identical second edition (London: Rivington, 1840), with the third edition (1874), i.e., the standard edition, given in square brackets.

31. *Jfc.*, 113 [101].

32. *Jfc.*, 160 [144].

33. *Jfc.*, 181 [160].

34. *Jfc.*, 230 [202]. Compare 249 [219].

35. *Jfc.*, 231–5 [203–7].

36. *Jfc.*, 81 [74].

37. *Jfc.*, 87–8 [79–80].

38. *Jfc.*, 91 [83].
39. *Jfc.*, 119–20 [107].
40. *Jfc.*, 282 [249].
41. *Jfc.*, 321–2 [282–3].
42. *Jfc.*, 276 [243].
43. *Jfc.*, 304 [267]; compare 306 [269] and *U.S.*, 176–201, 177–202 (Sermon nos. 10 and 11, which were delivered in 1839).
44. *Jfc.*, 278–9 [246].
45. *Jfc.*, 264 [225].
46. *Jfc.* (third edition), 226.
47. *Jfc.*, 334 [293].
48. *Jfc.*, 312 [274].
49. *Jfc.*, 318 [279].
50. *Jfc.*, 343 [302].
51. *Jfc.*, 316–17 [278].
52. A. E. McGrath, *Iustitia Dei: A History of the Christian Doctrine of Justification*, 2nd edn (Cambridge: Cambridge University Press, 1998), 312. McGrath devotes pp. 308–21 to an extensive critique of the *Lectures*, which he calls 'easily the most significant theological writing to emerge from the Oxford Movement', but he judges that 'Newman's historico-theological analysis appears to be seriously and irredeemably inaccurate'. Every aspect of this analysis was faulty, says McGrath, with respect to 'the doctrines of justification associated with Luther (and to a much lesser extent, with Melanchthon), with Roman Catholic theologians such as Bellarmine and Vásquez, and with the Caroline Divines', but 'supremely in the case of Luther himself' (see 309). He also faults Newman for neglecting the Reformed tradition, and especially for the paucity of references to John Calvin, with whom he also shared some important insights (see 317).
53. For a more extensive treatment of this question see T. L. Sheridan, 'Newman and Luther on Justification', *Journal of Ecumenical Studies* 38 (2001), 217–45.
54. Martin Luther, *Commentary on Galatians* (1519) in *Luther's Works* (St Louis: Concordia, 1964), xxvii:238.
55. Luther, *Commentary on Galatians* (1519), xxvii:252.
56. *Jfc.*, 386 [339–40]. For a detailed critique of this paragraph, see Alister McGrath, 'Newman on Justification: An Evangelical Anglican Evaluation', in T. Merrigan and I. Ker (eds.), *Newman and the Word* (Leuven: Peeters, 2000), 94–6.
57. J. Pelikan, *The Christian Tradition: A History of the Development of Doctrine* (Chicago and London: University of Chicago Press, 1984), iv:153–4, sums up Luther's view of faith as follows: 'The faith that justifies is no mere historical knowledge, but the firm acceptance of God's offer promising forgiveness of sins and justification. Luther set himself against scholastic theology with the simple antithesis: "Where they speak of love, we speak of faith". "Faith" here meant more than virtue or knowledge (though not less). It meant, above all, "a firm trust [fiducia]", for which "Christ is the object of faith, or rather not the object,

but, so to speak, the one who is present in the faith itself". Thus faith was "a sort of knowledge or darkness that can see nothing". It was, then, believing "in" Christ; that included, as Luther's exposition of the Apostles' Creed showed, believing "that" the life, death and resurrection of Christ were historically true – but above all that they were true "for me", a phrase that one was to "accept with a sure faith and apply to himself" without doubting'.

58. *Jfc.*, 26 [24].
59. Pelikan, *Christian Tradition*, iv:147.
60. Like almost of all his contemporaries, Pusey being one notable exception, Newman did not read German, so he was dependent upon the very poor translations of the time and secondary, probably polemic, sources.
61. For A. E. McGrath this polemical intent seriously compromises the value of the *Lectures*: 'Both in this work and in the earlier *Arians of the Fourth Century*, Newman uses historical theology as little more than a thinly-veiled foil for his own theological and ecclesiological agenda, which is firmly wedded to the realities of the Church of England in the 1830s'. See McGrath, 'Newman on Justification', 105.
62. W. J. Baker, 'Julius Charles Hare: A Victorian Interpreter of Luther', *South Atlantic Quarterly* 70 (1971), 91.
63. H. Chadwick, 'The Lectures on Justification', in I. Ker and A. G. Hill (eds.), *Newman after a Hundred Years* (Oxford: Clarendon Press, 1990), 297–8.
64. *Jfc.*, 3 [3].
65. *Jfc.*, 4 [4].
66. Baker, 'Julius Charles Hare', 238.

Further reading

Blehl, V. F. ed., *John Henry Newman: Sermons 1824–1843*. Volume ii: *Biblical History, Sin and Justification, Christian Way of Life, Biblical Theology*. Oxford: Oxford University Press, 1993.
Chadwick, H. 'The Lectures on Justification', in Ian Ker and Alan G. Hill. (eds.), *Newman after a Hundred Years*. Oxford: Clarendon Press, 1990, 287–307.
Dulles, A. 'Redemption, Justification, and Sanctification', in *John Henry Newman*. London and New York: Continuum, 2002, 16–33.
McGrath, A. E. *Iustitia Dei: A History of the Christian Doctrine of Justification*. Cambridge: Cambridge University Press, 1998.
   'Newman on Justification: An Evangelical Anglican Evaluation', in T. Merrigan and I. Ker (eds.), *Newman and the Word*. Leuven: Peeters, 2000, 91–107.
Morales, J. 'Newman and the Problems of Justification', in Stanley L. Jaki (ed.), *Newman Today*. San Francisco: Ignatius Press, 1989, 143–64.
Sheridan, T. L. *Newman on Justification*. Staten Island: Alba House, 1967.
   'Newman and Luther on Justification', *Journal of Ecumenical Studies* 38 (2001), 217–45.
Strange, R. 'Christ's Presence in the Believer', in *Newman and the Gospel of Christ*. Oxford: Oxford University Press, 1981, 134–67.

6 Development of doctrine

GERARD H. MCCARREN

Having decided to become a Roman Catholic, John Henry Newman laid aside his unfinished *Essay on the Development of Christian Doctrine*.[1] Neither he nor anyone in the Church knew that he had just articulated 'the classic discussion of doctrinal development' and fixed 'the almost inevitable starting point for an investigation of development of doctrine'.[2] Newman's *Essay* – and he considered it to be just that – enabled him to find intellectual warrant for his departure from Canterbury for Rome. The *Essay* possesses 'continuing relevance' for theology[3] because Newman both poignantly formulated the problem created by the collision of dogmatic Christianity with the historical consciousness that impressed itself upon Western culture in the nineteenth century, and advanced 'an hypothesis' towards an explanation.[4] In the estimation of Avery Dulles, the *Essay* remains unsurpassed in influence and 'in depth and thoroughness' among writings on development of doctrine.[5] The *Essay* framed subsequent confrontations with the problem; indeed the compatibility between Newman's *Essay* and the understanding of doctrinal development espoused by the Second Vatican Council is conspicuous.[6]

Newman's understanding of development was not entirely without precedent. Some patristic authors, most strikingly St Vincent of Lérins, came near the notion almost asymptotically but, like the medieval theologians who later drew near the theme in some way, they engaged in nothing resembling systematic reflection on it. Scholastic and neo-scholastic theologians cast the problem, to the limited extent that they perceived it, in logical terms, failing thereby to attain to the crux of the problem posed by the flux of history. In 1825 Johann Adam Möhler of the Catholic Tübingen School published *Die Einheit in der Kirche*, which approached the issue, yet neither this nor his more famous *Symbolik* of 1832 contended directly with the problem of history's clash with Catholic dogma's claim to immutability.[7] Only with Newman's publication of his *Essay* could it be said that history's inexorable bearing on Christian doctrinal claims was recognized and met with a somewhat tentative but imposing answer.[8]

THE THEME OF DEVELOPMENT IN NEWMAN'S EARLY WRITINGS

Newman's first book, *The Arians of the Fourth Century*, had come almost within reach of doctrinal development but had not grappled with it. Aware that the need to formulate doctrines with the specificity of creedal statements came upon the early Christians for good and for ill,[9] Newman applauded St Irenaeus's distinction 'between a tradition supplanting or perverting the inspired records, and a corroborating, illustrating, and altogether subordinate tradition'.[10] 'Newman was not yet occupied with the development of doctrine in its content', however.[11] He did not suggest development as a sort of middle way between discontinuity and mere explication. Similarly, Newman veered close to the idea of development when considering 'the line of conduct which is to be observed by the Christian apologist and missionary' in the face of the beliefs of pagans, whose writings might contain 'the ore in which the true metal was found',[12] but Newman did not pause to reflect on the process by which Christians refine it. Newman noticed heresy's effects upon the Church of 'requiring its authoritative judgment on the point in dispute'[13] and precipitating systematization of doctrine, but he did not go so far as to postulate development: 'a system of doctrine becomes unavoidable; being framed, let it be observed, not with a view of explaining, but of arranging the inspired notices concerning the Supreme Being, of providing, not a consistent, but a connected statement'.[14] When surveying the Arian controversy he marvelled at 'the gradual influence of truth over error' and especially at 'the remarkable manner in which Divine Providence makes use of error itself as a preparation for truth'[15] but approached the idea of development only tangentially: 'The very confidence which would be felt by Christians in general that Apostolic truth would never fail, – and that they held it in each locality themselves and the *orbis terrarum* with them, in spite of all verbal contrarieties, – would indispose them to define it, till definition became an imperative duty'.[16]

In his last University Sermon, Newman took up the topic directly. In 'The Theory of Developments in Religious Doctrine', Newman took as his text, 'But Mary kept all these things, and pondered them in her heart'. He observed that, 'The absence, or partial absence, or incompleteness of dogmatic statements is no proof of the absence of impressions or implicit judgments, in the mind of the Church. Even centuries might pass without the formal expression of a truth, which had been all along the secret life of millions of faithful souls.' He pointed out, for example, that 'the doctrine of the Double Procession was no Catholic dogma in the first ages, though it was more or less clearly stated by individual Fathers' but now is constitutive of the faith and as such must have been 'held every where from the beginning, and therefore, in a measure, held as a mere religious impression, and perhaps an unconscious one'.[17] Over time

> [o]ne proposition necessarily leads to another, and a second to a third; then some limitation is required; and the combination of these opposites occasions some fresh evolutions from the original idea, which indeed can never be said to be entirely exhausted. This process is its development, and results in a series, or rather body of dogmatic statements, till what was at first an impression on the Imagination has become a system or creed in the Reason.[18]

More important than the doctrinal statements that in combination define doctrine is the reality underneath those expressions; hence Newman articulated 'the distinction, yet connexion, between the implicit know-ledge and the explicit confession of the Divine Objects of Faith'.[19] Scripture itself contains doctrinal developments and in fact warrants further development by the use of reason in theological reflection.[20] Doctrinal development enshrines this progressive understanding.

THE ESSAY ON DEVELOPMENT

Newman elaborated his pioneering understanding of doctrinal devel-opment most fully in his *Essay on Development*,[21] which came starkly to grips with historical change:

> [W]e must determine whether on the one hand Christianity is still to represent to us a definite teaching from above, or whether on the other its utterances have been from time to time so strangely at variance that we are necessarily thrown back on our own judgment individually to determine what the revelation of God is, or rather if in fact there is, or has been, any revelation at all.[22]

Indeed the difficulty was his own insofar as he was coming to believe that the doctrines and practices of Roman Catholicism which he had hitherto dismissed as corruptive accretions to pure Christianity stood in legiti-mate continuity with the Christian faith of the apostles.[23] It was with the acknowledgement of 'certain apparent inconsistencies and alterations in its doctrine and its worship such as irresistibly attract the attention of all who inquire into it', 'which have to be explained',[24] that Newman commenced his treatise on the theology of development. He believed that the Church standing in real continuity with the primitive Church would have as a hallmark fidelity to the teaching of the apostles. But once the weight of history impressed itself on human consciousness, how could such an identity be ascertained? If the problem had hitherto been recognized at all, it had been resolved by a denial of historical variation in the manner of Bossuet's famously confident dismissal of it at the end of the seventeenth century.[25] Newman, in contrast, embraced historical fluctuation in the *Essay*, as its best known sentence proclaims: 'In a higher world it is otherwise, but here below to live is to change, and to be perfect is to have changed often'.[26] Newman countenanced change to the extent that it could be reconciled with his belief that the Church's later doctrines were in fact contained in the apostolic deposit; it should not be forgotten that the sentence immediately preceding that most famous line declared that 'a great idea' 'changes ... in order to remain the same'.[27] Having admitted the impact of the vicissitudes of history on Christian doctrine, Newman deemed doctrinal development the only hypothesis capable of explaining how Christianity could have remained faithful to its doctrinal patrimony.[28] Newman rejected out of hand the '[hypothesis] to the effect that Christianity has even changed from the first and ever accommodates itself to the circumstances of times and seasons' because it is 'difficult to understand how such a view is compatible with the special idea of revealed truth' which he assumed in his *Essay*.[29] Newman similarly excluded Protestantism from consideration because he summarily judged it 'not the Christianity of history', its doctrines being manifestly incongruent with 'antiquity, as it has come down to us',[30] 'Protestants [being] as little [able to] bear its Antenicene as its Post-tridentine period'.[31] Newman also considered whether or not the 'hypothesis' of the *disciplina arcani* was helpful 'for accounting for a want of accord between the early and the late aspects of Christianity',[32] since according to that primitive practice the mysteries of the faith were disclosed only to the converted. Acknowledging that 'this fact goes some way to account for that apparent variation and growth of doctrine', Newman judged that 'it is no key to the whole difficulty'.[33]

Newman found 'more plausible' the Anglican 'hypothesis' wherein 'all usages, ways, opinions, and tenets, which have not the sanction of primitive times', were excluded 'as corruptions'.[34] According to the famous dictum of Vincent of Lérins, 'revealed and Apostolic doctrine is "quod semper, quod ubique, quod ab omnibus"...'.[35] Yet Newman deemed the Vincentian Canon ultimately insufficient.[36] If Anglican apologists saw in it both the 'bulwark against Rome' and the 'assault against Protestantism' that they wanted, Newman had come to find 'difficulty' 'in applying it to particular cases'.[37] 'It admits of being interpreted in one of two ways', he wrote: if interpreted narrowly so as to exclude certain Catholic doctrines, it recoiled upon teachings of the Church of England, and if broadly so as to retain Anglican teaching, then its consistent application left room for Roman doctrines considered by Anglicans to be unwarranted accretions. With St Vincent's rule one could consistently hold both the doctrine of original sin and that of purgatory or neither; the Anglican affirmation of the former and denial of the latter could not stand.[38] Newman concluded that without prejudice to the truth and utility of Vincent's rule 'in his own age', in the present day '[t]he solution it offers is as difficult as the original problem'.[39]

Having excluded those 'hypotheses',[40] Newman embarked on his own attempt to show that the entire history of Christianity, despite its variations, preserves the truth of revelation. This enquiry was simultaneously his attempt to validate the gravitational pull Rome was exerting on him. Taking up a line of argument from the last of the *Oxford University Sermons*, the *Essay* now considered how the inexhaustible riches of a real idea defy full expression in words.[41] Hence 'the *primâ facie* dissimilitude of its aspects becomes, when explained, an argument for its substantiveness and integrity, and their multiplicity for its originality and power'.[42] Newman labelled the 'process ... by which the aspects of an idea are brought into consistency and form' by the mind in which it lives 'its development'.[43] Different perspectives afford new insights, and the idea develops. Ideas develop in interaction with their environment, which comprises the minds which possess them, the communities in which these people live, and related ideas.[44] Although an idea's exchange with its environment introduces the risk of corruption, it also constitutes the possibility of the idea's fuller display and comprehension, or for that matter of its continued intelligibility in a changing world.[45] Living ideas develop.[46] Should not Christian doctrines? Given the 'nature of the human mind' and the richness of 'the highest and most wonderful truths', development was inevitable.[47] After a penetrating analysis, especially of scriptural warrants for a theory of development, Newman answered conclusively: 'From the necessity, then, of the case, from the history of all sects and parties in religion, and from the analogy and example of Scripture, we may fairly conclude that Christian doctrine admits of formal, legitimate, and true developments, that is, of developments contemplated by its Divine Author'.[48] Newman supported his case with various historical 'instances in illustration'.[49]

Countering at the *Essay*'s outset those who summarily dismissed modern Christianity's claim to possess 'a real continuity of doctrine' with the primitive Church, Newman, acknowledging 'the abstract possibility of extreme changes', asserted: 'The *onus probandi* is with those who assert what it is unnatural to expect'.[50] 'Till positive reasons grounded on facts are adduced to the contrary, the most natural hypothesis, the most agreeable to our mode of proceeding in parallel cases, and that which takes precedence over all others', he claimed, is to assume fundamental continuity.[51] Considering 'the Historical Argument in behalf of the Existing Developments',[52] Newman reaffirmed his commitment to this approach,[53] assessing doctrines 'in proportion to the strength of the antecedent probability in their favour'.[54]

Applying this understanding of assumptions which would later become pivotal in his *Essay in Aid of a Grammar of Assent*, Newman declared: 'Now it is but a parallel exercise of reasoning to interpret the previous history of a doctrine by its later development, and to consider that it contains the later *in posse* and in the divine intention'.[55] Given development, Newman believed that one can make retrospective claims based on its outcome. Though by no means wholly uncritical,[56] his hermeneutic for evaluating primitive and undeveloped doctrines enabled him to offer a powerful alternative to sceptical interpretations of the history of doctrines. According to Newman, '[W]here a doctrine comes recommended to us by strong presumptions of its truth, we are bound to receive it unsuspiciously, and use it as a key to the evidences to which it appeals, or the facts which it professes to systematize, whatever may be our eventual judgment about it'.[57]

Newman's argument that the papacy was a true development of foundations present in the primitive Church illustrates how he employed his understanding of the valid use of antecedent probability. Anticipating objections to the effect that the apostolic deposit lacks sufficient evidence for the supremacy of the Bishop of Rome, Newman granted that 'it is a theory', principally 'a theory to connect the words and acts of the Antenicene Church with that antecedent probability of a monarchical principle in the Divine Scheme, and that actual exemplification of it in the fourth century, which forms their presumptive interpretation'.[58] Given that Newman found 'nothing in the early history of the Church to contradict it',[59] he contended that this 'presumptive interpretation' grounded a strong case in favour of the Roman Catholic belief that the papacy is divinely instituted.

Having established, by finding antecedent probability of development fulfilled in the facts of Christian history, what he termed the 'momentous fact' '[t]hat, beyond reasonable doubt, there are [developments of doctrine]',[60] Newman considered the question '*What* are they?' in light of the fact that true developments are not self-evident.[61] Referring to the 'tests' for distinguishing these from corruptions which he devised and which he would elaborate in the second part of his book, he observed that notwithstanding the usefulness of such 'tests', 'they are insufficient for the guidance of individuals in the case of so large and complicated a problem as Christianity'.[62] Since it would be incongruous that developments of the saving truths revealed by God be unrecogniz-able,[63] Newman claimed that 'an external authority', that is, 'the infal-libility of the Church', is to be expected 'to decide upon them, thereby separating them from the mass of mere human speculation, extrava-gance, corruption, and error, in and out of which they grow'.[64] Thus Newman posited the antecedent probability of 'an infallible developing authority'.[65] Carrying his argument forward, Newman claimed that the expected developments of Christian doctrine 'are found just where they might be expected, in the authoritative seats and homes of old tradition, the Latin and Greek Churches'.[66] Roman Catholicism more than other types of Christianity resembled 'the Church of the Fathers'.[67] 'Did St Athanasius or St Ambrose come suddenly to life', so Newman introduced a particularly especially captivating passage, 'it cannot be doubted what communion he would take to be his own'.[68]

Those developments, certified by the Church's teaching authority, were as reasonable as the concept of development itself. As such they did not depend utterly on their sanction by ecclesiastical authority for recognition. Examining the characteristics of true development, as dis-tinguished from corruption, or 'perversion of the truth',[69] Newman pro-posed his seven 'tests' of faithful development, which he would label 'notes' when he revised the *Essay* for republication in 1878. These would aid in distinguishing genuine development from mere historical succes-sion of one doctrine following upon another where the later doctrine does not preserve the substance of its antecedent.[70] Newman expected by the application of these tests to confirm that his 'hypothesis' of development in fact showed the identity of the Roman Catholic Church of his day and the primitive Church.[71] He hoped thereby to render acceptance of the Roman Catholic faith – precisely as the true representative of pristine Christian faith – inviting because reasonable. Here perhaps more clearly than in any other respect did the *Essay* go beyond Newman's last University Sermon, when he had preached: 'Nor am I here in any way concerned with the question, who is the legitimate framer and judge of these dogmatic inferences under the Gospel, or if there be any. Whether the Church is infallible, or the individual, or the first ages, or none of these, is not the point here, but the theory of developments itself.'[72] In both Newman sought to show that with the passage of time truth is preserved precisely as it is presented anew and with increasing penetration,[73] but in the *Essay* he set about 'assign[ing] certain characteristics of faithful developments, which none but faithful developments have, and the presence of which serves as a test to discriminate between them and corruptions'.[74] Seven 'tests' or 'notes' would provide 'the interpretative assistance' by which to show that the developments in Roman Catholicism, in the words of Aidan Nichols, 'enjoy a reasonable claim to be aspects of an authentic re-composition of the original Christian "idea" into new "consistency and form"'.[75] Newman's replacement of the 'tests' of the 1845 edition with what Nichols called 'the less ambitious "notes"' of that of 1878 would 'drive home the point' that 'the *Essay* does not offer a full criteriology of doctrinal development which will show Roman developments to be the genuine ones'.[76]

Newman labelled his 'first note of a genuine development' 'preservation of type'.[77] 'The analogy of physical growth' indicates how a plant or animal develops even as it remains the same. Newman noted that 'unity of type ... must not be pressed to the extent of denying all variation, nay, considerable alteration of proportion and relation, as time goes on, in the parts or aspects of an idea'.[78] A review of the history of the first ecumenical councils showed that precisely as Catholic bishops added to the creed against the objections of heretical parties, who claimed that by their refusal to sanction such development they remained more faithful to the primitive Church, the Catholic bishops in union with the pope preserved the true meaning of the scriptural formulae. Thus Newman freely juxtaposed the statement that 'the definition passed at Chalcedon is the Apostolic Truth once delivered to the saints' with the admission that

> the historical account of the Council is this, that a formula which the Creed did not contain, which the Fathers did not unanimously witness, and which some eminent Saints had almost in set terms opposed, which the whole East refused as a symbol, not once, but twice, patriarch by patriarch, metropolitan by metropolitan, first by the mouth of above a hundred, then by the mouth of above six hundred of its bishops, and refused upon the grounds of its being an addition to the Creed, was forced upon the Council, not indeed as being an addition, yet, on the other hand, not for subscription merely, but for acceptance as a definition of faith under the sanction of an anathema.[79]

No such penetrating insight had accompanied Newman's review in *Arians* of such patristic material.

'Continuity of Principles' constitutes Newman's second note of true development.[80] It is because development takes place 'on definite and continuous principles' that type is preserved.[81] Catholic principles engender true development. Newman found for example in the doctrine of the Incarnation several Gospel principles such as those of dogma, faith, theology, sacramentality, the mystical sense of Scripture, grace, asceticism, the malignity of sin, and matter's capability of sanctification.[82] These principles, according to Newman, 'are the very instruments of [doctrinal] development'. Doctrinal development, then, respects among other things faith's supremacy, the laws of reason, the dogmatic nature of Christianity and the spiritual interpretation of Scripture.[83] There is a sense in which principles even claim priority over specific doctrines. Hence Newman claimed: 'If it be true that the principles of the later Church are the same as those of the earlier, then, whatever are the variations of belief between the two periods, the later in reality agrees more than it differs with the earlier, for principles are responsible for doctrines'.[84] The second note 'comes to terms', according to Jaroslav Pelikan, 'with the stubborn fact of the doctrinal variety within every age of church history and between one age and another'.[85]

Another dynamic note is the third: 'Power of Assimilation'.[86] 'The idea never was that throve and lasted, yet, like mathematical truth, incorporated nothing from external sources', Newman asserted.[87] Far from losing its identity in its interaction with its various milieus, Christianity has demonstrated 'the power ... of absorbing its antagonists, as Aaron's rod'.[88] Through human meticulousness[89] and gracious Providence[90] the Church 'has been a treasure-house, giving forth things old and new, casting the gold of fresh tributaries into her refiner's fire, or stamping upon her own, as time required it, a deeper impress of her Master's image'.[91] From Power of Assimilation results 'Catholic fullness'.[92] The *Essay* displays a confidence not found in *Arians*.

Newman indicated by his fourth note, logical sequence,[93] that although doctrines do not ordinarily advance by syllogism, retrospective examination must be able to show that they proceed according to the rules of logic,[94] if not strictly, at least such that there is 'progress of the mind from one judgment to another, as, for instance, by way of moral fitness'.[95] Time will tell the true import of a doctrine as implications unfold according to logic.[96] As 'instances of one doctrine leading to another' Newman traced from the doctrine of baptism the development in sequence of pardons, penances, satisfactions, purgatory, meritorious works and the monastic rule.[97] Owen Chadwick observed that because

Newman interpreted logic in the widest sense, doctrines which proceed one from the other can be said to be truly new.[98]

Anticipation of future developments, Newman's fifth note,[99] follows upon the likelihood that 'under favourable circumstances' an idea will be displayed early in its history in richness ordinarily following upon a longer period of maturation, since 'developments are in great measure only aspects of the idea from which they proceed'.[100] Newman found the expectation fulfilled in various antenicene anticipations of allegedly later Catholic accretions.[101]

According to his sixth note, a true development is characterized by 'conservative action upon its past'.[102] Thus Newman quoted approvingly Vincent of Lérins's description of development as 'profectus fidei non permutatio'.[103] Hence in Newman's view 'a developed doctrine which reverses the course of development is no true development but a corruption'.[104] Genuine development involves 'addition', or 'change which is in one sense real and perceptible, yet without loss or reversal of what has gone before, but, on the contrary, protective and confirmative of it'.[105] Recalling that 'a strict correspondence between the various members of a development, and those of the doctrine from which it is derived, is more than we have any right to expect', just as '[t]he bodily structure of a grown man is not merely that of a magnified boy', Newman held that nonetheless there is real preservation. Development is a process of 'protecting', not of 'superseding'.[106]

Whereas corruption is 'a brief and rapid process' because it deviates from true development[107] and its variant, decay, though enduring, lacks 'vigorous action' altogether,[108] true development is marked by 'chronic vigour', its seventh note.[109] Thus Newman pointed out: 'The course of heresies is always short'.[110] When indeed they appear to contradict this rule, close observation will reveal that they do so only by vacillating between possibly contradictory ideas.[111] Therefore Newman ventured to state that an attempt to dismiss the longstanding peculiarly Catholic beliefs as corruptions would be to postulate a miracle indeed.[112]

THE APPLICATION OF THE THEORY OF DEVELOPMENT

Few of the many studies of Newman's *Essay* have brought sustained reflection to bear on its seven 'tests' or 'notes'. How do they really function in the *Essay*? The Roman Catholic Church's official International Theological Commission claimed in 1990 that the *Essay*'s 'notes' constitute 'a criteriology for dogmatic development ... that is useful ... for the ongoing contemporary interpretation of dogmas'.[113] So do other theologians, but close examination of the function of the 'tests' or 'notes' in the *Essay* indicates that they do not admit of so easy an application as might appear at a cursory glance. Scrutiny of Newman's editorial work on the *Essay* for its final edition suggests certain subtle adjustments in his understanding of the original edition's 'tests' corresponding to their recasting as 'notes', but perhaps more significant is Newman's admission that the 'notes' were 'of varying cogency, independence, and applicability'.[114]

Notwithstanding this lack of clarity, one can cautiously suggest guidelines for their application. With the *Essay* Newman was concerned primarily to confirm that the Roman Catholic Church as such could plausibly claim to embody authentic developments of doctrine, though it remains true that only some of the 'notes' apply to particular doctrines. In addition, the 'notes' for the most part must be applied together; it is hard to assess the applicability of just one or more of them to a doctrine or to the Church. Believing that 'they rather serve as answers to objections brought against the actual decisions of authority, than [as] proofs of the correctness of their decisions',[115] Newman tightly circumscribed their purpose. The 'notes' serve to dispel accusations that Roman Catholic doctrines are additions compromising the pristine apostolic deposit of faith. With the assistance of the 'notes' one can defend the plausibility of distinctively Catholic doctrines. Moreover, Newman's presentation of the 'notes' was not highly systematic. He did acknowledge them in 1878 to be 'seven out of various Notes, which may be assigned, of fidelity in the development of an idea'.[116] His impending reception into the Roman Catholic Church prompted him to rush the book to its conclusion, leaving it 'unfinished',[117] such that he moved progressively from a protracted exposition of the first 'note' to a cursory outline of the seventh.

Therefore, one may expect to find in the 'notes' qualities which may serve in a limited way as criteria for the recognition of genuine development of doctrine. On the one hand, one should not expect to construct upon them an ironclad proof. On the other hand, one should not undervalue them; to the extent that the application of the 'notes' can serve among the converging probabilities on the basis of which, as Newman argued in the *Essay* and more fully in his *Essay in Aid of a Grammar of Assent*, one can achieve certitude, they are modest but telling indicators. Newman's negative employment of the 'notes' should not prompt one to despair of their utility. The 'notes' have the important function of providing a check for a case constructed on other grounds. Newman conceived the *Essay* to refute objections to his becoming a Roman Catholic, not to discriminate between various faith options, and the book should be understood in that context. If one can employ the 'notes' with a presumption of the truth of doctrinal developments within the Church when one uses them as Newman did, i.e., retrospectively, upon doctrines embraced by the Church, using the 'notes' without reference to this intention carries much greater risk. If the 'notes' are applied to a doctrine that has not been embraced by the Church, one cannot attach such a presumption of truth to it. With such a presumption one might, after a favourable application of the seven 'notes' such that the doctrine seems tenable or reasonable, accept the developed doctrine as true, but without this presumption one would seem to be left merely with the claim that the doctrine in question is merely what the 'notes' can indicate: tenable because reasonable.

Given that careful examination of the 'notes' suggests that they are incapable of meeting the high expectations attached to them by the International Theological Commission and some contemporary theologians, how precisely may they be put to use in prospective application? Although they do not constitute a mathematical formula for adjudicating claims about possible developments of doctrine, Newman's 'tests' or 'notes' can serve at least to identify which such claims seem plausible and therefore worthy of further consideration and which appear to be unreasonable and therefore doubtfully authentic at best.

Indicative of Newman's view that his 'notes' constituted, in Dulles's words, not 'a set of laws' but 'rules of thumb'[118] was his option not to exploit them after 1845 in service of other theological issues. He did, however, give a succinct explanation of doctrinal development in his substantial letter of 1868 to Father John Stanislas Flanagan. Were St Paul queried about the 1854 definition of the Blessed Virgin's Immaculate Conception, his first answer might well reflect sheer incomprehension of the terminology, but his eventual response, upon hearing some explanation, would be affirmative.[119] In addition, shortly after he became a Roman Catholic, Newman submitted short chapters and theses encapsulating the argument of the *Essay* to the distinguished Roman theologian Fr Giovanni Perrone, SJ. Newman sought to gain approval of his rationale for becoming Roman Catholic and to clear up Roman misunderstanding of his *Essay*, which for reasons of language was known there more by hearsay than by direct acquaintance. Perrone's marginal comments suggested general acceptance of Newman's theology.[120]

Newman's 'hypothesis to account for a difficulty',[121] his articulation of doctrinal development, retains its influence not merely for its enduring place in Christian intellectual history, but because Newman's 'difficulty', despite recent theological advances, and indeed all the more because of such progress, remains a theological challenge today. Newman's statement of the problem continues to demand attention because the problem still calls for a solution, and because his answer to it, whatever its shortcomings, promises assistance to theologians who strive to explore the issue and to venture viable solutions.

Notes

1. See Ian Ker, *John Henry Newman: A Biography* (Oxford and New York: Oxford University Press, 1988), 301; and *L.D.*, x:781.
2. Jaroslav Pelikan, *Development of Christian Doctrine: Some Historical Prolegomena* (New Haven and London: Yale University Press, 1969), 13 and 3.
3. Thomas Guarino, *Revelation and Truth: Unity and Plurality in Contemporary Theology* (London: Associated University Presses, c. 1993), 181 n. 3. See also David Tracy, *Blessed Rage for Order: The New Pluralism in Theology* (New York: Seabury Press, Crossroad Books, 1975), 196 n. 46.
4. *Dev.*, 1st edn (London: James Toovey, 1845), 27 (hereafter *Dev.* (1845); *Dev.* 3rd edn (London: Longmans, Green, and Co., 1878) (hereafter *Dev.*), 90.
5. Avery Dulles, *Newman* (London and New York: Continuum, 2002), 79.
6. See especially *Gaudium et spes*, 62 and *Unitatis redintegratio*, 4, 6 and 17.
7. Jan Walgrave observed that Möhler neither analysed the process of development nor marshalled facts as Newman had done. J.H. Walgrave, 'Doctrine, Development of', *New Catholic Encyclopedia* iv (New York: McGraw-Hill Book Company, 1967), 943. See also Walgrave, 'L'originalité de l'idée Newmanienne du développement', in Heinrich Fries and Werner Becker (eds.), *Newman Studien*, vi (Nürnberg: Glock und Lutz, 1964), 83–96; Yves M.J. Congar, OP, *A History of Theology*, trans. Hunter Guthrie, SJ (Garden City, NY: Doubleday & Company, Inc., 1968), 188; and Henry Raphael Nienaltowski, OFMCap., 'Johann Adam Möhler's Theory of Doctrinal Development: Its Genesis and Formulation', The Catholic University of America Studies in Sacred Theology Series 2, no. 113 (S.T.D. diss. abstract, The Catholic University of America) (Washington, DC: The Catholic University of America Press, 1959), 72.
8. By writing tentatively that what '*may be* called the *Theory of Development of Doctrine*' 'has been at all times, perhaps, implicitly adopted by theologians, and, I believe, has recently been illustrated by several distinguished writers of the continent, such as De Maistre and Möhler', Newman indicated the essential originality of his *Essay. Dev.*, 29 and 30. Owen Chadwick deduced from 'that astonishing juxtaposition of names', of Möhler and de Maistre, that Newman was hardly familiar with the very different theologies represented. Owen Chadwick, *From Bossuet to Newman*, 2nd edn (Cambridge: Cambridge University Press, 1987), 112; see also 111 and 118–19.

9. *Ari.*, 36–8.
10. *Ari.*, 55.
11. J.H. Walgrave, *Newman the Theologian: The Nature of Belief and Doctrine as Exemplified in His Life and Works*, trans. A. V. Littledale (New York: Sheed & Ward, 1960), 45.
12. *Ari.*, 83 and 86.
13. *Ari.*, 141.
14. *Ari.*, 146; see also *Ari.*, 149–50, 154, 164, 179–80, 288, 367.
15. *Ari.*, 377. For a similarly confident expression of the providential triumph of truth over error, see *Ari.*, 392.
16. *Ari.*, 434.
17. *U.S.*, 323.
18. *U.S.*, 329.
19. *U.S.*, 337.
20. *U.S.*, 335.
21. Newman considered the *Essay* to be one of his five '"constructive" works'. *L.D.*, xxiv: 390–1, quoted in Ker, *John Henry Newman*, 636.
22. *Dev.*, 9.
23. See *Dev.*, 5–6. Newman's personal investment in his *Essay* ran deep. Sheridan Gilley, *Newman and His Age* (London: Darton, Longman and Todd, 1990), 231.
24. *Dev.*, 9 and 7.
25. Chadwick, *From Bossuet to Newman*, xviii, 1 and 73. The Roman theologians of Newman's time, Chadwick noted, were not sufficiently historically minded to face the implications of historical criticism. *Ibid.*, 184.
26. *Dev.*, 40.
27. *Dev.*, 40.
28. *Dev.*, 29–30.
29. *Dev.*, 10.
30. *Dev.*, 9, and Newman, *Church of the Fathers* (*H.S.*, i:418) quoted in *Dev.*, 9.
31. *Dev.*, 8.
32. *Dev.*, 27.
33. *Dev.*, 29.
34. *Dev.*, 10.
35. Vincent of Lérins, *Commonitorium*, 2, 6 quoted in *Dev.*, 10.
36. In the *Essay* Newman did not consider in a sustained way other texts of Vincent of Lérins which he might have found more adequate. See Thomas Guarino, 'Vincent of Lerins and the Hermeneutical Question', *Gregorianum* 75 (1994), 496. See also Yves M. J. Congar, OP, *Tradition and Traditions: An Historical and a Theological Essay* (New York: Macmillan, 1966), 210; and Thomas Guarino, 'Tradition and Doctrinal Development: Can Vincent of Lérins Still Teach the Church?' *Theological Studies* 67 (2006), 37–8, 63–5, 68–9 and 71.
37. *Dev.*, 11.
38. *Dev.*, 20; see *Dev.*, 11–24 for other striking examples.
39. *Dev.*, 27.

40. *Dev.*, 9.
41. *Dev.*, 35.
42. *Dev.*, 35.
43. *Dev.*, 38; see also *Dev.*, 39.
44. *Dev.*, 38–9.
45. *Dev.*, 39–40.
46. In *Dev.*, 41–54, Newman elaborated eight ways in which ideas develop. See T.J. Mashburn, 'The Categories of Development: An Overlooked Aspect of Newman's Theory of Doctrinal Development', *Heythrop Journal* 29 (1988), 33–43.
47. *Dev.*, 29–30.
48. *Dev.*, 74.
49. *Dev.*, 122–65.
50. He added that 'to be just able to doubt is no warrant for disbelieving'. *Dev.*, 6.
51. *Dev.*, 5.
52. *Dev.*, 99–121.
53. *Dev.*, 101.
54. *Dev.*, 101.
55. *Dev.*, 106. This claim, though edited for the 1878 edition, was present in the 1845 edition. *Dev.* (1845), 152. It therefore truly anticipated *G.A.*, published in 1870.
56. Nicholas Lash noted that Newman used antecedent probability merely to make negative claims, though sometimes his use of it appears to have constituted the basis for strong positive assertions. Nicholas Lash, *Newman on Development: The Search for an Explanation in History* (Shepherdstown, WV: Patmos Press, 1975), 41.
57. *Dev.*, 109–10. Moreover, Newman believed that his method of interpretation could attain the clarity Anglicans typically claimed for the Vincentian Canon. In language which would become central in the *Grammar*, Newman wrote: '[A] converging evidence in favour of certain doctrines may, under circumstances, be as clear a proof of their Apostolical origin as can be reached practically from the *Quod semper, quod ubique, quod ab omnibus*'. Vincent of Lérins, *Commonitorium* 2, 6 quoted in *Dev.*, 123.
58. *Dev.*, 154. Newman declared: '[T]he simple question is this, whether the clear light of the fourth and fifth centuries may be fairly taken to interpret to us the dim, though definite outlines traced in the preceding'. *Dev.*, 165. Newman believed his theory of development supplied a presumption constituting warrants for an affirmative answer.
59. *Dev.*, 154.
60. *Dev.*, 75. The perspective of the late twentieth century, in which 'development is now considered as a fact of life rather than as hypothetical explanation', should not be allowed to blunt appreciation of the 'momentous[ness]' of the 'fact' of development. John T. Ford, 'Faithfulness to Type in Newman's "*Essay* on Development"', in *Newman Today*, ed. with intro. Stanley L. Jaki (San Francisco: Ignatius Press, 1989), 33.

61. *Dev.*, 75; see also *Dev.*, 76.
62. *Dev.*, 78.
63. *Dev.*, 89 and 100.
64. *Dev.*, 78. See also *Dev.*, 79–80 and 85–6.
65. *Dev.*, 75.
66. *Dev.*, 93.
67. *Dev.*, 97.
68. *Dev.*, 97–8.
69. *Dev.*, 170.
70. *Dev.*, 171–2.
71. See Ford, 'Faithfulness to Type in Newman's "*Essay* on Development"', 19.
72. *U.S.*, 319–20.
73. *Dev.*, 169.
74. *Dev.*, 170.
75. Aidan Nichols, OP, *From Newman to Congar: The Idea of Doctrinal Development from the Victorians to the Second Vatican Council* (Edinburgh: T & T Clark, 1990), 51.
76. Nichols, *From Newman to Congar*, 47; John Coulson, 'Was Newman a Modernist?' in Arthur Hilary Jenkins (ed.), *John Henry Newman and Modernism*, Internationale Cardinal-Newman-Studien, 14 (Sigmarin-gendorf: Glock und Lutz, 1990), 78. With a broader emphasis, Jaroslav Pelikan deemed Newman's replacement of 'tests' by 'notes' significant and directed the reader to the Charles Frederick Harrold edition (New York, 1949) 'for a detailed comparison of the editions of 1845 and 1878'. Jaroslav Pelikan, *Development of Christian Doctrine: Some Historical Prolegomena* (New Haven and London: Yale University Press, 1969), 34 n. 70. According to Nichols, the later edition was 'notable for its emphasis that the theory of doctrinal development is not meant to prove the claims of Roman Catholicism. Rather was the *Essay* intended to dispel objections to [it]: not at all the same thing.' Nichols, *From Newman to Congar*, 45. Very insightful in connection with this question is Ford, 'Faithfulness to Type in Newman's "*Essay* on Development"'. For differences between the 'tests' of 1845 and the 'notes' of 1878, see Gerard H. McCarren, 'Are Newman's "Tests" or "Notes" of Genuine Doctrinal Development Useful Today?' *Newman Studies Journal* 2 (Fall 2004), 48–61.
77. *Dev.*, 171–8, 207–47.
78. *Dev.*, 173.
79. *Dev.*, 312.
80. *Dev.*, 178–85, 323–54.
81. *Dev.*, 324.
82. *Dev.*, 325–6.
83. *Dev.*, 326–52.
84. *Dev.*, 353.
85. Pelikan, *Development of Christian Doctrine*, 15. For all his appreciation of the *Essay*'s achievement, Pelikan ultimately judged its handling of doctrinal variation in history unsuccessful. Pelikan, *Development of*

Christian Doctrine, 2, 13 and 144–5; see also Jaroslav Pelikan, *Historical Theology: Continuity and Change in Christian Doctrine* (New York: Corpus; Philadelphia: Westminster; London: Hutchinson, 1971), 58, and Jaroslav Pelikan, *The Vindication of Tradition* (New Haven and London: Yale University Press, 1984), 38. Likewise, Nicholas Lash considered the possibility of admitting greater change in doctrine than Newman would have allowed. Nicholas Lash, 'Development of Doctrine: Smokescreen of Explanation?' *New Blackfriars* 52 (1971), 101–8.

86. *Dev.*, 185–9; 355–82.
87. *Dev.*, 186.
88. *Dev.*, 355; see also *Dev.*, 359.
89. *Dev.*, 366.
90. *Dev.*, 368–9.
91. *Dev.*, 382.
92. *Dev.*, 382.
93. In the 1845 edition, the fourth and fifth tests were reversed.
94. *Dev.*, 383.
95. *Dev.*, 383: 'Logical sequence means a vague but general intellectual coherence'. It is not 'the "logical implication" of the Scholastics', but merely 'harmony or congruity or "naturalness"'. Chadwick, *From Bossuet to Newman*, 157.
96. *Dev.*, 192–5.
97. *Dev.*, 384–99.
98. Chadwick, *From Bossuet to Newman*, 157; see also 193, 195. For a critique of Chadwick's equation of new doctrine with new revelation, see Jan Walgrave, *Unfolding Revelation: The Nature of Doctrinal Development* (Philadelphia: Westminster; London: Hutchinson, 1972), 306; Ian T. Ker, 'Newman's Theory – Development or Continuing Revelation?' in James D. Bastable (ed.), *Newman and Gladstone Centennial Essays* (Dublin: Veritas, 1978), 145–59; and H. Francis Davis, 'Is Newman's Theory of Development Catholic?' *Blackfriars* 39 (1958), 310–21. Paul Misner held that Chadwick's criticism, though ultimately unfounded, indicated an 'intellectualist constriction' on Newman's part. Paul Misner, 'Newman's Concept of Revelation and the Development of Doctrine', *Heythrop Journal* 11 (1970), 46. See also Gustave Thils, 'Autour de Newman', *Ephemerides Theologicae Louvanienses* 33 (1957), 352, and Avery Dulles, SJ, 'From Images to Truth: Newman on Revelation and Faith', *Theological Studies* 51 (1990), 266.
99. *Dev.*, 195–200, 400–18.
100. *Dev.*, 195.
101. *Dev.*, 401–18. Newman observed that from the doctrines concerning Christ's work of redemption follow Catholic doctrines sometimes accused of being corruptions: 'that of the resurrection of the bodies of His Saints, and of their future glorification with Him; next that of the sanctity of their relics; further, that of the merit of Virginity; and, lastly, that of the prerogatives of Mary, Mother of God'. 'All these doctrines',

he noted, 'are more or less developed in the Antenicene period'. *Dev.*, 401–10.
102. *Dev.*, 195–9, 410–36.
103. *Commonitorium*, 23, 54, quoted in *Dev.*, 201.
104. *Dev.*, 202.
105. *Dev.*, 420.
106. *Dev.*, 420.
107. *Dev.*, 203.
108. *Dev.*, 204.
109. *Dev.*, 203–6, 437–45. *Dev.* (1845), 90, employed 'Chronic Continuance' as the title of the seventh test.
110. *Dev.*, 204.
111. *Dev.*, 204.
112. *Dev.*, 438.
113. International Theological Commission, 'On the Interpretation of Dogmas', *Origins* 20 (1990), 13.
114. *Dev.*, 171.
115. *Dev.*, 78.
116. *Dev.*, 205–6.
117. *Apo.*, 234.
118. Dulles, *Newman*, 79.
119. *T.P.*, ii:159.
120. Newman, *De Catholici Dogmatis Evolutione (Utrum profecerit Ecclesia Catholica in cognitione sua fidei semel sibi ab Apostolis Traditae?)*, in T. Lynch (ed.), 'The Newman-Perrone Paper on Development', *Gregorianum* 16 (1935), 402–47; in Newman, *Roman Catholic Writings on Doctrinal Development*, ed. and trans. James Gaffney (Kansas City: Sheed & Ward, 1997).
121. *Dev.*, 30.

Further reading

Dulles, Cardinal Avery. *Newman*. London and New York: Continuum, 2002, 64–82.
Ford, John T. 'Faithfulness to Type in Newman's *"Essay on Development"'*, in Stanley L. Jaki (ed.), *Newman Today*. San Francisco: Ignatius Press, 1989, 17–48.
Ker, Ian. *John Henry Newman: A Biography*. Oxford and New York: Clarendon Press, 1988, 257–315.
  'Newman's Theory – Development or Continuing Revelation?' in James D. Bastable (ed.), *Newman and Gladstone: Centennial Essays*. Dublin: Veritas, 1978, 145–59.
Lash, Nicholas. *Newman on Development: The Search for an Explanation in History*. Shepherdstown, WV: Patmos Press, 1975.
McCarren, Gerard H. 'Are Newman's "Tests" or "Notes" of Genuine Doctrinal Development Useful Today?' *Newman Studies Journal* 2 (Fall 2004), 48–61.

Nichols, Aidan. *From Newman to Congar: The Idea of Doctrinal Development from the Victorians to the Second Vatican Council.* Edinburgh: T & T Clark, 1990, 17–70.

Walgrave, J.H. *Newman the Theologian: The Nature of Belief and Doctrine as Exemplified in His Life and Works.* New York: Sheed & Ward, 1960, 44–65, 'The Idea and Theory of Development in Newman's Works'; 241–77, 'Invariability and Development'; and 283–307, 'Newman in Contemporary Thought'.

7 The Church as communion

IAN KER

THE CHURCH AS SACRAMENTAL COMMUNION

Two years before the beginning of the Oxford Movement, Newman dismissed the idea of an individualistic Christianity. Any Christian who 'stands forth *on his own ground*, declaring himself as an individual a witness for Christ', would be 'grieving and disturbing the calm spirit given us by God', for Christians are called to 'unite together in one, and to shelter our personal profession under the authority of the general body'.[1] Two years later in 1833, the year Newman regarded as the formal beginning of the Movement, he is sure that you cannot separate Christianity from the Church: 'The Holy Church has been set up from the beginning as a solemn religious fact ... as a picture, a revelation of the next world, as itself the Christian Dispensation'.[2] Rejecting his former Evangelical conception of the real Church as invisible, the Tractarian Newman insisted that the Church 'is a visible body, and, to appearance, an institution of this world'.[3] For it is a 'Kingdom which Christ has set up', or, rather, 'a new Kingdom has been established, not merely different from all kingdoms before it, but contrary to them; a paradox in the eyes of man, – the visible rule of the invisible Saviour'.[4]

But although this visible communion has an institutional and regal aspect, nevertheless it is fundamentally sacramental: 'Christ formed a body. He secured that body from dissolution by the bond of a Sacrament. He committed the privileges of His spiritual kingdom and the maintenance of His Faith as a legacy of this baptized society.'[5] While rejecting any notion of an 'Invisible Church ... as if Scripture said one word, anywhere, of a spiritual body existing in this world separate from, and independent of, the Visible Church', Newman at the same time is well aware that the Church does indeed have an invisible dimension: 'No harm can come of the distinction of the Church into Visible and Invisible, while we view it as, on the whole, but one in different aspects; as Visible, because consisting (for instance) of clergy and laity – as Invisible, because resting for its life and strength upon unseen influences and gifts from Heaven.' For, although the Church 'is a visible body', yet it is 'invested with, or ... existing in invisible privileges', since 'the Church would cease to be the Church, did the Holy Spirit leave it', as 'its outward rites and forms are nourished and animated by the living power which dwells within it'.[6] Fundamentally, then, the Church is the Holy Spirit's 'especial dwelling-place',[7] since 'the Spirit came to make us one in Him who had died and was alive, that is, to form the Church'. The Church, therefore, is 'the one mystical body of Christ ... quickened by the Spirit' – 'one' by virtue of the Holy Spirit giving it life.[8]

This scriptural and patristic understanding of the Church as primarily the communion of those who have received the Holy Spirit in baptism was not abandoned by Newman when he entered the Roman Catholic Church of his day with its Tridentine stress on the Church as an institutional pyramid. Towards the end of his life he wrote a very lengthy 'Preface' (1877) to his Anglican *Lectures on the Prophetical Office of the Church viewed relatively to Romanism and Popular Protestantism* (1837), in which he attempted to account for the apparent discordance between the Roman Catholic Church's 'formal teaching and its popular and political manifestations', having already answered in his *Essay on the Development of Christian Doctrine* (1845) the other charge that he had brought against Rome in these lectures, namely, 'the contrast which modern Catholicism is said to present with the religion of the Primitive Church'. And it is striking how Newman takes as his starting-point not the institutional but the sacramental concept of the Church as Christ's 'mystical Body and Bride ... and the shrine and organ of the Paraclete'.[9] Given the Tridentine conception of the Church as first and foremost the hierarchical Church militant, one might have supposed that Newman would explain these apparent corruptions in Catholicism in a very different way. Having dealt with the alleged doctrinal corruptions in 1845, he now had to account for the superstitions and abuses of power which notoriously alienated his countrymen from Rome. And surely the most obvious explanation would have been to point out that the Catholic belief that the pope and bishops were the successors of Peter and the Apostles, in whose apostolic ministry the ministerial priesthood shared, meant that inevitably such power was open to corruption in a way that the Protestant ministry was not. It was, Newman might have argued, the unavoidably clerical and hierarchical nature of the Church which led inevitably to such abuses. A Catholic as opposed to a Protestant clergy were naturally tempted to keep the laity in submission by tolerating, even encouraging, superstition, just as papal and episcopal authority could easily be misused.

Now the striking thing about the 1877 Preface is that Newman does not attempt to employ that strategy. Far from speaking about the Church in the usual terms of clergy and laity, Newman instead begins the Preface by defining the Church as the Body of Christ, since he wants to argue that because the Church therefore shares in the three offices of Christ as prophet, priest, and king, it is the consequent difficulty of exercising this 'triple office' simultaneously that accounts for the apparent contradictions in Catholic theory and practice.[10] The Preface does not conceive of the Church in the usual institutional terms of clergy and laity. Even the regal office, which is seen by Newman as belonging pre-eminently to 'the Papacy and its Curia' (thus reflecting the papalism of the nineteenth-century Church), is not regarded as shared by the bishops, let alone the clergy.[11] Of the other two offices, the prophetical is assigned to the theologians, but nothing is said about whether they are clergy or laity. And, even more significantly, the priestly office 'is not particularly assigned to the ordained, as one might have expected'. Instead, initially, Newman 'attributes this office to the "pastor and flock", but in the main body of the Preface he focuses almost entirely on popular religion and on the beliefs of the simple faithful'.[12] Thus, rather than distinguishing clergy and laity, Newman says that the Church as a 'religion' has 'its special centre of action' in 'pastor and flock'.[13] From the point of view, then, of devotion and worship the Church is not conceived of as regulated or misregulated by the clergy and hierarchy but is regarded as pertaining to both priests and people together.

It is clear that Newman both as an Anglican and a Roman Catholic had the same sacramental conception of the Church as the Body of Christ, the temple of the Holy Spirit, or the communion of the baptized. Fundamentally, the same is true of the famous article, 'On Consulting the Faithful in Matters of Doctrine' (1859). This essay is usually held to be a classic text on the role of the laity in the Church. When it was first edited and reprinted over 100 years later,[14] the editor, John Coulson, took it for granted that the faithful are synonymous with the laity. Nor did he distinguish the clergy from the bishops with whom Newman's article was concerned, namely, the bishops at the time of the Arian heresy who, Newman claimed, had largely failed, unlike the 'faithful', to uphold the orthodox faith. In a subsequent book, Coulson represented Newman as protesting against the Church's being 'conceived as divided into two casts – the clerical or dynamic element; and the lay or passive element'.[15] However, Coulson does not conceive of the protest as being against such a division of the Church, but as being against the characterization of the laity as passive and the clergy as dynamic.

It is perfectly true that 'On Consulting the Faithful in Matters of Doctrine' was written as a result of a controversy over the English bishops' refusal to cooperate with a government commission concerning the state of primary education, in spite of the fact that Catholic schools received state aid. Newman thought the laity should be consulted on a matter concerning their children's education and deplored the hierarchy's scant regard for their rights. It is therefore true that in the essay Newman implicitly accepts the division of the Church into clergy and laity.

After his conversion in 1845, he had soon become aware of how clericalized the Catholic Church had become; by contrast the very different way the laity were treated in the Church of England was for him a distinct point in its favour. His feelings on this subject came to a head during his abortive rectorship of the Catholic University of Ireland. He came to believe that the principal cause of the damaging friction between him and Archbishop Cullen of Dublin was his desire to appoint a lay finance committee (the money for the university after all had to be raised from the laity), but even more seriously to appoint as many laymen rather than less able priests to chairs as possible, which meant appointing leading Irish nationalists who were anathema to Cullen. At the time of the controversy that led up to the writing of 'On Consulting', Newman's bishop in Birmingham responded to his complaint about the way the laity were treated by saying 'something like, "[w]ho are the laity?"', to which Newman replied, 'The Church would look foolish without them'.[16]

But in spite of Newman's strong views on the proper place of the laity in the nineteenth-century Church, what 'On Consulting the Faithful in Matters of Doctrine' also reveals is that he had a very clear understanding that such a clear-cut division was not characteristic of the early Church, and in particular that the 'faithful' are not synonymous with the laity. The argument of the essay is that in the fourth century 'the divine tradition committed to the infallible Church was proclaimed and maintained far more by the faithful than by the Episcopate'. It is true that Newman seems at times to equate the faithful with the laity, as when he goes on to say that 'the body of the episcopate was unfaithful to its commission, while the body of the laity was faithful to its baptism'. But in the same sentence he acknowledges that 'there were numbers of clergy who stood by the laity, and acted as their centres and guides'.[17] Later in the essay he cites an instance where *'there was a remarkable unanimity of clergy and people'* in rejecting the Arian bishop.[18] It is therefore not correct to say that the distinction in 'On Consulting the

Faithful in Matters of Doctrine' is between clergy and laity; it is between the bishops and the laity.

The second important point to make is that we need to be clear about whom Newman means by the laity. For when he comes to give his documentary 'proofs of the fidelity of the laity', it is striking that his very first text, a quotation from St Athanasius about the Alexandrian church, speaks about the Arian bishops physically attacking the '*holy virgins and brethren*'. Now in the terminology of Newman's day these 'virgins' and 'brethren' would be classed as 'religious'. In the same passage of Athanasius there is another reference to '*virgins*' in a later quotation. And it is noteworthy that in both these instances, as in the ones that follow, the words are italicized in order to indicate that this is proof of the fidelity of the *laity*. Similarly, the third of the texts quoted by Newman as examples of the fidelity of the laity refers to '*monks*'. Again, in the fifth text there is a reference to two upholders of the orthodox doctrine in Antioch 'who had embraced the ascetical life', in other words who were 'religious' in modern terms, but who are described as being '*in the ranks of the laity*', since they were 'not as yet in the sacred ministry'.[19]

When Newman came to republish his first book *The Arians of the Fourth Century* (1833) in 1871, he added an appendix which included a note containing part of 'On Consulting the Faithful in Matters of Doctrine' together with some amendments and additions. The latter include an extraordinary sentence in the first paragraph of the note: 'And again, in speaking of the laity, I speak inclusively of their parish-priests (so to call them), at least in many places; but ... we are obliged to say that the governing body of the Church came short'.[20] If the clergy are to be included in the laity, then any idea that the essay is a learned tract defending the laity against the clergy is absurd. The truth is that, in the historical examples Newman gives, the 'faithful' are by no means exclusively the laity, but rather include both priests and religious. Insofar as 'On Consulting the Faithful in Matters of Doctrine' is an attack on any part of the Church, it is an attack on the bishops. The article was written out of concern that the English episcopate had failed to consult the laity in a matter that concerned them. But at a deeper theological level Newman wanted to show how the faith did not belong to the bishops alone but to the whole communion of the baptized, a fact which was dramatically highlighted in the greatest crisis ever to face Christianity when that very part of the Church whose special responsibility it was to proclaim and teach the faith substantially failed to do so. But since the faith did not pertain to them alone, it was preserved by the body of the faithful, who included what we would now call 'priests' and 'religious', as well as laity.

AUTHORITY AND FREEDOM IN CREATIVE TENSION

Not only is the faith not the preserve of the episcopate, but the interpretation and development of doctrine does not pertain to the bishops alone. Newman's most extended treatment of the role of theologians and their relation to the magisterium or teaching authority of the pope and bishops is to be found in the final fifth chapter of his *Apologia Pro Vita Sua*. On the one hand, he is uncompromising about the infallibility of the teaching Church, calling it a 'power ... happily adapted to be a working instrument ... for smiting hard and throwing back the immense energy of the aggressive, capricious, untrustworthy intellect'. Similarly, the Church hierarchy's authority, 'viewed in its fulness' and 'viewed in the concrete, as clothed and surrounded by the appendages of its high sovereignty', is seen as 'a supereminent prodigious power sent upon earth to encounter and master a giant evil'. Although infallibility strictly only belongs to solemn dogmatic definitions, Newman professes to submit not only to the traditions of the Church, but also 'to those other decisions of the Holy See, theological or not ... which, waiving the question of their infallibility, on the lowest ground come to me with a claim to be accepted and obeyed'.[21]

On the other hand, this unequivocal assertion of Church authority provokes the obvious objection that 'the restless intellect of our common humanity is utterly weighed down' by such an authority, 'so that, if this is to be the mode of bringing it into order, it is brought into order only to be destroyed'. But Newman counters that in fact the 'energy of the human intellect ... thrives and is joyous, with a tough elastic strength, under the terrible blows of the divinely-fashioned weapon, and is never so much itself as when it has lately been overthrown'. The paradox is justified by the argument that, far from being mutually contradictory, authority and reason need each other precisely because each is actually sustained by conflict with the other:

> It is the vast Catholic body itself, and it only, which affords an arena for both combatants in that awful, never-dying duel. It is necessary for the very life of religion ... that the warfare should be incessantly carried on. Every exercise of Infallibility is brought out into act by an intense and varied operation of the Reason, both as its ally and as its opponent, and provokes again, when it has done its work, a re-action of Reason against it; and, as in a civil polity the State exists and

endures by means of the rivalry and collision, the encroachments and defeats of its constituent parts, so in like manner Catholic Christendom is no simple exhibition of religious absolutism, but presents a continuous picture of Authority and Private Judgment alternately advancing and retreating as the ebb and flow of the tide; – it is a vast assemblage of human beings with wilful intellects and wild passions, brought together into one by the beauty and the Majesty of a Superhuman Power, – into what may be called a large reformatory or training-school, not as if into a hospital or into a prison, not in order to be sent to bed, not to be buried alive, but (if I may change my metaphor) brought together as if into some moral factory, for the melting, refining, and moulding, by an incessant, noisy process, of the raw material of human nature, so excellent, so dangerous, so capable of divine purposes.[22]

Newman insists that an infallible authority is intended 'not to enfeeble the freedom or vigour of human thought in religious speculation, but to resist and control its extravagance'. He also emphasizes both the narrow limits of infallibility in defining as explicit doctrine what is already implicit in revelation, as well as its rare occurrence. And 'because there is a gift of infallibility in the Catholic Church', it does not necessarily follow that 'the parties who are in possession of it are in all their proceedings infallible'. On the contrary, Newman admits, 'history supplies us with instances in the Church where legitimate power has been harshly used'. Nevertheless, Newman quickly qualifies this admission by adding that it does not 'follow that the substance of the acts of the ruling power is not right and expedient, because its manner may have been faulty'.[23]

Carefully balancing the rival claims of authority and theological freedom, Newman develops his sharply antithetical argument. He continues by reinforcing the case for authority. Despite all abuses, he insists that ecclesiastical authority has been 'mainly in the right, and that those whom they were hard upon were mainly in the wrong'. For example, Origen (whose name 'I love') 'was wrong' and 'his opponents were right'. And yet – 'who can speak with patience of his enemy and the enemy of St John Chrysostom, that Theophilus, bishop of Alexandria? Who can admire or revere Pope Vigilius?' The contradiction is resolved by a shift of perspective:

> In reading ecclesiastical history, when I was an Anglican, it used to be brought home to me, how the initial error of what afterwards became heresy was the urging forward some truth against the

prohibition of authority at an unseasonable time. There is a time for every thing, and many a man desires a reformation of an abuse, or the fuller development of a doctrine, or the adoption of a particular policy, but forgets to ask himself whether the right time for it is come: and knowing that there is no one who will be doing any thing towards its accomplishment in his own lifetime unless he does it himself, he will not listen to the voice of authority, and he spoils a good work in his own century, in order that another man, as yet unborn, may not have the opportunity of bringing it happily to perfection in the next. He may seem to the world to be nothing else than a bold champion for the truth and a martyr to free opinion, when he is just one of those persons whom the competent authority ought to silence; and, though the case may not fall within that subject-matter in which that authority is infallible, or the formal condition of the exercise of that gift may be wanting, it is clearly the duty of authority to act vigorously in the case.[24]

This is bound to arouse criticism 'if the ruling power happens in its proceedings to evince any defect of prudence or consideration'. And so 'all those who take the part of that ruling authority will be considered as time-servers, or indifferent to the cause of uprightness and truth'. But that is not the conclusion of the sentence. The sting lies in the rest of the sentence which is aimed at those who would deny legitimate theological freedom: 'while, on the other hand, the said authority may be accidentally supported by a violent ultra party, which exalts opinions into dogmas, and has it principally at heart to destroy every school of thought but its own'.[25]

But authentic intellectual freedom is essential to the Church, for, Newman claims, it is 'individuals, and not the Holy See, that have taken the initiative, and given the lead to the Catholic mind, in theological inquiry'. 'Indeed', he points out to those who believe that all Catholic truth comes from the oracle of Rome, 'it is one of the reproaches against the Roman Church, that it has originated nothing, and has only served as a sort of *remora* or break in the development of doctrine. And it is an objection which I really embrace as a truth; for such I conceive to be the main purpose of its extraordinary gift.' Far from being distinguished for theological originality, Newman contends, 'the Church of Rome possessed no great mind in the whole period of persecution'. There was not a single great theologian until Pope St Leo, who taught only 'one point of doctrine'. Not even Pope St Gregory has a place in the history of theology. The greatest Western theologian, St Augustine, belonged, like the best early Latin theologians, to the African Church. Western theology, in fact, was formed to a considerable extent by heterodox theologians such as Tertullian, Origen, and Eusebius, with the result that heretical 'questionings' became 'salutary truths'. Even General Councils were guided by the 'individual reason' of a mere presbyter like Malchion or a young deacon like Athanasius. At the Council of Trent, too, particular theologians 'had a critical effect on some of the definitions of dogma'.[26]

By appealing to history to show how little authority in general has interfered with the freedom of theologians, Newman is arguing in effect for a balance to be kept between the teaching authority and theological freedom. He deliberately appeals to that most Catholic of periods, the Middle Ages:

> There never was a time when the intellect of the educated class was more active, or rather more restless, than in the middle ages. And then again all through Church history from the first, how slow is authority in interfering! Perhaps a local teacher, or a doctor in some local school, hazards a proposition, and a controversy ensues. It smoulders or burns in one place, no one interposing; Rome simply lets it alone. Then it comes before a Bishop; or some priest, or some professor in some other seat of learning takes it up; and then there is a second stage of it. Then it comes before a University, and it may be condemned by the theological faculty. So the controversy proceeds year after year, and Rome is still silent. An appeal perhaps is next made to a seat of authority inferior to Rome; and then at last after a long while it comes before the supreme power. Meanwhile, the question has been ventilated and turned over and over again, and viewed on every side of it, and authority is called upon to pronounce a decision, which has already been arrived at by reason. But even then, perhaps the supreme authority hesitates to do so, and nothing is determined on the point for years; or so generally and vaguely, that the whole controversy has to be gone through again, before it is ultimately determined.[27]

Having previously maintained that authority has sometimes to intervene when an idea is premature, Newman now puts the other side of the question. The individual theologian must have a certain space if ideas are to be considered and explored:

> It is manifest how a mode of proceeding, such as this, tends not only to the liberty, but to the courage, of the individual theologian or controversialist. Many a man has ideas, which he hopes are true,

and useful for his day, but he is not confident about them, and wishes to have them discussed. He is willing, or rather would be thankful, to give them up, if they can be proved to be erroneous or dangerous, and by means of controversy he achieves his end. He is answered, and he yields; or on the contrary he finds that he is considered safe. He would not dare do this, if he knew an authority, which was a supreme and final, was watching every word he said, and made signs of assent or dissent to each sentence, as he uttered it. Then indeed he would be fighting, as the Persian soldiers, under the lash, and the freedom of his intellect might truly be said to be beaten out of him.[28]

Anxious, however, to maintain the delicate balance between authority and freedom, Newman is careful to allow that, 'when controversies run high', then 'an interposition may ... advisably take place; and again, questions may be of that urgent nature, that an appeal must, as a matter of duty, be made at once to the highest authority in the Church'.[29] By the time Newman was writing communications had greatly improved with railways and the postal system, but he does not point out that this altered the balance between the teaching authority and the theologian, since theological ideas could quickly gain a wide currency that would have been impossible in the Middle Ages. In today's world of electronic communications the problem has been exacerbated: on the one hand, theologians can immediately propagate their views through the mass media, while on the other hand Rome is brought face to face with ideas that in the Middle Ages would have been confined more or less to the local church or university.

THE CHARISMATIC DIMENSION OF THE CHURCH

As an organic communion of the baptized, the Church must allow not only for theologians as well as bishops and popes, but also for the charismatic dimension alongside, albeit subordinate to, the hierarchical dimension. Newman's keen awareness of the importance of the charismatic dimension as a constitutive element of the Church was one of the ways in which he anticipated the Second Vatican Council. The Council's rediscovery of the concept of charisms in the first two chapters of its Constitution on the Church (*Lumen Gentium*) was one of its most important achievements. What had formerly been regarded as extraordinary, miraculous gifts are now recognized as less unusual, albeit special gifts of grace given by the Holy Spirit to the Church which is, in Newman's words, 'the especial dwelling-place' of the Spirit. Instead of the Church being seen as sustained primarily and almost entirely (except in extraordinary and miraculous instances) by the ministry and sacraments of the ordained ministry, it is now acknowledged also to be built up by the charisms given to the faithful.

The word 'charism' as used in *Lumen Gentium* is a transliteration of the New Testament Greek word *charisma* and was a new theological term for the Western Church which had previously used the Thomist phrase *gratia gratis data* ('grace freely given') to describe the New Testament concept of *charisma*. Not surprisingly, therefore, we do not find Newman using the term. Nevertheless, the idea of special graces given to individuals for the benefit of the Church was very much part of Newman's thinking both as an Anglican and as a Catholic.

In the *Apologia* Newman describes how as a boy of fifteen he became enamoured of the extracts from the Fathers which he read in Joseph Milner's *History of the Church of Christ* (1794–1809). The Fathers who were also bishops united in their persons both the hierarchical and the charismatic dimensions of the Church, whereas in succeeding centuries the two dimensions were rarely united in one person. It was to the Fathers that Newman turned in the first of his writings to propagate the Oxford Movement. Before writing any of the *Tracts for the Times*, he began a series of articles 'called the "Church of the Fathers" ... on the principle of popularity as an element of Church power, as exemplified in the history of St Ambrose'. Far from being clerical, the early Church, in Newman's vivid phrase, 'threw itself on the *people*'.[30] And indeed this is a very charismatic Church, in which there is a place for prophets: 'a child's voice, as is reported, was heard in the midst of the crowd to say, "Ambrose is bishop"'.[31] At the time Ambrose was governor of the province and had been called to quell a disturbance in the cathedral in Milan, where the people were meeting to elect a new bishop. Not only was Ambrose not in holy orders, he was still only a catechumen awaiting baptism. However, on the prophetic word of a child he was unanimously elected bishop. Here Newman points to a remarkable instance of charism preceding hierarchy.

The point of writing these sketches of the Church of the Fathers was to show how different the religion of the first centuries was from both Protestantism and the established Church of England. And one big difference that Newman highlights is the absence of the first great charismatic movement in the Church that appeared in the third century. With the end of persecution and the spread of Christianity, there was a danger of a dilution of the faith and 'one great purpose answered by' monasticism 'was the maintenance of the Truth in times and places in which great masses of Catholics had let it slip from them'. There was also the danger of Christians becoming 'more secular', and monasteries became 'the refuge of piety and holiness'. Indeed, Newman adds, 'such provisions, in one shape or other, will always be attempted by the more serious and anxious part of the community, whenever Christianity is generally professed'. In other words, the charismatic dimension of the Church is essential for Christians wishing to practise their faith in a more committed and devout way. Where no spiritual outlet exists for more serious Christians, they will be liable to 'run into separatism', 'by way of searching for something divine and transcendental', as in Protestant countries 'where monastic orders are unknown': 'Methodism has carried off many a man who was sincerely attached to the Established Church, merely because that Church will admit nothing but what it considers "rational" and "sensible" in religion'. The early Church, on the contrary, dealt 'softly with the arduous and impetuous, saying, in effect – "... You wish to live above the common course of a Christian; – I can teach you to do this, yet without arrogance."' By contrast, Newman complains, the Church of England is guilty of 'the tyranny of those who will not let a man do anything out of the way without stamping him with the name of fanatic'. In the early Church charism and hierarchy were in harmony and unity, with the result that 'enthusiasm' could flourish without getting out of control and without being suppressed. Thus St Antony, the founder of monasticism, would be condemned as an 'enthusiast' in the Church of England, with the result that he 'would be exposed to a serious temptation of becoming a fanatic': 'Longing for some higher rule of life ... and finding our present lines too rigidly drawn to include any character of mind that is much out of the way ... he might possibly have broken what he could not bend'. Antony, however, benefited from a hierarchical Church which accepted his charism but gave it 'form ... It was not vulgar, bustling, imbecile, unstable, undutiful; it was calm and composed ... full of affectionate loyalty to the Church.' Like *Lumen Gentium*, Newman is insistent that the charisms need the hierarchy to regulate them: 'enthusiasm is sobered and refined by being submitted to the discipline of the Church, instead of being allowed to run wild externally to it'.[32]

In his *Essay on the Development of Christian Doctrine*, Newman again wrote about monasticism, emphasizing the immense significance of this charismatic movement for the history of the Church: 'Little did the youth Antony foresee, when he set off to fight the evil one in the wilderness, what a sublime and various history he was opening, a history which had its first developments even in his own lifetime'. Antony had simply intended to be a hermit in the desert, 'but when others followed his example he was obliged to give them guidance'. The next stage in the development was when these hermits came together to form a community. There then followed further developments with St Pachomius and St Basil, until finally St Benedict consolidated these developments, as well as introducing the vital new element of education that was to be so crucial for the Church in the dark ages when the monasteries became the repositories of learning.[33]

Newman was well aware that the charisms are not given simply for the benefit of the recipient, but are intended for the whole Church. They therefore are the Holy Spirit's answer to the needs of the Church at a particular time. And so, while 'St Benedict had come as if to preserve a principle of civilization, and a refuge for learning, at a time when the old framework of society was falling, and new political creations were taking their place ... when the young intellect within them began to stir, and a change of another kind discovered itself, then appeared St Francis and St Dominic'. Finally, Newman concludes, 'in the last era of ecclesiastical revolution' the charism of St Ignatius Loyola was given to the Church to meet new needs: 'The hermitage, the cloister ... and the friar were suited to other states of society; with the Jesuits, as well as with the religious Communities, which are their juniors', the 'chief objects of attention' were new kinds of apostolate, such as teaching and the missions.[34]

There are half-a-dozen rhetorical passages in the *Essay on the Development of Christian Doctrine* where Newman offers an impression of the early Church and asks the reader whether it is not also a likeness of the modern Roman Catholic Church. It is significant that in the first two of these passages it is the charismatic aspect which is singled out as the most characteristic feature in common. The first, in which Newman appeals to the imagination of the reader, begins with the provocative assertion: 'On the whole, all parties will agree that, of all existing systems, the present communion of Rome is the nearest approximation in fact to the Church of the Fathers, possibly though some may think it, to be nearer still to that Church on paper'. He insists: 'Did St Athanasius or St Ambrose come suddenly to life, it cannot be doubted what communion he would take to be his own. All surely will agree that these Fathers ... would find themselves more at home with such men as St Bernard or St Ignatius Loyola ... or the holy sisterhood of mercy'. And a couple of pages later he asks whether the faith of the Roman Catholic Church is not the 'nearest approach, to say the least, to the religious sentiment, and what is called *ethos*, of the early Church, nay, to that of the Apostles and Prophets; for all will agree so far as this, that Elijah, Jeremiah, the Baptist, and St Paul are in their history and mode of life ... in what is external and meets the eye ... these saintly and heroic men, I say, are more like a Dominican preacher, or a Jesuit missionary, or a Carmelite friar, more like St Toribio, or St Vincent Ferrer, or St Francis Xavier, or St Alphonsus Liguori, than to any individuals, or to any classes of men, that can be found in other communions.'[35]

The success of the Oxford Movement raised, in Newman's view, a very serious problem: the Church of England's lack of the charismatic dimension. 'Give us monasteries', he demanded, otherwise there would be 'continual defections to Rome'. In 1842 he himself began what was in effect a 'monastic house' at Littlemore.[36] But next year he decided 'to master St Ignatius's Spiritual Exercises' as being 'very instructive'.[37] However, the charism of St Francis of Assisi had also already played a part in the process of Newman's conversion to Rome. In 1837 he had read with delight Manzoni's novel *I promesi sposi*; and two years later in the autumn of 1839, the time when his first serious doubts about Anglicanism as a *via media* had begun, he admitted to one of his closest friends: 'That Capuchin in the "Promesi Sposi" has stuck in my heart like a dart. I have never got over him.'[38]

After his conversion, Newman became an Oratorian. He was drawn to the charism of St Philip Neri with his mixture of 'extreme hatred of humbug, playfulness, nay oddity, tender love for others, and severity'.[39] Newman thought that the Oratorian charism was important in the Counter-Reformation for the reform of the diocesan clergy. Nevertheless, he also saw Oratorians as being in some respects like the early monks, who also did not take vows. For he thought the charism of St Philip was boldly to go back to primitive Christianity in its 'plainness and simplicity', not least in the informal 'exercises', consisting of singing, prayer, readings, talks, and discussion, in which, extraordinarily for the time, laymen participated.[40] Newman liked to contrast Philip's charism with the very different charism of St Ignatius Loyola, whose followers was disciplined soldiers as compared with the more individualistic, easy-going Oratorians.

Naturally, Newman had no illusion about which of the two charisms had been more important for the Church: in terms of influence and numbers there was no comparison between the Society of Jesus and the Oratory of St Philip Neri. In a sermon of 1850, 'The Mission of St Philip', he called Saints Benedict, Dominic, and Ignatius 'the three venerable Patriarchs, whose Orders divide between them the extent of Christian history'. Certainly Philip was a minor charismatic figure compared with the other giants, but nevertheless Newman points out that he 'came under the teaching of all three successively'. Although he did not have the term 'charism' in his theological vocabulary and although he lived at a time when the hierarchical dimension was exaggerated, Newman never underestimated the significance of the charismatic dimension. For these 'masters in the spiritual Israel', 'in an especial way ... had committed to them the office of a public ministry in the affairs of the Church one after another, and ... are, in some sense, her nursing fathers'. From his youth in Florence at San Marco, Philip imbibed the spirit of Dominic, whose vocation was 'to form the whole matter of human knowledge into one harmonious system, to secure the alliance between religion and philosophy, and to train men to the use of the gifts of nature in the sunlight of divine grace and revealed truth'. Such a Christian humanism was crucial in the age of the Renaissance, when 'a violent effort was in progress ... to break up this sublime unity, and to set human genius, the philosopher and the poet, the artist and the musician, in opposition to religion'. Leaving Florence, Philip came to live near Monte Cassino, where in turn he imbibed the simpler Benedictine spirit; 'and, as from St Dominic he gained the end he was to pursue, so from St Benedict he learned how to pursue it'. Philip's Oratory resembled the early independent monastic communities without formal vows and not organized in any order or congregation, which 'were simple in their forms of worship, and ... freely admitted laymen into their fellowship'. Finally, he met Ignatius Loyola in Rome, with whom 'in the care of souls he was one', as 'in theological traditions [he] was one with St Dominic'. Newman sums up the influence on Philip of these three great charisms: 'As then he learned from Benedict *what to be*, and from Dominic *what to do*, so let me consider that from Ignatius he learned *how he was to do it*'. To these he contributed his own special charism: '[he] had the breadth of view of St Dominic, the poetry of St Benedict, the wisdom of St Ignatius, and all recommended by an unassuming grace and a winning tenderness which were his own'.[41]

In 1855 Newman gave a lecture entitled 'The Three Patriarchs of Christian History, St Benedict, St Dominic, and St Ignatius', of which some notes survive.[42] He had had it in mind, he wrote fifteen years later, to write a book on the 'historical contrast of Benedictines, Dominicans, and Jesuits, which I suppose I shall never finish'. In the end, he only managed to write the part on the Benedictines, which was first published in *Atlantis*, the academic journal he founded at the Catholic University of Ireland, and then republished in the second volume of *Historical Sketches*.[43] It was a source of regret to him, he explained later, but, after what he had written on the Benedictines was criticized by a Benedictine abbot, he was nervous about trying to write about

Dominicans, Franciscans, and Jesuits. One can only regret that Newman was never able to complete this book on these three great charismatic movements in the history of the Church.

'The Mission of the Benedictine Order' was published in *Atlantis* in 1858 and 'The Benedictine Centuries' in 1859; they were later republished in *Historical Sketches* in 1873 under the titles of 'The Mission of St Benedict' and 'The Benedictine Schools'. Unlike the Church of the Fathers, this was not a period of history he knew well. His concern was chiefly educational, occupied as he was at the time with the Catholic University of Ireland. He thought that the history of Christian education could be divided into three periods, ancient, medieval, and modern, dominated by the names of Benedict, Dominic, and Ignatius. The monastic charism was 'a reaction from ... secular life', a 'flight from the world', it offered 'retirement and repose ... peace'. It was a 'poetical' charism, unlike the Dominican which was 'scientific' and the Ignatian which was 'practical'. It evoked the 'primitive age of the world' and 'was a sort of recognized emigration from the old world' ever since St Antony – and Newman uses a colourful contemporary image to convey the excitement Antony's charism had aroused – had found 'gold ... and on the news of it thousands took their departure year after year for the diggings in the desert'. It was more devotional than intellectual. But the charism was poetical not because the monks were 'dreamy sentimentalists, to fall in love with melancholy winds and purling rills, and waterfalls and nodding groves; but their poetry was the poetry of hard work', since Benedict's 'object ... was ... penance'. Still, monasticism was 'romantic' in its 'adventures' and history. And the paradox was that the very monasticism which had been a retreat from a dying world became 'in no small measure [the] very life' of the 'new order'.[44] So far as Newman was concerned, it was not the hierarchy but the charism of one man, who was not even a priest, that saved both the Church and Christian civilization.

Finally, it is noteworthy that Newman anticipated the charismatic phenomenon that was to sweep through the Catholic Church in the twentieth century, the so-called ecclesial movements and communities. They are called 'ecclesial' precisely because they reflect the understanding of the Church as an organic communion by virtue of their being open to all the baptized and not exclusive to priests or religious or laity. The ecclesiology of Newman anticipated that of the Second Vatican Council's Constitution on the Church, which also understood the Church as primarily consisting of those who 'are re-born ... from water and the Holy Spirit' in baptism, a 'messianic people' in whom the Spirit 'dwells as in a temple' (art. 9). But it was not only in his ecclesiology that

Newman anticipated the new ecclesial movements and communities. In practice, he himself led a movement in his own time, the Oxford or Tractarian Movement, which, far from being a clerical association as some of its initiators had wanted, consisted of both clergy and laity, some of its most prominent members being lay people. Later, at the time of the restoration of the Catholic hierarchy in 1850, Newman hoped that a similar kind of movement might arise to support the Catholic cause but the clerical nature of nineteenth-century Catholicism prevented this. Furthermore, Newman's understanding of the original nature of Philip Neri's Oratory shows how like a modern ecclesial community it had been to begin with. It had begun as an entirely lay community, not as a priestly order or congregation. From this original community emerged a smaller community of priests but still closely linked to the larger lay community. Together, the congregation of priests and the lay community constituted the Oratory.

Newman's understanding of the Church as an organic communion anticipated the teaching of the Second Vatican Council in its Constitution on the Church, which defined the Church as fundamentally and primarily sacramental, being the community of the baptized. Just as the word 'laity' is absent from the New Testament, so too the Constitution in its first two chapters that set out this definition avoids this term which implies a clerical institutional idea of the Church. Similarly, Newman's 'On Consulting the Faithful in Matters of Doctrine' clearly understands that the 'faithful' are not the equivalent of the laity but of the baptized. The baptized include both theologians and those endowed with special charisms as well as the hierarchy. Naturally, the Council does not go into the practical question of the interrelationships of the baptized with their different ministries, roles, and charisms. But the most pragmatic of theologians understood very well the inevitability of the conflicts and tensions that are endemic to such an organic communion, whose vitality depends on the various checks and balances that the different but interlocking parts of the Body of Christ provide.

Notes

1. *P.S.*, i:153.
2. *P.S.*, ii:66.
3. *P.S.*, ii:391.
4. *P.S.*, vi:313–14.
5. *P.S.*, vii:237.
6. *P.S.*, iii:207, 222, 224; v:41.

7. *P.S.*, iii:270.
8. *P.S.*, iv:170, 174, 171.
9. *V.M.*, 1:xxxix. Cf. Avery Dulles, 'Newman's Ecclesiology', in Ian Ker and Alan G. Hill (eds.), *Newman After a Hundred Years* (Oxford: Clarendon Press, 1990), 377.
10. *V.M.*, 1:xl.
11. *V.M.*, 1:xl.
12. Dulles, 'Newman's Ecclesiology', 380.
13. *V.M.*, 1:xl.
14. John Coulson (ed.), *On Consulting the Faithful in Matters of Doctrine* (London: Geoffrey Chapman, 1961).
15. John Coulson, *Newman and the Common Tradition: A Study in the Language of Church and Society* (Oxford: Clarendon Press, 1970), 129.
16. *L.D.*, xix:141.
17. *Cons.*, 75–6.
18. *Cons.*, 94.
19. *Cons.*, 86–8, 90.
20. *Ari.*, 445.
21. *Apo.*, 245–6, 250, 251.
22. *Apo.*, 252.
23. *Apo.*, 253, 257–8.
24. *Apo.*, 259.
25. *Apo.*, 260.
26. *Apo.*, 266.
27. *Apo.*, 266–7.
28. *Apo.*, 267–8.
29. *Apo.*, 268.
30. *L.D.*, iv:14, 18.
31. *H.S.*, i:343.
32. *H.S.*, ii:96, 98–9, 103, 164–5.
33. *Dev.*, 395–7.
34. *Dev.*, 398–9.
35. *Dev.*, 97–8, 100.
36. *L.D.*, vii:133, 264.
37. *L.D.*, ix:260.
38. *L.D.*, vii:151.
39. *L.D.*, xii:25.
40. *N.O.*, 186, 188, 203.
41. *O.S.*, 220–1, 224–5, 228, 240.
42. *L.D.*, xvi:378.
43. *L.D.*, xxv:228.
44. *H.S.*, ii:366, 373, 375, 384–5, 388, 398, 400, 436, 443.

Further reading

Coulson, J. *Newman and the Common Tradition: A Study in the Language of Church and Society.* Oxford: Clarendon Press, 1970, 55–131.

Dulles, A. 'The Threefold Office in Newman's Ecclesiology', in I. Ker and A. G. Hill (eds.), *Newman After a Hundred Years*. Oxford: Clarendon Press, 1990, 375–99.

Ker, I. *Newman on Being a Christian*. Notre Dame: University of Notre Dame Press, 1990; London: Collins, 1991, ch. 5.

'Newman on the *Consensus Fidelium* as "The Voice of the Infallible Church"', in T. Merrigan and I. T. Ker (eds.), *Newman and the Word*. Louvain: Peeters, 2000; Sterling, VA.: W. B. Eerdmans, 2000, 69–89.

'Newman and the Charismatic Dimension of the Church', in T. Merrigan and I. Ker (eds.), *Newman and Truth*. Louvain: Peeters, 2007; Sterling, VA: W. B. Eerdmans, 2007.

Miller, J. E. *John Henry Newman on the Idea of Church*. Shepherdstown, WV: Patmos Press, 1987.

8 Infallibility

FRANCIS A. SULLIVAN

For John Henry Newman, the difference between the infallibility of the Church and that of the pope, and between the claim of the one and the other on his act of faith, was no merely academic question. It was a very real issue that affected a great part of his life. Even as an Anglican, as we shall see, he believed that the Church enjoyed infallibility; but it was only some months after the definition by Vatican I that he could give his full assent to papal infallibility as a dogma of his faith. Our treatment of infallibility then falls into two parts, presenting first Newman's views on the infallibility of the Church, and second his views on papal infallibility.

THE INFALLIBILITY OF THE CHURCH

We begin with what Newman believed concerning the infallibility of the Church while still an Anglican. He expressed his mind on this most explicitly in the eighth of his *Lectures on the Prophetical Office of the Church*, entitled 'The Indefectibility of the Church Catholic'.[1] The main purpose Newman had in these lectures was to describe Anglicanism – in what he saw as its most authentic tradition, if not in actuality – as the *via media* between the deficiencies of Protestantism and the excesses of Roman Catholicism. The defect of Protestantism was its failure to recognize the need of a visible Church equipped with a 'prophetical office' to safeguard the purity of the apostolic faith against the errors inevitable in the exercise of private judgement on Scripture as a sole rule of faith. The excess of Romanism was its claim to possess an abiding and pervasive infallibility that would allow it to create new dogmas practically at will.

Against Protestantism, which exalts Scripture as the sole rule of faith, Newman argued from Scripture itself, which describes the Church as 'the pillar and ground of truth' (1 Tim 3:15), and tells us how Christ gave to the Church pastors and teachers so that all could come to unity and not be carried about by every wind of doctrine (cf. Eph 4:11–14). He concluded from these and other passages that Scripture presents the Church as the great and special support of truth, and assures us that a divine promise has been given that the word of truth given her shall never be lost.[2] The following passage of his lecture shows how 'high' a view he had of the role of the Church as guardian and teacher of revealed truth:

> Not only is the Church Catholic bound to teach the Truth, but she is ever divinely guided to teach it; her witness of the Christian faith is a matter of promise as well as of duty; her discernment of it is secured by a heavenly as well as by a human rule. She is indefectible in it, and therefore not only has authority to enforce, but is of authority in declaring it ... The Church not only transmits the faith by human means, but has a supernatural gift for that purpose; that doctrine, which is true, considered as an historical fact, is true also because she teaches it.[3]

What Newman meant by 'the Church Catholic' here, was the 'undivided Church' of Christian antiquity, which he believed continued to exist, although imperfectly united, in the three 'branches' (Eastern, Roman, and Anglican) which had maintained the apostolic faith and apostolic succession in ministry. He distinguished between two ways in which the 'Church Catholic' was 'unerring in its declarations of faith'. In antiquity, while it still enjoyed full unity, it could be described as infallible in such declarations of faith as it made in its creeds, and its conciliar definitions of the basic Trinitarian and Christological dogmas. However, when, during the course of history, the Church lost its unity, it also lost its prerogative of infallibility, and hence also its warrant to formulate new creeds or define new dogmas. But, since the apostolic faith, in its essentials, has a divine guarantee of being preserved through the 'prophetical office' of the Church, the Church Catholic must be indefectible in maintaining the apostolic faith. In other words, it must have a divine guarantee of remaining faithful to the essential dogmas already determined by the undivided Church of antiquity. For Newman as an Anglican, then, the true norm of faith is Scripture as interpreted by Christian antiquity.

Furthermore, he was convinced that the 'Church Catholic is unerring in its declarations of faith' in the sense that those Christian doctrines which all its branches teach as necessary to be believed for salvation are bound to be true, and that such agreement actually has always been had, and will always be had, but only in the essential dogmas that were already determined in Christian antiquity.

Having seen how Newman, as an Anglican, understood the indefectibility in faith which supernatural help guaranteed to the 'Church

Catholic', we must now see what new elements entered into his understanding of the Church's infallibility during the process that led to his becoming a Roman Catholic. In the event, it was his further study of and reflection on Christian antiquity that led him to the Catholic Church. The more deeply he came to understand the process by which the early Church rejected Arianism, Nestorianism, and Monophysitism as heresies, and hammered out the great Trinitarian and Christological dogmas of the creed, the more convinced he became that it must be God's plan that the Christian revelation should undergo development, whereby what was at first only obscurely or implicitly contained in the deposit of faith would come to be recognized as contained therein and thus become an object of explicit faith. It was while he was spelling out the implications and consequences of this insight in his *Essay on the Development of Christian Doctrine* that he reached his conviction that he must become a Roman Catholic, and that only the Catholic Church now enjoys the prerogative of infallibility. At the risk of over-simplification, I would summarize the process of his thought in the following way.

If the truths that are arrived at by a process of legitimate development of doctrine are really implicitly contained in the original revelation, it follows that they are really part of that revelation. Then Divine Providence, which safeguards the original revelation from being corrupted in its transmission in the faith of the Church, must also preserve the Church from error in its acceptance of such developments as articles of its faith. Such developments were already taking place in the ancient Church, as we see in the definition of the Trinitarian and Christological dogmas, and in the writings of the Fathers, who both prepared and subsequently defended and explained the conciliar decisions. If such development can rightly be seen as part of God's plan for the Church, there is no reason to restrict such development to a limited period of history. Actually such development has continued in the Roman Catholic Church, and the doctrines that are the fruit of such development can be shown to be homogeneous with the faith of Christian antiquity, and none can be shown to be a corruption of it. Of the three branches of what Anglicans call the Church Catholic, only the Roman Catholic Church truly corresponds to the Church of the first centuries; it is the only one that can invoke St Augustine's dictum: *Securus judicat orbis terrarum.* What the whole Roman Catholic Church believes and teaches as an article of apostolic faith must then be truly contained in the original revelation; indeed this Church must be infallible in its profession of faith and in the solemn definitions by which its teaching body proposes doctrines to be professed as articles of faith.

In his *Apologia Pro Vita Sua*, Newman describes the powerful impact the phrase *Securus judicat orbis terrarum* had upon him, and the role it played in the process of his conversion, comparing it with the *tolle lege, tolle lege* of St Augustine's *Confessions*.[4] As a Catholic, Newman came back to this dictum again and again, insisting that the *orbis terrarum* could only be identified with the Roman Catholic Church, since this was the only Christian body that was both spread over the whole world and at the same time united in faith and communion. The meaning of *securus judicat*, as he explained it, was 'that the deliberate judgement, in which the whole Church at length rests and acquiesces, is an infallible prescription, and a final sentence against such portions of it as protest and secede'.[5] He could put the same idea either negatively: 'What is not taught universally, what is not believed universally, has no claim on me',[6] or positively: 'As to faith, my great principle was: "Securus judicat orbis terrarium"'.[7] 'What bishops and people say all over the earth, that is the truth.'[8] He spoke of a 'passive infallibility' of the Catholic people, explaining this to mean that 'the body of the faithful can never misunderstand what the Church determines by the gift of active infallibility'.[9]

While Newman was convinced that the infallibility of the Church could only be understood as a supernatural gift, he also insisted that it did not involve a positive gift of inspiration, but that it was rather negative in character. In a letter to a friend, written almost a year after Vatican I, he explained how he conceived this negative aspect of infallibility:

> I have always thought, and think still, that the infallibility of the Church is an *inference* (a necessary inference) from her prerogative that she is the divinely appointed Teacher of her children and of the world. She cannot fulfil this office without divine help – that is, she never can be *permitted to go wrong* in the truths of revelation – This is a negative proposition – the very idea of infallibility is a negative. She teaches by human means, she ascertains the truth by human means – of course assisted by grace, but so is every inquirer, and she has *in kind* no promise of invincible grace, which a Father or a divine, or an inquirer has not – but she has this security, that, in order to fulfil her office, her *out come* is always true in the matter of revelation. She is not inspired – the word has sometimes been used, and in Councils especially, – but, properly speaking, inspiration is positive, and infallibility is negative; and a definition may be absolute truth, though the grounds suggested for it in the definition, the texts, the patristic authorities, the historical passages, are all mistakes.[10]

Precisely because infallibility is not inspiration, Newman insisted that it did not dispense the pope or bishops from the task of consultation and deliberation when they undertook the weighty responsibility of defining a dogma of faith. The preparatory work of the *schola theologorum* had an indispensable role to play in the process leading up to making final decisions on matters of faith. Nor could those enjoying the supernatural help assured to the Church's official teachers neglect the gift of reason possessed perhaps in extraordinary measure by individuals who did not share the bishops' gifts. From his intimate knowledge of the history of the early councils, Newman could affirm that, 'Ecumenical Councils ... have been guided in their decisions by the commanding genius of individuals, sometimes young and of inferior rank'.[11]

NEWMAN ON PAPAL INFALLIBILITY BEFORE VATICAN I

After he became a Catholic, the infallibility of the Catholic Church was for Newman a matter of the most absolute certitude. Strikingly different from this had been his state of mind about the infallibility of the pope. Even when the Vatican Council had defined this doctrine, he was not yet convinced that he must accept it with an assent of faith, since the council's final vote on this issue had lacked the moral unanimity he believed necessary for a conciliar definition. He arrived at certitude about papal infallibility only some months after the adjournment of the Vatican Council, when it had become clear that the Catholic Church accepted this as a dogma of its faith. In other words, it was his certitude about the infallibility of the Church that brought him to certitude about papal infallibility. How, then, did Newman describe his state of mind about the doctrine of papal infallibility during the previous twenty-five years since he became a Catholic? He answered this question quite often in his letters. The following are some examples of the way he expressed his mind about this between 1866 and 1868. 'I have ever thought it likely to be true, never thought it was certain.'[12] 'On the whole, then, I hold it, but I should account it no sin if, on grounds of reason, I doubted it.'[13] 'I hold the Pope's Infallibility, not as a dogma, but as a theological opinion; that is, not as a certainty, but as a probability.'[14] 'I have only an opinion (not faith) that the Pope is infallible.'[15]

Two questions arise, then. What were the reasons that led him to hold it as a theological opinion? Why did he not find them sufficient grounds for certitude? The following are some of the reasons that he gave, mostly in his private correspondence, to explain why he had held papal infallibility as a theological opinion. 'I think there is a good deal of evidence, on the very surface of history and the Fathers, in its favour.'[16] 'The fact that all along for so many centuries, the head of the Church and the teacher of the faithful and the Vicar of Christ has been allowed by God to assert virtually his infallibility, is a great argument in favour of the validity of his claim.'[17] 'I consider the self-assertion, the ipse dixit of the Popes for 1800 years, a great and imposing argument for the validity of their claims.'[18] 'The Popes acted as if they were infallible in doctrine with a very high hand, peremptorily, magisterially, fiercely ... They acted in a way that needed infallibility as its explanation.'[19]

It is this argument from the historical exercise of papal doctrinal authority that Newman consistently offered when he set out to explain why he had held papal infallibility as a theological opinion ever since he became a Catholic. It is obvious that he did not judge this argument sufficiently cogent to warrant an assent of certitude. There can be no doubt about Newman's familiarity with the arguments that Perrone and other Catholic theologians had offered in favour of papal infallibility. In fact, there are some references to such arguments in his letters and private notes, which, while brief and sometimes enigmatic, do suggest that he did not find them adequate to form the kind of convergence of probabilities that he required for certitude.

On the other hand, neither was he convinced by the arguments brought against papal infallibility by Döllinger and others, who claimed that it was contradicted by the serious doctrinal errors that various popes, such as Honorius, had made in their official pronouncements. In commenting on a pamphlet published in 1868 with the title 'The Condemnation of Pope Honorius', Newman wrote to its author, Peter Le Page Renouf: 'I certainly did not know how strong a case could be made out against Pope Honorius. But with all its power, I do not find it seriously interferes with my own view of Papal Infallibility ... You have brought out a grave difficulty in the way of the doctrine; that is, you have diminished its probability, but you have only diminished it. To my mind the balance of probabilities is still in favour of it.'[20]

Even though, during all this period, papal infallibility was not a matter of personal faith for Newman, he could say honestly that he 'held' it, and he did not hesitate to present it as Catholic doctrine and defend it against Protestant misrepresentations. On the other hand, he was strongly opposed to the effort being made by Archbishop Manning and others to have the Vatican Council define papal infallibility as a dogma of Catholic faith. One reason for this was his belief that for the council to declare that all Catholics were obliged to give this doctrine their assent of faith would place too heavy a burden on the faith of many Catholics, and especially of recent converts from Anglicanism. He argued that past councils had defined only such dogmas as were necessary to avert grave dangers to the faith, and that there was no such necessity to define papal infallibility.

The other reason was his fear that Archbishop Manning and his friends would succeed in having the council define papal infallibility in terms that would confirm the interpretation of this doctrine that William G. Ward had been propagating in his journal, *Dublin Review*. Newman had reason to believe that Manning and other bishops who were pressing for this definition understood the doctrine much as Ward did. Newman had two main objections to Ward's understanding of papal infallibility. It would allow the pope to define doctrines that were neither revealed nor necessary for the defence of revealed truth, and it would attribute infallibility to papal decrees lacking the solemnity of dogmatic definitions *ex cathedra*. Newman was convinced that Ward's interpretation of papal infallibility was excessive both with regard to the matters about which the pope could speak infallibly, and with regard to the kind of papal statements that ought to be recognized as infallible.

However, he did not publish his objections to Ward's position because he chose not to enter publicly into controversy with his fellow Catholics on questions concerning papal infallibility. The reason was that at that time there was no one answer being given by Catholic authors to several of these questions, and if Newman put forward his own opinion, he would have had either to criticize or to ignore opinions held by other Catholics. It was for this reason also that he decided not to publish the second part of his reply to Edward Pusey's *Eirenicon*, in which he would have answered Pusey's objections to the doctrine of papal infallibility. As he put it in his notes: 'I should not be writing against Pusey, but making a case against Ward, and every one would say so'.[21]

However, for a time he did contemplate writing a second reply to Pusey on the question of infallibility, and with that in view he compiled a fairly extensive volume of notes, which were first published in 1979.[22] In what follows, I shall rely on those notes to explain on what grounds Newman judged Ward's position on both of those issues to be excessive, and how he justified his own position.

Newman was convinced that the Church had the supernatural help that guaranteed her infallibility only with regard to the divine revelation that had been entrusted to her. As a Catholic, he recognized legitimate developments as belonging to the deposit of revelation. The gift of infallibility guaranteed that the Church would define as dogma only such developments as were legitimate. In addition to such developments, he also recognized certain kinds of 'dogmatic facts' as belonging to revelation, and hence as possible matters for infallible decision, provided that they were merely 'concrete expressions' or 'concrete exhibitions' of what was revealed. For example, in order effectively to reject the heresy of Jansenism, the Church had to be able to say definitively whether certain of the writings of Jansenius were heretical or not. The Church would not be able to speak infallibly at all if it could not determine with infallibility whether particular expressions were orthodox or heretical; this was merely the 'concrete exhibition' of the revealed truth. Questions of morality also belonged within the scope of infallibility; here Newman insisted that this does not apply to mere precepts, but only to 'general categorical enunciations' of moral doctrine; and only to such doctrine as is based on divine law and has to do with things necessary for salvation.[23]

Newman also recognized that, in order to be able to safeguard revelation itself, the Church needed to be able to speak with infallibility about certain matters which, while not in themselves revealed, were necessarily connected with revelation. Of these he used the Latin word *pomoeria*, which literally referred to the boundary zone which the ancient Romans left free of buildings inside and outside their city walls. Modern theologians generally speak of such matters as constituting a 'secondary object' of infallibility. With regard to such a 'boundary zone' of the subject-matter for infallible teaching, Newman's basic principle was: 'No declaration or proposition of the church is infallible except those which relate to the *res revelata*'.[24] But he saw that some propositions that were not in themselves part of the *res revelata* could be variously related to it. He distinguished between two kinds of such propositions, in the following way:

> Though the Church cannot increase the depositum fidei, there are two ways in which it can make positive enunciations beyond it (*viz.* by stating the *relations* of other propositions to it). In the first place, it can affirm that certain propositions are injurious to it. It does not affirm or deny their predicates of their subjects – but it affirms that the propositions, as they stand, are inconsistent with or injurious to the depositum. That is, it can condemn propositions.
>
> And next she can enunciate that certain other propositions are more or less connected with or congenial to the depositum; necessarily connected, or probably so, or morally, and therefore absolutely true, or certain, or probable, as the case may be.[25]

In all of this question concerning the limits of infallibility, what most deeply concerned Newman during the years leading up to the Vatican Council was the way that Ward was extending those limits so as to include matters that were neither revealed nor necessarily connected with revelation. Ward's line of argument ran as follows. Whenever the pope speaks with his authority as supreme teacher in the Church, he speaks infallibly. Since he exercises this teaching authority in his bulls, encyclicals, and allocutions, he also speaks with infallibility in such pronouncements. Therefore, whatever is the subject-matter of such authoritative statements is also the subject-matter of infallibility. It does not have to be contained in or necessarily related to the deposit of faith; all we have to know is that the pope has spoken with his supreme authority, and therefore with infallibility about it.

Newman vigorously rejected Ward's idea that whenever, and about whatever matter, the pope spoke with his authority as supreme teacher in the Church, he also spoke with infallibility. He came back again and again to this question in the theological notes that he wrote between 1865 and 1867. As we know, Newman did not want to enter into public controversy with Ward, but he did give his advice and encouragement to a younger priest of the Oratory, Fr Ignatius Ryder, who in 1867 published a work critical of Ward's extravagant views.[26] Some of the notes we are referring to were written for Ryder's use in his controversy with Ward. However, in the earlier part of the notes (which are all dated), Newman described the opinion which he objected to, without mentioning the names of its proponents. He said: 'Some have thought that the authoritative tone and wording of the Bulls and Briefs showed that they were infallible enunciations – but I cannot admit this argument at all'.[27]

Later on, in the notes which he wrote for Ryder's use, he was referring explicitly to Ward when he said: 'In other words, he does not allow that the Church can speak solemnly without speaking with her infallible voice. This then is the main proposition to which I shall direct my attention – *viz.*, to show that there is a department of teaching, in which the Church speaks, authoritatively indeed, but not infallibly.'[28] In further notes for Ryder, Newman says that he has no objection to Ward's holding the infallibility of encyclicals as his own private opinion, but he insists that Ward cannot declare this to be a matter of obligation for all Catholics, as he was in fact doing, unless he can prove it to be so; and he cannot prove it from the consensus of theologians, since it is an opinion that was 'unheard of till late centuries ... We can trace the authors in whose writings it arose, etc. etc. It is not generally received now.'[29] Many references in these notes show that Newman's understanding of the limits of papal infallibility was shared by such respected Catholic theologians as Giovanni Perrone of the Roman College.

PAPAL INFALLIBILITY AS DEFINED DOGMA

Newman's reaction, when he saw the decree defining papal infallibility as a dogma of faith, was one of relief at its contents, even though he was not pleased that it had been defined, nor was he yet convinced that it had the force of a conciliar definition, since it had not been approved by the bishops with the moral unanimity he believed to be required. However, as far as the wording of the decree was concerned, he was satisfied that it imposed no more on him that what he had already held. While he refrained from publishing his views on the Vatican dogma for several years after it had been defined, he did express his mind freely in his private letters to friends. The following are some of the comments he made to them.

'I saw the new Definition yesterday, and am pleased at its moderation, that is, if the doctrine in question is to be defined at all. The terms used are vague and comprehensive, and, personally, I have no difficulty in admitting it.'[30] 'The definition is what the Church has acted on for some centuries, and a very large body of Catholics have long held.'[31] 'You must not fancy that any very stringent definition has passed – on the contrary it is very mild in its tenor, and has been acted on by the Pope at least for the last 300 years.'[32] 'I agree with you that the wording of the Dogma has nothing very difficult in it. It expresses what, as an opinion, I have ever held myself with a host of other Catholics.'[33] 'Very little has been passed indeed – and they know this, and are disappointed who have been the means of passing it – but they use big words just now to conceal their disappointment, and they hope by speaking big and breaking down opposition, to open the way to passing something more. From what I heard at Rome, while the matter was going on, from almost the first authority, they hoped to get a decree which would cover the Syllabus, and they have not got it. They have only got authoritatively pronounced that which Fr Ryder maintained against Mr Ward.'[34] 'As to your friend's question, certainly the Pope is not infallible beyond the Deposit of Faith originally given – though there is a party of Catholics who, I suppose to frighten away converts, wish to make out that he is giving forth infallible utterances every day ... I have no hesitation in saying that, to all appearances, Pius IX wished to say a great deal more (that is, that the Council should say a great deal more) than it did, but a greater Power hindered it.'[35]

As the foregoing quotations attest, Newman was confident that the dogma as defined by the council could be correctly interpreted to put the limits on the exercise and the subject-matter of papal infallibility which he had been describing in his private notes. However, as some of his personal remarks also show, he knew that others (no doubt he had Ward and Manning in mind) had not abandoned their 'maximizing' views. Newman's concern in this regard was confirmed when Archbishop Manning on 13 October 1870 published a pastoral letter setting forth his interpretation of the Vatican decrees.[36] The passage in it that most disturbed Newman was the following:

> In like manner all censures, whether for heresy or with a note less than heresy, are doctrinal definitions in faith and morals, and are included in the words *in doctrina de fide vel moribus definienda*. In a word, the whole magisterium or doctrinal authority of the Pontiff as the supreme Doctor of all Christians is included in this definition of his infallibility. And also all legislative or judicial acts, so far as they are inseparably connected with his doctrinal authority; as, for instance, all judgments, sentences, and decisions, which contain the motives of such acts as derived from faith and morals. Under this will come laws of discipline, canonisation of Saints, approbation of religious Orders, of devotions, and the like; all of which intrinsically contain the truths and principles of faith, morals, and piety.
>
> The Definition, then, limits the infallibility of the Pontiff to his supreme acts ex cathedra in faith and morals, but extends his infallibility to all acts in the fullest exercise of his supreme magisterium or doctrinal authority.[37]

While this final sentence, if standing alone, would be susceptible of a moderate interpretation, in its context it can only mean that all the instances mentioned in the previous paragraph must be taken to be examples of the 'supreme acts ex cathedra' in which the pontiff exercises his infallibility. And this was put forward not as a theological opinion, but as the meaning of a dogma to which Catholics were obliged to give their assent of faith.

About a month after this pastoral appeared, Newman received a letter from a prominent member of Manning's archdiocese, Lady Simeon, who spoke of her distress at the contents of her archbishop's pastoral letter. Newman's reply contained the following very frank remarks on that subject:

> The Archbishop only does what he has done all along – he ever has exaggerated things, and ever has acted towards individuals in a way

which they felt to be unfeeling ... And now, as I think most cruelly, he is fearfully exaggerating what has been done at the Council. The Pope is not infallible in such things as you instance. I enclose a letter of our own Bishop, which I think will show you this ... Therefore, I say confidently, you may dismiss all such exaggerations from your mind, though it is a cruel penance to know that the Bishop where you are, puts them forth. It is an enormous tyranny.[38]

Although Newman expressed his mind so freely in private correspondence, he remained firm in his resolve not to enter into public controversy with Catholics, least of all with the Archbishop of Westminster. For the next four years he busied himself with other projects, such as preparing new editions of previous works. But in November 1874 a challenge presented itself that he felt he could not ignore, in the form of a pamphlet by the Prime Minister William Gladstone, entitled 'The Vatican Decrees in their Bearing on Civil Allegiance: A Political Expostulation'. Newman judged Gladstone's attack on the civil allegiance and personal freedom of Catholics to be based on a gross 'maximizing' of the meaning and consequences of the Vatican definition of papal infallibility. Thus Newman saw a golden opportunity presented him not only to defend his fellow Catholics against Gladstone's charges, but to put forth and to justify a moderate interpretation of the Vatican dogma, thus indirectly refuting Ward and Manning at the same time.

Towards the end of 1874, Newman had reason for added confidence that his 'minimizing' was legitimate, because during that year he had come to know of a work written by Bishop Joseph Fessler, entitled *The True and the False Infallibility of the Popes: A Controversial Reply to Dr Schulte*.[39] Schulte belonged to the 'Old Catholics' who rejected the Vatican dogmas; Fessler had been the Secretary-General of Vatican I, and had voted with the majority for the decree; but in answering Schulte had given a very moderate interpretation of papal infallibility. He had sent a copy of his work to Pius IX, who had it translated into Italian, read it, and wrote to Bishop Fessler giving it his full approval. Newman set his close friend Ambrose St John to work preparing an English translation, which he was able to use while writing his reply to Gladstone; at the same time he had the use of a French translation published in 1873.[40] Thus, at the very outset of chapter 9 of his *Letter to the Duke of Norfolk*, in which he gave his interpretation of the Vatican decree, he was able to appeal to Bishop Fessler's work in support of his own lifelong conviction that 'a moderation of doctrine, dictated by charity, is not inconsistent with soundness in the faith'.[41]

The twenty pages of Newman's chapter on 'The Vatican Definition' present his 'wise and cautious theology'[42] of infallibility. There is no need to go into detail here about the contents of this chapter of his reply to Gladstone, since it presents the same moderate understanding of papal infallibility that Newman had spelled out in his private notes against Ward. Newman himself declared, when he had seen the wording of the Vatican decree: 'It expresses what, as an opinion, I have ever held myself with a host of other Catholics'.[43] If the present article has made a contribution to the study of Newman's thought on infallibility, it will be to have demonstrated the truth of the statement we have just quoted, by illustrating, from his previous writings, and largely from his private letters and notes, that his interpretation of the Vatican dogma in 1874 was in fact what he had always believed with unshakeable faith about the infallibility of the Church, and what as a Catholic he had held as a personal opinion, even before the Vatican Council, about the nature and limits of papal infallibility.

Notes

1. *V.M.*, i:189–213.
2. *V.M.*, i:193.
3. *V.M.*, i:190.
4. *Apo.*, 110.
5. *Apo.*, 110.
6. *L.D.*, xxiii:275.
7. *L.D.*, xxiii:275.
8. *L.D.*, xxv:235.
9. *L.D.*, xxvii:338.
10. *L.D.*, xxv:309.
11. *Apo.*, 237–8.
12. *L.D.*, xxiii:157.
13. *L.D.*, xxiii:105.
14. *L.D.*, xxiv:92.
15. *L.D.*, xxiii:275.
16. *L.D.*, xxiii:105.
17. *L.D.*, xxv:168.
18. *L.D.*, xxv:186.
19. *L.D.*, xxv:299.
20. *T.P.*, ii:112.
21. *T.P.*, ii:112.
22. *T.P.*, ii:99–160.
23. *L.D.*, xxvii:214; see also *Diff.*, ii:331.
24. *T.P.*, ii:115.
25. *T.P.*, ii:142.
26. H.I.D. Ryder, *Idealism in Theology* (London, 1867).

27. *T.P.*, ii:118.
28. *T.P.*, ii:147.
29. *T.P.*, ii:149–50.
30. *L.D.*, xxv:164.
31. *L.D.*, xxv:170.
32. *L.D.*, xxv:173.
33. *L.D.*, xxv:174–5.
34. *L.D.*, xxv:224. Newman referred to the *Syllabus of Errors*, a list of propositions that Pius IX had condemned in his encyclicals, allocutions, etc., over a period of almost twenty years. This list was attached to his encyclical *Quanta cura* of 1864.
35. *L.D.*, xxv:297, 299.
36. Archbishop Manning, *The Vatican Council and its Definitions: A Pastoral Letter to the Clergy* (London, 1870). This was subsequently published, together with two previous pastoral letters by Manning, in one volume with the title *Petri Privilegium* (London, 1871).
37. Manning, *Vatican Council*, 89–90.
38. *L.D.*, xxiv:230. The 'letter of our own Bishop' to which Newman refers is probably the letter of Bishop Ullathorne of Birmingham that was published in the *Birmingham Daily Post* of 14 November 1870.
39. English translation from the German by A. St John (London, 1875).
40. Joseph Fessler, *La Vraie et la Fausse Infaillibilité des papes*, trans. and intro. E. Cosquin (Paris, 1873).
41. *Diff.*, ii:321.
42. *Diff.*, ii:332.
43. *L.D.*, xxv:174–5.

Further reading

Dibble, R. A. *John Henry Newman: The Concept of Infallible Doctrinal Authority*. Washington, DC: Catholic University of America, 1955.
Dulles, Avery. 'Newman on Infallibility', *Theological Studies* 51 (1990), 434–49.
Holmes, J. Derek. *The Theological Papers of John Henry Newman on Biblical Inspiration and on Infallibility*. Oxford: Clarendon Press, 1979.
Klausnitzer, Wolfgang. *Päpstliche Unfehlbarkeit bei Newman und Döllinger*. Innsbruck: Tyroliaverlag, 1980.
Page, John R. *What Will Dr Newman Do? John Henry Newman and Papal Infallibility*. Collegeville, MN: Liturgical Press, 1994.
Stern, J. 'L'infaillibilité de l'Église dans la pensée de J. H. Newman', *Recherches de Science Religieuse* 61 (1973), 161–85.
Strange, Roderick, 'Newman on Infallibility: 1870 and 1970', *Ampleforth Journal* 80 (1975), 61–70.

9 Authority in the Church

AVERY DULLES

For John Henry Newman the problem of authority in the Church was a lifelong preoccupation. He believed from boyhood in authoritative Scriptures and creeds, and as he grew older he pondered the question of authority in the Church. Was it located in bishops, in popes, in theologians, in lay persons, or in all together? In case of conflict, whose voice should prevail?

Committed though he was to an authoritative revelation, Newman cannot fairly be categorized as authoritarian. He was keenly aware of the rights of reason and the possibilities that authority would be abused. But he was sceptical enough to distrust the competence of pure reason in matters of religious truth. As we shall see, he generally preferred to use different authorities in the Church to supplement and counterbalance one another.

Newman believed that authority had a place even in pagan religions. Although revelation was present only in a vague and diffuse way in these 'natural' or 'traditionary' religions, God made his voice audible in them, enabling even the heathen to make acts of faith. In a sermon of 1830 he declared: 'The prerogative of Christians consists in the possession, not of exclusive knowledge and spiritual aid, but of gifts high and peculiar'. Although God's self-manifestation through the Incarnation is a singular and inestimable benefit, 'yet its absence is supplied to a degree ... in those various traditions concerning Divine Providences and Dispensations which are scattered through the heathen mythologies'.[1] In his first book, *The Arians of the Fourth Century* (1833), he quotes Clement of Alexandria and other Fathers to the effect that 'there never was a time when God has not spoken to man', creating the possibility of saving faith.[2]

In the present chapter we shall be dealing not with faith in the generic sense, but specifically with Christian faith.[3] All who are in a position to grasp the true nature of Christian revelation, Newman believed, are in principle bound to accept the channels that God has established for communicating revealed truth. As a Catholic, Newman accepted the standard doctrine that persons in invincible ignorance, including those raised in different religions and different Christian communities, could be saved if they believed whatever religious truth was accessible to them with the help of God's grace. But those who receive the grace to accept the divine claims of the Catholic Church had an obligation to act upon their lights. By failing to profess the Catholic faith, they would incur serious danger of losing their souls.[4]

Although the question of the possibility of faith and salvation without adherence to Christianity and the Catholic Church is of interest, it is not the theme of the present chapter. Our question has to do with the nature and locus of authority in the Christian Church, as treated in Newman's writings. What are the means that God has established for the transmission of his revelation in Christ? To what sources should Christians turn if they wish to find Christian revelation in its purity and fullness?

SCRIPTURE AND TRADITION

In his days as a student Newman accepted the doctrine of the Church of England that everything necessary for salvation is contained in the Bible or at least provable from it. But he never understood this doctrine as meaning that the bare text of Scripture, expounded with the tools of formal logic, suffices. He always read Scripture in light of the creed. When Newman was a young tutor at Oriel College, an older colleague, Edward Hawkins, drew his attention to the importance of the visible Church and its tradition for understanding the true sense of Scripture. In *The Arians of the Fourth Century*, Newman contended that Holy Scripture was written for the instruction and consolation of believers but was never intended to serve as the sourcebook of all revealed truth. From Christian antiquity, he believed, the illusion that the Bible alone can teach the word of God was the very seedbed of heresy.[5] It is presumptuous, according to Newman, to reject all helps in reading the Bible. Those who turn to it as a source of doctrine without previous formation are prone to misread it in idiosyncratic ways, falling into strange and perverse opinions. The theory of the sufficiency of Scripture lacks support in the Scripture itself.[6]

THE LOCAL BISHOP

The next question, for Newman, was to identify the various agencies other than Scripture that were given for the preservation of the word of God and its transmission to the faithful. Initially, Newman turned to the

Fathers of the Church. With the help of his friend Edward Pusey he obtained a good collection of patristic writings and set about reading them systematically in 1827, beginning with the Apostolic Fathers, who greatly influenced his ecclesiology. At the height of the Oxford Movement, in 1838, he wrote an article on 'The Theology of St. Ignatius' in which he quoted numerous passages on episcopal authority from Ignatius's letters to the Trallians, Philippians, Magnesians, Ephesians, and to Polycarp.[7] In these passages, he contended, Ignatius was not expressing his personal opinion but reflecting the teaching of the Lord himself. To separate oneself from one's bishop, he concluded, is to separate oneself from God. The episcopal structure of the ministry, which has withstood the test of 1,800 years of history, must continue to be normative for all churches, Eastern or Western, that make any claim to catholicity.

A high priority in the programme of the Oxford Movement was to revive the doctrine of episcopal authority in the Anglican Church. As Newman's friend John Keble pointed out in his famous sermon on 'National Apostasy', delivered on 14 July 1833, the Church of England had become abjectly dependent on the civil government. In a letter of 30 July 1833, Newman exclaimed, 'O that we had some bishops for us; the Clergy are dead'.[8] In another letter, written on 3 August 1833, he lamented: 'Even during the Arian heresy, there was a possibility of true-minded men becoming Bishops, which is now almost out of the question. If only we had one Athanasius, or Basil, we could bear with 20 Eusebiuses.'[9] In the *Tracts for the Times*, Newman often returns to the theme of apostolic succession.

In his sermons of this period, Newman exhorted the faithful to have reverence for their bishops. In a sermon published in 1835 he grieved that there were but few in the Church of England who still honoured the bishops as successors of the Apostles.[10] In another sermon, published in 1838, he declared: 'When we approach the Ministry, which He [Christ] has ordained, we approach the steps of His throne. When we approach the Bishops, who are the centres of that Ministry, what have we before us but the Twelve Apostles, present but invisible?'[11]

What Newman urged on others, he practised himself. He felt special allegiance to his own bishop, Richard Bagot of Oxford, not only for his personal traits but especially because of the authority of his office. Describing his own mentality during the 1830s, Newman wrote in his *Apologia Pro Vita Sua*:

> I loved to act as feeling myself in my Bishop's sight, as if it were in the
> sight of God ... I could not go very wrong while I had reason to believe

that I was in no respect displeasing him. It was not a mere formal obedience to rule that I put before me, but I desired to please him personally, as I considered him set over me by the Divine Hand. I was strict in observing my clerical engagements, not only because they were engagements, but because I considered myself simply as the servant and instrument of my Bishop. I did not care much for the Bench of Bishops, except as they might be the voice of my Church; nor should I have cared much for a Provincial Council; nor for a Diocesan Synod presided over by my Bishop; all these matters seemed to me to be *jure ecclesiastico*, but what to me was *jure divino* was the voice of my Bishop in his own person. My own Bishop was my Pope; I knew no other; the successor of the Apostles, the Vicar of Christ.[12]

THE BODY OF BISHOPS

Newman, however, could not long avoid the problem arising from the fact that bishops in the apostolic succession did not always speak with one mind. The French Abbé Jean-Nicolas Jager, in correspondence with Newman in 1835, pressed him to explain how he could affirm some ecclesiastical traditions while rejecting others. How could he accept the Nicene Creed without accepting that of Pius IV, based on the teaching of Trent? To meet this difficulty Newman excogitated a distinction between two kinds of tradition – episcopal and prophetical – a distinction of fundamental importance in Newman's *Lectures on the Prophetical Office of the Church*, published in 1837. Episcopal tradition, as he defines it, is handed down from bishop to bishop, and is forced upon the attention of every Christian. It is certified by the tests of catholicity, antiquity, and the consensus of the Fathers. Prophetical tradition, by contrast, includes interpretations and commentaries on the deposit of faith by private persons and groups of believers. It is subject to error in its details and is not binding on all Christians.[13]

From this concept of tradition Newman developed his 'branch theory' of the Church. The Catholic Church, he thought, has three branches – Greek, Roman, and Anglican – all three of which accept episcopal tradition. The Roman Church, however, errs by treating some prophetical traditions as though they too were obligatory. Newman gradually came to admit that the decrees of the Council of Trent, if strictly interpreted, may be seen as consonant with episcopal tradition. But until his conversion he continued to hold that Catholic theology and practice since the sixteenth century had attributed normative status to some accretions that belonged only to the prophetic tradition.

In the early stages of the Oxford Movement, Newman continued to express confidence in the Anglican bishops. In 1834 he wrote: 'Our prelates are still sound, and know the difference between what is modern and what is ancient'.[14] He dedicated his *Lectures on Justification* (1838) to Bishop Bagot. When Bagot delivered his charge at St Mary's Church, Oxford, later that year, Newman expected him to endorse the *Tracts for the Times*, of which Newman was the principal author. Bagot, however, admonished the Tractarians to take heed 'lest in their admiration of antiquity they revert to practices which heretofore have ended in superstition' – a veiled reference, it would seem, to the Church of Rome.[15] Newman, deeply hurt, confessed to a friend, 'What he said was very slight indeed, but a bishop's lightest word *ex Cathedra* is heavy'.[16] With the consent of his fellow Tractarian John Keble, he wrote to Bagot offering to withdraw any *Tract* that 'was judged to be offensive or even to suppress all of them'.[17] Bagot, surprised that his words were taken so seriously, gave assurances that he had no intent to censure the *Tracts*.

Sensing that the bishops were not always unanimous, Newman began to say explicitly that an individual bishop might fail to be a true witness to the faith. In a reply to an attack on the Tractarians, dated 22 June 1838, he wrote, 'No one person, not even a bishop *ex Cathedra*, may at his mere word determine what doctrine shall be received and what not. He is bound to appeal to the established faith.'[18]

While Newman was experiencing increasing tensions with the Anglican bishops, his attention was called to an article by Nicholas Wiseman, the future archbishop and cardinal, on 'The Anglican Claim to Apostolic Succession', published in the *Dublin Review* for August 1839. It quoted a principle used by St Augustine to refute the Donatists: 'The whole world judges with security' ('Securus iudicat orbis terrarum'). Although Newman rejected the parallelism between Anglicanism and Donatism, Augustine's words kept ringing in his ears in much the same way that the words 'tolle, lege' had for Augustine himself on the eve of his conversion.[19] He could not put out of his mind the apprehension that the Anglican Church might be in schism. He found it necessary to grant that 'the deliberate judgment, in which the whole Church at length rests and acquiesces, is an infallible prescription and a final sentence against such portions of it as protest and secede'.[20] To follow Anglican teaching where it diverged from the firm consensus of the Catholic episcopate as a whole would be to repeat the errors of the Donatists.

With these thoughts in mind, Newman made his last desperate effort to defend his Anglican allegiance and to stem the tide of young

Tractarians who were moving towards Rome. In January 1840 he published an article on 'The Catholicity of the Church'[21] in which he argues that because bishops stand in the apostolic succession, Christians are obliged by divine law to be subject to them. To rebel against one's bishop is to recede from the Church. Relying on a somewhat dubious interpretation of Cyprian, he maintains that each individual bishop, as a successor of Peter, is independent of the others. Intercommunion among bishops is a duty, and the breach of it a sin, but such intercommunion is not essential to catholicity. It is only a matter of ecclesiastical arrangement. If churches fall into separation from one another, they should strive to restore the broken unity. Anglicans are for the present kept from communion with Rome by their duty to their particular church and by the terms of communion that Rome forces on them.

Even while writing this article, Newman was aware that his defence of the Anglican settlement in this essay was vulnerable. Augustine, he admits, would not hold that separate parts of the Church were essentially complete even though not united with the main body. Newman concedes that if Rome reforms, 'it will be our Church's duty at once to join in communion with the continental Churches'.[22] At this stage, Newman, no longer repudiating any official teaching of the Roman Church, blames Rome only for encouraging certain exorbitant tenets and superstitious devotions. He is worried about Catholic practices regarding indulgences, the invocation of saints, and the worship of Mary, which he regards as unwarranted by apostolical tradition.

Newman's *Tract 90*, published in 1841, was a plea to interpret the confessional documents of the Church of England in the most Catholic sense that they would admit. The pamphlet aroused great indignation at Oxford and was bitterly attacked by many of the bishops, who urged Bishop Bagot to take action against Newman. To head off a formal condemnation, Newman agreed to suspend the *Tracts*. Lacking support in his own Church, and feeling himself to be adrift, he retired to Littlemore, where he worked on his translation of Athanasius and pondered what the future might hold.

Difficulties with the Anglican bishops continued to multiply. Failing to assert what Newman regarded as their apostolic authority, they allowed Parliament to decide what sees should be established or suppressed, as happened in Ireland. Then, in 1841, Parliament authorized the establishment of a bishopric in Jerusalem to be held alternately by Anglicans and by Lutherans. On the ground that Lutheranism was far from holding the Anglican view of apostolic succession and sacramental grace, Newman wrote letters of protest to the Archbishop of Canterbury and his own bishop.[23]

At Littlemore, Newman composed his masterly *Essay on the Development of Christian Doctrine* with a view to settling his remaining doubts about the Church of Rome. Newman at this point repudiates his previous position on the autonomy of individual bishops.[24] The apostolic succession, he teaches, cannot guarantee unity in the faith because some churches, while retaining that succession, are in schism or heresy. The episcopate must be catholic as well as apostolic. In the ancient Church, he asserts, bishops were not mere local officers, but possessed a quasi-ecumenical authority, extending wherever Christians were to be found. Ignatius of Antioch addresses letters to the churches along his way to martyrdom in Rome. Athanasius, exiled from his see, makes all Christendom from Trier to Ethiopia his home. Gregory Nazianzus refers to Cyprian as a universal bishop 'presiding not only over the Church of Carthage and Africa, but over all the regions of the West, and over the East, and South, and Northern portions of the world also'.[25] In the first centuries, Catholic bishops did not scruple to interfere in the affairs of schismatical or heretical dioceses. They addressed the members of such churches as though their bishops did not exist. 'The idea of acting upon the Donatists only as a body and through their bishops does not seem to have occurred to St Augustine at all.'[26]

Central to the *Essay on Development* was the issue of antiquity as a criterion of truth. As an Anglican, Newman gloried in professing the creeds and doctrines of the patristic age. But the great Trinitarian and Christological dogmas of the early councils went far beyond the clear teaching of Scripture. Anglicanism, in accepting these dogmas, committed itself to the principle that doctrine does develop. It looked upon itself as a *via media* between Protestantism, with its attachment to the letter of 'Scripture alone', and Romanism, which canonized additions to the apostolic faith. The Tractarians classified various modern Catholic doctrines, such as those concerning Transubstantiation and the pains of Purgatory, as accretions or corruptions.

The Anglican *via media*, Newman perceived, raised questions that he now felt it necessary to address. Why must the process of development stop in the first millennium? Could not the teachings of the Council of Trent and the Creed of Pius IV be understood as authentic continuations of the process of dogmatization at work in the early councils? In his *Essay on Development*, Newman concluded that the more recent Catholic doctrines had grown logically and organically out of the original deposit of faith. In consistency, therefore, Anglicans should accept them.

PAPACY

Remarkable in the *Essay on Development* is the strong emphasis Newman now gives to papal supremacy, a theme that had been all but absent in his previous writing. He is no longer satisfied, as he previously was, to appeal to the dictum of Vincent of Lérins that Christians were obliged to believe only what has been professed 'everywhere, always, and by all'.[27] Ancient Christianity, as he now presents it, was far from a harmonious chorus of Catholic bishops. It might better be described as an incessant struggle among hostile factions, freely anathematizing one another.[28] Arians, Semi-Arians, Macedonians, Manichaeans, Apollinarists, Pelagians, Novatianists, Donatists, and Priscillianists thrived at various times and in some regions became more numerous than Catholics. Each of these groups had its churches, its bishops, and its scholars. 'How', Newman asks, 'was the man to guide his course who wished to join himself to the doctrine and fellowship of the Apostles in the times of St Athanasius, St Basil, and St Augustine?'[29]

The first criterion, Newman suggests, is the title 'Catholic'. Heretics strove in vain to usurp that title for themselves. But people everywhere knew that the Arians, Nestorians, and Macedonians, however numerous, were not Catholic. Newman notes furthermore that the Catholics in the fifth and sixth centuries came to be denoted by the additional title of 'Roman', a title by which they meant communion with the Church of Rome.[30]

Newman's adduces the Council of Chalcedon as a palmary example of papal authority in action. The party of Eutyches had triumphed with virtual unanimity at the so-called 'Robber Council' of Ephesus in 449, with three of the four Eastern patriarchs favouring the restoration of Eutyches to his see. The fourth patriarch, Flavian of Constantinople, was on trial for his allegiance to the pope. Only the papal legates were in opposition, and they had to escape as best they could lest they suffer the kind of physical violence inflicted upon Flavian. Yet only two years later, with the support of the new emperor, Marcian, Pope Leo was able to bring about the convocation of a new council, that of Chalcedon. In Newman's words:

> The historical account of the Council is this, that a formula which the Creed did not contain, which the Fathers did not unanimously witness, and which some eminent Saints had almost in set terms opposed, which the whole East refused as a symbol, not once, but

twice, patriarch by patriarch, metropolitan by metropolitan, first by the mouth of above a hundred, then by the mouth of above six hundred of its Bishops, and refused upon the grounds of its being an addition to the Creed, was forced upon the Council ... for acceptance as a definition of faith under the sanction of an anathema, – forced on the Council by the resolution of the Pope of the day, acting through his Legates and supported by the civil power.[31]

Newman concludes this impressive chapter with the observation that if there is anywhere in the world today a form of Christianity in which, though 'heresies are rife and bishops negligent within its own pale', there is 'but one Voice for whose decisions people wait with trust, one Name and one See to which they look with hope, and that name Peter, and that see Rome; – such a religion is not unlike the Christianity of the fifth and sixth centuries'.[32]

After tracing the development of a number of distinctively Catholic doctrines and satisfying himself that they stood in continuity with the apostolic deposit of faith, Newman, leaving his book incomplete, made his submission to Rome on 9 October 1845. He wrote to Dr Wiseman, now a bishop, promising to obey the pope 'as I had obeyed my own Bishop in the Anglican Church'.[33]

For the next decade, Newman championed his new faith in rather triumphal tones. In his *Discourses to Mixed Congregations* (1849), he insists that a living and infallible magisterium is essential for Christian faith. In apostolic times, he writes, the gospel was believed on the word of the apostles, which was received as the word of God. 'In the Apostles' days the peculiarity of faith was submission to a living authority. If you will not look out for a living authority, and will bargain for private judgment, then say at once that you have not Apostolic faith.'[34] To believe on the word of a living authority is quite different from taking a book in one's hands and interpreting it for oneself. Protestants, when they profess to believe the Bible, reserve the right to explain it as they see fit. For this reason they do not have faith in the sense that it was exercised by the first Christians and is exercised by Catholics today. Newman therefore hesitates to say at this point that they can have the kind of faith that saves.

Christian faith, as Newman now describes it, is an unconditional submission to a present informant and guide. By its very nature it requires an infallible authority, which can be trusted to deliver the word of God. In making a revelation, God implicitly committed himself to establishing an organ that would prevent it from being corrupted by the capriciousness of human reason. Since the Catholic Church is the only body on earth that lays claim to such authority, the Christian has good reason to suppose that she might indeed be 'the pillar and the ground of truth'.[35]

In his first years as a Catholic Newman was inclined to make extreme claims on behalf of the papacy. In his conversion novel, *Loss and Gain*, he has the hero, Charles Reding, say of the pope: 'Catholics call him Vicar of Christ, Bishop of Bishops, and the like; and, I believe, consider that he, in a pre-eminent sense, is the one pastor or ruler of the Church, the source of jurisdiction, the judge of controversies, and the centre of unity, as having the powers of the Apostles, and especially of St Peter'.[36]

Until the first Vatican Council, there was considerable debate within the Church about the seat of infallibility. In his *Essay on Development*, Newman asserts the common teaching that the pope, acting together with an ecumenical council, could not err in matters of faith, but he refrains from taking a position on the disputed question of whether the pope could speak infallibly outside a general council. Again in the *Apologia* (1865), he eloquently defends the infallibility of the Church, but he does not commit himself as to whether the pope, acting alone, can impose a doctrine on all Catholics as a matter of faith.

As an adviser to Bishop William Ullathorne of Birmingham, who was attending the First Vatican Council, Newman expressed his view that there was no need to define papal infallibility. On learning that Cardinal Edward Manning and others were working for a definition, he reacted angrily in a private letter to Bishop Ullathorne: 'Why should an aggressive insolent faction', he asked, 'be allowed to "make the heart of the just mourn, whom the Lord has not made sorrowful"? ... If it is God's will that the Pope's infallibility should be defined, then it is His Blessed Will to throw back "the times and the moments" of that triumph for which He has destined His Kingdom; and I shall feel I have but to bow my head to His adorable, inscrutable Providence.'[37]

When the definition came, Newman's first reaction was to interpret the thunder and lightning that attended the definition as signs of God's wrath and to reckon that the loss of the papal states that same year was a divine punishment.[38] For some time he remained publicly silent, doubting whether the council had acted with sufficient unanimity for its definition to be binding. But when the dissident bishops submitted, Newman became convinced that the *orbis terrarum* (the whole world) had signified its consensus. Judged by the criterion that Augustine had used against the Donatists, the truth of the proclamation was secure.

The British statesman William E. Gladstone, together with some others, accused the council of having transferred to the papacy the functions of all the bishops, thus making them mere lackeys of the pope, contrary to historical precedent. In his *Letter to the Duke of Norfolk* (1875) Newman skilfully defends the Vatican Decrees, but in his defence he comes very close to admitting Gladstone's point. Ancient history, he contends, is no criterion of truth, because the Church and its doctrine must develop. By default the papacy has taken over the authority that formerly belonged to bishops such as Athanasius, Basil, Gregory Nazianzus, and Ambrose. The pope today is the sole heir of the ecumenical hierarchy of the fourth century. This concentration of powers has been providential. 'No one but a Master, who was a thousand bishops in himself at once, could have tamed and controlled, as the Pope did, the great and little tyrants of the middle age.'[39]

Later in the book, Newman moves on to defend the new dogma of papal infallibility. Giving it a moderate interpretation along the lines already marked out by the Secretary General of the Council, Bishop Joseph Fessler, Newman insists that the pope cannot claim to speak infallibly except under severe restrictions set forth in official explanations of the conciliar decree. Then he draws the conclusion that the identification and interpretation of irreformable statements always depends on the community of theologians. 'Theologians', he writes, 'employ themselves in determining precisely what it is that is condemned ... Instances frequently occur, when it is successfully maintained by some new writer, that the Pope's act does not imply what it has seemed to imply, and questions which seemed to be closed, are after a course of years re-opened.'[40] A little later he adds: 'All the dogmas of Pope or Council are but general, and so far, in consequence, admit of exceptions in their actual application, – these exceptions being determined either by other authoritative utterances or by the scrutinizing vigilance, acuteness, and subtlety of the *Schola Theologorum*'.[41] The last word, Newman seems to say, belongs to the community of theologians rather than to the hierarchical magisterium, whose determination is only penultimate.

Newman's *Letter to the Duke of Norfolk* accomplished its purpose. It shielded the Catholic Church in England from the storm of protest that engulfed it in several other countries. The Congregation for the Propagation of the Faith was dissatisfied with Newman's minimizing explanation, but Cardinal Manning and Bishop Ullathorne persuaded Rome not to publish its objections, which would have undone all the good effects of Newman's book.[42]

AUTHORITY OF THEOLOGIANS

In the course of his career, Newman spoke many times of the authority of theologians and its relation to that of the ecclesiastical magisterium. In his *Essay on Development*, he composed a short section on
theology in which he insists that reason has always been alert in the
Church, because the truths of faith clamour to be understood. The loving
inquisitiveness of theology, as it aspires to ascertain the meaning, grounds,
and implications of articles of faith, is praiseworthy and beneficial.[43]

A few years later, in his Lectures *On the Idea of a University*,
Newman analysed the respective functions of the hierarchical magisterium and the theological community. University theology, he asserted,
is easily drawn into rationalism and scepticism, as happened in the cases
of Abelard and David of Dinant in the Middle Ages.[44] But when theological inquiry is conducted in a loyal Catholic spirit, it performs a valuable
service. Especially in fields such as natural science, in which the Church
has no direct competence, the hierarchical leaders must exercise
patience and restraint, lest they repeat the errors that had been committed in the treatment of Galileo.[45] 'Error may flourish for a time, but truth
will prevail in the end.'[46]

In the final chapter of his *Apologia*, Newman eloquently discourses
on the dialectical interplay between authority and private judgement
that continually unfolds in the Church. 'Every exercise of infallibility',
he writes, 'is brought into act by an intense and varied operation of the
Reason' and unleashes a mighty effort to assimilate the definition.[47]
Infallibility is given to the magisterium 'not to enfeeble the freedom or
vigour of human thought in religious speculation, but to resist and
control its extravagance'.[48] Theology strives to cast the great body of
dogmatic teaching into the form of a science, with a distinct method and
terminology, as we find in the writings of St Athanasius, St Augustine,
and St Thomas.[49]

ROLE OF THE LAITY

Newman was a pioneer in investigating the responsibility of the laity
in matters of faith. He does not look upon lay persons as authoritative
judges of doctrine. In *The Idea of a University*, he remarks that although
lay persons have rarely excelled in strictly dogmatic theology, many of
them have been highly successful apologists, beginning with Justin and
Athenagoras and extending to René de Chateaubriand and Joseph de
Maistre.[50]

In 1859, during his brief editorship of *The Rambler*, Newman wrote his famous essay 'On Consulting the Faithful in Matters of Doctrine'. The immediate occasion was the controversy about the extent to which the views of the laity ought to be heard on the question of Catholic schools. In his article he broadened the discussion by considering the roles that lay Christians had played historically in the formation of Christian doctrine. He contended that the laity had often taken the initiative in promoting doctrines related to devotion, such as the divine motherhood of Mary, as defined at Ephesus, and the Immaculate Conception, recently defined by Pius IX. In treating the Arian crisis that racked the Church after Nicaea, Newman bluntly declared:

> There was a temporary suspense of the functions of the 'Ecclesia docens'. The body of Bishops failed in their confession of the faith. They spoke variously, one against another; there was nothing, after Nicaea, of firm, unvarying, consistent testimony, for nearly sixty years. There were untrustworthy Councils, unfaithful Bishops, there was weakness, fear of consequences, misguidance, delusion, hallucination, endless, hopeless, extending itself into nearly every corner of the Catholic Church.[51]

During this crisis, Newman contended, the laity did more than the bishops to sustain orthodoxy. His conclusion, which could hardly be demonstrated historically, aroused no little opposition from the hierarchical authorities of his day.

Some scholars have understood Newman in this essay as attributing an independent and infallible magisterium to the laity, but he stops short of any such claim. He asserts, however, that all faithful Christians, including the laity, receive from the Holy Spirit a kind of supernatural instinct inclining them to accept what is of faith and to reject what is contrary to faith. For this reason pope and councils, before defining doctrine, do well to consult the 'sense of the faith'. In proclaiming the Immaculate Conception, Pius IX called attention to the 'remarkable consensus' (*singularis conspiratio*) of the Catholic bishops and faithful as one ground for the definition. But Newman never attributes to the laity the power to adjudicate or define doctrine, which belongs exclusively to the ecclesiastical hierarchy.

BALANCE OF POWERS

Newman's final work on ecclesiology was his lengthy Preface to the third edition of his *Via Media of the Anglican Church* (1877), in which he responds to his own previous position in *The Prophetical Office of the Church*. This Preface takes the form of an eighty-page essay on the threefold office of the Church: the prophetic, the priestly, and the regal. Instead of concentrating all three functions in the episcopate, as Vatican II was to do, Newman distributes the functions among different segments of the Church. His position is neatly summarized in the following short paragraph:

> Christianity, then, is at once a philosophy, a political power, and a religious rite: as a religion, it is Holy; as a philosophy, it is Apostolic; as a political power, it is One and Catholic. As a religion, its centre of action is pastor and flock; as a philosophy, the Schools; as a rule, the Papacy and its Curia.[52]

In other words, the priestly function is centred in parish priests and laity; the prophetic in the theologians, and the regal in the pope and his curia. Where, then, do the bishops fit in? In the course of the essay, Newman refers to them as bearers of the regal office, with and under the pope, who is 'the Ecumenical Bishop and one Pastor of Christ's flock'.[53] The task of popes and bishops is to keep the flock in unity, sometimes tolerating deviations from strict correctness in teaching and worship for the sake of expediency. To excuse the doctrinal deviations of Popes Liberius and Honorius, Newman contends that their first duty was to maintain unity and peace among their faithful. This concern made them less firm and clear-sighted in matters of doctrine than would in theory be desired.[54]

Newman allows for the possibility that a bishop might also be a preacher and a spiritual guide, as was the case with Gregory Thaumaturgus, who combined in his own person something of all three offices. But normally the maintenance of the Church in the truth of the gospel requires the interaction of different classes of believers. The devotion of the lay faithful, the doctrinal insights of theologians, and the pastoral skills of popes and bishops supplement and correct one another's limitations. Newman thus finds in the Church something like the form of government that he cherishes in British constitutional monarchy, in which royal power is held in check by the two houses of Parliament.[55]

This final venture of Newman in ecclesiology is stimulating but problematic. In our day the laity are far more educated and more critical than the simple believers Newman has in mind. They are not manifestly more devout than clerics. Theologians, many of whom are laypeople, do not constitute anything like the medieval *schola theologorum*. They are not conspicuously 'apostolic' in their teaching. We do not commonly think of theologians as judges of orthodoxy, as was customary in the late Middle Ages, but rather as religious instructors and, in some cases, explorers whose hypotheses need to be critically assessed by the hierarchical magisterium. As for the pope and the bishops, we expect them to be guardians of revealed truth and not to yield to considerations of expediency. We connect the priestly office with the public liturgy rather than, as Newman did, with private devotions.

While Newman correctly identified different tendencies in the Church, his division of powers among bishops, theologians, and laity is not easily assimilable today. His position, moreover, can scarcely be reconciled with the Second Vatican Council, which taught that bishops 'in an eminent and visible way, take on the functions of Christ himself as Teacher, Shepherd, and High Priest and act in his person'.[56]

CONCLUSION

Newman's theology of the hierarchy cannot be understood apart from his career and the controversies in which he became involved. He writes not as a neutral observer indulging in cold speculation but in the heat of controversy, intent on defending some particular facet of the truth. He is not a serene systematician, seeking to build a comprehensive system, but an apologist or controversial theologian, addressing the needs of particular situations in which he was involved.

Newman's theology passes through a number of stages as it matures. In his youth as an Evangelical he concentrated on the gospel message and gave scant attention to the Church and its organs. As a young priest he discovered the importance of tradition and became enamoured of the Fathers. Then, as a leader of the Oxford Movement, he looked to his own local bishop as his supreme authority. When he encountered opposition from local bishops, he moved towards catholicity, seeking to find community with all bishops in the apostolic succession, whether Roman, Greek, or Anglican. In his early years as a Roman Catholic, he spoke glowingly of the pope as the oracle of God, correcting the bishops, who are prone to err when they act independently of Rome. After Vatican I, he accepted the infallibility of the pope. But as a British Catholic familiar with the 'balance of powers' he became wary of Roman clericalism. He therefore looked to the consensus of the faithful as a support for orthodoxy, even when the hierarchy fall short. When he found it necessary to quiet the turmoil stirred up by the First Vatican Council, he appealed to the body of theologians as the organ that interprets the true meaning of the conciliar decrees. Finally, responding to his own previous views on Roman corruptions, he maintained that the hierarchy, charged with maintaining unity within the flock, should not be blamed for benignly tolerating minor deviations.

Notwithstanding these variations, Newman's theology of authority exhibits a measure of constancy. From the beginning he was convinced that authority is of vital importance in Christian faith, since God has spoken and has entrusted his message to accredited witnesses. He never doubted that the government of the Church was by divine institution hierarchical and that the bishops were responsible for defining obligatory doctrine. All members of the Church were bound to submit to the authority of their bishops, as did Newman himself, with the eventual reservation that the bishops must speak in harmony with apostolic and catholic tradition. For the vitality of the Church, moreover, the hierarchy must give the theologians 'elbow room' in their search for truth and encourage the devotional initiatives of the lay faithful. Since theological speculation tends towards scepticism, and popular devotion towards superstition, both theologians and the laity are in need of mutual correction and hierarchical supervision.

Newman's convictions regarding authority in the Church undergo a cumulative development. In becoming an Anglican clergyman, he gains a sense of church office and tradition that he had lacked as a young Evangelical. As he moves from Anglicanism towards Catholicism he recognizes that each individual bishop, to speak with authority, must maintain communion with the whole body of Catholic bishops. He also becomes aware that the episcopate requires a visible head, who exercises universal authority in the name of the Lord. Thanks to the First Vatican Council, Newman comes to acknowledge that the pope can infallibly define doctrine when acting by his own authority and not only when acting together with his fellow bishops in council. But he also insists that papal infallibility is limited; it extends only to matters of faith and morals attested by Scripture and tradition. The hierarchy should not omit to consult the laity, who have certain insights from their own position. Doctrinal definitions, once made by the pastoral leaders, always allow for a margin of interpretation that must be probed by the reflection of theologians.

To profit from Newman's wisdom we should not be content to quote statements from one or another of his works. Since he is more a controversialist than a systematician, and since his own thought went through a series of developments, isolated passages do not do justice the full range of his thought. Sometimes he writes as an episcopalian, sometimes as a papalist, sometimes as a champion of the laity, sometimes as a spokesman for the theological community. In his long career he was able to call attention to different aspects of the truth in different works. For those who have the patience to familiarize themselves with the full corpus of his writing, he is a teacher almost without peer.

Notes

1. *U.S.*, 33.
2. *Ari.*, 80.
3. With the kind permission of the editor, Rev John T. Ford, CSC, I have incorporated into this article some sections from my article 'Newman and the Hierarchy', *Newman Studies Journal* 2 (2005), 8–19.
4. *Diff.*, 353–9.
5. *Ari.*, 50–1.
6. *Dev.*, 58–9.
7. *Ess.*, i:222–62, especially 254–7. As a Catholic Newman continued to use many of the same texts to the same effect; e.g., *O.S.*, 192–5.
8. *L.D.*, iv:13.
9. *L.D.*, iv:33.
10. *P.S.*, ii:401. The apostolic succession in the ministry is treated at greater length in *P.S.*, ii:300–19.
11. *P.S.*, iv:177.
12. *Apo.*, 51.
13. *V.M.*, i:249–52.
14. *Tract 41*, reprinted in *V.M.*, ii:35–48, at 38.
15. Bishop Bagot's charge is quoted in *L.D.*, vi:285–6.
16. Newman to John W. Bowden, 17 August 1838; *L.D.*, vi:291.
17. Newman to Archdeacon Clerke, 15 August 1838; *L.D.*, vi:289–90; see Newman to Richard Bagot, 21 August 1838; *L.D.*, vi:296–7.
18. Newman, 'Letter to the Margaret Professor of Divinity [Godfrey Gaussett] on Mr R. H. Froude's Statements on the Holy Eucharist', in *V.M.*, ii:195–257, at 200.
19. *Apo.*, 116–17.
20. *Apo.*, 117.
21. Newman, 'The Catholicity of the Anglican Church', reprinted in his *Ess.*, ii:1–73.
22. *Ess.*, ii:72.
23. *Apo.*, 141–6.
24. *Dev.*, 265–73.
25. *Dev.*, 266–7.
26. *Dev.*, 272.
27. Vincent of Lérins, *Commonitorium*, 2; PL 50:639.
28. In an essay published some years later on 'The Trials of Theodoret', Newman recounts how the bishops of that day appeared as 'antagonist hosts in a battle, not as angels of their respective Churches or as shepherds of their people'; see *H.S.*, ii:303–62, at 335. Francis McGrath, FMS,

a Newman scholar stationed at the Birmingham Oratory, informed me
that this essay was probably written about 1859.

29. *Dev.*, 248.
30. *Dev.*, 279.
31. *Dev.*, 312.
32. *Dev.*, 322.
33. *Apo.*, 51.
34. *Mix.*, 207.
35. *Dev.*, 87–9; cf. *Apo.*, 245–6.
36. *L.G.*, 394.
37. Newman to Bishop William Ullathorne, 28 January 1870; *L.D.*, xxv:18–19.
38. Newman to Mrs William Froude, 2 January 1871; *L.D.*, xxv:261–2, at 262.
39. 'A Letter Addressed to His Grace the Duke of Norfolk on Occasion of
    Mr. Gladstone's Recent Expostulation', *D.A.*, ii:171–378, at 212.
40. *D.A.*, 333.
41. *D.A.*, 334. Newman describes his concept of the *schola theologorum* in a
    letter to Henry N. Oxenham of 9 November 1865; *L.D.*, xxii:98–9. The
    description of the *schola* in this letter is reminiscent of the 'prophetic
    office', as described in Newman's Anglican works.
42. The relevant correspondence is printed in the original languages in *L.D.*,
    xxvii:401–11.
43. *Dev.*, 336–8.
44. *Idea*, 384.
45. *Idea*, 220; cf. *Apo.*, 264.
46. *Idea*, 478.
47. *Apo.*, 252.
48. *Apo.*, 253.
49. *Apo.*, 251.
50. *Idea*, 379.
51. *Cons.*, 77.
52. *V.M.*, i:xl.
53. *V.M.*, i:lxxxiii.
54. *V.M.*, i:lxxxii–lxxxiii.
55. In a letter to Frederic Rogers, Baron Blachford, dated 5 February 1875,
    Newman explained that the Catholic Church, like Great Britain, had a
    constitutional form of polity that protected her members against the
    excesses of the powerful. Just as lawyers and public offices preserve the
    body politic from the absolutistic tendencies of kings and lords, so,
    Newman argued, the theological schools (the *schola theologorum*) pro-
    tect the Church from the encroachments of popes and councils. *L.D.*,
    xxvii:211–13.
56. Vatican II, *Lumen gentium*, 21.

Further reading

Dulles, Avery. *Newman: Outstanding Christian Thinkers*. London and New York:
    Continuum, 2002.

Lease, Gary. *Witness to the Faith: Cardinal Newman on Teaching Authority of the Church*. Duquesne Studies: Theological Series 10. Pittsburgh: Duquesne University Press, 1971.

Miller, Edward Jeremy. *John Henry Newman on the Idea of Church*. Shepherdstown, WV: Patmos, 1987.

Misner, Paul. *Papacy and Development: Newman on the Primacy of the Pope*. Leiden: E. J. Brill, 1976.

Page, John R. *What Will Dr Newman Do? John Henry Newman and Papal Infallibility 1865–1875*. Collegeville, MN: Liturgical Press, 1994.

Patterson, Webster T. *Newman: Pioneer for the Layman*. Washington, DC: Corpus Books, 1968.

10 Conscience

GERARD J. HUGHES

Newman gives his views on conscience mainly in two contexts. As one would expect, he considers the role of conscience in moral decision-making. How does a person arrive at conscientious moral judgements? What is the content of such judgements? How should one resolve conflicts between one's own conscientious moral judgement and the views of others whom one accepts as authorities to whom one owes due respect? More surprisingly, Newman discusses the role which conscience might play in grounding a person's belief in God. How is one to account for the particular force which the claims of conscience make upon us, and the very personal nature of those claims? Is there any sense in which conscience must be thought of as the voice of God? The two main sections of this chapter will therefore consider Newman's views on the role of conscience in morality and in theology.

CONSCIENCE AND MORAL JUDGEMENT

Newman prefaces his discussions of conscience with two important sets of qualifications which he insists must be borne in mind throughout his entire treatment. One is concerned with academic discussions about the extent to which our conscientious judgements are conditioned; and the other is the less rigorous but perhaps more widespread assumption that nobody else is ever entitled to criticize one's own conscientious judgements.

Conscience and free will

One of the mistakes which Newman thinks is frequently made in academic circles is the denial of freedom and consequently of moral responsibility. Here are the final few sentences from his attack on such views, common in universities and repeated by subversive 'public writers':

> We are told that conscience is but a twist in primitive and untutored man; that its dictate is an imagination; that the very notion of

guiltiness, which that dictate enforces, is simply irrational, for how can there possibly be freedom of will, how can there be consequent responsibility, in that infinite eternal network of cause and effect, in which we helplessly lie? And what retribution have we to fear, when we have had no real choice to do good or evil?[1]

As he here presents matters, neither Newman nor the people he is attacking even consider the more modern view that responsibility might be compatible with determinism. Newman is a libertarian, who believes that determinism is false and that anyone who performs an action for which they can be held morally responsible must at the moment of acting have been able to act otherwise than they in fact did. His opponents are those who would now be described as 'hard-determinists' or 'incompatibilists'. Newman claims that when someone acts freely, neither the external circumstances in which they are placed nor their own desires and beliefs at that time made that piece of behaviour inevitable. Though he does not say so here, he would probably have accepted the traditional doctrine that to the extent that one has in the past been responsible for the formation of long-established habits of thought or of desire one can be held responsible for the actions which are caused by those habits, even if at the time it would have been impossible for the person to act otherwise than they did.

Conscience 'truly so called'
In his *Letter to the Duke of Norfolk* Newman dismisses two ways of explaining the nature of conscience. The first, he says, is prevalent in academic circles. He rejects it in the following terms:

The rule and measure of duty is not utility, nor expedience, nor the happiness of the greatest number, nor State convenience, nor fitness, order and the *pulchrum*. Conscience is not a long-sighted selfishness, nor a desire to be consistent with oneself, but a messenger from Him who, both in nature and in grace, speaks to us behind a veil ...

Words like these are idle empty verbiage to the great world of philosophy now. All through my day there has been a resolute warfare, I had almost said conspiracy, against the rights of conscience, as I have described it. Literature and science have been embodied in great institutions in order to put it down. Noble buildings have been reared as fortresses against that spiritual, invisible influence which is too subtle for science and too profound for literature. Chairs in universities have been made the seats of an antagonist tradition.[2]

This scathing passage obviously expresses a total disdain for a great deal of what he took to be the academic fashions of the time. In these passages, Newman simply rejects without elaboration the whole gamut of ethical theories current in his day: Hobbesian egoism, utilitarianism, Kantian ethics, Darwinian selection and the rest. But the rhetoric does not make it easy to disentangle exactly what it is that he most dislikes, let alone to see the reasons he might have given for his rejection.

Perhaps one clue lies in the way in which he contrasts conscience truly so called with the role he takes to be ascribed to it in all the academic discussions of ethical theory. The true notion of conscience is, he says, too subtle for science and too profound for literature. In a broad sense, most of the ethical theories he rejects probably did have some pretensions to scientific exactitude. Bentham, Mill, and the later utilitarians were reacting against various earlier accounts of moral perceptiveness. By offering what they termed a calculus, in contrast to what they regarded as the undefended and often indefensible claim made by earlier philosophers to possess a clarity of moral perceptiveness, they saw themselves as putting ethics firmly on a rational, almost a scientific, basis. Utilitarianism, as Bentham puts it, had as its object 'to rear the fabric of felicity by the hands of reason and of law. Systems which question it deal in sounds instead of sense, in caprice instead of reason, in darkness instead of light. But enough of metaphor and declamation: it is not by such means that moral science is to be improved.'[3] The target of Bentham's criticism here, with his stress on calculus, reason, law and science, is just the kind of view which Newman wants to reinstate in the teeth of academic fashion. Newman would have had much the same to say about the aim of many Darwinians to fit ethics into the evolutionary scheme of things, and thus again make it 'scientific'. Hobbesian egoists stressed the critical use of moral reason. As Hobbes himself had said, 'The science of virtue and vice is moral philosophy; and therefore the true doctrine of the laws of nature is the true moral philosophy. But the writers of moral philosophy, though they acknowledge the same virtues and vices; yet, not seeing wherein consisted their goodness ... place them in a mediocrity of passions as if not the cause but the degree of daring made fortitude; or not the cause but the quantity of a gift made liberality.'[4]

As the phrase 'a mediocrity of passions' makes clear, the view Hobbes is attacking is just that version of Aristotelianism which Newman wished to promote.[5] Of course, the judgements of conscience which Newman defends as 'too subtle for science' could easily be represented as being too subject to the whims of an individual to be in any important sense rational at all. Newman wishes to argue that moral judgements are indeed not numerically *calculable* nor are they *logically* derivable. The 'subtlety' which he wishes to defend depends upon a nicety of judgement which cannot be reduced to any scientific terms or process. His critics would regard this kind of claim as little better than enshrining old-fashioned sentiments and prejudice. It remains to be seen whether Newman can defend himself with more than the rhetoric he uses in the passages just cited.

So conscience 'truly so called' is not, in Newman's view, widely fostered by academics. But he does not believe the correct view is widespread among the common people either:

> Now let us see what the notion of conscience is in this day in the popular mind. There, no more than in the intellectual world, does 'conscience' retain the old, true, Catholic meaning of the word. There too, the idea of a moral governor is far away from the use of it, frequent and emphatic as that use of it is. When men advocate the rights of conscience, they in no sense mean the rights of the Creator, nor the duty to him, in thought and deed, of the creature; but the right of thinking, speaking, writing and acting, according to their judgement and their humour, without any thought of God at all. They do not even pretend to go by any moral rule, but they demand, what they think is an Englishman's prerogative, for each to be his own master in all things, and to profess what he pleases, asking no one's leave and accounting priest or preacher, speaker or writer, unutterably impertinent, who dare say a word against his going to perdition, if he likes it, in his own way.[6]

If Newman's problem with the academics was their insistence on some kind of scientific accuracy, insufficiently subtle for the nuances of the moral life, it appears from this passage that neither is he about to allow just any kind of appeal against the rigour of would-be scientific rules. Yet it is not obvious that the attack in this passage is precisely directed against loose living; the real focus of his criticism is the claim to an autonomy and independence which feels no reverence at all for the Creator. Even if the 'popular mind' pays little attention to the Creator, Newman believes that his 'high' view of conscience is shared at any rate by the main body of Christians, who are agreed that it

> is founded on the doctrine that conscience is the voice of God, whereas it is fashionable on all hands now to consider it in one way or another the creation of man. Of course, there are great and broad

exceptions to this statement. It is not true of many or most religious bodies of men; especially not of their teachers or ministers. When Anglicans, Wesleyans, the various Presbyterian sects in Scotland, and other denominations among us speak of conscience, they mean what we mean, the voice of God in the nature and heart of man, as distinct from the voice of Revelation. They speak of a principle planted within us before we have had any training, although training and experience are necessary for its strength, growth, and due formation. They consider it a constituent element of the mind, as our perception of other ideas may be, as our powers of reasoning, as our sense of order and the beautiful, and our other intellectual endowments. They consider it, as Catholics consider it, to be the internal witness of both the existence and the law of God.[7]

In short, he takes his view to be one which is solidly established in mainstream Christian tradition, in contrast to the secularism of Hobbes, Bentham, and the Darwinians. Scientific ethics fails on two counts, then. First it pretends to a rigour which is insufficiently nuanced (if that is the point of his use of 'subtle') to be useful in practice. Secondly, it fails to see that the strength of moral demands derives not from scientific rationalism but from God to whom all human beings owe total obedience. His concluding remarks are in exact accord with the Thomist view which he cites,[8] and with the wholly Aristotelian background which he presupposes. For it is crucial to both Thomas Aquinas and Aristotle that although the basic ability to make sound moral judgements is innate in humans, it cannot be properly exercised except after careful training and experience.

We can compare Aristotle:

A young man is not a suitable person to take a course on how to run a city, for he is inexperienced in the affairs of life (which are the starting point and subject matter of the course). Besides, since he tends to be led by his feelings, attending the course will be pointless and unprofitable, since the aim of the course is not knowledge but action. It makes no difference whether he is young in years or immature in character. The problem is not a matter of time, but of a life-style which pursues one thing after another as feelings dictate.[9]

It is no trivial matter, then, that we form habits of one kind or another right from childhood; on the contrary it is very important, indeed all-important.[10]

And Newman:

> But the sense of right and wrong, which is the first element in
> religion, is so delicate, so fitful, so easily puzzled, obscured, perverted,
> so subtle in its argumentative methods, so impressible by education,
> so biased by pride and passion, so unsteady in its course, that, in the
> struggle for existence amid the various exercises and triumphs of the
> human intellect this sense is at once the highest of all teachers and
> the least luminous.[11]

Newman's view of conscience 'truly so called'[12] is very close to Aristotle's
notion of *phronēsis*, practical wisdom. *Phronēsis*, too, is the ability to
make sound moral judgements. In Aristotle's view, it is an intellectual
virtue, a quality of rational reflection. The person whose conscientious
judgements are sound will through childhood training have gradually
achieved the emotional balance without which moral judgements are
likely to be distorted; and their intellectual grasp of moral situations
will have been informed by a considerable experience of the complexities
of life. Only this carefully nurtured combination of sensibility, experience, and intellectual acumen will result in the possession of 'conscience
in the true sense'; the ability to make moral judgements upon which the
person is entitled to rely.[13]

Somehow, then, Newman intends to harmonize the following claims:

(1) Conscience is nuanced and subtle rather than rigorous, scientific and
governed by the laws of any 'theory' of morals.
(2) Conscience requires careful education, emotional balance, and intellectual clarity if it is to function correctly.
(3) Conscience 'truly so called' expresses within us the demands of God.

The tensions are not difficult to find. For it will appear that in his view
conscientious judgements do not conform to the terms of a precise set of
moral laws: yet he appears to urge the claims of the commandments of
God as a challenge to the insistence of so many people to 'profess what
they please' rather than follow any moral rule. So what is his view of
the relationship between moral rules and the conscientious judgements
of the person of practical wisdom trying to do the will of God?

Conscience and moral judgement

Newman develops his account of conscientious moral judgements in
two principal places. One is in the discussion of the relationship between
conscience and authority in the *Letter to the Duke of Norfolk* already
mentioned. The other, perhaps rather more unexpectedly, comes towards

the end of *A Grammar of Assent*. Newman here, perhaps rather optimistically, takes it that his views on conscience are clear and would be widely accepted; so he can easily use them to illustrate his much more controversial views on what he calls the 'Illative Sense'. But for our present purposes we shall do better to work the other way round, and consider what light his extended treatment of the Illative Sense throws on the notion of conscience which he takes most sensible people to accept.

A Grammar of Assent sets out to break away from the assumption that epistemology requires all arguments aimed at establishing truth to be modelled on the arguments of formal logic. Newman points out that the arguments of formal logic succeed only to the extent that the terms are given a totally precise sense and the rules of legitimate inference are equally precisely defined. This can be achieved only by making the terms as abstract as possible; the argument 'All A's are F, B is an A, therefore B is F' follows strictly and precisely because 'A', 'B', and 'F' are purely abstract notions, shorn of any empirical content. 'No process of argument', he says 'is so perfect as that which is conducted by means of symbols'.[14] When we try to construct similar arguments using words instead of the rigid symbols of mathematics or logic, the inference will succeed only to the extent that we manage to restrict the words artificially: the variations and subtleties of meaning which they have in ordinary discourse are excluded so as to avoid any risk of equivocation. In either case, all we are doing is exploring the relationships between our concepts. Crucially, he claims that it is 'a fallacy that whatever can be thought can be adequately expressed in words'.[15] I think he must mean not only that all our concepts for things other than mathematical or logical abstractions are inevitably 'fuzzy' at the edges, but also that the strength of the evidence for a conclusion is not captured by an abstract rule of inference. There are always and inevitably going to be borderline cases where it is not in advance clear whether the concept is correctly applied or not, and whether the evidence really is cogent. With this in mind, he speaks of premisses involving terms referring to real things as being 'assumed' – taken to be true even if we realize they are inaccurate and may not strictly apply at all. 'Inference comes short of proof in concrete matters because it has not a full command over the objects to which it relates, but merely assumes its premisses.'[16]

Newman illustrates his view by drawing a contrast between an argument in formal logic or mathematics and the process by which we might argue about the correct reading of a Shakespearean text of which the extant manuscripts give different versions. He emphasizes the very many types of consideration which contribute to the formation of such judgements, and the artificiality of reducing them to the precision of mathematics or formal logic. When we are thinking about the real world, he says,

> We have to do with things, far more than with notions. We are not solitary, left to the contemplation of our own thoughts and their legitimate developments ... But how is an exercise of mind, which is for the most part occupied with notions, not things, competent to deal with things except partially and indirectly?[17]
>
> It is by the strength, variety, or multiplicity of premises, which are only probable, not by invincible syllogisms – by objections over-come, by adverse theories neutralised, by difficulties gradually clear-ing up, by exceptions proving the rule, by unlooked for correlations found with received truths ... by all these ways, and many others, it is that the practised and experienced mind is able to make a sure divination that a conclusion is inevitable, of which his lines of reasoning do not actually put him in possession.[18]

When someone is trying to understand the real world and explain what happens in it, the evidence which they will consider relevant and whose force they try to assess is normally manifold. Exactly why, for instance, a juror might conclude that a witness was hiding something important, and that it might be of sufficient importance to require a different overall verdict, is something which perhaps the juror herself might find it difficult even to put into words. Her process of thought cannot with any plausibility be represented as a piece of syllogistic reasoning. Newman's point is that what is important is whether the evidence supports the charge being made. The level of support is not numerically quantifiable, nor expressible in logical terms, but the assess-ment might still be entirely reasonable. Metaphors such as 'weighing' the evidence (which suggests that the various pieces have pre-defined weights), or 'drawing the logical conclusion' (which suggests a kind of formal inference) are in Newman's view quite inappropriate if they are taken in more than a general metaphorical sense. What it is reasonable or unreasonable to say or believe about the real world is discovered by a process of assessment which is quite unique and cannot be reduced to any formula. Rational assessment is not somehow a 'second best' to formal logic. On the contrary, it is the proper way in which to think about the real world.

If this is a correct interpretation of Newman's intentions, however, it is surely unfortunate that the passage given above concludes with the comment that these lines of reasoning do *not* actually 'put us in possession' of the inevitable conclusion. Newman's contrast between 'possession' and 'sure divination', and indeed the very use of a term like 'divination' with its somewhat misleading overtones, do tend to mislead his reader. What he is trying to do is to contrast a process of reasoning leading to a rational assessment of the force of the evidence for a particular conclusion with the process of *deducing* that conclusion from premisses. To have the premisses is in a sense *already* to be in possession of the conclusion which those premisses deliver. Assessing the import of evidence about things in the real world requires the person to 'reach' a conclusion. But this process of 'reaching' is in no sense a second best.

Newman's view of the Illative Sense has been severely criticized. Patrick Fitzpatrick takes issue with several points, two of which are specially important.[19] The first is that Newman's examples of conclusive informal reasoning – that Britain is an island, that the earth is a globe, that there are cities called London and Paris, that the future is affected by the past[20] – are not typical. Fitzpatrick concedes that in such cases we do indeed reason in the way that Newman suggests, by a simple assessment which is not and need not be expressed as a formal argument; but he insists that many other cases do not exactly fit this model, and in some the process is quite different – 'It is a matter of degree'. Often our conclusions – about the emendation of Shakespearean texts, or the diagnosis of complex mechanical failures – require very careful and complex and cooperative investigation. They require a precision which makes Newman's model of a simple, immediate personal grasp of the force of the evidence seem very far from how such inquiries are actually conducted.

However, it may be possible to lessen the force of this criticism. Newman does not particularly wish to oversimplify the discussion about the correct version of the Shakespearean text, nor does he suggest that arriving at the correct conclusions is a matter for the almost effortless solitary insight of the individual rather than from the work of a body of scholars. The final act of assessment is simple only in the sense of being irreducible to anything more fundamental.

Fitzpatrick's other criticism is that Newman presents the Illative Sense as infallible, whereas we do not possess any such faculty.[21] This criticism, too, can be blunted. The point is similar, as we shall see, to a point that might be made about Aristotle's *phronēsis* (practical wisdom). Moral judgements made by the exercise of practical wisdom are indeed correct. But this is not because we possess an infallible faculty: *phronēsis* is not a faculty, it is an intellectual virtue. By that Aristotle means that it is an acquired disposition of our power to judge which actions ought to be performed. The judgements of the young, or of adults whose upbringing has been faulty, are liable to be mistaken; acquiring the ability to get such things right is a process which any given individual might or might not have completed. So it is, I would suggest, with Newman's Illative Sense, which he describes as 'the perfection or virtue of the ratiocinative faculty'.[22] It is not a special 'faculty of infallibility' but rather the ability to assess evidence which the perfect thinker has gradually developed. Newman does not suggest that Shakespearean editors can function without years of training and experience. One might indeed wonder whether such intellectual perfection is ever attained, as one might equally well wonder whether any individual actually achieves the perfection of the virtue of moral discernment. Newman's point is not that we always have such a perfected ability at our disposal, but that nevertheless there are many times when a person is justified in their assessment of complex evidence without there being any possibility, or need, to demonstrate that justification in formal logical terms. Progress in soundness of judgement is 'a living growth, not a mechanism; and its instruments are mental acts, not the formulae and contrivances of language'.[23]

Newman expects this rather unfashionable epistemological doctrine to be made more palatable by what he clearly thinks people already believe about moral judgements, where he takes the situation to be precisely similar. He cites what he calls 'the grand words of Aristotle':

> We are bound to give heed to the undemonstrated sayings and opinions of the experienced and aged, not less than to demonstrations; because, from their having the eye of experience, they behold the principles of things.[24]

And Newman's comment:

> Instead of trusting logical science, we must trust persons, namely, those who by long acquaintance with their subject, have a right to judge.[25]

The text which Newman uses here is part of a general summing up of Aristotle's account of moral judgement. The use of 'undemonstrated' requires some explanation. An Aristotelian *apodeixis*, 'demonstration', starts from accepted premises which are true of necessity and proceeds by strictly defined logical steps to reach conclusions which are equally necessary. Suppose it is known that water is H_2O; the idea would be that, with that basic starting-point (no doubt along with other similar ones), one would be able to show that the other properties of water – its ability to dissolve many other substances, its boiling point, and so on – followed logically. This type of explanation of why things are as they are is a 'demonstration'. Even in the case of physics, Aristotle did not believe that physicists will have employed demonstration as a method for *discovering* that water is H₂O. To discover that, one needs to have spent time examining water in various circumstances, and eventually to have the insight that all would be explained if water were H₂O. Once that is achieved, then demonstrations can proceed from necessary premises to necessary conclusions in order to exhibit the value of the insight involved. It is this model that Aristotle says does *not* fit ethics, for two reasons: particular moral conclusions do not follow from moral principles by necessity; and the principles themselves are not true of necessity. That is why Aristotle says that the *undemonstrated* opinions of the experienced are to be respected. Reliable moral judgement, in Newman's view and in Aristotle's, like any other judgement about the complex realities of life, requires the growth of lifelong experience more than logic, and a reliable grasp of the fundamental values in human life, 'the principles of things'. The comparison is made quite explicitly in the *Grammar*. Aristotle calls our ability to make correct assessments in matters of conduct 'by the name of *phronēsis* or judgement' and Newman describes, develops and endorses it in these terms:

> What it is to be virtuous, how we are to gain the just and right idea and standard of virtue, how we are to approximate in practice to our own standard, what is right and wrong in a particular case, for the answers in fullness and accuracy to these and similar questions, the philosopher refers us to no code of laws, to no moral treatise, because no science of life, applicable to the case of an individual, has been or can be written. Such is Aristotle's doctrine, and it is undoubtedly true ... The authoritative oracle, which is to decide our path, is something more searching and manifold than such jejune generalisations as treatises can give, which are most distinct and clear when we least need them.²⁶

The various points made in the first sentence of this paragraph are perhaps not to be taken as merely rhetorical elaborations. How we are to grow in understanding of dispositions such as courage, or generosity, or loyalty is one issue; by what criterion progress in virtue is to be distinguished, what is meant by living by this standard, and 'What should I do now?' are related issues, to be sure; but they are not identical. What they have in common, in Newman's view, is that there is no neat way of answering any of these questions. Appropriate emotional responses to situations, the tests to be applied when making moral decisions, what a fulfilled life is like – these are matters which cannot be adequately put into words or codified in a way that makes further interpretative insight unnecessary. The undemonstrated judgements of the wise are to be heeded because of what the wise can 'see', not because of any argument they might have been asked to produce. In this paragraph, then, Newman neatly combines some essential Aristotelian points: (i) what it is to be virtuous and which standards of virtue are the true ones, can be derived only from our many judgements in individual cases; (ii) no code of laws or set of moral principles can possibly guarantee their correct application to particular instances; and (iii) our judgement in individual cases is, at least in those of us who are older and sufficiently experienced, more demanding and searching than any set of jejune generalities could possibly be.

In understanding Aristotle in this way, Newman interprets him as holding some version of the position in contemporary moral philosophy which would be termed 'particularism'. The basic moral judgement is the assessment by the person of mature conscience, the *phronimos*, of what is to be done on this particular occasion. Moral principles are summaries of the individual decisions already made – 'universals come from particulars' as Aristotle puts it.[27] It is therefore not the case that one simply starts with a moral principle and from it deduces what is to be done in the particular case. Of course, it will in general be true that our moral principles employ a set of categories in terms of which individual cases can be interpreted; and in that sense the adult will come to the assessment of particular cases armed with a whole range of moral terms at their disposal. It is Aristotle's contention, though, that these moral terms – 'killing', 'unjust', 'generous' 'courageous' and so on – get their meanings from our past experience and from the individual judgements we have already made in interpreting that experience morally. So when we are faced with a particular situation now, our experience, which is a necessary aid to our judgement, certainly does not make that judgement automatic. We will come to a decision with all these patterns of thought at our disposal: we have concepts like 'killing', 'unjust', 'foolhardy', 'adultery'. But we might still have to wonder about situations involving a life-support machine, or taxation policy, risking one's life to save a friend or living in a second marriage. In the assessment of these situations we may or may not come to make further refinements in our understanding of our moral principles and of the terms they contain. Is switching off this life-support now properly to be described as 'killing'? But Newman's key claim is this: in making such judgements, we do not make a decision which is in any way in conflict with our principles, for the principles themselves are now interpreted in the light of this decision as well as our earlier ones. 'Killing' (or any of our other concepts) may come to have a slightly different application for us than it previously did; and so the moral principles may come to have a different sense precisely because of what we have seen to be required in individual cases:

> I should decide *according to the particular case, which is beyond all rule, and must be decided on its own merits.* I should look to see what theologians could do for me, what the Bishops and clergy around me, what my confessor; what friends whom I revered: and if, after all, I could not take their view of the matter, then I must rule myself by my own judgement and my own conscience.[28]

The person of practical wisdom will take every means – advice, reading, precedent, experience – to enhance their ability to reach a good decision. Sound judgement does not come automatically. Still, particular cases are 'beyond all rule' in the sense that no moral rule can guarantee its correct application to each particular set of circumstances. So, according to the *Letter*, the manuals of moral theology, even though they are doubtless 'drawn up by theologians of authority and experience', are 'little more than reflexions and memoranda of our moral sense'.[29]

For just this reason, Newman rejects Gladstone's claim that the authority of the pope as defined in the First Vatican Council undermines the judgements of conscience made by Catholics:

> I observe that conscience is not a judgment upon any speculative truth, any abstract doctrine, but bears immediately on conduct, on something to be done or not done. 'Conscience', says St Thomas, 'is the practical judgment or dictate of reason by which we judge what *hic et nunc* is to be done as being good, or avoided as evil'. Hence conscience cannot come into direct collision with the Church's or the Pope's infallibility, which is engaged on general propositions and in the condemnation of particular and given errors.[30]

Probably the words 'hic et nunc' ('here and now') are italicized as being in a foreign language; but the italics might equally well serve to emphasize the epistemological primacy of the experienced and wise person's insight into the present, irreducibly particular, situation. Unless a pope were to condemn precisely this individual action in these particular circumstances, his infallible statements cannot contradict a person's conscientious judgement, because the understanding of the terms in any such statement depends not merely upon past experience and precedent, but on a person's insight into the particular cases with which they are confronted. Gladstone's criticism, that the doctrine of papal infallibility in morals undercuts individual judgement and controls from afar the lives of citizens who owe him allegiance, misses the mark entirely because it fails to understand the process of making a moral judgement. The point is not a theological but a straightforwardly philosophical one.

Some criticisms and replies

It might be argued that there are problems with Newman's position.

(1) How does he reconcile his statement that the moral judgement is 'beyond all rule' with his own criticism of some modern thinkers who 'do not even pretend to go by any moral rule'?

(2) Exactly what is the relationship between those basic moral values which are in his words 'the principles of things' and judgements about what ought to be done in any particular case?

(3) Does Newman believe that there is anything distinctive about a Christian ethic?

I shall consider these one at a time.

The role of 'moral rules'

Newman's use of 'principles' here links the notion of a moral rule to the Aristotelian notion of an *archē; archai* in Aristotle's ethics are 'starting-points', and he says that the starting-points of moral reasoning have the form 'since the end is of such and such a kind'.[31] These 'ends', Aristotle says, are not clear except to the virtuous person; and virtues are habits of appropriate emotional response to situations. 'Virtue makes the end right, and practical wisdom those things which are for the end.'[32] To have appropriate emotional responses to situations is already to find oneself responding to what is morally significant about each situation. Examples of 'starting-points' expressing the ends of action might be such statements as 'Generosity towards others is a virtue' and 'Foolhardiness is a vice'. I suggest, then, that when Newman thinks of moral judgement as being 'beyond all rule' he is claiming that such 'principles' are in themselves no more than starting-points. One still needs to *think* about how to be generous here, or how not to do something foolhardy at this point. So Newman says that all practical judgements must be in accord with practical wisdom:

> In buying or selling, in contracts, in his treatment of others, in giving and receiving, in thinking, speaking, doing, and working, in toil, in

danger, in his pleasures, every one of his acts, to be praiseworthy, must be in accord with this practical sense. Thus it is, and not by science, that he perfects the virtues of justice, self-command, magnanimity, generosity, gentleness and all others. *Phronēsis* is the regulating principle of every one of them.[33]

I take it that the criticism that some – perhaps many – of Newman's contemporaries consider themselves bound by no moral rule amounts to saying that they believe that they are justified in taking decisions which take no account of such virtues. He contrasts his own view with theirs precisely on those grounds. These virtues are the starting-points, the *archai*, of sound moral judgements, precisely because the emotional dispositions in which virtues consist open our eyes to the morally significant features of the situations in which we find ourselves. A psychopath, who is unable to have emotional responses, simply cannot see situations in moral terms at all, cannot even 'get started' morally speaking; and the young, whose emotional responses to situations are often far from appropriate, will find their moral judgements skewed as a result. However, like Aristotle, Newman does not believe that even the possession of wholly appropriate emotional responses to situations is sufficient to guarantee right judgement in particular cases. One needs experience, and often one needs to profit from the wisdom and experience of others. The moral judgement should take all of that into account; but is itself 'beyond all rule'.

The relationship between 'rules' and moral judgements
Newman makes two very significant remarks in this context:

> [a] [Practical wisdom] is formed and matured by practice and experience; and it manifests itself not in any breadth of view, or any philosophical comprehension of the mutual relations of duty towards duty, or any consistency in its teachings, but it is a capacity sufficient for the occasion, deciding what ought to be done here and now by this given person under these given circumstances.
>
> [b] [Practical wisdom] has an elasticity, which, in its application to individual cases, is, as I have said, not studious to maintain the appearance of consistency.[34]

Newman is here speaking of judgements expressing moral conclusions about what one should do here and now, as distinct from moral judgements concerning virtues or moral values. But what exactly is meant by his repeated denial of the importance of consistency in reaching one's moral conclusions? There are several possibilities: that the weight given to any given type of moral consideration – truthfulness, for instance – might vary from one case to another; or that a consideration which is admittedly relevant in one case – that someone will be offended, for instance – might not even be relevant in another; or that a consideration – for instance that nobody else knows what is being done – might be a reason in favour of what is done in one case, and a reason against it in some other case. It seems to me that Newman has little interest in any of these details, despite the emphasis he places upon individual circumstances, and the considerable theoretical importance of distinguishing them.[35] I think the most that can be established from his text and the various examples he offers is along the following lines. Someone who is thinking about, or trying to explain to someone else, why they should do A, will select one or more considerations which they take to be relevant to this case, assess their relative importance, and so decide; but though the process of reflection might indeed involve considerable thought and require that quite a large number of facts need to be taken in to consideration, the act of reaching a conclusion on the basis of all those considerations cannot itself be further analysed. Aristotle describes it as a 'perception' in a broad sense, and I think this is the view that Newman takes.[36] He also wishes to make it clear that in an apparently similar case the assessment of the relevance and importance of the various considerations might be seen to be different, and to lead to a different conclusion, without there being any further explanation for why they are seen to be different.

Newman is far from thinking this process is infallible. He is well aware that one's best efforts in reflecting and deciding can go wrong for a variety of reasons; the person may be factually ill-informed, emotionally immature, emotionally involved in a way that would cloud their judgement, or simply lacking in experience of life. That is why he counsels taking advice, praying, reading well-established authorities. He admits that one's most conscientious judgements may indeed be mistaken, but insists that even so one has a duty to act in accordance with them.[37]

On the other hand, it cannot be said that Newman's lengthy discussions of whether or not he has a duty to accept some important papal documents are a particularly good or edifying example of how his accounts of conscience might work in practice. The considerations he discusses are indeed complex; and it is clear that he finds himself in a particularly awkward position, as a convert, prominent, and yet in some Catholic quarters nonetheless suspect. All the same, at times he gives the impression of being less than candid in his attempt to defend the indefensible, and of resorting to a narrow legalism in an attempt to dodge the central issues.[38] If he were faced with this criticism, what could he say? He would point out that my view, that he was over-cautious and bending over backwards to be loyal, is an opinion which I could no more *prove* than he could prove that he was right. The matter can of course be discussed, and various relevant, or possibly relevant considerations can be advanced. But at the end of the day, there is nothing more one can appeal to than one's honest perception of what one should do in the light of all the various considerations. There is no moral algorithm for reaching correct decisions, nor any series of syllogisms which would not simply assume what has to be established. I might well be right in my view: but if he cannot see that fact, there is nothing more he can say.

In general terms, Newman holds the Aristotelian view that morality depends upon features of our human nature as thinking social animals, since it is those facts about us which will determine how we can live fulfilled lives. A morally admirable life consists in living in such a way that our human capacities at every level are exercised harmoniously to their fullest extent. One can give a general characterization of how such a life would be, in terms of physical and mental health, mature emotional balance, the exercise of our minds both in practical matters and in trying to understand the deepest questions about the nature of our world and the meaning of human life.

The distinctive character of a Christian ethic

In presenting Newman's account of the way in which judgements of conscience are formed, I have made it clear that in my view the framework within which he discusses conscience is heavily indebted to Aristotle. A story is related of another well-known Oxford don, William Spooner, who from 1867 to 1930 was a Fellow and later Warden of New College, that he returned to the pulpit having just finished a sermon, and apologised to the congregation: 'In the places in which I said "Aristotle" I did of course mean "St Paul"'. Could Newman have been guilty of a similar confusion? What few clues Newman gives to the actual content as distinct from the method of his ethics suggest that his views were rather conventional, conforming to the standards of educated Victorian society, much as Aristotle's might be thought to correspond to those of a cultivated Greek of his time. Speaking of pride under the training of modesty, Newman writes,

It is no longer such a restless agent, without definite aim; it has a large field of exertion assigned to it, and it subserves those social interests which it would naturally trouble. It is directed into the channel of frugality, honesty and obedience; and it becomes the very staple of the religion and morality held in honour in a day like our own. It becomes the safeguard of chastity, the guarantee of veracity, in high and low; it is the very household god of society, as at present constituted, inspiring neatness and decency in the servant girl, propriety of carriage and refined manners in her mistress, uprightness, manliness, and generosity in the head of the family.[39]

His sermons, however, as distinct from this lecture to a university audience, are much more biblically based, and their moral tone derives more from the Sermon on the Mount and the parables of Jesus than from Aristotle. He accepts that contemporary social decency has indeed been influenced by the great Western tradition in philosophy, which has also influenced Christian ethics. But this influence, in itself a good thing, can easily mislead even Christians into thinking that in all conscience they need look no further. Newman offers two principal criticisms of contemporary morality. The first is that

> it has taken the brighter side of the Gospel, – its tidings of comfort, its precepts of love; all darker, deeper views of man's condition and prospects being comparatively forgotten. The is the religion *natural* to a civilized age, and well has Satan dressed it and completed it into an idol of the Truth. As Reason is cultivated, the taste formed, the affections and sentiments refined, a general decency and grace will of course spread over the face of society, quite independently of the force of Revelation ... Thus elegance is gradually made the test and standard of virtue, which is no longer thought to possess an intrinsic claim on our hearts, or to exist *further* than it leads to the quiet and comfort of others. Conscience is no longer recognised as an independent arbiter of actions, its authority is explained away.[40]

Conscience is replaced by some theory of a moral sense, and the conviction of guilt and the stern forewarning of future punishment which it should sound in our ears is muted or forgotten altogether. What he calls 'elegant accomplishments' satisfy our minds, as do thoughts of heroism and virtue; but they lack the *impact* of the truly Christian conscience. Hence, his second criticism of contemporary morality is that it has severed its link with God:

> This is what is meant by the peace of a good conscience; it is the habitual consciousness that our hearts are open to God, with a desire that they should be open. It is confidence in God, from a feeling that there is nothing in us which we ought to be ashamed or afraid of.[41]

To sum up. Newman does not have a *theory* of ethics, nor is he particularly intent on correcting the mistaken moral conclusions of many of his contemporaries (though he is scathingly critical of the positions advocated by many academic moralists). The judgements of Newman's conscience are neither radical nor revolutionary. What he emphasizes is the delicacy and sensitivity of the mature conscience to the particular demands of each situation, a view which he finds in Aristotle. There is also what is almost a Kantian strand in Newman. Kant argues that it is a central feature of our moral experience that we believe it to be somehow morally offensive that virtue and happiness so often fail to coincide in our world; and Kant goes on to suggest that we cannot make any satisfying sense of our moral experience unless we see it as pointing beyond our world to God, the guarantor and vindicator of morality.[42] As we shall now see, Newman takes a similar position with much less hesitancy than Kant.

CONSCIENCE AND THE EXISTENCE OF GOD

Newman gives only grudging approval to what might be termed the traditional arguments for the existence of God. His lack of enthusiasm stems not so much from doubts about their validity or force, but from the very limited conclusions about the nature of God to which they can lead. Starting from the kinds of premises which are available to everyone, they conclude only to an impoverished one-size-fits-all notion of God, far removed from the God of Christian belief. Starting from the phenomenon of change and impermanence in the world of our experience, we might well argue for the existence of an uncaused cause, or a prime mover, a necessary being or an artificer of the ordered cosmos. But where is the religious significance of such conclusions?[43]

In his discussion of the history of Arianism, Newman discusses a pastoral strategy which he calls 'The Economy'. It consists in an

> accommodation to the feelings and prejudices of the hearer, in leading him to the reception of a novel or unacceptable doctrine. It professes to be founded in the actual necessity of the case; because those who are strangers to the tone of thought and principles of the speaker cannot at once be initiated into his system, and because they must begin with imperfect views; and therefore if he is to teach them at all, he must put before them large propositions, which he has afterwards to modify, or make assertions which are but parallel or analogous to the truth rather than coincident with it.[44]

One instance of what Newman takes to be an acceptable use of this approach is Paul's speech to the Athenians in the Areopagus, where Paul uses as his starting-point the Athenian altar dedicated to the 'The Unknown God'; Newman goes on to give several more examples, taken from the early Church Fathers. He concedes that this kind of gradual and conciliatory approach can be useful; but he is equally clear that it can be abused if the hearer is led to believe something which is in fact false (as distinct from not being from the start shown where his beliefs are in error). But plainly Newman has no doubt that this approach is of only limited utility, and at most might provide a helpful first step in preaching the gospel. It will necessarily fail to deliver the full riches of the Christian experience of God.[45] He outlines and comments less than enthusiastically on some 'economic' proofs for the existence of God:

> What are the phenomena of the external world, but a divine mode of conveying to the mind the realities of existence, individuality, and the influence of being on being, the best possible, though beguiling the imagination of most men with a harmless but unfounded belief in matter as distinct from impressions on their senses. This is at least the opinion of some philosophers, and whether the particular theory be right or wrong it serves as an illustration here of the great truth which we are considering. Or what, again, as others hold, is the popular argument from final causes but an *Economia* suited to the practical wants of the multitude, as teaching them in the simplest way the active presence of Him, who after all dwells intelligibly, prior to argument, in their heart and conscience? And though, on the mind's first mastering this general principle, it seems to itself at the moment to have cut all the ties that bind it to the universe, and to be floated off upon the ocean of interminable scepticism; yet a true sense of its own weakness brings it back, the instinctive persuasion that it must be intended to rely on something, and that therefore the information given, though philosophically inaccurate, must be practically certain.[46]

This is far from an easy passage to follow. The first argument he mentions seems intended to be that of Bishop Berkeley – though if it is, it seriously misrepresents him – which Newman interprets as trying to show that there are no good grounds for believing in the independent existence of matter or of the material world, because the ultimate reality of everything consists in the fact that it exists in the mind of God. Berkeley's argument is indeed comparatively simple: a material substance just is the total of all possible sensations of that thing; but sensations are properties of conscious minds; hence a material substance exists primarily in consciousness rather than 'out there', independently of any mind. Since we are not constantly perceiving every object in the universe, such things must exist in the mind of God who is aware of them all the time. Berkeley insists that this is more direct than arguments that start from the *independent* existence of matter, which, he claims, lead to scepticism, or to a kind of misleading scientism and ultimately to atheism. But Newman himself is not 'beguiled' by this argument, nor does he take our belief in the existence of matter to be 'unfounded'. I suppose he thinks that these misleading features of the argument are distracting rather than helpful; the simplicity of arguing that all things depend immediately upon the consciousness of God is outweighed by the disadvantages of such an approach.[47]

Again, the traditional argument from design might indeed instil wonder at the orderliness of the universe, but fail to establish the existence of the true origin of that order. Newman echoes Berkeley's fear of the scepticism which can be induced by placing too much emphasis on these 'economic' arguments which claim to start with what everyone already is disposed to believe; but, if my interpretation of the present passage is correct, he thinks that Berkeley himself falls into the very trap he warns us against; Newman takes the same view of William Paley's famous version of the argument from design. Here is Newman criticizing Paley, while claiming that the same criticism does not touch his own view about the immediate experience of God through conscience:

> It is to be considered whether this feeling of conscience as involving a Personal Governor is peculiar e.g. to the Anglo-Saxons. Have the Germans it? Have the Chinese? It may be objected that in arguing from the analogy of an earthly friend, I am committing the same mistake as Paley who argues Design in the universe from the case of a watch. But the cases are not parallel. It is first the very intricacy, vastness, perfection of nature which takes it out of parallelism with human work – and secondly, if there is a God, *design* is a finite idea to include in the notion of him. On the other hand in the argument which I am urging I am not speaking of any attribute or work internal or proper to him, but what I feel towards him. It is hardly any assumption to say that an Infinite Being cannot have a design – It is no assumption to say that he *may* excite certain feelings in us.[48]

The lack of parallelism with human work is just the kind of shortcoming which might in the end lead to scepticism; we know perfectly well that watches or cars have been designed: but, the objection goes, it is not at all so clear that the universe has been designed. Reliance on that parallel is as likely to induce doubt rather than belief. By contrast, Newman thinks that it is quite obvious that if there is a God, we can at once assume that that God can act on us. The mind has a 'true sense of its own weakness' which leads it to abandon arguments like those of Berkeley and Paley and to turn instead to one whose force is more immediately and directly felt. In the experience of conscience, we directly experience the action of God.

Two of the phrases Newman uses in these passages are especially important. One occurs in his claim that God dwells in the human heart and conscience intelligibly, *'prior to argument'*; and the other in his criticism of what he takes to be Berkeley's contrast between the *'unfounded belief'* in matter and the 'impressions on the senses'. A helpful way to understand what Newman is getting at here is to compare him with the recent development of 'Reformed Epistemology' in the hands of such philosophers as Alvin Plantinga and Nicholas Wolterstorff.[49] Newman argues that we do not *infer* the existence of an external world from the experience of our own senses. The experience of our senses just *is* the experience of an external world. Similarly, Plantinga and Wolterstorff both deny that belief in the existence of God is *inferred* from religious experience; they insist that some experiences just are, and are known to be, experiences of God. Wolterstorff writes,

> Deeply embedded in the Reformed tradition is the conviction that a person's belief that God exists may be a justified belief even though that person has not inferred that belief from others of his beliefs which provide good evidence for it. After all, not all the things we are justified in believing are inferred from other beliefs.

Plantinga, in the same vein, says,

> It is not exactly right to say that belief in God is properly basic: more exactly what are properly basic are such propositions as 'God disapproves of what I have done' which self-evidently entail that God exists ... Perhaps such items as 'There are trees' are not properly basic, but instead such propositions as 'I see a tree'.[50]

It is the immediacy of being spoken to by God which is basic. What is striking about these two contemporary authors is the way in which their views mirror those of Newman. Newman does not wish to *infer* that there is a God from the experience of conscience; that is why he explicitly denies that he 'has faith in' his conscience, or in his sense experience:

Sentio ergo sum.[51] To call this an act of argumentation or deduction, and to say that it implies faith in the reasoning process which is denoted by the symbol of the 'ergo' seems to me a fallacy. I do not advance from one proposition to another when I know my existence from being conscious of my feeling, but one and the same act of consciousness brings home to me that which afterwards at leisure I draw out into two propositions, denoting two out of many aspects of the one thing.[52]

Newman takes exactly this line when speaking of conscience:

By conscience I mean the discrimination of acts as worthy of praise or blame. Now, such praise or blame is a phenomenon of my existence, one of those phenomena through which, as I have said, my existence is brought home to me. But the accuracy of praise or blame in the particular case is a matter not of faith, but of judgment. Here then are two senses of the word conscience. It either stands for the act of moral judgment, or for the particular judgment formed. In the former case it is the foundation of religion, in the latter of ethics.[53]

The last sentence is of central importance. The foundation of religion is the experience of being under moral obligation – the lived experience of subjection, not the content of the obligations to which I take myself to be subject. These latter are the starting-points of ethics, and Newman sees very well that they will differ widely from one culture and indeed from one individual to another, and that they are not infrequently false. But the experience of being obliged to a Being far greater than oneself is, he argues, common to us all.

He makes his character Callista express the point as follows:

You may tell me that this dictate is a mere law of my nature, as is to joy or to grieve. I cannot understand this. No, it is the echo of a person speaking to me. Nothing shall persuade me that it does not ultimately proceed from a person external to me. It carries with it the proof of its divine origin. My nature feels towards it as towards a person. When I obey it, I feel a satisfaction; when I disobey, a soreness – just like that I feel in pleasing or offending some revered friend. The echo implies a voice, the voice a speaker. That speaker I love and fear.[54]

In Newman's view, then, the experience of conscience is simply one aspect of a complex experience of God:

I have said – assumed if you will – that this feeling of a *law*, whatever its dictates, and which I call conscience is, not a law of my mind, but one of those phenomena which like thought or consciousness are bound up with or convey to me the idea and the fact of my being or existence. Now I say that, as consciousness of thoughts is a reflex act implying existence (I think therefore I am), so this sensation of conscience is the recognition of an obligation involving the notion of an external being obliging. I say this not from any abstract argument from the force of the terms (e.g. 'A Law implies a Lawgiver') but from the peculiarity of that feeling to which I give the name conscience.[55]

This passage is Newman's attempt to express in more formal philosophical terms ideas which, as he puts it, he has already put in hortatory or popular form.[56] Its key features are as follows:

(1)   There is no *inference* from the experience of moral obligation to the existence of the Supreme Lawgiver, any more than Descartes's *cogito* should be interpreted as an inference. In both cases what is being spelt out is an aspect of a complex experience.

(2)   In what is almost a Wittgensteinian manner, Newman insists that 'as there is no *faith* properly in these exercises of my being, so there is no scepticism about them properly – and it is as absurd to speak of being sceptical of consciousness, reasoning, memory, sensation as to say that I am sceptical whether I am'. Wittgenstein similarly maintains that certain propositions 'hold fast' for us, in that one simply cannot make sense of what it might be to doubt them. There is nothing more basic to which appeal might be made.[57]

Newman claims that these considerations have been his 'chosen proof of that fundamental doctrine for thirty years past'. 'Proof' here, I take it, cannot be used in the sense of a logically conclusive argument nor indeed of an argument at all. His intention is to claim that the experience itself provides the *sufficient rational basis* for other religious beliefs; and some of the most fundamental religious beliefs are simply ways of spelling out aspects of the basic experience itself. Newman points out that 'all men know what the feeling of a bad or good conscience is, though they may differ most widely from each other as to *what* conscience enjoins' and goes on to say that it is the force of conscience rather than the content of any given moral judgement which is important for his position.[58] Judgements of conscience are precisely not like judgements of taste, since judgements of taste do not involve the experience of giving personal offence and of being open to judgement, sanction or punishment. To experience conscience is to experience God as father, lawgiver, and judge.

It is not difficult to find objections to this position, just as there have been many objections to the similar views of Plantinga and Wolterstorff. The fundamental problem is that the argument would seem to make it possible to claim almost anything as a properly basic belief and thereby put it beyond challenge. Hence Plantinga is at pains to defend himself from the criticism that his claim that belief that God has spoken to him is properly basic is no more secure than someone else's belief in voodoo, or that the Great Pumpkin returns every Hallowe'en.

The criticisms of Newman's and Plantinga's position may not be unanswerable. Consider the claim that it makes no sense to doubt that as I write this I am seeing a computer screen in front of me, or the claim that the world has existed for many centuries before I was born. Of course, one could indeed construct unusual situations in which I am not in fact seeing a computer screen but am subject to some carefully planned illusion, or suffering from some severe mental disturbance. So my claim is not *totally* beyond questioning; but neither is it one which in normal circumstances can be rationally questioned. If it were always rationally legitimate to doubt someone's claim to see an object in front of them, then anything one might use to settle the matter would be similarly open to doubt. Moreover, as the second example also makes clear, we do not hold our beliefs as separate items unconnected with one another. They form a network of interconnected beliefs which to a large extent would stand or fall together. One good reason for querying a particular belief would be its incompatibility with a much wider network of beliefs which one does not believe can be open to reasonable challenge. Our beliefs about the existence of the external world, or the age of the earth, or that there are other persons, belong to just such a network. In the light of considerations of this kind, then, it might be argued, as Plantinga does, that the kinds of religious claims which he (and Newman) have in mind should be believed unless there are good reasons for disbelieving them. The burden of proof is on the challenger. Newman and Plantinga need to insist on immediacy, but not upon infallibility.

The key issue, therefore, is whether there are good grounds for questioning Newman's account of his experience of conscience. It would be difficult to suggest that he himself was subject to mental disturbance or delusion. More reasonably, one might want to suggest that the feelings of obligation and sanction of which Newman makes so much are in fact the result of childhood conditioning rather than aspects of a direct experience of God. Where Newman is mistaken, the criticism would go, is not in his claim that he does immediately have such feelings, but that alternative explanations for them might be readily available which would be less contentious than the claim that they were directly experiences of God. He might in turn have replied to this suggestion by saying that such explanations in terms of childhood upbringing would ultimately reduce conscience to no more than a matter of taste or social pressure, for these too have doubtless been inculcated from childhood; whereas it is simply immediately given in the experience of conscience itself that more is at stake than that. It is here that the crucial element in his account lies. He maintains that he is not *arguing* for a particular interpretation of his moral experience over against other possible interpretations, he is claiming that any reflective human will *immediately recognize* the uniquely personal and over-riding importance of moral obligation even while fully accepting that the content of various moral codes may differ widely.

The great advantage of his view, as he sees it, is that it appeals to the whole person and requires no abstruse philosophical skills to understand. The traditional arguments are unhelpfully abstract, disconnected with our immediate experience:

> Why am I to begin with taking up a position not my own, and unclothing my mind of that large outfit of existing thoughts, principles, likings, desires and hopes which make me what I am? If I am asked to use Paley's argument for my own conversion, I say plainly that I do not want to be converted by a smart syllogism; if I am asked to convert others by it, I say plainly I do not care to overcome their reason without touching their hearts.[59]

Newman goes on immediately to describe Paley's argument as 'clear, clever, and powerful', but insists that such purely intellectual considerations about whose cogency someone is asked to give a speculative judgement will never lead to a true conversion, in which someone is committed to acting on the conclusions he has reached, and not just to believing them. Conversion, as he puts it, involves a real, and not just a notional assent. His own preferred route, then, has two related advantages, he believes: the experience of God as Lawgiver on which it is based is universal and cannot seriously be questioned; and appropriating that experience is a true conversion, a transformation of one's life rather than a move in a purely speculative game.

Nonetheless, even philosophers who would perhaps not be convinced by the assertion that the experience of being morally obliged is no more than the product of early education, to be explained in terms of the development of one's superego, might still not wish to concede Newman's case. Once again, the obvious example would be Kant. He writes, along lines quite similar to Newman's:

> Every man has a conscience, and finds himself watched, threatened and, in general, kept in an attitude of respect (of esteem coupled with fear) by an inner judge. And this power watching over the law in him is not something that he himself (arbitrarily) *makes*, but something incorporated in his being. It follows him like his shadow when he plans to escape. He can indeed numb himself or put himself to sleep by pleasures and distractions, but he cannot avoid coming to himself or waking up from time to time, and when he does he hears at once its awful voice. He can at most, in the extremity of corruption, induce himself to pay no more attention to it, but he still cannot help hearing it.
>
> Now this inherent intellectual and (since it is a thought of duty) moral disposition called *conscience* has this peculiarity to it: although its business is an affair of a man with himself, man yet sees himself necessitated by his reason to carry it on as if at the command of *another person* ... Now since such a moral being must also have all power (in heaven and on earth) in order to give his law its due effect (a function essential to the office of judge) and since such an omnipotent moral being is called **God**, conscience must be conceived as a subjective principle of responsibility before God for our deeds. In fact the latter concept will always be contained (even if only in an obscure way) in the moral self-awareness of conscience.[60]

Kant here agrees with Newman about the character of the experience of being under moral obligation. Much more explicitly than many other philosophers, he accepts that the experience of being morally obliged does indeed have the character of coming from outside oneself, of being absolutely authoritative and inescapable, and as deriving from God himself. But there is one crucial difference between Newman's claim and what Kant here is willing to accept. In saying that this experience must be interpreted in terms of God, Kant is not willing to concede either that it is an immediate experience of God, or that a valid argument can be constructed to show that it is an experience of God. He denies that this experience 'entitles a man to *posit* such a Supreme Being as really existing outside himself'.

This highlights the double difficulty in Newman's position. Many modern philosophers would be much less willing than was Kant to concede that the experience of conscience involves the feeling of being subject to a Supreme Lawgiver; and even if they were, would certainly not concede Newman's claim that the experience of conscience is directly an experience of God, and that this can be known without any argument at all. Newman might reply that Kant is perhaps wrong to downplay the experience of conscience for the reasons he does. Kant's reasons go back to his general epistemology and the kind of defence he tried to offer against a Humean empiricism which, in Kant's view, would have totally undermined the achievements of Enlightenment science. Kant believed that he had vindicated the appeal to causation in explaining the patterns of events in the world, but that his vindication did not extend beyond the realm of our possible *sense* experiences; in particular, then, since what someone takes to be an experience of God would not be a *sense* experience, it could not legitimately be used to vindicate causal arguments to establish the existence of God, nor could it make sense of the notion of God's causal activity. In reply, of course, Newman's defenders would try to point out that Kant might have difficulty in showing that he can consistently claim both that there is such an immediate experience of the authoritative voice of conscience while denying that there can be an immediate experience of God, which is no less immediate for not being a sense experience.

CONCLUSION

The salient feature of both Newman's discussions of conscience is the degree of reliance which he is willing to place on it. Both in ethics and in religion he does not, I believe, deny that such reliance is often called into question. On the narrowly religious point he believes that the questioning would have no rational basis and that the reflective person already knows that it does not; on the ethical point, although the individual's judgements of what ought to be done in particular circumstances are indeed often mistaken, there is no higher court of appeal than to the insight into the individual case on the part of someone who is well informed, well trained, and emotionally balanced. Consistently with this, Newman exhibits something of a distrust of philosophical systems. His dismissal of the various academic systems of ethics is a corollary of his insistence that he wishes to deal with things, not notions, with the concrete particular and not just the relationships between ideas. His description of even valid arguments in philosophy as 'smart syllogisms' and his preference for experience recognized as religious is another aspect of the same approach.

It would be a mistake, however, to conclude that Newman is in some deep sense anti-intellectual. The whole project of the *Grammar* is to argue that a proper understanding of how we think cannot normally be reduced to the formal structures of logic or mathematics, and that the attempt to do so is highly misleading. It is in this sense that I suggest that there is a parallel between Newman and the later Wittgenstein. The starting-point for philosophy is to be found in how we as a matter of fact talk and think and reflect. Our actual practice has to be taken seriously, both in ethics and in religion, and not forced into some epistemological straitjacket, as if deductive logic were the only method of reasoned thinking. This is of course not to say that Newman's own conclusions, whether in ethics or in religion, are somehow beyond rational assessment; nor would he for a moment claim that they are. But he is right to insist that the notion of evidence, and the relationship between evidence and interpretation, is often richer and more complex than in our analytical moments we are tempted to allow.

Notes

1. *Diff.*, ii:249.
2. *Diff.*, ii:248–9.
3. Jeremy Bentham, *An Introduction to the Principles of Morals and Legislation*, ed. J. H. Burns and H. L. A. Hart (Oxford: Oxford University Press, 1996), 11.
4. Thomas Hobbes, *Leviathan*, ed. A. P. Martinich (Peterborough: Broadview Press, 2002), 118 (I, §15).
5. 'Moral virtue is concerned with passions and actions, and in these whereas one can go wrong either by excess or by deficiency, it is what is in the middle that is praised and is right.' See Aristotle's *Nicomachean Ethics*, II, 6, 1106b24–6. Hereafter referred to as *NE*. Unless otherwise indicated, all translations of the texts of the *Ethics* are the author's own. For an extensive discussion of the *Ethics*, including the texts under consideration here, see Gerard J. Hughes, *Aristotle on Ethics* (London: Routledge, 2002). What Aristotle intends by 'in the middle' is considerably more complex than this text might suggest; but it is nonetheless clear that it is some version of this view that Hobbes is attacking, and some version of it which Newman wishes to defend.
6. *Diff.*, ii:249–50.
7. *Diff.*, ii:247–8.
8. 'Conscience is the practical judgement or dictate of reason by which we judge what *hic et nunc* is to be done as good, or avoided as evil' (*Diff.*, ii:256) paraphrases St Thomas Aquinas, *Summa Theologiae*, I, 79, 13.
9. *NE*, I, 3, 1095a2–11.
10. *NE*, II, 1, 1103b24–5.

11. *Diff.*, ii:253–4.
12. *Diff.*, ii:257.
13. Aristotle's account of *phronēsis* is to be found in his *Nicomachean Ethics*, VI. I offer what I hope is an accessible commentary in Hughes, *Aristotle on Ethics*, ch. 5. For the importance of moral education, see *NE*, II, 1, 1103b21–5.
14. *G.A.*, 265.
15. *G.A.*, 264.
16. *G.A.*, 269.
17. *G.A.*, 277–8.
18. *G.A.*, 321.
19. P. J. Fitzpatrick, 'Newman's *Grammar* and the Church Today', in David Nicholls and Fergus Kerr, OP (eds.), *John Henry Newman: Reason, Rhetoric and Romanticism* (Bristol: The Bristol Press, 1991), 109–34.
20. *G.A.*, 277.
21. 'Unfortunately, to think about a special faculty is particularly tempting if we have defined the faculty in terms of its successful exercise – obviously so, because we then seem to be awarding ourselves an infallible means of drawing conclusions, do we but employ it.' Fitzpatrick, 'Newman's *Grammar* and the Church Today', 115.
22. *G.A.*, 345, 353.
23. *G.A.*, 350.
24. *NE*, VI, 1143b11–14. This is the translation of Aristotle provided by Newman in *G.A.*, 341–2.
25. *G.A.*, 341–2.
26. *G.A.*, 354.
27. *NE*, VI, 11 (1143a22–b5). This passage is central to an understanding of Aristotle's account of *phronēsis*. The interpretation of it is, however, still controversial. A convenient summary of the discussion is to be found in D. Bostock, *Aristotle's Ethics* (Oxford: Oxford University Press, 2002), 88–98.
28. *Diff.*, ii:243–4 (my italics).
29. *Diff.*, ii:242, 243.
30. *Diff.*, ii:256.
31. *NE*, VI, 12, 1144a26–b1.
32. *NE*, VI, 12, 1144a6–9.
33. *G.A.*, 356.
34. *G.A.*, 354–5.
35. For a very careful and much more nuanced discussion of all such issues, see Jonathan Dancy, *Morality Without Principles* (Oxford: Oxford University Press, 2004).
36. *NE*, VI, 8, 1142a30.
37. See *D.A.*, 257–61.
38. See the discussion of the authoritativeness of specific documents in the *Letter to the Duke of Norfolk*, chs 6–10; see *Diff.*, 262–347.
39. *Idea*, 207 (Discourse 8).
40. *P.S.*, i:311–12. The sermon is entitled 'The Religion of the Day'.

41. *P.S.*, v:319. The sermon is entitled 'The Thought of God, the Stay of the Soul'.

42. Immanuel Kant, *Critique of Practical Reason*, nos. 265–9.

43. See the passages mentioned by Edward Sillem in *P.N.*, ii:32 note 6.

44. *Ari.*, 71–2.

45. Edward Sillem points out that this was not Newman's original position. Newman originally held that consideration of the experience of conscience pointed only to an impersonal deity. See *U.S.*, 18–19, 22–3. The point is already somewhat weaker in *P.S.*, i:193; and *P.S.*, xi:11, 18, 64–7, 217.

46. *Ari.*, 75–6.

47. Bishop George Berkeley, *Principles of Human Knowledge*, in A. A. Luce and T. E. Jessop (eds.), *The Works of George Berkeley* (London: Thomas Nelson, 1949), vol. ii, Part I, §133–4.

48. *P.N.*, ii:60 (*Proof of Theism*).

49. See, for instance, Alvin Plantinga. 'Is Belief in God Properly Basic?' in *Nous* 15 (1981), and Nicholas Wolterstorff, 'Is Reason Enough?' *The Reformed Journal* 31 (1981). These are conveniently reprinted, with comments from Robert Pargetter and a dissenting article by Stewart Goetz, in R. Douglas Geivert and Brendan Sweetman (eds.), *Contemporary Perspectives in Religious Epistemology* (Oxford: Oxford University Press, 1992). The quotation from Plantinga occurs on p. 138, that from Wolterstorff on p. 149 of Geivert and Sweetman.

50. Plantinga in fact refers to a list of ten propositions of which the one I have mentioned about offending God is only one. I have abbreviated his remarks while leaving the overall sense and syntax unchanged.

51. Literally, 'I feel, therefore I am'.

52. *P.N.*, ii:35. The passage forms part of a series of reflections entitled *Proof of Theism*.

53. *P.N.*, ii:47 (*Proof of Theism*).

54. *Call.*, 244.

55. *P.N.*, ii:59 (*Proof of Theism*).

56. See *P.N.*, ii:51 where Newman refers to *U.S.*, 17–19; *P.N.*, ii:53 where he refers to *O.S.*, 64–5; and *P.N.*, ii:59 where he cites the passage from *Callista* quoted above (*Call.*, 314–15).

57. *P.N.*, ii:37 (*Proof of Theism*). Compare Wittgenstein, *On Certainty* (Oxford: Oxford University Press, 1969), 191–234 with *G.A.*, 318: 'Yet, though our certitude of the fact is quite as clear, we should not think it unnatural to say that the insularity of Great Britain is as good as demonstrated or that none but a fool expects never to die. Phrases indeed such as these are sometimes used to express a shade of doubt, but it is enough for my purpose if they are also used *when doubt is altogether absent*' (my italics). See also Cyril Barrett, 'Newman and Wittgenstein on the Rationality of Religious Belief', in Ian Ker (ed.), *Newman and Conversion* (Edinburgh: T & T Clark, 1997), 89–99.

58. *P.N.*, ii:49 (*Proof of Theism*).

59. *G.A.*, 424–5. The reference to Paley's argument is, of course, to the example he gives of finding a watch, whose complexity and purposiveness leads one to infer the existence of a designer.

60. Immanuel Kant, *The Doctrine of Virtue: Part II of the Metaphysic of Morals*, trans. Mary J. Gregor (New York: Harper & Row, 1964), 104–5.

Further reading

Alston, William P. *Perceiving God*. Ithaca, NY: Cornell University Press, 1991.

Barrett, Cyril. 'Newman and Wittgenstein on the Rationality of Religious Belief', in Ian Ker (ed.), *Newman and Conversion*. Edinburgh: T & T Clark, 1997, 89–99.

Boekraad, Adrian J., and Henry Tristram. *The Argument from Conscience to the Existence of God according to J. H. Newman*. Louvain: Nauwelaerts, 1961.

Engberg-Pedersen, Troels. *Aristotle's Theory of Moral Insight*. Oxford: Clarendon Press, 1983.

Fields, Stephen. 'Image and Truth in Newman's Moral Argument for God', *Louvain Studies* 24 (1999), 191–210.

Finnis, John. 'Conscience in the *Letter to the Duke of Norfolk*', in Ian Ker (ed.), *Newman After a Hundred Years*. Oxford: Clarendon Press, 1990, 401–18.

Hughes, Gerard J. *Aristotle on Ethics*. London: Routledge Philosophy Guidebooks, 2002.

Newman, John Henry. *The Philosophical Notebook*. Ed. Edward Sillem. Louvain: Nauwelaerts, 1969–70.

Nicholls, David and Fergus Kerr (eds.). *John Henry Newman: Reason, Rhetoric and Romanticism*. Bristol: The Bristol Press, 1991.

Plantinga, Alvin. *Warranted Christian Belief*. Oxford: Oxford University Press, 1988.

Rorty, Amélie Oksenberg (ed.). *Essays on Aristotle's Ethics*. Berkeley: University of California Press, 1989.

11 Theology in the university

GERARD LOUGHLIN

Theology has no place in the university of the twenty-first century. She is out of place in such a place, a pre-Enlightenment relic, an uncomfortable reminder of what the modern university was meant to abolish. As long ago as 1772, Baron d'Holbach, in *Le Bon sens*, declared the 'science' of theology to be 'a continual insult to human reason',[1] and reason is the bedrock of the modern university, which is home to all true science. Theology is no science at all but a chimera of the imagination,[2] an aberration in the place that banishes all such fantasies. Immanuel Kant, in his late satire, *The Conflict of the Faculties* (1798), was less dismissive than d'Holbach, allowing theology her queenly place in the university, with even philosophy as a handmaid. But whether carrying 'her lady's torch before or her train behind' he would not say.[3]

D'Holbach's antipathy to religion is still with us more than 250 years later. Richard Dawkins still opposes science to religion, reason to faith.[4] Though Dawkins, as the Charles Simonyi Professor of the Public Understanding of Science at Oxford, teaches in a university of medieval foundation, he rightly understands it as committed to the tenets of the modern research university, the idea of which came into being at the turn of the eighteenth century, and was given form in the University of Berlin (1810). Wilhelm von Humboldt is usually credited with establishing Berlin University, but he gave form to ideas that were generally abroad and had already affected the universities of Halle (1694) and Göttingen (1737). These were the ideas of enlightened men like d'Holbach, but more importantly of Kant, Johann Gottlieb Fichte and Friedrich Schleiermacher. It is one of the ironies of this story that the man who would become the father of modern theology was himself responsible for securing the very institution that, while it was required to teach theology, was ideologically disposed to despise the theology it taught as at best unscientific and at worst superstition.[5] Yet Schleiermacher did secure theology a place in the research university, if at a price.

The price that theology paid was to become like its fellow disciplines, a scientific servant of the State. Theology became *wissenschaftliche*

Theologie and its primary role was the preparation of pastors for service in the national church, 'tools of government' contracted to teach what the government wanted.[6] Of course this arrangement was not unique. Church and State were also conjoined in England, with university theology serving the one through the other, providing clerics for the shepherding of the monarch's subjects.[7] And theology had always considered herself a science, indeed the *regina scientiarum*. But as such she was an Aristotelian undertaking, working from axioms she had *received*.[8] Modern science is an altogether different creature. Enlightenment *Wissenschaft* was answerable to nothing other than reason, which is 'by its nature free and admits of no command to hold something as true (no imperative "Believe!" but only a free *credo*)'.[9] Moreover, it sought to understand all things through understanding the 'principles and foundations of all knowledge'.[10] It sought a total, unified comprehension, an *encyclopaedic* science.[11]

That which reason taught was at first less restricted than it later became. *Wissenschaft* included the social sciences (*Geisteswissenschaften*) along with the natural, and could encompass any discipline that aspired to 'rigorous, systematic enquiry'.[12] It was only as the nineteenth century progressed that the ambit of *Wissenschaft* was increasingly restricted to those 'hard' sciences that disdained tradition, being solely governed by reason and experience (repeatable experiment), and pretending to *Voraussetzungslosigkeit* (presuppositionlessness).[13] Many have pointed out that there is no thinking without presupposition, that reason requires some kind of faith in order to get a purchase on the world.[14] But this would be of little avail to theology in the modern university. Theology ceased to be a science when 'science' became an ideology.

Theology kept its place in the university, but only by becoming something other than it had been.[15] As *Wissenschaft* it still served the Church, but through a State organization. It still answered to the Church's faith, but as a science that sought to know the mind of God through a self-sufficient reason. It refused 'unfathomable mystery'. That last is Fichte at the beginning of the nineteenth century, who held that there was no place in the university for a science that could not understand and penetrate 'to its ultimate ground' that which it was given to think.[16] At the end of the century, Adolf von Harnack would welcome theology's separation from the Church, as only thus enabled to 'contribute to the edifice of modern German science and culture'.[17] We may think that the scientific refiguration of theology has itself been refigured, or was weakened or never took hold in many universities. But for some, that which university theology has become is so unlike what it was and should be that it has ceased to be theology at all. Most forcefully, Gavin

D'Costa declares that university theology is a masquerade. 'Theology, properly understood, cannot be taught and practiced within the modern university.'[18] In this D'Costa agrees with the French *philosophes* and the German idealists.

In the light of this story it is instructive to turn from Prussia to Britain, and from Protestant to Catholic theology, and again consider John Henry Newman's adventures in the idea and practice of the university. For unlike those who think that theology has no place in the university, or at least in the modern university,[19] Newman argued that there is no university where there is no theology.

MIXED EDUCATION

When Newman wrote on the university he treated of its 'essence'.[20] But he also wrote about particular universities. He wrote about the university he loved, Oxford; about the university he detested, London; and about the university he was to bring into being in Dublin. He also had in mind the Catholic University of Louvain (1425; but closed in 1797 and reopened in 1834), in which he saw a model for Ireland's Catholic University, and with whose rector he was to correspond. It was in April 1851 that Dr Paul Cullen, Archbishop of Armagh, wrote to Newman seeking advice on the setting up of a Catholic university in Ireland, and invited him to Dublin to give a series of lectures 'against Mixed Education'.[21] Shortly afterwards Cullen met Newman and invited him to become the founding rector of the Catholic University of Ireland.[22] Newman accepted, but had to wait until 1854 for his formal installation as rector.[23]

The lectures that inaugurated the new venture were given on successive Mondays in May and early June 1852. The last five were not delivered but published as pamphlets, as were the first five, with all of them bound into a book in the following year – though it bore the previous year's date – and published as *Discourses on the Scope of University Education* (1852). The lectures were written during a period of considerable strain for Newman, not only because of the university undertaking but also because of Newman's imminent trial for libel. He was accused of defaming Giacinto Achilli (b.1803) – an ex-Dominican Don Juan, whose supposed confinement by the Inquisition was presented to the English public as the suffering of a Protestant hero at the hands of the old Roman enemy, that was again astir with the re-establishment of the Catholic hierarchy in November 1850.[24] Newman feared that his 'Irish engagement would be completely disarranged by a year's imprisonment'.[25] In the event the trial did not come to court until late June, after Newman had delivered the first five of his lectures, but then he had to wait until November to be found guilty. However, after failing to secure a retrial, he was only fined £100; the press generally conceded him the moral victory.[26] But it was throughout this latter period that he was working on the *Discourses*; the 'most painful of all' his books to write.[27] Tellingly it was dedicated to those who through their 'prayers and penances ... stubborn efforts ... [and] munificent alms' had 'broken for him the stress of a great anxiety'.

It is thus a testament to Newman's facility that his discourses on the university are so beguiling. For many, the idea of a university is Newman's idea. It is one he subsequently enlarged as he sought to make the idea a reality. In 1859 he published a further ten *Lectures and Essays on University Subjects*, and it was these he added to the earlier discourses – though with the original fifth and appendix of historical examples removed – to produce *The Idea of a University* in 1873.[28] But by then Newman had ceased to be the rector of the Catholic University in Dublin. He had come to feel that he lacked the support of both the Irish and English hierarchies. The university was 'abused in Ireland for being English, and neglected in England for being Irish'.[29] In April 1857 Newman signalled his intention to resign, and did so on 12 November 1858. But the idea of the university remained even if its shadow faded.[30]

Newman had been invited to lecture against 'mixed education'; not against the mixing of the sexes, but against the mixing of Catholic and Protestant men.[31] Newman had to address this issue, even if his own interest – and that of later readers – was in the university considered 'in the *abstract* and in its idea'.[32] Thus Newman writes sometimes of the 'university' and sometimes of the 'Catholic university', and sometimes the distinction is lost to view.[33] There is a tension between Newman's interest in the essence of the university, and the demands of the context in which he explored that essence. He was required to champion the idea of a Catholic university against the background of the Queen's Colleges, which had been conceived by Robert Peel, and established by 1849 in Belfast, Cork and Galway.[34] They were State funded and open to all. They answered to what Newman saw as the temptation of the Catholic but 'liberal' statesman. 'Since his schools cannot have *one* faith, he determines, as the best choice left to him, that they shall have *none*.'[35] And in Ireland many lay Catholics and some clerics – including until his death in February 1852 the Archbishop of Dublin, Daniel Murray[36] – were in favour of the Queen's Colleges, since what the 'respectable' laity wanted for their sons was an education that would fit them for professional life,[37] while many nationalists hoped that the Queen's Colleges would foster a united Irish culture.

Newman of course was not opposed to partisan education, having as an Anglican defended Oxford's right to exclude Dissenters when their admittance had been proposed in 1834. But now he was to favour a Catholic partisanship. This he did by arguing for the necessity of theology in any university worth the name, and so the necessity for a Catholic university, since Catholic theology in a 'mixed' university was unthinkable. Newman worried about the reception of his argument, but reported the success of his first lecture,[38] and his pleasant surprise with the 'great cleverness of the Irish', which far surpassed anything he had seen elsewhere. 'The very ticket-taker in the room followed my arguments, and gave an analysis of the discourse afterwards.'[39]

Newman began his argument by defining a university as a place for *'teaching* universal *knowledge'*.[40] Many would be unhappy with this definition, which seems to suppose a grasp of universal knowledge that is now, if not already in Newman's day, impossible; and which seems to exclude research, and so – today – resource. The first concern is easily met, for Newman did not suppose it possible for any one person to gain universal knowledge. Nor did he suppose that it was possible for any one university to teach it, but allowed that universal knowledge might have to be pursued across a range of institutions, and so the lack of a particular subject might not signal a disaster for the university.

But Newman does not allow that a university – a real university – would give up on the *idea* of teaching universal knowledge. Thus if a university lacked some departments, it would understand itself to be but a partial realization of the true university, in which 'all branches of knowledge were presupposed or implied, *and none omitted on principle'*.

Newman's seeming denial of research in the university is more curious, for surely all real universities are 'research universities', as exemplified by the University of Berlin? But for Newman, the object of the university is the 'diffusion and extension of knowledge rather than the advancement'. If the object of the university is 'scientific and philosophical discovery', why should it have students?[41] Newman's idea of the researcher is somewhat arcane, since he imagines a secluded individual, free from the distractions of society, living in a cave or tower, or wandering among trees.[42] No doubt many professors aspire to such an idyll, and wish for nothing more than to be left alone with their laptop and books, but it hardly matches to the requirements of most modern research, especially in the social and physical sciences. Nor does it really match with either Newman's imagined university or the actual Catholic

University of Ireland, as it functioned under Newman's leadership. For in Newman's university the student is to breathe a 'pure and clear atmosphere of thought', which is produced through the 'assemblage of learned men', who, 'zealous for their own sciences, and rivals of each other, are brought, by familiar intercourse and for the sake of intellectual peace, to adjust together the claims and relation of their respective subjects of investigation'.[43] It is unlikely that such men would not engage in research. And so it proved in the realization of Newman's idea, when, for example, the university's journal, *Atlantis*, began to publish scientific research in 1858. Indeed, Newman's idea of the university became so capacious that he likened it to the ordered multitudes of the Roman empire, a vast 'sphere of philosophy *and research*'.[44]

Newman imagines that knowledge is advanced through the work of institutions that may be connected with universities, as subordinate 'congregations', but need not be. Such independent or semi-independent institutions contemplate science, not students.[45] The object of the university, on the other hand, is to take students and turn them into 'something or other', to mould their characters, form their habits, educate their hearts through educating their minds.[46] The university imparts knowledge, not just for its own sake, but also in order to create a 'culture of the intellect'.[47]

Newman did not foresee a time of mass education in Britain, when there would be more university students studying theology and religious studies than were studying across all subjects in his day, and when more than half of them would be women. Newman's students were to become 'gentlemen', shorthand for cultivated minds. Newman was concerned with the strengthening, knitting together and toning of boys' intellects;[48] turning youth into men of 'good sense, sobriety of thought, reasonableness, candour, self-command, and steadiness of view ... entering with comparative ease into any subject of thought, and of taking up with aptitude any science or profession'.[49] Equipped with these transferable skills, a gentleman would be able to withstand the 'random theories and imposing sophistries and dashing paradoxes' of modern culture, promulgated, in Newman's day, by the 'periodical literature'.[50] If we allow that such skills are not the preserve of gentlemen alone, then Newman's vision can still speak to our condition. His university is a place where universal knowledge is taught in order to create subjects with the skills of divination and discernment, the ability to reason and judge, in short, to exercise the ancient virtue of prudence (*prudentia*), that is still necessary for combating contemporary sophistries and seeking out truth.[51]

THEOLOGY IN ITS PLACE

That the university should make some pretence to universal knowledge would seem implicit in its name, Newman suggests, even though its name is more properly derived not from the cosmos but from the corporate body of scholars and students in which the cosmos is known. But it is a nice conceit, as Newman more or less admits.[52] The university is to be that place in which the universe is thought, and given this aspiration it follows that theology must be one of its subjects, since theology, for Newman, is a branch of knowledge. There can be no pruning of the university tree. Thus Newman asks if it is 'logically consistent in a seat of learning to call itself a University and to exclude Theology from the number of its studies?'[53] Newman of course was aware that there were such universities in his day, as in ours.[54] But for Newman, a university without theology is either trading under a false name or assuming that the 'province of Religion is very barren of real knowledge'.[55]

This of course is the assumption of all who have opposed university theology, from d'Holbach to Dawkins. Newman was also aware of a practical atheism amongst intellectuals, which he ascribed to a growing tendency to view religion as a matter of sentiment rather than reason, a tendency that began with the Protestant Reformation and was in his day promulgated by the 'Liberal or Latitudinarian'. When such a tendency prevails it is as unreasonable 'to demand for Religion a chair in a University, as to demand one for fine feeling, sense of honour, patriotism, gratitude, maternal affection, or good companionship, proposals which would be simply unmeaning'.[56] Newman had a profound, ironic insight into theology's plight, its reduction to mere opinion in a sceptical climate.[57] Dawkins is hardly more eloquent than Newman in describing the (supposed) futility of pursuing the divine: 'A small insect, a wasp or a fly, is unable to make his way through the pane of glass; and his very failure is the occasion of greater violence in his struggle than before'.[58]

Newman was well aware that the object of theological knowledge is of a different order from those of other sciences,[59] and that the way to such knowledge differs in part from the ways of those other sciences, but he was in no doubt that theology is knowledge, and so demands its place in the university that teaches universal knowledge. And the object of universal knowledge is truth, which Newman glosses as 'facts and their relations, which stand towards each other pretty much as subjects and predicates in logic'. These facts include everything, from 'the internal mysteries of the Divine Essence down to our own sensations and consciousness ... from the most glorious seraph to the vilest and most noxious of reptiles'. And all these facts hang together, forming 'one large system or complex fact', and it is the knowledge of this truth, which the human mind seeks to contemplate. We cannot take in this single fact as a whole, but must traverse it slowly, short-sightedly, by means of our sciences, which give us 'partial views or abstractions', which sometimes look to the horizon, and sometimes focus on the ground beneath our feet. Moreover, the sciences show us things by showing us their relations, and so they never tell us everything that may be told, nor escape the medium of their telling.[60]

The labour of knowledge is divided among the sciences, and when 'certain sciences are away' we have a 'defective apprehension' of the truth.[61] All sciences are needed for the seeking of truth, in the university where it is sought. Thus Newman's view is of a unified existence, of creation in relation to its creator, which must be studied by us – as particular, limited creatures – through a myriad of interrelated sciences: a truly interdisciplinary labour for the truth. And this common labour includes the co-dependence of theology on other disciplines, through which in part it learns its own proper object through their learning of the world that the creator has made and makes to be.[62] On Newman's account, theology does not appear as the 'queen of the sciences', but as the first amongst equals, for the truth that is to be known in theology is a fundamental condition for all knowledge.[63] When Newman does invoke the idea of a ruling science, an architectonic 'science of sciences', he gives it the name of philosophy.[64] This philosophy is not so much a body of knowledge, distinct from other sciences, as the cast of mind by which those sciences are apprehended and thus united. It is 'an intellectual ... grasp of many things brought together in one'.[65] It is not the unity of a general theory of everything, but of a community. Indeed, it is the university as such, in its universal scope and *idea*. '[I]t is the home, it is the mansion-house, of the goodly family of Sciences, sisters all, and sisterly in their mutual dispositions.'[66]

> Not Science only, not Literature only, not Theology only, neither abstract knowledge simply nor experimental, neither moral nor material, neither metaphysical nor historical, but all knowledge whatever, is taken into account in a University, as being the special seat of that large Philosophy, which embraces and locates truth of every kind, and every method of attaining it.[67]

But today the university seems a less sisterly place, and even when more sororal, theology is the one sister with whom the others are less willing to play. The 'Liberal or Latitudinarian' view prevails, and theology is seen as at best 'fine feeling' and so unreasonable in its demand for a university place.[68] Of course theology has responded by becoming less the learning of God and more the learning of the learning of God, the history of the texts, beliefs and practices of those who thereby learn God. 'Religious studies' was precisely developed in order to offer a social-scientific approach to religion that would be acceptable in the modern university. And Newman allowed for just such an approach, for teaching about religion as a 'branch of knowledge'.[69] This would be an historical rather than doctrinal study, providing the Catholic who was not reading theology with a knowledge of his faith sufficient to 'keep up a conversation' with educated Protestants.[70] By extension this is a 'religious studies' that would today fit any student with a knowledge of religious peoples, and the problems attendant upon their study. But of course Newman also argued for theology proper, for 'natural' and 'revealed' theology:[71] the 'science of God'.[72]

Yet Newman does little to defend his claim that theology is knowledge. He thinks it sufficient to note that unbelief rests upon a 'mere assumption', that philosophy has yet to show the unattainability of 'religious truth', and that the *onus probandi* lies with those who think otherwise.[73] Newman's argument for theology in a Catholic university is uncontroversial, but he presses to an argument for theology in the university as such,[74] and for this to have its full force in a world grown wary if not weary of religion, we have to press for the university as that place which seeks to ask the question of the universe *without limit*.[75] Christian faith – as indeed other faiths – presses to this question even though it seemingly already has an answer in God, for 'God' is more the name of a question than of an answer. 'God' is a name for the final incomprehensibility of the universe, for the mystery of existence as such, when recognized as such;[76] and that this mystery comes to us, and for us, in Jesus, is the venture of the 'research project' named 'church'. To exclude the rigorous thinking of this venture from the university would be to exclude a tradition of knowledge from the very place that aspires – or should aspire – to think the totality of the given.[77]

THE UNIVERSITY WITHOUT AN IDEA

Today universities are very different from those that Newman knew and imagined. Today they are more likely to teach 'Shakespeare and Milton' than 'Virgil and Horace'.[78] Today they admit women and are urged to be engines of social mobility. But in other ways they are surprisingly similar. They still train up people for the government and judiciary, the clubs that rule a country. And remarkably nearly all are examples of what was once London University's prerogative, the university as 'bazaar, or pantechnicon',[79] enticing students with the variety and mix of its wares. Today's university no longer offers a unified education, for there is little consensus as to what this might entail, little sense of a shared culture for which it might fit people. Today universities offer vocational courses, but little or no sense of vocation, of being *called* to a way of life, let alone a way of life for others, and through others for God. Today universities seek merely to meet the tastes of their customers and the whims of their paymasters. Today the university lies in ruins.

This at least is the view of Bill Readings, who argues that the university of excellence has replaced that of culture – Newman's university – and that of reason, from which Newman's idea emerged.[80] The university of excellence is the university without an idea, since it pursues only excellence rather than any excellent thing. Excellence as such is a null category, and so answers to the interests of global capital, which turns all it touches into the means of its own acceleration. The university of culture served the interests of the State, inculcating a national culture that it both formed and reflected. But with the decline of the nation-state and the rise of transnational corporations and multiculturalism there is little by way of any agreed culture to reproduce,[81] and the civilization that Newman linked with the West is now utterly mercantile.[82] For Newman the university exists to form discerning minds, and the study by which this is done is not as important as its doing, though Newman favoured the arts, the classics, since their efficacy for the 'real and proper cultivation of the mind' is shown by 'long experience' while that of the 'experimental sciences' is yet to be proved.[83] But now no university aspires to cultivate its students, but to make them as flexible as the market requires, by fitting them with the requisite skills for the 'knowledge economy'. The university tempts with the promise of increased earnings, and is itself judged by its contribution to the flourishing of the market. Research is judged by its profitability. Capital is now the universal that the university serves.

Stanley Fish agrees with Readings's analysis, but unlike Readings he welcomes the university of excellence.[84] For all ideas can flourish in the university without an idea, and as an administrator, Fish's role is to see that they flourish excellently. But beyond that he has no preferences, no idea as to what the university is for. His motto: 'Have Skills, Will Travel'.[85] And in such a context, theology no longer has to justify itself. It just has to do what it does excellently.[86] The Enlightenment project is vanquished in the university without an idea. For all truths (and falsehoods) may be spoken when truth has no value, and only money matters.[87] But this then is the objection that Stanley Hauerwas raises against Fish's blithe acceptance of the postmodern condition: that he elides the university's complicity in producing subjects for the modern state and corporate interest.[88] The university without an idea becomes a university without questioning.

There is a sense in which Newman envisaged a university without an idea, but never one without questioning. Newman said that if he had to choose between a university that awarded degrees for knowledge gained and a university that simply brought 'young men together for three or four years', he would choose the latter; the university that 'did nothing'.[89] For such a university – as Oxford showed – better produces men of natural virtue, business acumen and cultivated taste; it better produces men who can 'subdue the earth' and 'domineer over Catholics'.[90] This is a university that reproduces a culture through association; but in the ideal university – in Dublin rather than Oxford – the culture reproduced is also one of questioning, of learning to see and say things as they are, 'of discriminating between truth and falsehood ... of arranging things according to their real value, and ... of building up ideas'.[91] In this Newman is as much a father to the university of culture as he is to the university envisaged by thinkers as different as Bill Readings and Alasdair MacIntyre.

Readings's vision of the university is bleak, since for him the national cultures (English or Irish) that Newman's universities reproduced are no more, or fast disappearing, and there is no possibility of giving 'culture back its reason', of retrieving the *Wissenschaft* that was to unify a people through totalizing its knowledge.[92] We necessarily live amongst the ruins of the past, and so the university becomes the question of those ruins, the place where culture and the university itself are in question, where 'we' are in question.[93] The university becomes a 'dissensual community', where traditions of enquiry are pursued beside one another, in dialogue with one another, but without the illusion of 'transparent communication', of an identity already achieved.[94] The university is not an 'ideal speech situation'. Unlike Newman, Readings will not say that the university pursues truth (though he would have it pursue the truth of our dissensus), but his blunt assertion that the business of the university is 'evaluation, judgement and self-questioning'[95] recalls Newman's cultivation of discernment. Moreover Readings's understanding of people has a religious ring to it, as he himself notes.[96] People, for Readings, are given as singularities within networks of infinite obligation, to the extent that they are even responsible for the acts of their forebears.[97] This gives Readings's university a decidedly 'ethical atmosphere',[98] and seems to suggest that even a university of dissensus might constitute a kind of culture.

Alasdair MacIntyre has a similarly bleak view of our condition, and a surprisingly similar account of the university as a place of learned disagreement. For MacIntyre the university is 'where conceptions of and standards of rational justification are elaborated, put to work in the detailed practices of enquiry, and themselves rationally evaluated, so that only from the university can the wider society learn how to conduct its own debates, practical or theoretical, in a rationally defensible way'. And for this the university must be a place 'where rival and antagonistic views of rational justification ... are afforded the opportunity both to develop their own enquiries, in practice and in the articulation of the theory of that practice, and to conduct their intellectual and moral warfare'.[99] MacIntyre is no doubt happier than Readings to imagine that the 'intellectual and moral warfare' he envisages might issue in some kind of dialectical progress, but both are agreed that there is no unified culture for the university to reproduce, that it must reproduce disunity, and that this might be an ethical endeavour.[100]

Newman imagined a university in pursuit of universal knowledge. This was not the universality of the Enlightenment, which resides in the knowing subject who would comprehend all things encyclopaedically, but of an older tradition that looked to know the universe, and through the universe, the universe's creator, who alone has universal knowledge. The unity of all resides in that which is sought, not in those who seek, who can only participate in a 'science' that always exceeds them. This tradition is an affront to human pride, but not a denial of reason. Indeed faith demands reason because it holds that we are given to know by that which we would know: reason is given in the gift of our being. At the same time this tradition is contested, but that contestation must be staged and elaborated in the university that would not foreclose on the question, but pursue universal knowledge, harbour all traditions of enquiry, and be a community of dissensus. In this way theology proves to be the measure of a liberal education in the university without an idea other than to ask *the question* (of the universe). And a truly Catholic university is but a more intense realization of this, since its asking of the question is not framed by the subject of a universal reason but by the mystery of the universe that is *given* for our learning.

Notes

1. Baron d'Holbach, *Good Sense*, trans. Anna Knoop (New York: Prometheus Books, 2004 [1878]), 13; cited in Thomas Albert Howard, *Protestant Theology and the Making of the Modern German University* (Oxford: Oxford University Press, 2006), 2.
2. D'Holbach, *Good Sense*, 14.
3. Immanuel Kant, *The Conflict of the Faculties* (1798) in Allen W. Wood and George di Giovanni (eds.), *Religion and Rational Theology* (Cambridge: Cambridge University Press, 1996), 233–327, at 255. Kant, of course, looked for the day when the last would be first, when philosophy as 'the lower faculty would be the higher' (261).
4. See Richard Dawkins, *The God Delusion*, 2nd edn (London: Black Swan, 2007 [2006]). For a French equivalent in the tradition of d'Holbach see Michel Onfray, *In Defence of Atheism: The Case Against Christianity, Judaism and Islam* (London: Serpent's Tail, 2007 [2005]).
5. See Hans Frei, *Types of Theology*, ed. George Hunsinger and William C. Placher (New Haven: Yale University Press, 1992), 101. Schleiermacher secured the (medieval) fourfold division of the university into the ('higher') faculties of theology, law and medicine, and the ('lower') faculty of philosophy (formerly arts, which traditionally encompassed grammar, rhetoric and logic, together with geometry, arithmetic, astronomy and music).
6. Kant, *Conflict of the Faculties*, 248.
7. The arrangement was however less direct than in the Prussian system. Clergy did not have to pass a state examination in order to pastor their flocks.
8. See further Gerard Loughlin, 'The Basis and Authority of Doctrine', in Colin E. Gunton (ed.), *The Cambridge Companion to Christian Doctrine* (Cambridge: Cambridge University Press, 1997), 41–64, at 57–9.
9. Kant, *Conflict of the Faculties*, 249.
10. Friedrich Schleiermacher quoted in Howard, *Protestant Theology*, 28.
11. On the Enlightenment project of the encyclopaedia, see further Alasdair MacIntyre, *Three Rival Versions of Moral Enquiry: Encyclopaedia, Genealogy, and Tradition* (London: Duckworth, 1990).
12. Howard, *Protestant Theology*, 28. Howard, on whom I rely at this point, offers an enlightening overview of the history of *Wissenschaft* in the nineteenth and early twentieth centuries (28–35).
13. W. G. Ward, writing in 1867, was one of the first English writers to use 'science' in the limited sense that is now commonplace: 'as expressing physical and experimental science, to the exclusion of theological and metaphysical'. Ward cited from *The Dublin Review* in the *Oxford English Dictionary*'s definition of 'science' (sense 5).
14. '[A]lmost all we do, every day of our lives, is on trust, i.e. faith.' John Henry Newman, 'Religious Faith Rational', *P.S.*, i:190–202, at 193. See further Gerard Loughlin, '"To Live and Die upon a Dogma": Newman and Post/modern Faith', in Ian Ker and Terrence Merrigan (eds.), *Newman and Faith* (Louvain: Peeters, 2004), 25–52, at 33–4, 50–2.

15. With Kant, religion became a mode of morality, an expression of the duties that reason dictates. 'A rational theologian ... is one *versed in reason* with regard to faith, which is based on inner laws that can be developed from every human being's own reason' (Kant, *Conflict*, 262).

16. Wilhelm Gottlieb Fichte, 'Deduced Scheme for an Academy to be Established in Berlin', in G. H. Turnbull (ed.), *Educational Theory of J. G. Fichte* (London: Hodder & Stoughton, 1926), 170–259; quoted in Frei, *Types*, 105.

17. Adolf von Harnack, 'Über die Bedeutung der theologischen Fakultäten', *Preussische Jahrbücher* 175 (March 1919), 362–74; quoted in Howard, *Protestant Theology*, 15.

18. Gavin D'Costa, *Theology in the Public Square: Church, Academy, and Nation* (Oxford: Blackwell, 2005), 1 and 20. D'Costa admits that his assertion prompts an 'uncomfortable' (5) question as to the status of his own theologizing, but he forgoes a comfortable answer.

19. The problem may not be uniquely modern, since D'Costa – drawing on the work of Jean Leclercq and Prudence Allen – argues that the rot set in when theology moved from the monastery to the university in the twelfth and thirteenth centuries. Theology was divided from worship, and from other knowledge, which was itself divided into the faculties of the university. See D'Costa, *Theology in the Public Square*, 10–11.

20. John Henry Newman, *Discourses on the Scope and Nature of University Education Addressed to the Catholics of Dublin* (Dublin: James Duffy, 1852), v (see *Idea*, ix).

21. Newman cited in Fergal McGrath, SJ, *Newman's University: Idea and Reality* (London: Longmans, Green & Co., 1951), 104.

22. A written invitation was sent in November. See McGrath, *Newman's University*, 123.

23. Newman was installed on 4 June 1854. See McGrath, *Newman's University*, 313–15.

24. Newman had supposedly libelled Achilli in the fifth of his lectures 'On the Present Position of Catholics in England', delivered in Birmingham on 5 July 1851.

25. Newman to James Hope Scott, 25 November 1851; see *L.D.*, xiv:436.

26. The Achilli affair was just a little unseemly, with Newman dispatching the devoted Miss Maria Giberne to the Continent to round up as many as possible of the women whom Achilli had debauched so that they might testify in Newman's defence. See further *Ward*, i:275–304; and Sheridan Gilley, *Newman and his Age* (London: Darton, Longman & Todd, 1990), 269–74.

27. Newman to Sr Mary Imelda Poole, 22 October 1852; see *L.D.*, xv:183.

28. Newman may have cancelled the original fifth lecture because some thought that, in the words of Cardinal Wiseman, it treated theology as 'one class of science, which must be restrained of trenching on the right of other sciences' (Wiseman cited in McGrath, *Newman's University*, 174). The excised appendix was replaced with a series of historical essays illustrating the idea of a university. These were first published in the *Gazette* during 1854 and then in 1856 as a book, *Office and Work of*

Universities, and republished as 'Rise and Progress of Universities' in the
third volume of Newman's *Historical Sketches* (1872).

29. Newman, *L.D.*, xviii:228; cited in Gilley, *Newman and his Age*, 291.
Wilfrid Ward believed that Newman had formed the idea that the university was 'doomed to failure' from as early as February 1854, four
months before his formal installation as rector. See *Ward*, i:355.

30. Of course the university continued after Newman's leaving. But 1879
saw the establishment of the Royal University of Ireland, an examining
body for its constituent colleges, which came to include University
College (1882), the successor to the Catholic University's University
House. This would survive until the creation of the National
University of Ireland in 1908, which had colleges in Dublin, Cork and
Galway. See further McGrath, *Newman's University*, ch. 20.

31. While a number of women attended Newman's lecture, he seems to have
taken some delight in failing to acknowledge their presence. 'There were
a number of ladies, and I *fancied* a slight sensation in the room, when I
said, not Ladies and Gentlemen, but Gentlemen.' Newman to Ambrose
St John, 11 May 1852; see *L.D.*, xv:84.

32. From Newman's introduction to the pamphlet version of Discourse VI,
and which survives in some copies of the 1852 book. See McGrath,
Newman's University, 173.

33. See McGrath, *Newman's University*, 170–2.

34. The parliamentary bill for their establishment was introduced in 1845.
See further McGrath, *Newman's University*, ch. 2.

35. Newman, *Discourses on the Scope and Nature of University Education
Addressed to the Catholics of Dublin* (1852), 38.

36. Cullen succeeded Murray as Archbishop of Dublin.

37. In a letter of 16 April 1852, Robert Ornsby provided Newman with an
assessment of 'Dublin Catholic society'. '[It] may be distributed into four
classes: 1. the clergy; 2. Society properly so called; 3. the citizen class;
4. the poor. The second class, which I call "Society" consists of two sets:
a few families of true distinction ... a very limited number of whom indeed
are for the University, and the rest is the Castle set; the other division is
more numerous, and makes up the bulk of Catholic society in the place,
barristers, solicitors, employés, people who have made their futures ...
There is no traditional knowledge of matters perfectly familiar in English
society, even among those who do pretend to learning ... They don't
feel the deficiencies that would strike English society; the same words,
"education," "university," and the like, don't convey to their minds the
same ideas that they convey to ours ... The citizen class are men still in
business. The clergy mix with them more than with the rest of society.
They are very deficient in education, and of course about as remote from
understanding such questions as the University as anything that could
be conceived. But ... I am sure the generosity of this class is beyond all
praise. And of the poor the same may be said.' Ornsby cited in McGrath,
Newman's University, 143–7.

38. Newman to Ambrose St John, 11 May 1852; see *L.D.*, xv:83–4.

39. Newman to Nicholas Darnell, 16 May 1852; see *L.D.*, xv:88.

40. *Idea*, ix; Newman's emphases.
41. *Idea*, ix.
42. *Idea*, xiii.
43. *Idea*, 101.
44. *Idea*, 459; emphasis added. On the theme of research in the university, see Ian Ker, 'Newman's Idea of a University: A Guide for the Contemporary University?' in David Smith and Anne Karin Langslow (eds.), *The Idea of a University* (London: Jessica Kingsley, 1999), 12–16.
45. *Idea*, xii.
46. *Idea*, xiv.
47. *Idea*, xv. While Newman made much of the distinction between liberal and useful knowledge – insisting that the university is concerned with the former rather than the latter, with knowledge apprehended as beautiful rather than as powerful (*Idea*, 217) – he nevertheless found that liberal knowledge has utility in fitting men for society. The art of the university is 'the art of social life, and its end is fitness for the world'. See *Idea*, 177.
48. *Idea*, xvi.
49. Newman, *Idea*, xviii; see also Newman's masterly description of the fruits of a university education at the conclusion of Discourse VII (178). It may be noted that while these fruits are cast as virtues, Newman did not think it was the duty of the university *as such* to teach moral virtue. The university teaches universal knowledge. It is the associations necessary for this teaching – the colleges and fraternities of the university – that inculcate moral virtue, especially when graced with common worship (as in the University of Ireland).
50. *Idea*, xx.
51. In this Newman agrees with Thomas Jefferson, for whom education in general, and the university in particular, is necessary for defending democracy; for giving 'every citizen the information he needs for the transaction of his own business', of course, but also for knowing 'his rights; to exercise with order and justice those he retains; to choose with discretion the fiduciary of those he delegates; and to notice their conduct with diligence, with candour, and judgment; and, in general, to observe with intelligence and faithfulness all the social relations under which he shall be placed'. Thomas Jefferson, 'Report of the Commissioners for the University of Virginia (4 August 1818)', in *Writings* (New York: The Library of America, c. 1984), 457–73, at 459. So, similarly, Newman taught that the university 'is a place to fit men of the world for the world'. See *Idea*, 232.
52. 'As to the meaning of the word ["university"], authors are divided in opinion; some explaining it of a universality of studies, others of students. As, however, it is the variety of its schools which brings students from all parts, and the variety of its members which demands so many subjects of teaching, it does not matter much how we settle the *derivation* of the word.' See Newman, *Discourses on the Scope and Nature of University Education Addressed to the Catholics of Dublin* (1852), Appendix, 381.

53. *Idea*, 21.
54. Thomas Jefferson's academy of American virtue – the University of Virginia at Charlottesville – had been founded in 1819 without a Professor of Theology. The American Constitution granted equality and freedom to all religious sects, and this precluded preferring any one of them with a professorship. But there was to be a Professor of Ethics who could teach the basic doctrines of deism, 'common to all sects': the existence and rule of a supreme being. (See Jefferson, 'Report of the Commissioners for the University of Virginia', 467.) Closer to home, and of more concern to Newman, London University had been founded in 1826 with no denominational tests, and no teaching of theology.
55. *Idea*, 21.
56. *Idea*, 29.
57. *Idea*, 388.
58. *Idea*, 389. And no one is more astute than Newman in observing that when Christianity is believed to be the 'bane of true knowledge' there arises a 'feeling, not merely of contempt, but of absolute hatred, towards the Catholic theologian and the dogmatic teacher' (389, 390).
59. 'Theology teaches ... a doctrine ... so mysterious as in its fullness to lie beyond any system, and in particular aspects to be simply external to nature, and to seem in parts even to be irreconcilable with itself, the imagination being unable to embrace what the reason determines.' See *Idea*, 63.
60. *Idea*, 45–6.
61. *Idea*, 47.
62. *Idea*, 50–1.
63. *Idea*, 69–70. 'Theology is one branch of knowledge, and Secular Sciences are other branches. Theology is the highest indeed, and widest, but it does not interfere with the real freedom of any secular science in its own particular department.' See also Newman, *Discourses on the Scope and Nature of University Education Addressed to the Catholics of Dublin* (1852), 152–3.
64. *Idea*, 51.
65. Newman, *Discourses on the Scope and Nature of University Education Addressed to the Catholics of Dublin* (1852), 144.
66. Newman, *Discourses on the Scope and Nature of University Education Addressed to the Catholics of Dublin* (1852), 140.
67. Newman, *Discourses on the Scope and Nature of University Education Addressed to the Catholics of Dublin* (1852), 153.
68. *Idea*, 29.
69. *Idea*, 374.
70. *Idea*, 375.
71. *Idea*, 26. Newman claims that the case for teaching revealed theology is stronger than that for natural because it includes historical as well as metaphysical facts.
72. *Idea*, 61. 'I speak of one idea unfolded in its just proportions, carried out upon an intelligible method, and issuing in necessary and immutable results; understood indeed at one time and place better than at another,

held here and there with more or less of inconsistency, but still, after all, in all times and places, where it is found, the evolution, not of half-a-dozen ideas, but of one' (see *Idea*, 67).

73. *Idea*, 390. Today some of Newman's arguments will seem to beg the question, as when he argues (*Idea*, 33–5) that 'human science leads to belief in a Supreme Being' (*Idea*, 35).

74. Newman makes it clear that his argument is for theology in the university before it is an argument for Catholic theology in a Catholic university. See *Idea*, 60. But there is an implicit argument (or assertion) that a real university is a Catholic one, since only Catholicism fully comprehends the 'Religious Truth' that is for Newman 'a condition of general knowledge' (*Idea*, 70). The world is not really known until it is known as created and redeemed. For a robust ('in your face') version of this argument, see John Milbank, 'The Conflict of the Faculties: Theology and the Economy of the Sciences', in Mark Thiessen Nation and Samuel Wells (eds.), *Faithfulness and Fortitude: In Conversation with the Theological Ethics of Stanley Hauerwas* (Edinburgh: T & T Clark, 2000).

75. The idea of the university as a place of unrestricted questioning derives from Jacques Derrida. For an account of the consonance between this and Newman's idea, see further Gerard Loughlin, 'The University Without Question: John Henry Newman and Jacques Derrida on Faith in the University', in Jeff Astley, Leslie Francis, John Sullivan and Andrew Walker (eds.), *The Idea of a Christian University: Essays on Theology and Higher Education* (Milton Keynes: Paternoster Press, 2004), 113–31, at 126–31.

76. On recognizing the question of the mystery of the world, see further Denys Turner, *Faith, Reason and the Existence of God* (Cambridge: Cambridge University Press, 2004).

77. Equally, of course, the university should also make room for other religious traditions that think the mystery of the universe, most obviously in the Western context the Judaic and Islamic, but not excluding the Asian and East Asian as well. For lack of space I restrict myself to Newman's concern with Catholicism.

78. Compare *Idea*, 260. 'Even to this day Shakespeare and Milton are not studied in our course of education; but the poems of Virgil and Horace ... were in schoolboys' satchels not much more than a hundred years after they were written.'

79. See Newman, *Discourses on the Scope and Nature of University Education Addressed to the Catholics of Dublin* (1852), 139.

80. Bill Readings, *The University in Ruins* (Cambridge, MA: Harvard University Press, 1996).

81. For Readings the rise of 'cultural studies' is a sure sign of culture's demise. Anything and everything is the subject of cultural studies and so there is no one thing – culture – that it studies. See Readings, *University in Ruins*, ch. 7.

82. My use of the definite article is misleading because for Newman there is really only one civilization and it is Western. No other civilization – neither the 'Hindoo' nor the 'morose' Chinese – has a legitimate claim on

the name, since they are but 'outlying portions' – 'fragmentary, unsociable, solitary' – of the 'grand central formation'. See *Idea*, 252.
83. *Idea*, 262–3.
84. Stanley Fish, 'Take This Job and Do It: Administering the University without an Idea', *Critical Inquiry* 31 (2005), 271–85, at 279. See further Stanley Fish, *Political Correctness: Literary Studies and Political Change* (Oxford: Clarendon Press, 1995).
85. Fish, 'Take This Job and Do It', 280.
86. Fish, 'Take This Job and Do It', 281–2.
87. The point is almost Newman's when he writes that the 'great advantage of an age in which unbelief speaks out' is that 'Faith can speak out too; that, if falsehood assails Truth, Truth can assail falsehood' (see *Idea*, 382).
88. Stanley Hauerwas, *The State of the University: Academic Knowledges and the Knowledge of God* (Oxford: Blackwell, 2007), 82–8.
89. *Idea*, 145.
90. *Idea*, 146.
91. *Idea*, 152.
92. Readings, *The University in Ruins*, 122.
93. Readings's analysis is resonant with Jean-François Lyotard's account of the postmodern condition, as a time when grand narratives have collapsed and smaller stories proliferate, with none gaining universal legitimacy. See Jean-François Lyotard, *The Postmodern Condition: A Report on Knowledge*, trans. Geoff Bennington and Brian Massumi (Manchester: Manchester University Press, 1984 [1979]); and Bill Readings, *Introducing Lyotard: Art and Politics* (London: Routledge, 1991).
94. Readings, *The University in Ruins*, 127, 180–93.
95. Readings, *The University in Ruins*, 133.
96. Readings, *The University in Ruins*, 188.
97. Readings, *The University in Ruins*, 186.
98. *Idea*, 147. The 'ethical atmosphere' of Readings's university is that of Emmanuel Levinas.
99. MacIntyre, *Three Rival Versions*, 222. MacIntyre finds a realization of this ideal university in thirteenth-century Paris, when 'Augustinians and Aristotelians each conducted their own systematic enquiries while at the same time engaging in systematic controversy' (*Three Rival Versions*, 232). It was thus not a place where knowledge simply fractured (see note 19 above) but where that fracturing became a tradition of enquiry.
100. It may be noted that MacIntyre imagines different traditions of enquiry developing in different universities, so that the contest between them would take place not in any one university but in meta-university 'forums in which the debate between rival types of enquiry was afforded rhetorical expression' (*Three Rival Versions*, 234). But this is to imagine the university either grown synonymous with society or its collapse, since no one place would be the university of dissensus that Readings and MacIntyre look for.

Further reading

Astley, Jeff, Leslie Francis, John Sullivan and Andrew Walker, eds. *The Idea of a Christian University: Essays on Theology and Higher Education*. Milton Keynes: Paternoster Press, 2004.

D'Costa, Gavin. *Theology in the Public Square: Church, Academy and Nation*. Oxford: Blackwell, 2005.

Howard, Thomas Albert. *Protestant Theology and the Making of the Modern German University*. Oxford: Oxford University Press, 2006.

Kant, Immanuel, 'Conflict of the Faculties' (1798), in Allen W. Wood, and George Di Giovanni, (eds.), *Religion and Rational Theology*. Cambridge: Cambridge University Press, 1996.

MacIntyre, Alasdair. *Three Rival Versions of Moral Enquiry: Encyclopedia, Genealogy, and Tradition*. London: Duckworth, 1990.

Milbank, John, 'The Conflict of the Faculties: Theology and the Economy of the Sciences', in Mark Theissen Nation and Samuel Wells (eds.), *Faith and Fortitude: In Conversation with the Theological Ethics of Stanley Hauerwas*. Edinburgh: T & T Clark, 2000, 39–58.

Newman, John Henry, *The Idea of a University Defined and Illustrated: (I) in Nine Discourses Delivered to the Catholics in Dublin (II) in Occasional Lectures and Essays Addressed to the members of the Catholic University*, ed. with intro. I. T. Ker. Oxford: Clarendon Press, 1976.

12 Preaching

DENIS ROBINSON

Few preachers in the history of the Church, and even fewer from the nineteenth century have enjoyed as far-reaching and long-lasting a reputation as John Henry Newman. First as an Anglican pastor and then as a Roman Catholic priest, Newman's sermons provided and continue to provide spiritual and enlightening reading more than 100 years after his death. Much of this is undoubtedly due to Newman's great facility with language. Equally, however, this fame must be attributed to Newman's unique method, the particularities of which are only becoming apparent in our time, in light of contemporary homiletic theory. Like many of his contemporaries, Newman published his sermons. The first volume of *Parochial and Plain Sermons* appeared in 1834.[1] Additional volumes continued to be published and remained in print throughout Newman's life. Newman also published other volumes of sermons and hundreds of his sermons remain unpublished in manuscript form in the archives of the Birmingham Oratory. Newman was a popular preacher, attracting great crowds to his Sunday sermons in St Mary's University church in Oxford and later at Littlemore, and still later at the Oratory in Birmingham. Newman's preaching struck a chord with his age, and any appreciation of his preaching must be seen in light of its original, nineteenth-century, British context.

This chapter will explore the preaching of Newman in three steps. First, we will provide a brief examination of the context of Newman's preaching. Second, we will examine Newman's preaching method. Finally, the meaning of Newman's preaching will be considered in light of its ultimate purpose, the *realization* of the first principle of Christianity, the Incarnation of the Word of God.

THE CONTEXT OF NEWMAN'S PREACHING

Newman's preaching has been described as 'reactionary',[2] in that he used his various pulpits as a means to confront the crises in the Anglican Church of his time as he understood them. The stimulus for the emergence of the Oxford Movement, which was dedicated to the reassertion of the Catholic character of the Church of England, was political in character, namely, the question of whether or not the Church should be established.[3] In its early phase, the movement (also called Tractarianism) was intended to be a populist one, in line with the power of the ordinary Christian in the early Church, 'as exemplified in the history of St Ambrose'.[4] Tracts were the natural way of initiating a popular movement and arousing the interest of the people. Preaching was another way. In both endeavours, Newman proved himself to be a master strategist.[5] This was true even before the formal inauguration of the Movement. 'Although the sermons between 1829 and 1831 are a defence of a beleaguered, established, visible Church against intellectual heterodoxy and "schismatic" Dissent, this is not to say that Newman was *unequivocally* upholding the "powers that be".'[6] Rather, Newman's preaching during this period was directed against both those who would compromise the authority of the Church and those who espoused a utilitarian culture of 'national apostasy'. Newman was as appalled by the 'comfortable' and popular forms of the Christianity of his day as he was by the secularized government's attempts to overwhelm the authority of the bishops.[7] He was also convinced that the same challenges that had plagued the early Church were still present in his own age. Nevertheless, he maintained an absolute confidence in the capacity of committed believers to understand and assimilate Christian truth. The full force of the Scriptures and the tradition of antiquity must be brought to bear upon the contemporary situation. In Newman's estimation, although the ways of approaching the task of preaching may have altered over time, the core issues remained the same.

One of the important writings in the development of Newman's preaching was J. B. Sumner's *Treatise on Apostolical Preaching*.[8] Sumner's work grounds not only the aims of preaching, but its style and techniques in patristic sources.[9] Some important themes in Sumner were to be of lasting influence on Newman's attitude towards the task of preaching. The first was a positive image of the assembly.[10] Sumner proposed that the preachers of the post-New Testament period had a more or less positive attitude towards their assemblies. They did not see the hearers of the sermon as merely passive, but as able to participate and make judgements on their own. The second theme was of the understanding of preaching as a theological task. For Newman, this translated into the positive injunction to presume a certain level of sophistication among the congregants and a growing conviction that preaching is a theological task in its own right, a kind of performative theology worked out in the midst of the people.

THE CHARACTER OF NEWMAN'S PREACHING

In line with his conviction that preaching involved an appeal to the intellect, Newman was suspicious of the Evangelical understanding of preaching as emotional persuasion. For Newman, 'preaching was not the way to convert people, but to prepare them for conversion'.[11] It was part of a delicate and complex task of formation. Newman identifies the three qualities of a good sermon in Chapter 6 of *The Idea of a University*. First, a sermon must exhibit a sense of earnestness. This earnestness is expressed in a definiteness of purpose. For Newman this earnestness is bound up with the character of the preacher. Invoking Aristotle, Newman insists that persuasiveness is a direct result of 'personal traits of an ethical nature evident in the orator'.[12] Secondly, the sermon ought to convey a particular goal or aim on the part of the preacher. 'As a marksman aims at the target and its bull's-eye, and at nothing else, so the preacher must have a definite point before him, which he has to hit.'[13] Finally, the sermon must be adapted to the needs of the specific audiences. For Newman this was a matter of observing that 'personal influence requires personal acquaintance, and the minute labour a discretionary rule'.[14] While Newman recognized a certain commonality among hearers in light of their shared condition as 'children of Adam', he nevertheless insisted that audiences varied and that the preacher had a responsibility to know the hearers. This was especially true regarding the ethical imperative in the sermon:

> A preacher should be quite sure that he understands the persons he is addressing before he ventures to aim at what he considers to be their ethical condition; for, if he mistakes, he will probably be doing harm rather than good. I have known consequences to occur very far from edifying, when strangers have fancied they knew an auditory when they did not, and have by implication imputed to them habits or motives which were not theirs.[15]

What was it like to hear Newman preach?[16]

Newman's preaching at St Mary's became legendary and many descriptions were written of it, the most famous being Matthew Arnold's retrospective romantic evocation of 'the charm of that spiritual apparition, gliding in the dim afternoon light through the aisles of St Mary's, rising into the pulpit, and then, in the most entrancing of voices, breaking the silence with words and thoughts which were a religious music, – subtle, sweet, mournful'.[17]

As an Anglican, Newman preached almost every Sunday from the time he was ordained until his retirement to Littlemore in 1843. 'The church was full when Newman preached, thronged usually by not less than 500 or 600 graduates, besides other members of the congregation'.[18] His sermons were characterized by their clarity. 'Newman's sermons are distinguished not for vague platitudes and pious aspirations, but for their utter concreteness and definiteness.'[19] This is especially true of the imaginative way in which Newman handled his texts. He was almost calculating in the presentation of his images and the dependability of his structure. The sermons, in their attention to structure and the careful handling of language, had the quality of poetry. This might be seen as a concrete expression of Newman's conviction that religion was primarily poetical.[20]

THE STRUCTURE OF NEWMAN'S SERMONS

Newman almost invariably structured his sermons in the same way. The expository section of every sermon presents a dilemma, a problem to be resolved in the context of the life of the Church. These dilemmas vary widely from sermon to sermon, but Newman was determined that they must be made in some way *real* to the hearers, that is to say, something that touched on their daily lives. Even a casual glance at the *Parochial and Plain Sermons* reveals the technique at work.

The first four sermons of the fifth volume are the Advent sermons of 1839, which used a common text, Isaiah 33:17, 'Thine eyes shall see the King in His beauty; they shall behold the land that is very far off'. The first sermon, 'Worship, A Preparation for Christ's Coming', presents the dilemma in terms of the darkness of the season and the promise of the coming of Christ in light. Newman first draws this out in terms of the order of nature, and then in terms of an analogy with the human spirit. The question of the sermon becomes: How does one reconcile the despair that is a real aspect of human life and the hope of the Christian promise? In the second sermon, 'Reverence, A Belief in God's Presence', Newman creates a dilemma between two types of people mistaken about God's forgiveness. In the third sermon, 'Unreal Words', the dilemma is presented in terms of the shadows of former times and the bounty of the Christological age to come. In the fourth Advent sermon, 'Shrinking from Christ's Coming', he juxtaposes anticipation and fear. This presentation of a dilemma in the form of two terms or two images was Newman's starting-point.

In the second part of each sermon, he expands upon the basic dilemma using vivid word-pictures, which, although drawn from the biblical texts, are invariably set up to link the biblical discourse with the situation in the Church of Newman's time. This was Newman's opportunity to demonstrate that he knew his hearers, sometimes uncomfortably well. It is easy to imagine that when Newman was in his high ironic form, these sections of his sermons could have been most uncomfortable for the assembly.

In the third section of each sermon, Newman applies the impact of the dilemma to his hearers. What does this dilemma mean to us? How are the hearers to *respond* to these images and these dilemmas? For the most part, Newman left this question unresolved or used it as a starting-point for subsequent sermons in a series.

Approaching the sermons of Newman, one notices the number of rhetorical devices he employed. These devices were employed to lure the hearer into a kind of dialogue with the preacher. They have the power not only to engage the hearer but at times even to shock.

One of these devices was the use of *binaries and ternaries*, combinations of two or three ideas or images. Newman often places two or three terms together, drawing dramatic contrasts and inviting comparison, yet remaining rather vague as regards the way in which the terms actually fit together. In fact, almost all of Newman's sermons deal with an underlying primordial binary, the connection between the 'real' and the 'unreal'.[21] Often in Newman's sermons, these binaries and ternaries are introduced and are either left unresolved or are resolved only in the context of the introduction of a further confounding element. It remains the task of the hearers (or readers) to discover how these elements are connected. For example, in the Advent sermons mentioned above, Newman uses the binary or the ternary device more than 150 times. These varied uses allow for a range of possible outcomes in terms of the assembly of the elements.

A second device Newman frequently employed might be described as *hypertextuality*. In postmodern literary theory, a hypertext is one which derives from or is related to other texts (if only by means of subtle allusions). In Newman's case, hypertextuality seems to be an appropriate term to describe his practice of employing a word in two different ways or choosing a word that has a variety of meanings and which might therefore lead his hearers down completely different paths. This technique is at play in Newman's Advent sermons, where he employs images that are able to evoke a variety of responses and thereby expand the possible horizons of meaning for the hearer.

A third device was Newman's use of *paradigmatic moments and figures from history* that would resonate with the contemporary context and serve to illustrate a sermon's purpose. So, for example, Newman might mention the word 'Arian' or 'Alexandrian' in a sermon to refer to the past, though it is clear that the example invoked would also serve to conjure up associations for the congregation of Newman's time. The historical allusion has contemporary implications. This was one of Newman's most frequently employed devices and was useful not only in the sermons, but in his discursive writings as well.

A fourth device used by Newman was the persistent *counsel of patience* on the part of his hearers.[22] Indeed, patience and the concomitant theme of constancy were significant motifs in Newman's sermons. He counselled, 'Nothing is more difficult than to be disciplined and regular in our religion'.[23] Too much of religion, in Newman's estimation, was governed by 'fits and starts', themselves the products of presumptuous fancy and emotionalism. The key to the correct appropriation of religious truth was patience and perseverance. Where these are present, religious truth has the opportunity to penetrate the mind and the heart. 'Is not holiness the result of many patient, repeated efforts after obedience, gradually working on us, and first modifying and then changing our hearts?'[24]

A final and crucial device employed by Newman was one that cannot be observed on the basis of a reading of his sermons, namely, his frequent and purposeful use of *pauses*, 'which sometimes lasted long enough to thrill his hearers to an almost unbearable degree'.[25] Ker ascribes this practice to Newman's 'sheer intensity of thought'.[26] It was certainly not an element introduced by Newman for mere effect. Newman was almost immune to the impact of the dramatic gesture. He was not interested in promoting the theatrical qualities of the preacher. He was consistently and doggedly interested in the impact of *words* on the hearer.[27]

This complicated series of devices contributed to what might be called the inductive dimension of Newman's homiletic practice. The role of the preacher is to provide a whole range of images, each of them rich, real and varied and all of them together, at least initially, able to confound the hearer with their dizzying interplay of relationships. The preacher chooses the images carefully, drawing upon his pastoral knowledge of the community's life. Newman's own anxiety about his pastoral responsibilities testify to his concern in this regard.[28] Having presented the various images, and drawing upon the devices discussed above, Newman employed the pause to give his hearers the opportunity to process the material before the introduction of the next element. This is the *open ending*. Reading Newman's sermons, one is sometimes left with the sense that there is an element missing, an element that the hearers themselves must supply. Elsewhere, Newman employed the image of an inventory to discuss the way in which the Church deals with religious truths. 'All is given to us in profusion; it remains for us to catalogue, sort, distribute, select, harmonize, and complete.'[29] This inductive method-ology reflects Newman's confidence in the ability of the assembly to manage and assimilate the images into a meaningful whole.[30]

Newman's homiletic approach is an extension of his ideas about Scripture and revelation. Revelation, for Newman, was always perceived in light of its companion, Mystery. 'Religious truth is neither light nor darkness, but both together.'[31] Scripture, for Newman, involved the interplay between the known and the mysterious, the systematic and the unsystematic. This tension is indeed characteristic of the scriptural text.[32] Revelation insinuates itself, as it were, in the space opened up by this tension. This necessitates a process of interpretation and reinterpre-tation, a 'working out and through' that is reminiscent of the method-ology employed in the preaching of the patristic period. The goal of this preaching, like Newman's own, was the disclosure of revealed truth. The nature of that truth is the subject of the following discussion.

THE GOAL OF THE SERMONS: THE INCULCATION OF INCARNATIONAL FAITH

All of Newman's homiletic devices and methodology were directed to one central goal, the unveiling of the mystery of the Incarnation. For him, 'the preacher's aim was to present the person of Christ not in an "unreal way – as a mere idea or vision", but as "Scripture has set Him before us in His actual sojourn on earth, in His gestures, words and deeds"'.[33] Christ must be presented in the full paradox of his being, as at once God and man. The Incarnation is at the heart of the ongoing life of the Church. 'Henceforth He is the one principle of life in all His servants, who are but His organs.'[34]

The issue of orthodox Christology was vitally significant for Newman. He had already dealt extensively with this topic in his first full-length writing, *The Arians of the Fourth Century*. In his historical treatment of the Arian crisis and the resulting Council of Nicaea, Newman drew distinct parallels between the theological controversies of the early Church and those of his own day. Newman's concerns about the way in which the reality of Christ was preached in the Church was essentially a pastoral concern. He believed that a correct understanding of Christology was essential to the authentic practice of Christian faith. The sermons were a primary means of promoting this correct understanding.

Both the content of his sermons and the homiletic techniques he employed were designed to encourage the faithful appropriation of the paradoxical truth of the Incarnation. This was especially evident in his development of a number of themes, including the idea of the God-Man, the cross, the 'hiddenness' of Christ and, perhaps most memorably, the humiliation of the Son of God. His reflections on the latter constitute his most moving treatment of Christology. They are to be found in a sermon preached in 1835 and entitled 'The Humiliation of the Eternal Son'. In this sermon, Newman's homiletic skills are most vividly displayed.

Newman employs all of the devices of homiletic rhetoric at his disposal to encourage his listeners to 'realize' the central principle of Christianity, namely, the truth of the Word made Flesh. In Newman's vocabulary, the verb 'to realize' is almost a technical term denoting a personal grasp of the reality of a particular object or truth, a grasp so profound that it can move the believer to action. Newman begins his sermon by declaring that, 'the chief mystery of our holy faith is the humiliation of the Son of God to temptation and suffering'.[35] The terms of the argument are stated here in the first sentence. The mystery is invoked by an appeal to two seemingly contradictory terms: 'humiliation', with its evocation of earthliness, and 'Son of God', with its evocation of otherworldliness. Newman goes on to describe the Son's humiliation as a mystery that is more overwhelming than that of the Trinity, by virtue of our familiarity with one of its terms. He is careful to note that it is not a greater mystery (for it is a mystery of the same type), but one that is in some sense more accessible to us. In this way, the mystery remains, but it is at the same time somewhat demystified. In the next section, Newman introduces a device that he will employ throughout the sermon, the use of the conjunction 'but' to indicate contrary motions.

> When the mystery of the Trinity is set before us, we see indeed that it is quite beyond our reason; but, at the same time, it is no wonder that human language should be unable to convey, and human intellect to receive, truths relating to the incommunicable and infinite essence of Almighty God. But the mystery of the Incarnation relates, in part, to subjects more level with our reason; it lies not only in the manner

how God and man is one Christ, but in the very fact that so it is. We think we know of God so much as this, that He is altogether separate from imperfection and infirmity; yet we are told that the Eternal Son has taken into Himself a creature's nature, which henceforth became as much one with Him, as much belonged to Him, as the divine attributes and powers which He had ever had.[36]

The divine mystery eludes human language but it is nevertheless spoken of; the 'mystery of the Incarnation' is rendered accessible by the 'very fact' of it; that which is 'altogether separate from imperfection and infirmity' has 'taken into Himself a creature's nature'. The binaries are lined up to indicate the kind of disjunction with which the imagination must grapple if it is to do justice to this holy truth. It is on this disjunction that Newman will dwell in the sermon. The mystery of the Incarnation, its real sense, lies somewhere *between* what we know and what we do not know. Here is a statement of the essence of the nature of Christ. Christ, like the mystery in which he is inculcated, lies somewhere between what we know, that is, the sensible world of which we are a part, and the divine realm in which we do not take part, at least not yet. He is both between and within the human and the divine. It is the same with all human 'knowledge'. What we know moves between the earth ('a sentence caught up here, and an argument heard there'), and the horizon of the infinite (a knowledge 'too excellent for us'). The event of Christ, like our minds, oscillates between a 'certain time', the here and now of 'human flesh', and the 'everlasting', the eternal 'glory with the Father'. As Newman proceeds, binaries proliferate and are countered by others. In a replication of the action of the mind confronted by this overwhelming mystery, the progression of the argument becomes very nearly unchartable. The mystery of Christ is not something remote, but a movement that is being played out within us. The sermon has drawn us into that movement.

Newman not only displays the complexity of the engagement with the mystery, he revels in it. 'And as the doctrine of our Lord's humiliation is most mysterious, so the very surface of the narrative in which it is contained is mysterious also, as exciting wonder, and impressing upon us our real ignorance of the nature, manner, and causes of it.'[37] Once again the epistemological reality replicates the Incarnation, and the one who contemplates the mystery is caught between the binaries of wonder, which is excited by the mysterious interchange, and our real ignorance. Here Newman hints at a point he will later drive home. The most grievous mistake that the enquirer can make regarding this mystery is to fail to admit the tension between wonder and ignorance. The most grievous mistake the preacher can make is to relax the tension. Those who reduce the Incarnation to one or the other of the terms are heretical, be they denizens of the fourth century or the nineteenth. 'In consequence we are too often led, as a matter of necessity, in discoursing of His words and works, to distinguish between the Christ who lived on earth and the Son of God Most High, speaking of His human nature and His Divine nature so separately as not to feel or understand that God is man and man is God.' The fruitless quest for the so-called historical Jesus in the nineteenth century was inspired by the relaxation of the tension between the Word and the Flesh. The truth about Christ, according to Newman, is to be found precisely in the willingness to sustain it. Drawing upon history to drive home his point, Newman says of those who dissolve the tension that they 'begin by being Sabellians, that they go on to be Nestorians, and that they tend to be Ebionites and to deny Christ's Divinity altogether'. Newman insists that orthodoxy is reducible to neither strictly rational categories nor to human passions. Indeed, 'the so-called religion of the heart, without orthodoxy of doctrine, is but the warmth of a corpse, real for a time, but sure to fail'.[38]

In the next section of the sermon, Newman carries the discourse forward by introducing a series of questions that he does not answer. In fact he admits that 'these and many other questions admit of no satisfactory solution'.[39] The reality of Christ's mystery lies in the paradox, that is, in the suspension of solutions in favour of further relational enquiry. The satisfaction of 'knowing' Christ comes in the mystery of connections, such as that between the binary of temptation and the Holy Spirit. Questions generate questions in Newman's homiletic economy. One question leads to another. The question of Christ's baptism leads, inexplicably, to his descent into Hell. None of the questions is answered. Instead, in Newman's preaching, they have rather the cumulative effect of drawing the enquirer deeper into the mysterious relationship. Newman reveals his methodological focus: 'I bring together these various questions in order to impress upon you our depth of ignorance on the entire subject under review'.[40] However, Newman never implies that this dizzying process is without rewards. The preacher's task is not to confound, but to inculcate the largeness, indeed the inexhaustibility of the Object. 'Enlarge upon them we ought, even because they are few and partial, not slighting what is given us, because it is not all (like the servant who buried his lord's talent), but giving it what increase we can.'[41] The purpose of the 'one or two partial notices' that we have is to entice us more deeply into the relationship with the inexhaustible mystery of the God-man. The rational theologian or those who quest for the historical Jesus refuse the invitation to enlarge upon what paltry evidence 'fact' and 'history' give. Instead they manifest 'the narrow spirit of that slothful servant at the present day, in which is strangely combined a profession of knowing everything with an assertion that there is nothing to know concerning the Incarnation'.[42] Newman then states the terms of the mystery again:

> Bearing in mind, then, that we *know nothing* truly about the manner or the *ultimate ends* of the humiliation of the Eternal Son, our Lord and Saviour, let us consider what that humiliation itself was.[43]

Newman then continues with a host of binaries and ternaries comparing and contrasting the two natures of Christ, and relating them again to the seemingly double action of the human mind that is both grounded in the present and looks forward to the future. The mystery is now set against the backdrop of history, as Newman moves between reflection on the patristic era and his own. In this way he connects the past with the present. Just as attitudes towards the Son of God can be transported across time, so can the living and inviting reality of Christ be meaningful then and now. It remains what it was precisely in the movement. Once again Newman mentions that his purpose is not to explain the mystery 'but to facilitate your *conception* of Him who is the subject of it, to help you towards contemplating Him as God and man at once, as still the Son of God though He had assumed a nature short of His original perfection'.[44] Newman uses the word 'conception' very deliberately, juxtaposing the actual conception of the Son of God, that is, the first instance of his humiliation, with our 'conception' of him. We know something of Christ, Newman is saying, but there is infinitely more to know and our lives must be spent in that knowing, just as the life of the Son of God was spent in 'knowing' the human condition. It is only when 'we contemplate our Lord and Saviour, God and man, as a really existing being, external to our minds, as complete and entire in His personality as we show ourselves to be to each other, as one and the same in all His various and contrary attributes, "the same yesterday, today, and for ever"', that we can be said to '*realize* that Object of faith, which is not a mere name on which titles and properties may be affixed without congruity and meaning, but has a personal existence and an identity distinct from everything else'.[45] Not surprisingly, Newman concludes by asking still more questions:

> In what true sense do we 'know' Him, if our idea of Him be not such as to take up and incorporate into itself the manifold attributes

and offices which we ascribe to Him? What do we gain from words, however correct and abundant, if they end with themselves, instead of lighting up the image of the Incarnate Son in our hearts?[46]

The sermon ends with a prayer that restates the terms of the mystery. The 'realization' of what it means to call Christ the Son of God is unfolded in the combination of heart and intellect. His humiliation is relived in our homiletic rediscovery of him:

> May God, even the Father, give us a heart and understanding to realize, as well as to confess that doctrine into which we were baptized, that His Only-begotten Son, our Lord, was conceived by the Holy Ghost, was born of the Virgin Mary, suffered, and was buried, rose again from the dead, ascended into heaven, from whence He shall come again, at the end of the world, to judge the quick and the dead.[47]

All of Newman's preaching was centred on the mystery of the Incarnation. The key to his success as a preacher must, however, be sought in his own 'realization' of the truth of this mystery and his ability to draw others into it.

Notes

1. The first volume of the sermons appeared as *Parochial Sermons* in 1834 (London: Printed for J. G. F. & J. Rivington & J. H. Parker, Oxford, 1834). Volume ii came out the following year (London: Printed for J. G. F. & J. Rivington & J. H. Parker, Oxford, 1835); volume iii appeared in 1836 (London: Printed for J. G. F. & J. Rivington & J. H. Parker, Oxford, 1836), volume iv was first published in 1839 (London: Printed for J. G. F. & J. Rivington & J. H. Parker, Oxford, 1839), volume v in 1840 (London: Printed for J. G. F. & J. Rivington & J. H. Parker, Oxford, 1840) and volume vi in 1842 (London: Printed for J. G. F. & J. Rivington & J. H. Parker, Oxford, 1842). The individual volumes each went through numerous editions and were excerpted and recombined many times. The six volumes appeared as a set in 1843 and were reprinted together in 1848. The first collected edition titled *Parochial and Plain Sermons* came out in 1868 (London, Oxford and Cambridge: Rivington, 1868) in eight volumes. Fifteen subsequent editions or imprints of the various volumes appeared during Newman's life. No modern critical edition has appeared.
2. Stephen Thomas, *Newman and Heresy: The Anglican Years* (Cambridge: Cambridge University Press, 1991), 27. Newman remarked that preaching was usually only tolerable 'till it comes home'. See *P.S.*, iv:299–300.
3. See Ian Ker, *John Henry Newman: A Biography* (Oxford: Oxford University Press, 1988), 80. For Newman's understanding of the Erastianism of the

Anglican Church, see *Diff.*, i:105–13, and *Ath.*, i:310–12. Newman claims
that the State is clearly the overlord of the Church of England.
4. *L.D.*, iv:418.
5. Ker, *John Henry Newman*, 81.
6. Thomas, *Newman and Heresy*, 33.
7. *D.A.*, 10–13.
8. See Ker, *John Henry Newman*, 22.
9. Background material may be found in Christiane D'Haussy, 'Panorama
du sermon anglais au XIXe siècle', *Études Newmaniennes* 17 (2001), 9–17.
10. Newman remarks in *The Idea of a University* that the task of preaching
should not be undertaken without adequate knowledge of the congregation. See *Idea*, 418.
11. Ker, *John Henry Newman*, 113.
12. *Idea*, 408.
13. *Idea*, 407.
14. *Campaign*, 37.
15. *Idea*, 418.
16. Robert D. Middleton, 'The Vicar of Saint Mary's', in G. Wheeler (ed.),
Newman Centenary Essays (London: Burns, Oates and Washbourne,
1945), 127–38. Middleton provides an excellent selection of contemporary sources relating the experience of those who heard Newman preach
in St Mary's. Newman viewed preaching as a holistic exercise, that is,
one that engaged the whole preacher and not just the intellect. See
Newman, *Idea*, 413.
17. Ian Ker, *The Achievement of John Henry Newman* (Notre Dame:
University of Notre Dame Press, 1991), 75.
18. Middleton, 'The Vicar of Saint Mary's', 130.
19. Ker, *Achievement*, 76.
20. 'Revealed Religion should be especially poetical – and it is so in fact.' See
Ath., i:23.
21. Ker, *Achievement*, 79.
22. See Ramon Mas, 'Parole et silence chez Newman', *Études Newmaniennes*
10 (1994), 43–52. See also R. Michael Olson, 'Newman's Patient Mind',
The Newman Rambler 5 (2001), 13–17.
23. *P.S.*, i:252.
24. *P.S.*, i:11.
25. Archbishop Temple quoted in Middleton, 'The Vicar of Saint Mary's', 131.
26. Ker, *Achievement*, 75.
27. D.M. Whalen, 'John Henry Newman: The Rhetoric and the Real',
Nineteenth-Century Prose 8 (1991), 1–9.
28. For Newman's various pastoral perspectives see Dermot Fenlon, 'The
Aristocracy of Talent and the Mystery of Newman', *Louvain Studies* 15
(1990), 203–25.
29. *V.M.*, i:23.
30. An excellent account of the inductive methodology in modern homiletic
theory can be found in Fred B. Craddock, *Preaching* (Nashville:
Abingdon Press, 1990).
31. *Ess.*, i:41–2.

32. *D.A.*, 125.
33. Ker, *Achievement*, 83. See *P.S.*, iii:130–1.
34. *Jfc.*, 196.
35. *P.S.*, iii:157.
36. *P.S.*, iii:157.
37. *P.S.*, iii:159.
38. *P.S.*, iii:159.
39. *P.S.*, iii:160.
40. *P.S.*, iii:160.
41. *P.S.*, iii:161.
42. *P.S.*, iii:159.
43. *P.S.*, iii:161.
44. *P.S.*, iii:166. Emphasis in the original.
45. *P.S.*, iii:170. Emphasis added.
46. *P.S.*, iii:171.
47. *P.S.*, iii:173.

Further reading

Harrold, Charles F. *John Henry Newman: An Expository and Critical Study of His Mind, Thought and Art*. London: Longmans, Green & Co., 1945, 318–51.
Ker, Ian. *John Henry Newman: A Biography*. Oxford: Clarendon Press, 1988, 90–100.
  The Achievement of John Henry Newman. Notre Dame: University of Notre Dame Press, 1991, 74–95.
Robinson, Denis. 'The Mother of Wisdom: Exploring the Parabolic Imperative in the Early Works of John Henry Newman', *Louvain Studies* 27 (2002), 153–70.

13 Newman in retrospect

DAVID B. BURRELL

INTRODUCTION: NEWMAN AND THE LOGIC OF FAITH

Writing in the heyday of 'modernist rationalism', John Henry Newman's analysis of the fiduciary roots of all inquiry – an argument reproduced in our century by Hans-Georg Gadamer – offers us a benign understanding of the 'postmodern': that one ought not simply oppose knowing and believing, notably when the object of belief is divine revelation. Yet in finding room for faith, his mode of argument resists including any belief whatsoever under that rubric. So the quality of discernment whereby one discriminates among different modes of faith represents a primary and indispensable use of reason.

Like Socrates, Newman believed in the capacity of human intelligence to discriminate, with proper tutelage and catechesis, the relevant from the spurious.[1] In fact, one always hears the tutor in his writings, as he poses issues in commonplace ways only to lead us to greater appreciation of the nuances needed to move beyond oppositional clichés or crude descriptors like 'modernist rationalism' (found in the opening sentence of this chapter). Newman's preponderant legacy, I suggest, lies in teaching us how to elude distracting oppositions by effectively neutralizing their appeal.

The clichés which abounded in Newman's time are reflected in the ways he poses questions, only to recast them before we can respond to them effectively. In his *Achievement of John Henry Newman*, Ian Ker notes that:

> Newman was much more prolific as a theologian than as a philosopher of religion, and yet the justification of religious belief always remained the subject which was closest to his heart and which was never far from his thoughts throughout his life. In the face of increasing secularization and unbelief, he came to feel that the fundamental religious problem of the modern age was the crisis of faith.[2]

Yet the ways he proposes to resolve such a pervasive 'crisis' are hardly dogmatic, and proceed by his characteristic way of 'deconstructing' the very problematics which may have inadvertently incited the crisis. In the process, as we shall see, 'the justification of religious belief' becomes a genial conversation, replete with reminders of things we already realize. Note how he gently mocks standard strategies for 'justification of belief' in his eleventh Oxford University Sermon (1839), 'The Nature of Faith in Relation to Reason':

> It is usual at this day to speak as if Faith were simply of a moral nature, and depended and followed upon a distinct act of Reason beforehand, – Reason warranting, on the ground of evidence, both ample and carefully examined, that the Gospel comes from God, and *then* faith embracing it. On the other hand, the more Scriptural representation seems to be this, which is obviously more agreeable to facts also, that, instead of there being really any such united process of reasoning first, and then believing, the act of Faith is sole and elementary, and complete in itself, and depends on no process of mind previous to it.

For consider:

> The Word of Life is offered to a man; and on the grounds of its being offered, he has Faith in it. Why? On these two grounds, – the word of its human messenger, and the likelihood of the message. And why does he feel the message to be probable? Because he has a love for it, his love being strong, though the testimony is weak. He has a keen sense of the intrinsic excellence of the message, of its desirableness, of likeness to what it seems to him Divine Goodness would vouchsafe did He vouchsafe any, of the need of a Revelation, and its probability.

Nor is Newman unaware of the interlocking set of presumptions in this account:

> Thus Faith is the reasoning of a religious mind, or of what Scripture calls a right or renewed heart, which acts upon presumptions rather than evidence, which speculates and ventures on the future when it cannot make sure of it.[3]

Yet how can this complex description amount to a 'justification of religious belief'? Indeed, Newman freely admits that

> this instance ... seems very fully to justify the view of Faith which I have been taking, that it is an act of Reason, but of what the world

would call weak, bad, or insufficient Reason; and that, because it rests on presumptions more, and on evidence less.[4]

Yet to lead us out of 'the common opinion of men [who] rather consider Faith to be weak Reason', he asks us to consider

the instance of St Paul preaching at Athens: he told his hearers that he came as a messenger from that God whom they worshipped already, though ignorantly, and of whom their poets spoke. He appealed to the conviction that was lodged within them of the spiritual nature and the unity of God; and he exhorted them to turn to Him who had appointed One to judge the whole world hereafter. This was an appeal to the antecedent probability of a revelation, which would be estimated variously according to the desire of it existing in each breast.[5]

Newman contrasts this intentional attitude with those who

regard the pursuit of truth only as a syllogistic process, and failure in attaining it as arising from merely a want of mental conformity with the laws in which just reasoning is conducted. But surely there is no greater mistake than this. For the experience of life contains abundant evidence that in practical matters, when their minds are really aroused, men commonly are not bad reasoners. Men do not mistake when their interest is concerned ... They may argue badly, but they reason well; that is, their professed grounds are no sufficient measures of their real ones. And in like manner, though the evidence with which Faith is content is apparently inadequate to its purpose, yet this is no proof of real weakness or imperfection in its reasoning. It seems to be contrary to reason, yet is not; it is but independent of and distinct from what are called philosophical inquiries, intellectual systems, courses of argument and the like.[6]

The strategy invoked here will be developed nearly three decades later (1870) in his extended *Essay in Aid of a Grammar of Assent*, which eases one into the peculiarities of assenting to faith by noting that the touted process of reasoning itself depends upon a bevy of prior assents. Newman evidences an abiding trust in the discernment of 'ordinary people', whose philosophical skills may be underdeveloped, yet whose reasoning from 'real grounds' makes up for their inability to profess these quite adequate grounds. The fact that we invariably reason from presumptions which are often more implicit than explicit, and that most people possess a 'homing instinct' for what is true for them, which philosophy may indeed be used to refine, but which the most astute philosophical reasoning already presumes in practice – these are part of Newman's arsenal in defending the 'rationality of faith' without reducing it to a *rationality* which can pass universal muster. For, in effect, no reasoning process can do that, since each one presumes premises only implicitly present yet nonetheless operative. Nicholas Lash offers firm guidance on this point when he invokes John Coulson to help interpret the complex paragraph we have just seen: 'Newman's distinction is not between rational cognition and some other activity which is non-rational ... It is rather ... between two modes of rationality or, in his own words, between two habits of mind.'[7]

NEWMAN AND POSTMODERNITY

Newman's *Grammar of Assent* is manifestly the best document from which to offer a philosophical assessment of his legacy, though it will have been useful to compare and contrast this extended treatment with that of the *Oxford University Sermons*, delivered nearly three decades earlier. Citing from Newman's letter to 'his old friend Maria Giberne: "I have done five constructive works in my life, and this is the hardest"' (16 February 1870),[8] Lash helps us to appreciate the difficulties involved, from a larger cultural context:

> In an intellectual climate in which post-enlightenment rationalism is presumed to be normative for the exercise of human rationality, Newman's lifelong hostility to rationalism is bound to be misunderstood. In such a climate, emphasis on 'the personal conquest of truth' is invariably misconstrued as 'subjectivism'. It is therefore not surprising that, from the Modernist crisis to our own day, Newman has frequently been charged with 'irrationalism', 'fideism', and cognate vices.[9]

Yet in the intervening quarter-century since this Introduction was composed, that 'intellectual climate' has shifted in such a way that we all now imbibe a 'postmodern' cultural context, despite the various meanings that term can convey. Yet Newman's *Grammar of Assent* can be taken as key to opening us to a benign reading of 'postmodern', assisted by astute critics like George Steiner with philosophers like Pierre Hadot.[10] What has taken place? A heightened sensitivity to context (Hans-Georg Gadamer) and to the inescapability of 'tradition-directed inquiry' (Alasdair MacIntyre), notably in assessing the works of those who thought they had 'overcome' tradition.[11] To appreciate this positive use of a postmodern ethos, allow me a scheme which reorients our standard way of constructing the history of philosophy.

Regularly teaching a course in ancient and medieval philosophy has led me to identify the difference between these two periods quite clearly: the presence of a free creator. Jewish, Christian, and Muslim thinkers converged in their efforts to find place for a free creator in the apparently seamless Hellenic philosophy they inherited. (Josef Pieper's observation that 'creation is the hidden element in the philosophy of St Thomas' should have alerted us decades ago to this operative difference from Aristotle, yet many Thomists managed to overlook it in their anxiety to demarcate philosophy from theology.[12]) Yet if we can say, schematically, that the presence of a free creator divides medieval from ancient philosophy, what marks the subsequent transition to modern philosophy? Many things, of course, but to continue speaking schematically, 'moderns' wanted to distinguish themselves by eliminating theological overtones of 'scholastics', so proceeded by avoiding reference to a creator. Yet the creator is a bit large to overlook, so the gradual tendency was to deny its relevance, as evidenced in Enlightenment fascination with 'the Greeks', even though they seemed more a construct than an historical reference. Aristotle, after all, had managed quite well without a creator. Now if that be the case – again, speaking quite schematically – we can characterize modern philosophy as 'post-medieval', where the 'post-' prefix carries a note of denial – in this case, of a creator, either directly or implicitly. A cursory look at the strategies whereby modern philosophers compensated for the absence of a creator, however, shows them to lead inescapably to foundational grounds, be they 'self-evident' propositions or 'sense-data' or whatever. Once these proved illusory, we cannot but enter a 'postmodern' world. Yet if our presumptions regarding 'philosophy' itself are inherently linked to such strategies, then we will inevitably regard a postmodern context as one in which 'anything goes'.

Here is where Newman puts flesh on our schema: if modern philosophy can be seen as 'post-medieval', then 'postmodern' philosophy will have to be read as 'post (post-medieval)'. And while the 'post-' prefixes may not connote the same sort of denials, we will be directed to a sense of 'postmodern' which bears affinities with medieval inquiry. Put more positively and less schematically, both medieval and postmodern inquiry find themselves quite at ease with Gadamer's contention that any inquiry whatsoever rests on fiduciary premises. In practice, this means that faith may be regarded as a way of knowing, though like any other way of knowing, never uncritically; however startling such a contention would sound to Descartes! Ironically enough, however, those forms of inquiry we call 'Thomist' owed more to Descartes and the context of modernity than to Aquinas himself, for they sought a metaphysical way of attaining the very certitude which Descartes had postulated epistemologically. By way of revenge, Cartesian failure would spell Thomistic failure as well. If there can be no viable epistemology without metaphysics, a postmodern ethos can be shown to direct us (albeit negatively) to see that there is no way to move to the level of metaphysics without a critical faith. But this carries us well beyond Newman's struggles in the second half of the nineteenth century, well before Pope Leo XIII's clarion call to follow the philosophy of St Thomas (in his encyclical letter, *Aeterni Patris* [1898]), though it is an undisputed fact that Newman's inability to hew to the 'potted Thomist' line extant in his day led many Catholics to question his full assimilation into the Catholic Church! What becomes clear to us, however, with the help of Pierre Hadot's reminders about ancient philosophy demanding a cognate 'way of life', is the way Newman's having been steeped in a patristic mode of thought led him more naturally into a posture of reciprocity between faith and reason which characterizes the work of Aquinas, by contrast with neo-Thomist reconstructions. Clement of Alexandria, after all, had no scruples denominating his reflections on sacred doctrine 'philosophy', as they called upon all the skills which Pierre Hadot has identified as required for executing philosophy among the ancients; that is, exercises embodying a way of life consonant with one's beliefs.

What I have dubbed the 'additive picture', whereby theology is demarcated from philosophy by the presence of premises taken from faith, reflects the modern presumption of 'pure reason', now acknowledged (thanks largely to Gadamer) to be chimerical, whereas Newman's characterization is far more fluid or 'dialectical':

> Now, in attempting to investigate what are the distinct offices of Faith and Reason in religious matters, and the relation of the one to the other, I observe, first that undeniable though it be, that reason has a power of analysis and criticism in all opinion and conduct, that nothing is true or right but what may be justified, and, in a certain sense, proved by it, and undeniable, in consequence, that, unless the doctrines received by Faith are approved by reason, they have no claim to be regarded as true, it does not therefore follow that faith is actually grounded on reason in the believing mind itself; unless, indeed, to take a parallel case, a judge can be called the origin, as well as the justifier, of the innocence or truth of those brought before him. A judge does not make men honest, but acquits and vindicates them: in like manner,

Reason need not be the origin of Faith, as Faith exists in the very persons believing, though it does test and verify it.[13]

The phrase which sets Newman apart from his nineteenth-century interlocutors, and aligns him with a post-Wittgensteinian legacy is the following: 'it does not therefore follow that faith is actually grounded on reason in the believing mind itself'. That is to say, reason has a role to play other than a foundational one; in fact, a critical one. Yet the example reminds us that this role is largely practical rather than speculative, for that is how judges operate. One might indeed characterize Newman as restoring Aristotelian 'practical reason' in a climate where those uses of reason had been eclipsed by deductive models. This will be elaborated in the following section.

NEWMAN AND THE RETRIEVAL OF PRACTICAL REASON

The Grammar of Assent is perhaps best known for the strategic distinction among *assents* as either *real* or *notional*, reserving 'real assent' for matters of faith and practice. Yet a great deal of work concerning inference and judgment precedes this famous distinction, to give it proper philosophical bite. The key text is as follows:

> In comparison of the directness and force of the apprehension, which we have of an object, when our assent is to be called real, Notional Assent and Inference seem to be thrown back into one and the same class of intellectual acts, though the former of the two is always an unconditional acceptance of a proposition, and the latter is an acceptance of the condition of an acceptance of its premises. In its notional assents as well as in its inferences, the mind contemplates its own creations instead of things; in real, it is directed towards things, represented by the impressions which they have left on the imagination. These images, when assented-to, have an influence both on the individual and on society, where mere notions cannot exert.[14]

Philosophical readers will detect traces of the scholastic distinction between the *intentional* and *real*, as well as Hume's emphasis on 'impressions', while the composition is Newman's own. A characteristic biblical reference is to

> the confession of the patriarch Job, when he contrasts his apprehension of the Almighty before and after his afflictions. He says he had indeed a true apprehension of the Divine Attributes before as well as

after; but with the trial came a great change of character of that apprehension: – 'With the hearing of the ear', he says, 'I have heard Thee, but now mine eye seeeth thee; therefore I reprehend myself, and do penance in dust and ashes' (Job 42:5–6).[15]

What characterizes any assent, we shall see, is that it must be unconditional, while what distinguishes 'real assents' is 'that they are of a personal character ... proper to the individual'.[16] Newman characterizes the way the inferences involved culminate, to bring one to such an unconditional assent, as 'severally the co-incidents of many laws ... but what is not clear is how all these various conditions met together in a particular case'.[17] Here is where the *practicality* inherent to 'real assent' figures so prominently:

> After all, man is *not* a reasoning animal; he is a seeing, feeling, contemplating, acting animal. [Indeed,] life is not long enough for a religion of inferences; we shall never have done beginning, if we determine to begin with proof. [Yet] why we are so constituted that faith, not knowledge or argument, is our principle of action, is a question with which I have nothing to do; but I think it is a fact (90–1).[18]

We can enlist the services of Bernard Lonergan, who freely celebrated his inspiration by Newman, and especially by this text, to elucidate the inherently practical character of 'real assent', as well as Newman's initially puzzling demand that any assent be *unconditional*.[19] In deference to Newman and to a philosophical tradition stemming from Aristotle, Lonergan insists that any judgment must be unconditional, yet underscores the character of fallible human judgments by elucidating them as 'virtually unconditioned'. That is, to be straightforward, an assertion must indeed assert that something is the case. Yet it is a feature of progressive human understanding, consonant with our experience, that we are able to recognize when objections to our assertions meet their mark or not. Yet this recognition is thoroughly 'virtual', in that we cannot be conscious of all that we have (or have not) taken into consideration in making particular judgments, yet as objections emerge, we are nonetheless able to recognize whether we have met them or not. In this way, any particular judgment will in principle be open to revision (its 'virtual' side) while in fact a developed capacity to meet objections, in a non-defensive way, converges to unconditionality. Fred Lawrence identifies Lonergan's intellectual debt to and development of Newman as follows:

> Lonergan was enabled to grasp Aquinas's achievement on reflection and judgment because of his prior familiarity with John Henry

Newman's appropriation of Aristotle's *phronēsis* in working out the 'illative sense' in *An Essay in Aid of a Grammar of Assent*.[20] There is a direct kinship between Newman's elucidation of 'arguments too various for direct enumeration, too personal and deep for words, too powerful and concurrent for refutation', and Gadamer's rehabilitation of prejudice.[21] Newman's proposal that Aristotle's analysis of *phronesis* as a concrete mode of human knowing is appropriate not just in the realm of moral judgment but in all fields of human knowing anticipated Heidegger, Gadamer, and Lonergan. Because Gadamer espouses Heidegger's disclosure-model of truth as *a-letheia*, the difference between insight and interpretation and reflective understanding and judgment was not a central issue for him.

For Lonergan, as for Heidegger and Gadamer, the hermeneutic revolution implies that the epistemological question is no longer the first relevant question about human knowledge. As Lonergan agreed, the genuine issue is not the *quaestio juris* but the *quaestio facti*: not *whether* we know but What do we do when we know? Quite early on, Lonergan learned both from Augustine's early dialogues at Cassiciacum and especially from Newman's *Grammar of Assent* that questions about the nature of human knowledge can only be answered by reflecting on one's own experience of coming to know. Newman thus preceded Heidegger and Gadamer in carrying out the hermeneutic explication of performative acts of consciousness, thereby convincing Lonergan that Newman's discoveries about apprehension and assent were congruent with his own experience of knowing.[22]

All of this reflection comes to a point in Lonergan's articulation of *judgment* as 'virtually unconditioned', seen here as a refinement of Newman's insistence on uniting both unconditionality with adventitiousness in *judgment*, under the neologism of 'the Illative Sense'. As Newman puts it:

> Judgment then in all concrete matter is the architectonic faculty; and what may be called the Illative Sense, or right judgment in ratiocination, or one branch of it.[23]

Finally, Lonergan's cryptic comment that 'I had become something of an existentialist from my study of Newman's *A Grammar of Assent*' offers a clue to his guiding observation at the beginning of *Insight* defining it as a 'performative' work, whose pointers must be executed if one ever hopes to grasp their point.[24] It is not, in short, a treatise on epistemology, but a recipe for becoming conscious of the act which defines our reach as humans: understanding. That guiding inspiration comes manifestly from Newman.

The next figure connecting us to Newman and Newman to us has to be Ludwig Wittgenstein. James Cameron's observations set the stage:

> Language, then, for Newman is a set of tools well enough adapted to the furthering of particular practical or even speculative purposes, but compelled to strain itself to breaking point when it attempts to speak of God or the soul or faith. Language is framed to deal with our ordinary commerce with the world of things and persons, not with the subject-matter of theology. It is the tragedy of the vocation of the theologian – or the philosopher – that he must proceed by way of analysis and definition; but the nature of language is such that every comment he makes is an oblique one, every description a travesty, every definition a mutilation ... Newman has the view of language as a set of tools the function of which are determined by needs arising out of the way of life of those who use the language, and this view is close to that elaborated by Wittgenstein in his later work.[25]

But there is much more. Not only do they share views of how language works, but this view is constantly reflected in the ways they approach issues, beginning with a devastating deconstruction of standard – usually 'theoretical' – problematics, designed to return one to the paths which we find inscribed in our actual quest for understanding. Newman's impatience with 'philosophical accounts', especially of reasoning, will be echoed by Wittgenstein's insistent attempts to move questions out of the parameters into which they had been constrained by 'philosophers', so that they have a chance of meeting the actual needs of inquirers. What is at stake here is recovering 'philosophy as a way of life', a staple of Wittgenstein's approach, embodied in the title of Pierre Hadot's essays illustrating an effective way of taking philosophy to heart.[26] Moreover, by focusing on practice and judgment, Wittgenstein's strategies can facilitate a hermeneutical retrieval of classical texts, reminiscent of the ways in which Newman's sensitive ways of reading such texts can bring them to life, as his retrieval of developments in Christian doctrine had a profound impact on his life and that of countless others in the nineteenth century.

Cyril Barrett explores in some detail the relation between these two thinkers. Wittgenstein rarely cited others, even those whom he appreciated, so the cryptic remark in *On Certainty*, 'a curious [*komische*] remark of H. Newman', offers but a slim lead, yet affinities between the

Philosophical Investigations are Newman's characteristic ways of pars-
ing 'understanding' are everywhere to be remarked. Barrett's comparison
turns principally on the apparently circular character of Newman's
attempts (notably in the *Grammar*) to 'justify' religious belief, for this
is at once where both thinkers appear most vulnerable and yet made their
signal contributions to this endeavour. But one will miss those very
contributions if one insists on reading 'justify' as 'offering proof' or a
foundation. Barrett notes this, and suggests that 'here might be a better
way of describing what [Newman] is doing':

> This would be to say that what he was giving was not a piece of
> information and cumulative reasoning in support of religious belief
> so much as a *rational account* of the basis of Christian belief: why
> Christians believe what they do and what that implies. In other
> words, if the *Grammar of Assent* is seen as a rational exposé of
> what Christian belief implies and involves, and not as a cumulative
> argument, there can be no question of circularity, since nothing is
> being proved, even informally.[27]

Barrett goes on to compare this 'non-foundational' use of reason to
Anselm's famous exercise of reason in his *Proslogion*, miscast (since
Kant) as 'the ontological argument'.

> What makes it look like an argument (or rather, arguments) is that
> he dragged in the fool who said in his heart 'there is no God'. This
> made it look like a refutation, whereas Anselm was speaking to
> his fellow monks, all of whom believed in God, and, had they not,
> would have been unimpressed by his arguments (as would the fool).
> What Anselm was in effect proving was that believing in God involved
> belief in a necessary, all-perfect, eternal being, and that that made
> sense. Implied in this account is its rationality. This is precisely what
> Wittgenstein had in mind when he wrote, 'I think that what *believers*
> who have furnished such proofs have wanted to do is give their
> "belief" an intellectual analysis and foundation, although they them-
> selves would never had come to believe as a result of such proofs'.[28]

And what is here described as 'coming to believe as a result of proof'
is what we normally call a 'foundational' use of reason. Barrett's description of how Anselm wanted his 'argument' to function not only illustrates a sensitive reading of the *Proslogion* in its larger context, as well as
noting how the preliminary chapters of that classic work are intended to
direct our interpretation of his endeavour, but can also remind us how
singular are Newman's and Wittgenstein's way of relating reason to faith

in the climate of 'philosophy of religion' which seems to have perdured from their day to ours!

Pierre Hadot can supply yet another link to Newman's way of modelling and stimulating our understanding of matters religious, by reminding us how crucial are 'spiritual exercises' to doing philosophy, thereby showing how contemporary such a 'classical' paradigm can be.[29] We know such exercises from Socratic dialogue as well as our own efforts to carry on something similar in our own efforts to reach students. Indeed, the very term, 'exercises', introduces a notion of inquiry shaped by intellectual virtues, endorsing a style of teaching geared to helping students acquire virtues requisite to the inquiry in question. Of another order than the 'decision algorithms' endemic to formal logic, acquiring these virtues will demand a quality of judgment akin to the *phronēsis* at the heart of all moral virtues.[30] Moreover, that same quality of judgment emerges at the heart of Aquinas's understanding of the analogous use of terms, as Etienne Gilson insisted.[31] It may help to illustrate this elusive yet pervasive practice of judgment from that of translating, which must have been a practice at which Newman was adept, given his mastery of classical languages.

Those who have tried their hand at translating quickly come to realize that there are no rules for doing it.[32] I call it 'hermeneutics where the rubber hits the road'. For as one seeks to ascertain what the author in question means, one does so by casting about for an idiom which will convey that sense as perspicuously as possible to one's contemporaries. And where the distance is cultural as well as chronological, as in the author whom I have translated most, al-Ghazali, one is engaged in making complex and imbedded judgments. They will be shaped by what one has come to learn of the context of the work, which will help illuminate how the work itself serves as context for the sentences one must render into another language and a contemporary idiom. So the endeavour cannot be solitary; indeed, it cannot but embody multi-disciplinary efforts, ideally as a team but inescapably involving consultants to the work. Moreover, these efforts will have a duplex goal: to render al-Ghazali intelligible to contemporary readers with a different cultural formation, and at the same time to invite those very readers to enlarge their working presumptions by enticing them into the author's culture.

Listen to the appeal which opens al-Ghazali's commentary on a central Muslim practice, reciting the 'ninety-nine beautiful names of God':

> Praise be to God, alone in His majesty and His might, unique in His sublimity and His eternity, who clips the wings of intellects well

short of the glow of his glory, and who makes the way of knowing Him pass through the inability to know Him; who makes the tongues of the eloquent fall short of praising the beauty of His presence unless they use the means by which He praises Himself: His names and attributes which He has enumerated. And my blessings be upon Muhammad, the best of his creatures, and on his companions and his family.[33]

It should be clear how an entire set of practices as well as a tradition of reflection is imbedded in this text, carefully crafted to inaugurate his commentary on the practice of reciting a canonical list of 'names' for the divinity culled from the Qur'an itself. They are indeed *attributes* but also names which enjoy the authority of God naming God's own self. Hence they allow us to engage in an activity which far surpasses our own powers: of praising God, and expecting that praise to attain its object. And any efforts to praise God will also bless the Prophet, whose recitation (*Qur'an*) delivered these very names to us so as to leave their divine provenance undiluted. Indeed, their divine origin will privilege these attributes as *names*, and lead al-Ghazali to invest his commentary on each of them with a correlative 'Admonition' sketching ways in which those reciting them might assimilate themselves to that divine attribute, in as much as humans can. So the practice of recitation of the divinely given names on the part of Muslims – that is, those seeking to respond faithfully to the revelation of God in the Qur'an – at once calls attention to the gulf between creator and creatures as well as the call to those who recognize the gift of creation to return everything to the One from whom they received everything. In short, this opening appeal limns the heart of Islamic reflection on the 'straight path' offered by the Qur'an and itself announced in Sura 1 (*Fatiha*) – lineaments translators must detect if they would lead readers to appreciate them. Indeed, the elegance of the original appeal must also inform the English rendering, if the appeal is to do its work – a demand which actually facilitates the effort of translating, even while it helps assure that the project will seldom meet the standards it sets for itself.

One is immediately reminded of Newman's invocation of Scripture to illuminate transitions in human life and understanding, like the way he took Paul's preaching in the *agora* in Athens to be exemplary:

Now, what was the evidence he gave, in order to concentrate those various antecedent presumptions, to which he referred, in behalf of a message which he brought? Very slight, yet something; not a miracle, but his own word that God had raised Christ form the dead; very like the evidence given to the mass of men now, or rather not so much. No one will say it was strong evidence; yet, aided by the novelty, and what may be called originality, of the claim, its strangeness and improbability considered as a mere invention, and the personal bearing of the Apostle, and supported by the full force of the antecedent probabilities which existed, and which he stirred within them, it was enough. It was enough, for some did believe, – enough, not indeed in itself, but enough for those who had love, and therefore were inclined to believe. To those who had no fears, wishes, longings or expectations, of another world, he was but a 'babbler'; those who had such, or in the Evangelists' words in another place, were 'ordained to eternal life', 'clave unto him, and believed'.[34]

So it is the lived context of conversation which can constitute 'sufficient evidence', and the introduction of *love* reminds one of a related sermon: 'Love: The Safeguard of Faith against Superstition', which addresses the objection that his way of articulating the reasonableness of faith

> may be made an excuse for all manner of prejudice and bigotry, and leads directly to credulity and superstition; and on the other hand, in the case of unbelief, that it affords a sort of excuse for impenetrable obduracy. Antecedent probabilities may be equally available for what is true, and what pretends to be true ... They seem to supply no intelligible rule what is to be believed, and what not; or how a man is to pass from a false belief to a true.[35]

> It is plain that some safeguard of Faith is needed, some corrective principle, which will secure it from running (as it were) to seed, and becoming superstition or fanaticism ... What, then, is the safeguard, if Reason is not? I shall give an answer, which may seem at once common-place and paradoxical, yet I believe is the true one. The safeguard of Faith is a right state of heart. This it is which gives it birth; it also disciplines it.[36]

This anticipates Lonergan's crucial distinction between '*quest* for understanding' and a '*need* for certitude', which reminds each of us that psychological needs may be distracting in the journey to faith, even if we cannot simply (with Freud) dismiss that journey as an irresponsible catering to such needs. What Newman calls a 'right state of heart' Lonergan will match with 'the unrestricted desire to know', for what gives that 'state of heart' its rightness are the disciplines which help us dissolve projections in seeking what is right and true. And here is where

Hadot's reminder of 'spiritual exercises' and Newman's search for an authentic ecclesial tradition coalesce. It can also remind us that the *certitude* which Newman celebrates and which Lonergan denigrates are far from the same thing. As the extensive treatment of *certitude* in Chapter 7 of *Grammar of Assent* makes clear, it is not something one claims to possess, but a spontaneous 'law of my mind to seal up the conclusions to which ratiocination has brought me'.[37] *Certitude* for Newman is not something I claim, but something which rightly claims me. It is in fact 'attainable as regards general and cardinal truths'.[38] Yet it

> does not admit of an interior, immediate test, sufficient to discriminate it from false certitude. Such a test is rendered impossible from the circumstance that, when we make the mental act expressed by 'I know', we sum up the whole series of reflexive judgments which might, each in turn, successively exercise a critical function towards those of the series which precede it ... It seems then that on the whole there are three conditions of certitude: that it follows on investigation and proof, that it is accompanied by a specific sense of intellectual satisfaction and repose, and that it is irreversible. If the assent is made without rational grounds, it is a rash judgment, a fancy, or prejudice; if without a sense of finality, it is scarcely more than an inference; if without permanence, it is a mere conviction.[39]

Moreover, Newman joins Plato to insist that 'the multitude of men confuse together the probable, the possible, and the certain, and apply these terms to doctrines and to statements almost at random. They have no clear view what it is they know, what they presume, what they suppose, and what they only assert.'[40] So what is required for any intellectual inquiry, and especially to 'seal it', are skills which are eminently human, but require keen development, so that we shall use our powers to discern properly.

In this respect, Newman's work offers a paradigm example of 'tradition-directed inquiry', to anticipate the astute ways in which Alasdair MacIntyre, Charles Taylor, and Martha Nussbaum can retrieve classical texts for contemporary illumination.[41] His manner of writing reveals how much he would resonate with Martha Nussbaum's exemplary way of using narrative to offer philosophical elucidation of central human issues. What all these thinkers have in common is a sense that philosophical inquiry proceeds best when it imbeds itself in a tradition, always critically but never presuming to 'go it alone'. I have tried to show how this governing conviction can be seen to be 'postmodern', rejecting the utterly 'autonomous' picture of philosophy (and of 'the self') which governed modern inquiry. For a final illustration of

Newman's intellectual legacy, let us turn to John Paul II's encyclical *Fides et Ratio* ('Faith and Reason').

Fides et Ratio has been the subject of numerous commentaries, one of which I shall feature, by Jorge Garcia.[42] What Karl Wojtyla highlights in his exploration of 'faith and reason' is their reciprocal relation to one another, which can be one of 'mutual illumination'. While insisting on the proper 'autonomy of philosophy', he also suggests 'how faith can help philosophy remain true to its vocation by remaining on the trail of the answers it seeks and drawing close to them'. Here Garcia remarks that 'the very suggestion that religious faith might actually assist philosophy is shocking to those who see philosophy as religion's enemy, [for] as many philosophers today view religious faith with contempt, so many religious people view philosophy with suspicion'.[43] Continuing his commentary, Garcia asks:

> What, according to this pope, can faith give philosophy? First, and most important, John Paul II maintains, is a Christocentric anthropology ... [For] Jesus' was a life lived in love, devotion to the good of persons. His love of God was expressed as utter obedience in which his own will harmonized with the Father's. [And] that means that self-fulfillment depends on the truth about the human being's origin, essence, and vocation. For John Paul II's personalism, the personal presupposes the interpersonal ... Here, human personhood in loving relationship mirrors the internal life of the three divine persons ... Whatever [faith's] epistemic disadvantage as compared with belief based either in logical demonstration or in direct empirical evidence, faith is more human precisely in being interpersonal.[44]

All of these features of philosophical reason informed by faith, and of a faith made critically available by judicious use of rational strategies, are deeply redolent of Newman's consistent practice. So the fact that one can identify portions of his legacy in so many contemporary thinkers, some explicitly linked to the practice of Christian faith, and others not so linked, or even linked to other faith traditions, can only remind us of the central role which this Catholic inquirer has played in helping us wend our way in a confusing and turbulent intellectual and interfaith milieu.[45]

A final note regards the perspective which Newman's life and writings can give us regarding professional philosophy. His way of giving short shrift to 'formal reasoning' while engaging in a good bit of it himself, is reminiscent of the way Søren Kierkegaard can denigrate 'philosophy' while employing philosophical strategies with acuity. The explanation is really quite simple: when the 'philosophy' taught in universities was in fact 'potted Hegel', the critique had to sidestep this elephant as it limned a fresh way of retrieving the promise which Socrates had brought to philosophy.[46] For Newman, when the 'uses of reason' had been unduly restricted to formal reasoning in the name of 'philosophy', he was forced to retrace Socrates' steps to recover the well-springs of human reasoning, and in his case, this would amount to retrieving Aristotle's 'practical reason'. Here especially is where he can appear so timely to us today, in a 'postmodern' context in which attention to the practices of reason is slowly coming to the fore, to eclipse philosophers' predilection for 'theories', in the wake of Wittgenstein. Again, however, university practice of 'philosophy' may be slow to adopt these changes, so Newman's task of deconstruction, and then of restored attention to practice, remains perennially ours.

Notes

1. For an inspired use of 'catechesis', see Paul Griffiths, 'How Reasoning goes Wrong: A Quasi-Augustinian Account of Error and its Implications', in Paul Griffiths and Reinhard Hutter (eds.), *Reason and the Reasons of Faith* (New York and London: T & T Clark, 2005), 145–59.
2. Ian Ker, *The Achievement of John Henry Newman* (Notre Dame: University of Notre Dame Press, 1991), 35.
3. *U.S.*, 202–3. For a cognate assessment of the role of *praeambula fidei*, see Guy deBroglie, SJ, 'La vraie notion thomiste des *praeambula fidei*', *Gregorianum* 34 (1953), 341–89.
4. *U.S.*, 204.
5. *U.S.*, 203.
6. *U.S.*, 211–12.
7. Nicholas Lash, 'Introduction' to John Henry Newman, *An Essay in Aid of a Grammar of Assent* (Notre Dame: University of Notre Dame Press, 1979), 15. Lash refers to *G.A.*, 98–9, and to Sermon X, 'Faith and Reason Contrasted as Habits of Mind', of *U.S.*, 176–201. See also John Coulson, 'Belief and Imagination', *Downside Review* 90 (1972), 1–14.
8. Lash, 'Introduction', 1 n. 3.
9. Lash, 'Introduction', 8; for references Lash directs us to his study, *Newman on Development* (London: Sheed & Ward, 1975), 11, 148–9.
10. See George Steiner, *Real Presences* (London: Faber and Faber, 1989). For an illuminating introduction to the work of Pierre Hadot in English, see *Philosophy as a Way of Life*, ed. Arnold Davidson (Cambridge, MA: Blackwell, 1995); for a synopsis, see his *What is Ancient Philosophy?* (Cambridge, MA: Belknap Press of Harvard University, 2002).
11. Alasdair MacIntyre, *Whose Justice? Which Rationality?* (Notre Dame: University of Notre Dame Press, 1988).
12. Josef Pieper, *The Silence of St Thomas: Three Essays* (New York: Pantheon, 1957): 'The Negative Element in the Philosophy of St Thomas', 47–67 (reissued: South Bend, IN: St Augustine's Press, 2002).

13. *U.S.*, 182–3: Sermon X: 'Faith and Reason Contrasted as Habits of Mind'. For a development of this 'dialectical relation', see David Burrell, 'Philosophy', in Gareth Jones (ed.), *Blackwell Companion to Modern Theology* (Oxford: Blackwell, 2004), 34–46.

14. *G.A.*, 75.

15. *G.A.*, 80. For a recent study of Job which exploits this crucial distinction, see David Burrell, *Deconstructing Theodicy* (Grand Rapids, MI: Brazos Press, 2007).

16. *G.A.*, 83.

17. *G.A.*, 84.

18. *G.A.*, 94.

19. Bernard Lonergan, *Insight: A Study of Human Understanding*, chapters 10 and 11. See Frederick Crowe and Robert Doran (eds.), *Collected Works*, vol. iii (Toronto: University of Toronto Press, 1992), 304–71 (original edition (fifth, revised and augmented): London: Longmans, Green, & Co., 1957). For a critical summary of Lonergan's intent in *Insight*, see Edward M. McKinnon, SJ, 'Understanding According to Bernard J.F. Lonergan, S.J.', *Thomist* [Part I] 28 (1964), 97–132; [Part II] 28 (1964), 338–72; [Part III] 28 (1964), 475–522.

20. Bernard Lonergan, '*Insight* Revisited', in William Ryan and Bernard Tyrell (eds.), *Second Collection* (Philadelphia: Westminster Press, 1974), 263–78. Recapping the long-term steps to *Insight*, Lonergan notes: '[I] read several times the more theoretical passages in Newman's *A Grammar of Assent* ... His illative sense later became my reflective act of understanding [i.e., judgment]' (263); and 'I had become something of an existentialist from my study of Newman's *A Grammar of Assent*' (276).

21. Joseph Dunne has developed the parallel more broadly in *Back to the Rough Ground: Practical Judgment and the Lure of Technique* (Notre Dame: University of Notre Dame Press, 1993).

22. Fred Lawrence, 'The Hermeneutic Revolution and the Future of Theology', in Andrzej Wiercinski (ed.), *Between the Human and the Divine: Philosophical and Theological Hermeneutics* (Toronto: The Hermeneutic Press, 2002), 326–54, at 337–48.

23. *G.A.*, 342.

24. Lonergan, *Insight*, Preface.

25. James Cameron, *Night Battle* (Baltimore: Helicon Press, 1962), 204–5.

26. Pierre Hadot, *Philosophy as a Way of Life*, trans. and presented Arnold Davidson (Oxford: Blackwell, 1985).

27. Cyril Barrett, 'Newman and Wittgenstein on the Rationality of Religious Belief', in Ian Ker (ed.), *Newman and Conversion* (Edinburgh: T & T Clark, 1997), 98.

28. Barrett, 'Newman and Wittgenstein', 98–9. The Wittgenstein reference is to *Culture and Value* (Oxford: Oxford University Press, 1980), 85.

29. Pierre Hadot, *What is Philosophy?* (Cambridge, MA: Harvard University Press, 2003); for a hermeneutical application, see David Burrell, *Exercises in Religious Understanding* (Notre Dame: University of Notre Dame

Press, 1974), featuring readings (in the manner of Wittgenstein and of Lonergan) of Augustine, Anselm, Aquinas, Kierkegaard, and Jung.

30. See Linda Zagzebski, *Virtues of the Mind: An Inquiry into the Nature of Virtue and the Ethical Foundation of Knowledge* (Cambridge: Cambridge University Press, 1996).
31. This idea is developed in David Burrell, 'From Analogy of "Being" to the Analogy of Being', in John O'Callaghan and Thomas Hibbs (eds.), *Recovering Nature* (Notre Dame: University of Notre Dame Press, 1999), 253–66.
32. See the illuminating set of essays collected by Rainer Schulte and John Biguenet, *Theories of Translation* (Chicago: University of Chicago Press, 1992) where renowned writers and translators conspire to undermine the title of the collection.
33. *Al-Ghazali: The Ninety-nine Beautiful Names of God* [*al-Maqsad al-asna fi sharh asma Allah al husna*], trans. David Burrell and Nazih Daher (Cambridge: Islamic Texts Society, 1995, and Louisville, KY: Fons Vitae, 2000).
34. *U.S.*, 203–4.
35. *U.S.*, 232.
36. *U.S.*, 233–4.
37. *G.A.*, 229.
38. *G.A.*, 240.
39. *G.A.*, 255, 258.
40. *G.A.*, 234.
41. MacIntyre, *Whose Justice?*; Charles Taylor, *Sources of the Self: the Making of Modern Identity* (Cambridge, MA; Harvard University Press, 1989); Martha Nussbaum, *Love's Knowledge: Essays on Philosophy and Literature* (Oxford: Oxford University Press, 1990). For a discussion with others, see also Charles Taylor, *A Catholic Modernity*, ed. James Heft (New York: Oxford University Press, 1999).
42. J. L. A. Garcia, 'Death of the (Hand)maiden: Contemporary Philosophy in Faith and Reason', *Logos: A Journal of Catholic Thought and Culture* 2 (1999), 11–19.
43. Garcia, 'Death of the (Hand)maiden', 15.
44. Garcia, 'Death of the (Hand)maiden', 15–16.
45. See Terrence Merrigan's contribution to Ian Ker (ed.), *Newman and Conversion*, 'The Anthropology of Conversion: Newman and the Contemporary Theology of Religions', for one perspective on how Newman's 'antecedent probabilities' analysis might be applied to other religious convictions, as he himself does to 'paganism'.
46. See John Macquarrie, 'Newman and Kierkegaard on the Act of Faith', in Ker (ed.), *Newman and Conversion*, 75–88.

Further reading

Burrell, David. *Exercises in Religious Understanding*. Notre Dame: University of Notre Dame Press, 1974.

Dunne, Joseph. *Back to the Rough Ground: Practical Judgment and the Lure of Technique*. Notre Dame: University of Notre Dame Press, 1993.

Hadot, Pierre. *Philosophy as a Way of Life*, ed. Arnold Davidson. Cambridge, MA: Blackwell, 1995.

Ker, Ian. 'Newman and the Postconciliar Church', in Stanley L. Jaki (ed.), *Newman Today*. San Francisco: Ignatius Press, 1989, 121–42.

Lash, Nicholas. 'Tides and Twilight: Newman since Vatican II', in Ian Ker and A. G. Hill (eds.), *Newman after a Hundred Years*. Oxford: Clarendon Press, 1990, 447–64.

Index

For EU product safety concerns, contact us at Calle de José Abascal, 56–1°, 28003 Madrid, Spain or eugpsr@cambridge.org.

www.ingramcontent.com/pod-product-compliance
Ingram Content Group UK Ltd.
Pitfield, Milton Keynes, MK11 3LW, UK
UKHW020337140625
459647UK00018B/2190